CANADIAN POLITICAL ECONOMY

Edited by Heather Whiteside

In *Canadian Political Economy*, experts from a number of disciplinary backgrounds come together to explore Canada's empirical political economy and the field's contributions to theory and debate. Considering both historical and contemporary approaches to CPE, the contributors pay particular attention to key actors and institutions, as well as developments in Canadian political-economic policies and practices, explored through themes of changes, crises, and conflicts in CPE. Offering up-to-date interpretations, analyses, and descriptions, *Canadian Political Economy* is accessibly written and suitable for students and scholars. In 17 chapters, the book's topics include theory, history, inequality, work, free trade and fair trade, co-operatives, banking and finance, the environment, indigeneity, and the gendered politics of political economy. Linking long-standing debates with current developments, this volume represents both a state-of-the-discipline and a state-of-the-art contribution to scholarship.

HEATHER WHITESIDE is an assistant professor in the Department of Political Science at the University of Waterloo and Fellow at the Balsillie School of International Affairs.

Canadian Political Economy

EDITED BY HEATHER WHITESIDE

UNIVERSITY OF TORONTO PRESS
Toronto Buffalo London

© University of Toronto Press 2020
Toronto Buffalo London
utorontopress.com
Printed in Canada

ISBN 978-1-4875-0479-3 (cloth)   ISBN 978-1-4875-3091-4 (EPUB)
ISBN 978-1-4875-2348-0 (paper)   ISBN 978-1-4875-3090-7 (PDF)

Library and Archives Canada Cataloguing in Publication

Title: Canadian political economy / edited by Heather Whiteside.
Names: Whiteside, Heather, 1982– editor.
Description: Includes bibliographical references and index.
Identifiers: Canadiana (print) 20200309196 | Canadiana (ebook)
    20200309382 | ISBN 9781487504793 (cloth) | ISBN 9781487523480
    (paper) | ISBN 9781487530914 (EPUB) | ISBN 9781487530907 (PDF)
Subjects: LCSH: Economics – Canada. | LCSH: Canada – Economic
    conditions – 21st century. | LCSH: Canada – Politics and
    government – 21st century.
Classification: LCC HC115 .C274 2020 | DDC 330.971 – dc23

This book has been published with the help of a grant from the Federation
for the Humanities and Social Sciences, through the Awards to Scholarly
Publications Program, using funds provided by the Social Sciences and
Humanities Research Council of Canada.

University of Toronto Press acknowledges the financial assistance to its
publishing program of the Canada Council for the Arts and the Ontario
Arts Council, an agency of the Government of Ontario.

 Canada Council
for the Arts
Conseil des Arts
du Canada

 ONTARIO ARTS COUNCIL
CONSEIL DES ARTS DE L'ONTARIO
an Ontario government agency
un organisme du gouvernement de l'Ontario

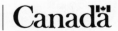 Funded by the   Financé par le
Government   gouvernement
of Canada   du Canada   Canadä

 MIX
Paper from
responsible sources
FSC   FSC® C016245
www.fsc.org

Contents

Section 1: Approaches to Canadian Political Economy

Section 2: Agents in Canadian Political Economy

Section 3: Applications of Canadian Political Economy

Tables

Figures

CANADIAN POLITICAL ECONOMY

Introduction: Changes, Crises, and Conflicts in Canadian Political Economy

HEATHER WHITESIDE

Synopsis

This book seeks to reinvigorate the distinct interdisciplinary field of Canadian political economy (CPE).[1] As such, it is oriented around the empirical political economy of Canada and Canada's contribution to theory and debate in political economy. Political economy recognizes and celebrates the ontological interconnection between politics and economics in society, and Canada has its own story to tell. The Canadian political economy story as presented in this book is narrated and analysed by authors from a number of disciplinary backgrounds, dealing with historical and contemporary approaches to CPE, the agents (institutions and actors) in Canada's political economy, and developments in the application of Canadian political-economic policies and practices. The following subjects animate the book's treatment of CPE: theories and debates, historical political economy, Indigenous and gendered scholarship, provinces and cities, public sectors and public administration, inequality, work and workers, corporations, co-operatives, non-profits, free trade and fair trade, money and finance, resources and the environment, social policies, industrial and research and development (R&D) policy, and the North American/global context. Themes of conflict, change, and crisis (3Cs) are woven throughout the book.

Political Economy

Political economy is not only an acknowledgement that politics and economics are interrelated; it is also a lens through which social phenomena may be analysed. As Robert Cox (1996, 87) succinctly describes, "theory is always for someone and for some purpose." Although "political economy" encompasses multiple theoretical perspectives, as

---

1 We thank the Canadian Political Science Association for supporting a book planning workshop at Congress 2018. And thanks to Melsen Babe for assistance with the indexing.

a field of study its purpose is, centrally, to understand the theory, practice, history, and implications of capitalist development and its alternatives – capitalism being primarily oriented around profit, prices, and private property. Regardless of theoretical lens, political economy insists that the "economic" and the "political" cannot (or ought not to) be reduced to binary states plus markets, or antagonistic states versus markets. Economic activities are inherently political, and state activities guide and constrain private markets. Further, formal and informal (cultural, social) political-economic power is interlaced with issues of race, class, gender, power, contestation, and other socio-institutional characteristics that demand an interdisciplinary approach.

The term "market," a venue of exchange, is typically but not exclusively used here to refer to private for-profit markets derived through capitalism as a mode of production based on private property and the capitalist division of labour. Markets distributing goods and services through other modes of production (e.g., slave, feudal, communal) have existed in the past and likely would continue to exist under alternative modes of production (e.g., socialist, anarchist, techno-futurist). Thus the "market" cannot be apprehended as either ahistorical or transhistorical. Similarly, the "state" is expedient shorthand typically denoting a particular form of governmental configuration of political-institutional dynamics (e.g., the capitalist state, the colonial state). Other qualifiers and attributes are equally important (e.g., the neoliberal state).

Capitalism might be dominant, but it is not the only way of producing, consuming, and relating, politically and economically. Between unpaid household labour, volunteer labour, unfree labour, intra-organizational state and corporate bureaucratic activity, not-for-profit production, and myriad other ways of determining the "who gets what, when, how, and why" of political economy, much economic activity remains beyond the realm of market prices, private property, and profit-making ambitions central to capitalism. The realm of the "social economy," constituting both a practice and a perspective, involves "economic activity neither controlled directly by the state nor by the profit logic of the market, activity that prioritizes the social well-being of communities and marginalized individuals over partisan political directives or individual gain" (McMurtry 2010a, 4). Co-operatives, non-profits, mutual aid organizations, and volunteer-based enterprises are central to the social economy.

Social reproduction, beyond and within market relations, is equally important for the study of capitalism. Feminist political economy identifies and analyses "social relations as they relate to the economic system of production" (Luxton 2006, 12), thus revealing or clarifying how gender determines or influences social and political relationships, structures of power, and the diverse and unequal economic effects that flow from these relationships and structures. To give but one well-known statistical example of non-market social reproduction, Waring (1990) estimates that, in capitalist countries, unpaid work makes up as much as 40 per cent of the time spent producing goods and services. Feminists have been tireless (and absolutely correct) in their theoretical and empirical conviction that social reproduction (often provided by women's unpaid domestic labour) fundamentally supports the wage-market system (see, for example, Cohen 1988; Folbre 1994).

Likewise, political economists who emphasize the importance of the free gifts of nature's bounty to the formation of capitalism in its early days (Harvey 2005b), and the work of political ecologists on the ongoing commodification of nature (Dempsey 2016), identify important motors of profit making beyond capitalist production itself.[2] Studies in the field of political ecology tend to focus on five subjects related to the environment: degradation and marginalization, conservation and control, conflict and exclusion, subjects and identity, and political objects and actors (Robbins 2012, 22). Although each invokes elements of political economy, the final item – political objects and actors – is said to involve how "political and economic systems are shown to be underpinned and affected by the non-human actors with which they are intertwined" (ibid).

Capitalism is, of course, not only relevant for its structural, material, and market dimensions; the outlook of economic participants, or the ideational component of capitalist social relations, is equally important. Max Weber ([1905] 2009) famously considered the socio-cultural transformation that was ushered in with the rise of the Protestant work ethic to be an essential component of the "spirit" of capitalism in its early days. Karl Polanyi's *Great Transformation* targets the system of ideas constructed by classical political economists – what he calls the "liberal creed" – as necessary for a market society and the operation of self-regulating markets (less historical reality than ideal). The liberal state is also a core institution of the market system because it separates political and economic spheres based on a *laissez-faire* ideology (the doctrine of minimal government), reducing social relations to the rule of private property (Polanyi [1944] 2001). Even when implementing protectionist

---

2 Commodification renders divisible and exchangeable a good, service, idea, or other aspect of human and natural life not intentionally produced for the market.

policies of economic nationalism, or "practices to create, bolster and protect national economies in the context of world markets" (Pryke 2012, 281), the capitalist state might still remain fundamentally a liberal state in the sense that the core tenets of liberal political economy are not violated: primacy of the individual, equal opportunity (as opposed to equal outcome), and an emphasis on individual freedoms determined through the rule of law within the formal political realm (Howlett, Netherton, and Ramesh 1999, 14–16).

The liberal state becomes responsible for the general interest, and delineates democratic decision making – and is also responsible for naked coercion, as cruel but often legal relations of settler colonialism and militaristic or carceral politics demonstrate. A settler colonial relationship is one where "power – in this case, interrelated discursive and nondiscursive facets of economic, gendered, racial, and state power – has been structured into a relatively secure or sedimented set of hierarchical relations that continue to facilitate the dispossession of Indigenous Peoples of their land and self-determining authority" (Coulthard 2014, 6–7; see also Starblanket and Coburn, in this volume). Canada, for example, is clearly settler-colonial, even if liberal-capitalist, as Coulthard (2014, 4) powerfully recounts:

[T]he reproduction of the colonial relationship between Indigenous Peoples and what would eventually become Canada depended heavily on the deployment of state power geared around genocidal practices of forced *exclusion* and *assimilation* ... For example ... Canada's repeated attempts to overtly uproot and destroy the vitality and autonomy of Indigenous modes of life through institutions such as residential schools; through the imposition of settler-state policies aimed at explicitly undercutting Indigenous political economies and relations to and with land; through the violent dispossession of First Nation women's rights to land and community membership under sexist provisions of the Indian Act; through the theft of Aboriginal children via racist child welfare policies; and through the near wholesale dispossession of Indigenous Peoples' territories and modes of traditional governance in exchange for delegated administrative powers to be exercised over relatively minuscule reserve lands. All of these policies sought to marginalize Indigenous people and communities with the ultimate goal being our *elimination*, if not physically, then as cultural, political, and legal *peoples* distinguishable from the rest of Canadian society. These initiatives reflect the more or less unconcealed, unilateral, and coercive nature of colonial rule during most of the nineteenth and twentieth centuries.

The actually existing features of liberal public policy might vary a great deal, while state-market relations remain liberal; thus the convergence or divergence of policy forms and capitalist relations is an issue of structural, ideational, gendered, and racialized investigation. Keynesian political economy, firmly in the liberal camp, diverted from classical liberalism quite significantly, carving out a much more interventionist role for the state, whether in the form of countercyclical spending to even out the booms and busts of capitalism or welfare state policies that encouraged consumption and investment through income support, public health insurance, social services, public education, and unemployment insurance. Conversely, Marxian political economy highlights, among other things, dialectical class struggle, the theft of surplus value produced by labour through private property rights, and the contradictions inherent in capitalism. And yet, socialist and social democratic parties inspired by Marx's insights in practice might emphasize bargaining through legalized trade unions, an expansion of the welfare state, and forms of economic nationalism.

The range of policy options available to capitalist states becomes most obvious when state intervention is viewed from a historical perspective. The chapters in this book often deal with developments over the neoliberal era (the 1980s and since), although some contrast this with the previous era of the post-war Keynesian welfare state (1950s–1970s) or earlier. Thus the term "neoliberalism" appears throughout this book – indeed it would be difficult to deal with Canadian political rconomy, both theory and empirics, since the 1980s without in some way invoking it. And yet, for many, the privilege given to neoliberalism as a concept in academia ought to be questioned, as ought its stylized description of complex, messy reality. In his book devoted to neoliberalism, Eagleton-Pierce (2016, iii) writes that, despite the popularity of this concept, its exact definition and implications remain "confusing, the product of contested histories, meanings, and practices." Le Gales (2016) and Storper (2016) raise similar concerns. In most countries, we can identify common trends over the past forty years that fit within the neoliberal rubric identified by Harvey (2005a) – e.g., public asset privatization, fiscal austerity, market liberalization – but it is equally true that policy over this same period has been inconsistent, contradictory, and variegated (Brenner, Peck, and Theodore 2010; Peck 2010; Peck and Tickell 2002). There is evidence, in some cases, not of less state regulation but of far more, not only of miserly public sector spending but of new forms of redistribution (Braithwaite 2008). Thus "neoliberalism" should be employed with caution, but the term remains useful as shorthand summarizing forms of profit making and regulation in capitalism that

- privatize aspects of the public sector and non-market rights and resources (dispossession, commodification);
- turn everyday life into financial instruments (financialization);
- combat unionization and cut wages to the bone (labour market devaluation);
- free capital markets and trade flows from tight nation-state regulation and shift production to low-wage countries (deregulation, liberalization, and offshoring);
- impose stringent balanced budget and debt-reduction strategies on the public sector (austerity);
- privilege interest and inflation rates over unemployment dynamics (monetarism); and
- rely on personal indebtedness to fuel household consumption for the many, in marked contrast to the hoarding of wealth and income at the top (inequality).

Neoliberalism is also associated with the "marketization" of the public sector: (re)arranging internal state operations so as to be more "market-like." Largely, this means taking bureaucratic reform cues from a branch of public administration theory known as new public management (NPM), with significant ramifications for staffing, spending, procurement, the workplace, planning, public works and service delivery, and other core elements of the public service and public sector (see Borins 1999; Hood 1991; Hughes 2003; Osborne and Gaebler 1992). Canada was an early adopter of NPM, which sought to overturn older established styles of public administration with its emphasis on hierarchical management, "one best way" of working, the direct delivery of pubic services by public servants, and a professional bureaucracy offering employment for life. NPM replaced traditional public administration thought through a reversal on nearly all fronts: disaggregating the bureaucracy and "letting the managers manage," fostering competition within and between units in the public sector, importing private sector management styles, encouraging the recruitment of private sector employees and business school graduates, and adopting strict cost control and fiscal discipline.

Government bureaucracies now emphasize value for money, efficiency, competition, choice, and market mechanisms. They are to "steer," rather than to "row," by becoming the purchasers of private commodities rather than the direct providers of public services. Contracting out, or outsourcing, commercialization, public asset shedding, joint ventures, public-private partnerships, and other forms of privatization and marketization become key public policy expressions of the new orientation in public management. Transformed government, as opposed to less government, is the result (see Evans, in this volume).

Just as NPM is set against its opposite, traditional public administration, to some extent neoliberalism ought to be understood in relation to its twentieth-century counterpart, Keynesianism. Much has been written on Keynesianism and its similarities to and differences from neoliberalism (see, e.g., Mann 2017; McBride 2005). Suffice it to say that post-war profit making and regulation often took the opposite approach on most of the points above: state sectors expanded, rather than contracted; massive gains in productivity within production drove high growth rates (the "Golden Age" of capitalism), and wage gains that matched productivity growth were often secured through strong unions and labour markets; merchandise trade flowed by state agreement and financial capital was tightly controlled (embedded liberalism); state spending was seen as an important component of national growth and welfare state activities were marshaled to buoy domestic consumption; and taxation schemes often redistributed some degree of wealth and income from top to bottom. Keynesianism was not socialism, however, and the ideals of this era, particularly in retrospect, were often out of synch with the historical practice of its public policy – not to mention that the story can be quite different when seen through a gendered or racialized lens. (Evans, Graefe, Joy and Shields, McBride, and Smardon, in this volume, address some of these differences.)

A broad-sweeping epochal gloss cannot adequately detail the granular, nor can it easily bring out the contingent and contradictory elements of actual practice and experience. Nevertheless, returning to our orienting concept of "political economy," it is evident that markets and politics are intertwined and that capitalism cannot be adequately appreciated from an isolated economics or political science vantage point. And thus, "political economy, at its best, connects the economic, political, and cultural/ideological moments of social life ... political economy is historical and dynamic ... [it] seeks out tensions and contradictions within society that produce struggles and resistance to the prevailing order" (Clement 1997a, 3). Markets are socially embedded institutions; "they are not self-regulating, but in fact demand the exercise of political power in order to enforce contracts and protect private property" (Graefe 2007, 20; see also Ingham 2008; Polanyi [1944] 2001). A glib answer to Clow's (1984, 136) question – "what is the relative importance of political domination versus economic process?" – might be that these are inseparable dynamics. A more considered approach would subject social institutions to contextualization: the specific political economy under investigation matters. Canada's political economy tells a distinct story, whether at the local, regional, or national level or in terms of Canada's involvement in global capitalist relations; and, as the next section details, the Canadian theoretical tradition equally offers unique contributions to the field of political economy.

Political Economy of/in Canada

The settlement of the prairies, the provision of an all-Canadian transportation system, and finally, the adoption of a protective tariff policy are all ... major and related elements of policy in the structure of the Canadian economy. (Mackintosh 1939, 7)

From inception, the Canadian state has played an active (colonial-liberal) role in capitalist market development. Confederation itself was intended to create an economy where the whole would be greater than the sum of its parts through interregional (domestic) trade, and industrialization encouraged by a protective tariff. The Hudson's Bay purchase was intended to stimulate Dominion development, and a transcontinental railway project, financed by private bonds but underwritten by Treasury funds, linked Atlantic to Pacific (Mackintosh 1939). The post-war Keynesian era, in Canada as elsewhere, is often pointed to as an example of a "mixed" economy, one with flourishing public and private sector markets and property rights (see McBride 2005). As the story goes, neoliberalism in the 1980s and beyond sought to upend this dynamic, with capital pushing and policy makers opting for a return to the "residual" state of the nineteenth and early twentieth centuries (Guest 1980; cf. Graefe, on social policy, in this volume). The transformation of property relations holds significant consequences, as property cannot be understood as merely a "thing," but instead is a system of social relations (Macpherson 1978). Although it is certainly true that a wave of public property privatization and austerity-induced public sector clawbacks, not to mention trade liberalization and market deregulation, distinguishes the neoliberal period from the post-war era (McBride and Whiteside 2011), a longer historical vantage point equally reveals tangled public-private relations. Canada has always had a "mixed" economy: "the state in British North America had a large role in propelling development long before such a role became universal with the arrival of the monopoly-capitalism phase" (Clow 1984, 127).

And the Canadian state remains an important economic actor today – notwithstanding key forms of public sector and public service reconfiguration (see Evans; Joy and Shields; and Graefe, in this volume).

Along with prices and profits, a fundamental aspect of capitalist development is the rule of private property relations. Private property relations reflect the important wage labour dynamic: how and by whom the economic value produced by workers' labour is captured (see Smith, in this volume); and on this front, Canada has long had a capitalist economy. As Panitch (1991, 273) describes, "this society was from the beginning constituted in terms of free wage labour or tendentially free wage labour."

Another aspect of private property is land itself. The enclosure of the commons in England (Marx [1867] 1977) and colonial land and resource grabs in Canada (see Carter; and Starblanket and Coburn, in this volume) serviced capitalist production and underpin its origins. However, in contrast to the unfettered private rights to land offered through the English feudal tradition and American-style land sales systems, private rights to Canadian land have been circumscribed over four hundred years of colonial-capitalist development (Vogt 1999; Whiteside 2017b). During the initial period of colonial governance, bargains made with private railway developers and settler farmers meant Crown land rights were often surrendered to private parties, and Indigenous rights to collective ownership were frequently ignored or intentionally dispossessed. In 1867, the British North America Act solidified the rights of the federal and provincial governments and the division of power between the two (along with Indigenous-state relations). Much land, including urban land, became part of provincial government jurisdiction, with federal holdings retained in the northern territories and scattered around the country in urban and rural settings (e.g., federal activities relating to transportation, heritage, national defence, etc.). Over the next 150 years, provincial governments in turn surrendered most of their Crown rights to city and agricultural land through a system of freehold tenure (long-term tenancy legally recognized through fee-simple purchases), but retained ownership of all subsoil resources. Profit making from surface resources (water, timber, minerals, energy) is now typically granted only through lease or licence by the provinces.

By the early twentieth century, groups within the business community were expressing their fear of "a general assault upon the rights of private property" (Armstrong and Nelles 1973, 21) when governments began seizing land to widen public operations through the activities of Crown corporations in sectors ranging from hydro to rail. The number and range of sectors occupied by Crown corporations would only

increase after the Second World War, but concerns from private industry would prove unfounded: most Crown corporations were used to
support private markets and capital accumulation. As Vogt (1999, 45–6)
explains: "Historically, Canadians have granted to governments a
major economic and social role and have accepted fairly uncritically the
creation of state property that accompanies such a role. For several
decades after Confederation [in 1867] the state played what has been
called a promotional role. It facilitated capital accumulation and the
building of substantial [public and private] infrastructure." Several factors urged an active role for the Canadian state in economic development, including: a lack of domestic market linkages, the need to
integrate distinct colonial economies into a single national economy
after Confederation, the attempt to forge a national identity, and an
effort to overcome domination by American entrepreneurs and minimize economic dependency (Whiteside 2012; cf. McBride; Smardon, in
this volume). Crown corporations would similarly function to "bind
the nation (together), to develop and market its resources, and to retain
some measure of the profits and rents" (Taylor 1991, 97). The first
Crown corporation established in Canada was the 1821 government of
Lower Canada initiative to build and operate the Lachine Canal to support the Hudson's Bay Company in its fur trade – a telling origin (Gordon 1981, 7).

The political economy of Canada is not simply that of a strong state
guiding a domestic market – world economic conditions have had a
tremendous influence on Canadian governments. After the booms of
the gold rush (1850s) and post–US Civil War reconstruction, a series of
global economic depressions hit in the 1870s, 1880s, and early 1890s. By
1895, global income expansion positioned Canada as a recipient of foreign investment and natural resource export demand, and industrialization soon picked up in raw product refining and textile manufacturing,
although wheat, mining, and lumber remained major employers at the
turn of the twentieth century (Mackintosh 1939). With the 1929 stock
market crash, and particularly the onset of the Great Depression in the
1930s, Canada experienced the other side of the coin: with one-third of
national gross domestic product derived through exports (primarily
raw materials), Canadian income was highly vulnerable to world price
fluctuations, international demand, and the tariff policies of trade partners (Mackintosh 1939, 57). Needless to say, this was a time of price
deflation, demand slump, and mercantilist autarky, and Canada was
dragged into depression. In contrast, Clarkson (2002, 16), recanting a
similar story as Mackintosh narrated at the time, uses this same CPE
history to argue that "Canadian governments have never fully

controlled their economy, which has had high levels of trade dependence linked to imperial control." Whatever the interpretation of the power and prowess of the Canadian state, two world wars would soon bring a devastating human toll but also generate significant world demand for Canadian exports and ideological support for far greater state intervention to direct supply-and-demand markets and investment decision making across the country (see McBride 2005 for how Keynes came to Canada; see also McBride, and Smardon, in this volume).

Neoliberal free trade agreements integrating Canada with the US and continental economy (see Fridell, in this volume), and emphasizing the Canadian comparative advantage in staples and resource extraction (see Carter, in this volume), have reinforced Canada's vulnerability to world market prices. Even today, despite industrialization and a sophisticated service-based economy with a strong domestic banking sector (see Seccareccia and Pringle, in this volume), along with corporate and co-operative sectors (see Brownlee, and MacArthur, in this volume), significant provincial disparities remain. There is a lack of internal trade, protectionist interprovincial barriers remain, and the domestic economy continues to be geared to north-south continental links, rather than to east-west Canadian integration (see Bemrose, Brown, and Tweedle 2017). Urban capacities are equally diverse (Fanelli and Hudson, in this volume). This varied combination of public-private capitalism and differential forms of accumulation make the Canadian political economy a clear example of combined and uneven development. As described by Trotsky ([1906/1930] 1962, 31), the "force of uneven development operates not only in relations of countries to each other, but also in the mutual relationships of the various processes within one and the same country."

Early Canadian "hewers of wood and drawers of water" – not to mention fish catchers, fur trappers, wheat growers, and land enclosers – gave way to an urban population boom in Montreal, Toronto, Winnipeg, and Vancouver in the early twentieth century, matched by relative and absolute declines in population and economic conditions in the Maritime provinces. Banking and financial services, headquarters, and distribution sites were concentrated in Montreal and Toronto by 1920. With the rise of the US steel industry, "the task of the tariff maker, already heavy because of regional differences of interest, was made still more difficult by the fact that Canadian manufacturers found it hard to either live with or without the United States manufacturing industry" (Mackintosh 1939, 34). The deindustrialization of the Maritimes and assignment of "bread basket" status to the Prairies were undertaken in large part not through geographical necessity but because of national capitalistic policies. Clow (1984) holds federal governments responsible for systematically blocking and thwarting development in the Maritimes in favour of central Canada. Deindustrialization by the 1920s occurred through the "concentration and centralization of capital in Montreal [that] produced a pattern of destruction and 'branch planting' of Maritime manufacturing which led to the de-industrialization of the region" (Jim Sacouman, quoted in Clow 1984, 118). Clow's point resonates beyond the historical development of this particular region – it applies to the Canadian political economy as a whole, then and now. "Confederation pulled the Maritime economies into an 'alien' continental economic of the new British North American dominion, the political framework of the Canadas, and the problems and priorities of the Canadian bourgeoisie" (124). English Canada was not a monolith with uniform interests. "Ccombined development" implies that interaction between societies (provinces, cultures) determines their development and reproduction, and unevenness results through a dialectical process leading to differences and variation (reviewed in Anievas and Nişancıoğlu 2015).

The creation of Canada was fundamentally political and economic, cultural and ideological; and this combined and uneven development of a national economy is also reflected in the national story of the field of political economy in Canada.

> [T]the term "Canadian" is something of a misnomer; a Canadian political economy of genuinely transcontinental scope has yet to be written. The label "Canadian" has been an umbrella under which the political economies of the country's many regions have sheltered; Canadian political economy has remained as unevenly developed as its subject ... What has usually passed as "national" political economy in English Canada has tended to be written from the perspective of the imperatives of Montreal-Toronto – if not just those of Southwest Ontario. (Clow 1984, 134)

Whether this assessment is fair or not is up to the reader. Suffice it to say that Harold Innis, at the University of Toronto, and W.A. Mackintosh, at Queen's University, both writing from Southern Ontario, are early and influential liberal Canadian political economists, known most famously for their description of and contribution to "staples theory" (e.g., Innis 1956; Mackintosh 1939). A liberal interpretation of development and underdevelopment, a staples economy is one that is reliant upon the export of unprocessed or relatively unprocessed resources. The staple good determines the pace of growth, mainly through exposure to world market volatility, and dictates infrastructure needs, state revenue sources, reliance on foreign investment, and so on. Canada's history of political-economic development through cod, fur, wheat, and lumber leaves little mystery as to why the staples thesis was developed by Canadians.

The Classical period in CPE thought (1920s–1950s) was dominated by Innis and the staples approach (cf. Helleiner, in this volume); the 1970s and beyond were led by more critical theorists. Kari Levitt's *Silent Surrender* (1970) put Canadian dependence upon American multinational corporations in the crosshairs. The New Canadian Political Economy (NCPE) of the 1970s and 1980s was heavily left nationalist in its inflection and linked in the 1970s to socialist political activism through the Waffle party (Mahon 1990). Numerous commentators have described early NCPE as a mix of staples theory, dependency theory, and Marxist state theory and critique of capital, the combination of which sought to theorize and explain Canada's position as a rich, underdeveloped country: how to explain the paradox of Canada's condition as a "rich dependency"? (Mahon 1990). NCPE was a dominant influence on political-economic thought in Canada and of Canada, but was not without its critics and drawbacks. Some called it bourgeois for its use of liberal theory (Schmidt 1981); others questioned the application of Latin American dependency theory to the history of Canadian class development (Panitch 1981); and its relative silence on issues of gender and race were notable lacunae (Mahon 1990). Later NCPE writing (1990s and beyond) would take a more intersectional approach, with an expanded role for feminist theorizing, environmentalism, and sensitivity to Indigenous histories and experiences (see Abele 1997; Adkin 1994; Bezanson and Luxton 2006; Green 2003; Smith 1989; Vosko 2002; Wallace and Shields 1997; Williams 1992; see also Coburn 2016; Hurl and Christensen 2015). Core texts forming NCPE include: Levitt (1970; cf. Kellogg 2005); Clement (1997); Clement and Drache (1978); Clement and Vosko (2003); Clement and Williams (1989b); Drache and Clement (1985); Laxer (1991); Panitch (1977a); Teeple (1972).

For better or worse, the field of political economy in Canada has become less coherent since the early NCPE heyday. Some aspects remain the same, such as the focus on the capitalist state and public sector restructuring (see Evans, and Graefe, in this volume), capitalist class and union struggles (see Brownlee, and Smith, in this volume), and trade and resource extraction (see Carter, and Fridell, in this volume). However, as neoliberalism and NPM bring changes to the university and academic publishing, the hegemony of positivism and liberalism in economics and political science combine to position political economy in an (increasingly isolated) oasis of intersectional and interdisciplinary thought in Canada. With equally seismic changes in the political economy of Canada since the 1970s, topics of study for political economists in and of Canada have also converged with comparative and international political economy, reflecting commonly shared experiences in national capitalisms: privatization, financialization, austerity, deindustrialization, trade liberalization, climate change and resource exhaustion, the pressures of globalization and urbanization (see Fanelli and Hudson, in this volume), enhanced reliance on non-profit and charitable organizations to provide much-needed social services (see Joy and Shields, in this volume), and socio-economic inequality (see Peters, in this volume). Indigenization in political-economic thought and across the humanities and social sciences is an especially important step forward witnessed of late (see CPSA 2018; Starblanket and Coburn, in this volume). Convergence with broader political-economic thought and developments beyond Canada's borders chips away at the uniqueness of CPE while heightening its relevance through connections to more global trends and discussions.

Canadian Political Economy

This book brings together experts from across the field of CPE, with contributors working in a number of disciplines in universities across Canada and beyond, combining breadth and depth by linking their strengths and specializations to form a unique, coherent, and timely reassertion of Canadian political economy in the twenty-first century. Covering a wide range of subjects and disciplines is important not only as a way of distinguishing this book, but also for adequately elucidating themes in the development of Canada's political economy and Canadian political-economic thought. As such, this book aims to involve readers in "state of the art" and "state of the discipline" debates.

The core and commonly cited CPE-specific texts in the field are: *The Canadian State* (Panitch 1977a), *A Practical Guide to Canadian Political Economy* (Clement and Drache 1978), *The New Canadian Political Economy* (Clement and Williams 1989b), *Understanding Canada* (Clement 1997b), *The Political Economy of Canada* (Howlett, Netherton, and Ramesh 1999), *Changing Canada* (Clement and Vosko 2003), *Uncle Sam and Us* (Clarkson 2002), *Inside Capitalism* (Phillips 2003), and *Paradigm Shift* (McBride 2005). Although these are stellar sources, and referenced in chapters throughout this book, many are quite dated – some are thirty to forty years old – and thus are silent on important twenty-first century developments. Books published more recently, such as *Private*

Affluence, Public Austerity (McBride and Whiteside 2011), *The Servant State* (McCormack and Workman 2015), *Purchase for Profit* (Whiteside 2015), and a new addition anticipated for the *New Canadian Political Economy* book series (Thomas et al. 2019), deal with topics related to contemporary CPE, but are of more limited scope than what this book addresses – namely, CPE as a contested and evolving field over multiple eras within several ideological traditions, with varied historical and contemporary empirical arcs, covering a full range of theories, institutions, actors, policies, and practices.

The chapters in this book are organized by major subject area in order to uncover real world experiences of/in Canadian political economy and the theories and debates that form the academic field of Canadian political economy. As an edited collection, each chapter can be read as a stand-alone piece; however, the book as a whole is more than the sum of its parts. Together each subject links long-standing and cutting-edge developments and debates in Canadian political economy through three common themes: *changes, crises,* and *conflicts.*

Section 1, *Approaches to Canadian Political Economy,* opens with Chapter 1 by Eric Helleiner on "Historical Canadian Political Economy," wherein he emphasizes change and continuity over three eras of CPE thought. Across these eras, thinkers in Canada have claimed a distinctive "Canadian" approach to political economy arising from the study of their country: the 1970s, when "New Canadian Political Economy" emerged; the inter-war period, when a "staples approach" first appeared; and the era leading up to the introduction of the 1879 National Policy. While CPE was associated with different ideologies in each era, some features of CPE are thought have been common across all three: an openness to foreign ideas, a historical and multidisciplinary orientation, and an interest in Canada's place in the broader international political economy.

Chapter 2, "Dependent Technological Change: The Long Arc of Canadian Innovation and Political Economic Development," by Bruce Smardon, examines long-run historical changes in Canadian technological capacity and economic development and the conflicts that have emerged along the way. Also discussing three distinct periods of Canadian capitalist development, this chapter reviews how technological borrowing and low domestic technological capacities were and continue to be built into the fabric of the Canadian political economy. Canada's low levels of R&D and original innovation compared to those of other advanced capitalist economies are traced from the initial rapid period of industrialization in the National Policy era through to the current period of neoliberal restructuring. Smardon reviews key interpretations of the Canadian political economy, and concludes that they have not accounted sufficiently for how development over time has combined both dependent and autonomous features.

Chapter 3, "Canada's Continental Political Economy," by Stephen McBride, delves into the changing, but subordinate, position of Canada in the hierarchical international and North American political economy context over many decades, and the conflicts that have emerged over solutions to related crises and instability. As McBride argues, this subordinate position has required a degree of state management of Canada's relationship with hegemonic powers, particularly the United States. Historically, the Canadian state adopted strategies and instruments to modify the impact of market forces while fostering capital accumulation. From the 1980s, a "free trade" strategy, continued in the North American Free Trade Agreement and the United States-Mexico-Canada Agreement, led to increased economic integration and vulnerability and to the partial constitutionalization of Canada-US relations in ways that diminished the sovereignty and policy capacity of the Canadian state. Despite the strategy's unimpressive economic results and its problematic political impact, initial public opposition has faded. Continentalism now seems to be hegemonic.

Chapter 4, "'This country has another story': Colonial Crisis, Treaty Relationships, and Indigenous Women's Futurities," by Gina Starblanket and Elaine Coburn, foregrounds Indigenous analyses of the colonial present and imaginings of Indigenous futures, identifying conflicts over land rights and treaty interpretations. It begins with an overview of the interrelated social, political, and economic logics of colonialism, and explores these dynamics through contested interpretations of treaties. From these, it draws out alternate ideas of political economy grounded in treaties as ongoing dialogical relationships. Starblanket and Coburn then turn to Indigenous women's voices as offering vital insights into Indigenous relationality with Creation, in and beyond treaties. The authors consider these to be the starting point for a brief engagement with Indigenous feminist futurities, beyond the colonial present.

Chapter 5, Angela V. Carter's "Canadian Ecological Political Economy," focuses on the environmental crises generated by natural resource exploitation at the heart of Canadian political-economic development, but underappreciated in CPE. She writes of how some of Canada's most difficult political-economic dilemmas are, in essence, ecological, yet traditionally the field of Canadian political economy has viewed the environment narrowly as mere "natural resources" to fuel extractive-based development. Ecological political economy (EPE) provides a corrective to that tendency. Although EPE is aligned with Canadian political economy's commitment to analysing structural power and redistribution, it also offers a more dynamic theorization of capitalism's consequences, given its dual focus on ecological degradation and multilayered social injustice and on fostering sustainable and equitable modes of production. Carter traces out major currents in Canadian EPE, and illustrates how the approach is being applied in analyses of Canada's oil sector. Given how well-equipped EPE is to confront our complex eco-political-economic moment, students of political economy will find it valuable to foreground EPE's theoretical approaches and analytical practices.

Section 2, *Agents in Canadian Political Economy*, begins with Chapter 6, "The Politics of Public Administration: Constructing the Neoliberal State," by Bryan Evans, on emphasizing the changes in public administration studies and within the public sector proper that have helped construct the Canadian neoliberal state. Evans argues that public administration, as practised and taught in Canada, tends to present itself as a technocratic discipline. The more explicitly political and ideological aspects of public administration – specifically, the array of forces that shape the structure and policy work of the administrative state – are given only modest consideration. This entails an acceptance of the broader structural context as an immutable given. The application of a political economy lens to the study of public administration yields insights into the state, not as neutral machinery standing above the fray of class and other conflicts, but as the distillation of political and economic forces that reflect the imbalance of forces in the larger societal context.

Crises, conflicts, and changes in labour relations are treated in Chapter 7, "Political Economy and the Canadian Working Class," by Charles W. Smith. As Smith describes, since the early formation of the union movement in Canada there has been a tacit agreement among working-class activists that the state and the law could be used to restrict the power of both capital and the state to promote collective workers' freedoms. Yet the militancy of Canada's working class – which once shook the very foundations of how capital and the state functioned – has declined along with a drop in labour organization, as workers today are far less likely to belong to a union than at any time since the end of the Second World War. In examining these circumstances, Smith seeks to expose workers' contradictory dependency on state law to protect their collective abilities to organize, bargain, and strike, arguing that overreliance on such law – both as a tool to preserve past gains and to advance workers' collective freedoms – is weakening the ability of workers and their unions to respond to government-driven anti-union-ism in the current era.

Chapter 8, "Corporations and Corporate Power," by Jamie Brownlee, addresses the conflicts and concerns that have emerged in Canada through increasingly problematic concentrations of corporation power. In Canada, and to varying degrees in nations throughout the world, the economy, the state, and the political system are now heavily influenced by corporations. Corporate power has reached unprecedented levels, influencing decisions about who governs and how, the production process, how resources are distributed, the quality and quantity of jobs, and the content of media and communication systems. Brownlee explores the modern corporation in Canada, focusing on three key empirical issues in the Canadian political economy literature: (i) the economic, social, and political dimensions of corporate power; (ii) the relationship between corporations and economic inequality; and (iii) the changing nature of corporate regulation in the context of neoliberal-ism and globalization.

In Chapter 9, "Co-operatives," Julie L. MacArthur examines the pos-sibility of change to the corporate status quo through an exploration of the nature and significance of co-operatives in Canada's political econ-omy, an area long neglected in CPE scholarship due to its largely nationalist and state-level focus. Co-operatives are diverse, contested, and adaptable organizations, part of a centuries'-old social movement. They are united in an institutional design that connects members' needs to decision-making power. However, they also occupy a contested space in terms of their contribution to post-capitalist futures, given sig-nificant diversity in their practice. This chapter traces the emergence and contours of the Canadian co-operative sector, examining its varied forms, functions, and characteristics.

Chapter 10, "The Political Economy of the Non-profit Sector," by Meghan Joy and John Shields, examines the nature of the non-profit sector through a political economy lens, taking up the issue of how non-profits in capitalist society have changed over time, and how they both absorb and reflect conflicts and crises in capitalism. Rarely subject to critical analysis in the orthodox literature, the non-profit sector, as the authors show, is strategically positioned to shed new light on the ongoing contradictions and struggles of capitalist society. The chapter thus explores the book's three themes of changes, crises, and conflicts through a historical analysis of the shifting social role of the non-profit sector in capitalist society. Joy and Shields conclude with a reflection on the current period of advanced neoliberal capitalism and the role it has set out for the non-profit sector to facilitate austerity politics. They also consider social justice dynamics within the sector and the possibility these might help to shift dominant political projects towards more progressive ends.

Section 3, *Applications of Canadian Political Economy*, begins with Chapter 11, "Inequality," by John Peters. Citizens and public officials have long debated economic inequality, and even today there are major conflicts over its causes and solutions. Over the past thirty years, however, with the widening gap in wages and incomes, and in light of the 2008 global financial crisis, new research has emerged on inequality, re-evaluating its causes, trends, and consequences. Peters reviews some of this recent international research as well as contemporary critical political economy literature in Canada, highlighting what is happening to economic inequality and why. He also notes the many areas where further research on inequality in Canada is required, as this important issue remains in some ways underaddressed in the CPE literature.

In Chapter 12, "Urban Political Economy, Poverty and Inequality in Canada," Carlo Fanelli and Carol-Anne Hudson examine changes in how the "urban" is approached in CPE, along with crises of inequality in Canadian cities and the changes needed to address urban poverty in Canada. Within the broad tradition of Canadian political economy, the "urban question" has long been relegated to the margins as issues of national identity and trade dependency on the British and, later, American empires dominated the period from the 1930s to the 1970s. Although a distinctively Canadian approach to urban political economy has yet to materialize, the broader "new" political economy revival of the 1970s went a long way towards establishing the significance of the "urban question" as a space for critical engagement in and of itself. In this regard, the chapter's aim is threefold: (i) to provide an overview of the "new" critical urban political economy approach of the 1970s; (ii) to locate this approach in the broader context of poverty and inequality in Canada's largest cities; and (iii) to evaluate the strengths and weaknesses of current poverty reduction strategies in Canada's largest urban centres.

In Chapter 13, "The Political Economy of Social Policy in Canada," Peter Graefe analyses conflicts over the role and interpretation of social policy. Social policies have a contradictory place in capitalism, drawing resources away from accumulation on the one hand, while ensuring the reproduction of necessary inputs for production on the other. Political economists studying Canadian social policy in the present neoliberal moment tend to emphasize one side of this contradiction. For some, social policies are "rolling out" new institutions that enable capitalist social relations to colonize more of the lifeworld. For others, new social policies are creating an "inclusive liberalism" that flanks neoliberalism by mopping up social dislocation. Graefe argues for a more open form of analysis that recognizes that social conflicts shape how social policies relate to neoliberalism in terms of the extent to which they roll out or flank neoliberalism, or indeed open the door to alternative social imaginaries.

In Chapter 14, "Canadian Trade and Trade Agreements: Free or Fair?" Gavin Fridell examines the free trade/fair trade debate in Canada and conflicts over the meaning and goals of trade agreements, and how change in the dominant regime is possible but requires progressive underpinnings. Although "free trade" is widely popular as an *idea*, political economists have questioned whether we actually live in a free trade world and whether this is something positive to which we should aspire. Canadian trade policy has often been driven by goals at odds with genuine free trade, and trade agreements have been opposed by movements demanding a "fair trade" vision that places social and environmental rights first. Drawing examples from major trade agreements, Fridell examines how the goals of trade policy emerge not out of neutral policy debate, but out of struggles between dominant and subordinate sectors of society.

A looming crisis in the once-resilient Canadian banking sector is presented in Chapter 15, "Money and Finance," by Mario Seccareccia and David Pringle. Despite the Canadian financial system's having displayed relative resiliency during the global financial crisis, current levels of household indebtedness are creating vulnerability and instability. The chapter's narrative focuses on the 1975–2018 period, and investigates the evolving structures and social processes operating within three spheres of the political economy of Canadian finance: the chartered banking industry, lender-borrower relations at the macroeconomic level, and monetary policy conducted by the Bank of Canada. The sectoral balance framework and the financial fragility hypothesis are employed as analytic tools. The combined insights offer an interpretation of the present risks facing the Canadian system.

In "Conclusion: Advancing Canadian Political Economy," Heather Whiteside sums up the aims and ambitions of this book and its contribution to Canadian political economy through the 3Cs.

SECTION 1

Approaches to Canadian Political Economy

1 Historical Canadian Political Economy

ERIC HELLEINER[1]

Introduction

Any history of Canadian political economy (CPE) must first stake out a definition of CPE itself. One approach might be to define CPE as the study of political economy *in* Canada. Alternatively, CPE can refer to the study of the political economy *of* Canada. In this chapter, I am interested in how the term CPE has been often used in a third and more specific way to refer to a claim that a distinctive intellectual approach has arisen from the study of political economy both *in* and *of* Canada.

What is the history of this idea of CPE as distinctive intellectual approach? This chapter highlights that there have been three separate eras when thinkers in Canada have claimed the existence of a distinctive "Canadian" approach to political economy arising from the study of their own country. I begin by describing two that are better known: the 1970s period, in which a "New Canadian Political Economy" (NCPE) was born, and the inter-war period, when a distinctive "staples approach" to political economy first became prominent in Canadian intellectual circles. I then turn to examining in more detail even earlier discussions of the need for a "Canadian" approach to political economy in the nineteenth century, discussions which have been neglected in more contemporary CPE scholarship.

---

1 I am very grateful for the comments of an anonymous reviewer, as well as those of Angela Carter, Jennifer Clapp, Peter Graefe, Stephen McBride, John Peters, Bruce Smardon, Charles Smith, and Heather Whiteside. I am also grateful to the Killam Fellowship Programme and the Social Sciences and Humanities Research Council of Canada for supporting this research.

In addition to deepening the history of this idea of CPE as a distinctive intellectual approach, I am interested in exploring the common features of CPE thought across the three periods (beyond the claim of Canadian distinctiveness). In other words, can we speak of a genuine long-standing CPE intellectual tradition that dates back to the nineteenth century? If such a tradition exists, I argue that it cannot be defined in ideological terms because, across time, CPE has been characterized by ideological diversity rather than by conformity. Although CPE was associated with conservativism in the nineteenth century, it became more associated with liberal thought in the inter-war period and then with left-of-centre politics in the post-1970 era. Looking at CPE through this ideological lens, *change* is thus a key theme. When viewed in a long historical trajectory, however, there is also some continuity. A CPE tradition can be defined with reference to some other features that have been common across all three eras: a willingness to combine claims of Canadian distinctiveness with an openness to foreign ideas, an embrace of a historical and wide multidisciplinary approach to the study of political economy, and a strong interest in analysing Canada's place in the broader international political economy.

The "New" and the "Old" CPE

Contemporary NCPE scholarship has its roots in the 1970s. At the start of that decade, the study of CPE was very limited in Canadian universities. Robin Neill and Gilles Paquet (1993) describe how an earlier tradition of political economy (see below) became sidelined in Canadian economics departments in the 1950s and 1960s by the growing dominance of neoclassical "scientific economics." A survey of sixty-five Canadian political science departments in 1973 also revealed that at least 90 per cent had no focus on Canadian political economy (Drache 1978, 8). Moreover, some universities, such as Queen's and McGill, which had long-standing departments integrating economics and political science, split these departments into two units representing the two separate disciplines in the 1960s – others, such the University of Toronto's Department of Political Economy lasted longer, splitting into two in 1982 (Germain 2009). The *Canadian Journal of Economics and Political Science* also split in 1967, creating one journal for economics and one for political science.

Into this vacuum stepped the pioneers of NCPE in the 1970s. A number of important publications helped to encourage the new interest in CPE at this time (see Whiteside's Introduction to this volume, as well as Coburn 2016; Hurl and Christensen 2015). The growth of NCPE was also marked by the creation of a political economy section in the Canadian Political Science Association in 1976 and the establishment of a new journal, *Studies in Political Economy*, in 1979. Another sign of the new respectability and popularity of the field was the production of CPE textbooks (e.g., Clement and Williams 1989b; Howlett and Ramesh 1992).

Those associated with the birth of NCPE saw it as an effort to carve out a distinctive Canadian approach to political economy. In an influential survey of the emerging field in 1978, Wallace Clement and Daniel Drache put it this way: "For many years the social sciences in Canada have been dominated by perspectives and concerns emanating from the United Kingdom and the United States. The point has now been reached, however, where there exists in Canada a critical number of researchers and teachers able to sustain a distinctly Canadian perspective" (Clement and Drache (1978, ii). Similarly, Mel Watkins, another important promoter of NCPE, argued that Canadian economics had become "a branch plant of U.S. economics," and critiqued those "who too deeply embrace the metropolitan paradigm" (Watkins 1982, 17; 1978, S112).

The content of much NCPE thought in this period reflected these nationalist sentiments. Scholars analysed Canada's "dependence" and "silent surrender" to the United States (Levitt 1970), as well as its status as an American "colony" (Teeple 1972, xiii). The heavy focus of the Canadian economy on exporting resources to the United States was said to be one cause of the country's subordination. NCPE scholars also argued that Canada's sovereignty was undermined by the large presence of American multinational corporations in the Canadian economy, including in the manufacturing sector, where foreign ownership was blamed for inhibiting innovation and creating a distorted and dependent kind of industrialization.

These nationalist themes often intersected with left critiques of the Canadian bourgeoisie for having a "colonial mentality" and a "comprador" position that was subordinate to American capital and serving its interests (Teeple, 1972, xii; Watkins 1978, S91). Many NCPE thinkers sought to cultivate popular nationalist forces that could help build a more independent Canadian economy. The left-of-centre ideological orientation of the dominant strand of NCPE was apparent from the subtitle of the journal *Studies in Political Economy: A Socialist Review*. Legacies of this early work remained in the NCPE tradition as it evolved after the 1970s; as Kellogg (2015, 4) puts it, "[t]he CPE tradition is quite accurately captured through the couplet 'left nationalism.'"

At the same time that they highlighted the "Canadian-ness" of their thought, NCPE scholars also openly highlighted how they drew upon and adapted foreign ideas in the context of studying Canadian problems. For some NCPE thinkers, debates in European Marxist political economy were particularly significant. Others drew on ideas associated with the "dependency school" that had become increasingly popular in Latin America and other poorer regions of the world during the 1960s and 1970s (Hurl and Christensen 2015). As Clement and Drache (1978, ii) put it, the NCPE approach was thus "not a parochial one."

The dominant methods of NCPE were historical and multidisciplinary, drawing not just on politics and economics, but also sociology, geography, history, and other fields. This methodological orientation contrasted with trends in many US universities at this time, where "political economy" came to be associated with formal modelling using rationalist assumptions emulating the practices of neoclassical economics (Howlett and Ramesh 1992). In addition to reflecting the foreign intellectual sources from which NCPE drew some inspiration, the historical and multidisciplinary orientation of NCPE also had local roots. NCPE scholars trumpeted how they were building upon the methods and approach of an earlier Canadian intellectual tradition from the inter-war years: the staples approach of Harold Innis.

Innis and the Staples Approach

Born in rural Ontario in 1894, Innis had become a central figure promoting Canadian political economy from the time he joined the University of Toronto's Department of Political Economy in 1920 until his death in 1952. He analysed many dimensions of Canada's economic history in works published during the inter-war years (his focus became broader after this, including issues relating to communications). He also devoted enormous energy to encouraging others to study CPE, including through the creation in 1928 of a new publication titled *Contributions to Canadian Economics* (which morphed into the *Canadian Journal of Economics and Political Science* in 1935) (Neill 1972; Watson 2006).

Like NCPE scholars in the 1970s, Innis was particularly keen to promote perspectives on political economy that reflected Canadian experience and needs, rather than those of dominant powers. He was concerned that social scientists in Canada's growing universities at the time were often trained abroad in ways that left them with little knowledge of Canada and inadequate tools for understanding its issues (Neill 1972, 15). Here, for example, is the case he made in 1929:

> A new country presents certain definite problems which appear to be more or less insoluble from the standpoint of the application of economic

theory as worked out in the older highly industrialized countries ... [T] here is evidence to show that the application of the economic theories of old countries to the problems of new countries results in a new form of exploitation with dangerous consequences. The only escape can come from an intensive study of Canadian economic problems and from the development of a philosophy of economic history or an economic theory suited to Canadian needs. (Innis [1929] 1956, 3)

Innis's staples approach to the study of Canadian economic history was his contribution towards this goal. The approach suggested that Canada's history and development were shaped heavily by the successive staples it exported – such as fish, fur, minerals, lumber, and wheat – to meet the demands of more highly industrialized countries at the centre of the world economy. He highlighted how each staple export was associated with distinct technologies, industrial structures, patterns of demand, rents, forward and backward linkages to the rest of the economy, overhead costs associated with infrastructure, and so on. Innis was also interested in the important role played by public authorities in supporting the large investments associated with each new staples-exporting process, as well as in scaling down commitments (including debts accumulated) in declining staples sectors (for an overview, see Neill 1972; Watkins 1963).

Innis highlighted a number of problems associated with Canada's reliance on staples exporting. One was the country's dependence on external demand as a driver for its economic development, a dependence that he argued inhibited self-sustaining growth and left the country vulnerable to unstable boom-and-bust cycles. Innis was also concerned about the rigidities associated with institutions established in each staple's export phase and the painful and costly adjustments associated with shifting from one phase to the next. He put the case as follows in a widely quoted passage: "Concentration on the production of staples for export to more highly industrialized areas in Europe and later in the United States had broad implications for the Canadian economic, political, and social structure. Each staple in its turn left its stamp, and the shift to new staples invariably produced periods of crises in which adjustments in the old structure were painfully made and a new pattern created in relation to a new staple" (Innis [1950] 1972, 5–6).

Innis's staples approach has long been seen as one of the most important distinctive contributions to political economy to have emerged from Canada – and it has been used to study the political economy of other staples-exporting countries. His ideas emerged from his detailed inductive studies of Canadian economic history, as well as those of some of his Canadian colleagues, notably W.A. Mackintosh, whose 1923 work on staples exports inspired Innis's initial interest in this approach (Neill 1972, chap. 3). Innis's development of the staples approach also benefited from the broader intellectual environment of a small but growing community of Canadian professional economists who were sympathetic to the methods of the "German historical school" within political economy. The latter was sceptical of the abstractions of neoclassical economics, and praised inductive work that was sensitive to distinct historical and institutional contexts that shaped countries' different economic evolution (Neill 1991, 97, 119–25). Innis himself rarely referred to the German historical school, but Neill (1998, 186) notes that this Canadian intellectual environment "generated the tolerance that Innis needed" for his work.

Innis was also influenced by the American political economist Thorstein Veblen, whose ideas he encountered as a graduate student at the University of Chicago (Bonnett 2013; McNally 1981; Neill 1972; Watson 2006, 153–63). Veblen was well known at the time as a leading critic of the focus in neoclassical economics on marginal utility theory and on static states of equilibrium. Innis drew on Veblen's alternative ideas about the institutional context for individual values and the price system, as well as his emphasis on the historical evolution and transformation of economic systems. Also important were Veblen's ideas about the role of the diffusion of technology from rich to poor countries in the economic development of the latter.

The Staples Approach and NCPE

Innis's ideas played an important role in facilitating the emergence of the NCPE scholarship in the 1970s (Watkins 1982). Many of the pioneers of the NCPE had been trained by Innis or his disciples. NCPE scholars were also inspired by Innis's deep commitment to studying Canada and developing theories that were tailored to the Canadian experience. Innis's style of analysis also appealed to scholars seeking a build a new kind of historically minded, multidisciplinary political economy that challenged neoclassical economics. In addition to highlighting various disequilibria and market failures, Innis was very critical of the short-term static analytics of neoclassical economics, which he felt overlooked the influence of culture, history, politics, and geography on the meaning and content of the price system (Neill 1972, 79).

Innis's analysis of the limitations of staples-led development also provided intellectual ammunition for NCPE scholars to criticize

Canada's reliance on commodity exporting to the United States. In addition, they were able to quote him in support of their critiques of US foreign investment in Canada. In a 1948 lecture, Innis had famously argued that "Canada moved from colony to nation to colony" when discussing how "American capital investors" had established branch plants in Canada that took advantage of the country's tariff and access to British imperial markets (Innis [1948] 1956, 405]. Just before his death, Innis had also suggested that "[w]e can only survive by taking specific action at strategic points against American imperialism in all its attractive guises" (quoted in Watkins 1978, S97fn22).

Although the appeal of Innis for NCPE scholars was clear, his ideological orientation was different from that which characterized much NCPE scholarship (e.g., McNally 1981). Innis had shown little interest in the Canadian political left during his career, and was sceptical of government intervention in the economy and centralized planning (Neill 1991, 134). As Watkins (1982, 18) put it, Innis was "a liberal, albeit a liberal with a difference." He was also more wary of nationalism than were many NCPE scholars in the 1970s (Howlett and Ramesh 1992).

The liberal orientation of staples theory was even more evident in the work of some of Innis's colleagues, including W.A. Mackintosh, the scholar often seen as a "co-founder" of this approach (Ferguson 1993, 208). Like Innis, Mackintosh's thinking had been influenced by Veblen, but also by the "frontier thesis" of US historian Frederick Jackson Turner. Where Innis was pessimistic about Canada's economic future, Mackintosh was more optimistic, arguing that staples-led development could set the stage for Canada to shift to a more diversified economy and self-sustaining industrial growth over time, following the US example (Drache 1978, 3; Ferguson 1993). This more positive version of the staples thesis had little appeal for most NCPE scholars in the 1970s, who were more inclined to embrace what Watkins (1981, 62) called a "dependency version of the staples model." Watkins himself, however, noted that the staples approach itself was not determinist on this issue. Indeed, some Latin American critics of dependency theory drew on the Canadian staples approach when arguing that commodity exporting could generate positive long-term development outcomes for their countries (Conde 1992, 168–71).

In addition to his more positive view of staples exporting, Mackintosh was also more interested than Innis in combining the staples approach with broader Anglo-American liberal reformist thought at the time, which backed forms of public management of the economy to address market failures, poverty, and unemployment (Ferguson 1993). His interest in these ideas encouraged Mackintosh to become active in advising the Canadian government after the mid-1930s, including in the 1940s on the introduction of both Keynesianism and the US-led Bretton Woods order, which was designed to reconcile liberal multilateral principles with new kinds of active public economic management. Once again, this liberal orientation departed from the ideas of the dominant strand of NCPE scholarship in the 1970s. The direction of Mackintosh's thinking in this period was also very different from that of Innis, who became increasingly sceptical of US power and the centralizing tendencies and short-term orientation of Keynesian planning (Neill 1972, chap. 5).

An Even Older CPE

Most CPE textbooks and surveys of CPE thought trace the historical origins of CPE no further back than the staples approach of Innis and Mackintosh. Here, however, I argue that this approach overlooks active intellectual discussions that took place earlier, in the nineteenth century, about a distinctly Canadian approach to political economy arising from the study of the country. These discussions reached their peak around the time of the introduction of the Conservative Party's National Policy in 1879 and its much higher tariff.

This new trade policy, introduced by Prime Minister John A. Macdonald, was controversial in many circles because it challenged prevalent free trade thinking. To defend the tariff, supporters of the National Policy depicted free trade theory as an overly abstract idea that had been imported from Europe, while arguing that the case for trade protectionism was grounded in local Canadian realities and priorities (Heaman 2014, 213–7). Conservative politicians in the federal Parliament advancing this theme quoted the words of a Scottish critic of liberal political economy, Samuel Laing: "Political economy is not a universal science, of which all the principles are applicable to all men under all circumstances, and equally good and true for all nations, but every country has a political economy of its own, suitable to its own physical circumstances of position on the globe, climate, soil and products, and to the habits, character, and idiosyncrasy of its inhabitants, formed or modified by such physical circumstances."[2]

---

2 See Prince Edward Island's George Howlan and Ontario's James Patterson in Canada (1878, 327; 1879, 645). For the original, whose wording is slightly different, see Laing (1852, 293).

Laing's idea that "every country has a political economy of its own" had been made in 1852 in the context of his defence of Danish protectionist policies that insulated the country's manufacturing and commercial sectors from foreign competition. Although free trade would have lowered prices and boosted efficiency in these sectors, Laing had argued that protectionism was justified because it boosted employment and supported guilds that reflected "ancient social arrangements and regulations to which their populations are accustomed, and regard not merely with favour, but as rights" (Laing 1852, 293). Challenging the priorities of liberal political economy, which was dominant in his home country, Laing argued: "the national wealth – that is, the means to raise the public revenue and meet the exigencies of the state – may be less, yet the national well-being may be greater, the diffusion of employment, subsistence, comfort, and civilized habits and tastes may be greater under their system of political economy than under ours" (Laing 1852, 307).

Laing's ideas were cited not just by Canadian critics of free trade, but also by some in the United States, including Henry Carey, who emerged in the 1850s and 1860s as the leading American advocate of protectionism – or what was known as the "American system" of political economy (e.g., Carey 1858, 1:50–1; 2:111–15; 1859, 3:260, 343–5; see also *Commercial and Financial Chronicle* 1875, 74; Bowen 1856, v). Carey (1858) argued that protectionism could cultivate local industry and create a more balanced, domestically focused economy that fostered diverse employment opportunities and social harmony within the country. His defence of a more inward-looking development strategy even extended to environmental issues, as he critiqued monocrop, export-oriented agriculture for exhausting local soils (e.g., Carey 1858, 1:83, 87, 308–11, 329, 368; 2:206).

Canadian protectionists often drew heavily on Carey's ideas, including the Hamilton-based merchant Isaac Buchanan, who was the leading Canadian advocate of higher tariffs for many years before the introduction of the National Policy (Goodwin 1961, 49; Helleiner 2019; Henley 1989; Kealey 1980, 10–11, 126, 155–7, 161; Palmer 1979, 101). A conservative nationalist, Buchanan (1864) highlighted the employment benefits of tariffs, which could build up local industry in ways that reduced the Canadian economy's dependence on staples exports. Like Carey, he promoted an ideal in which Canadian farmers, workers, and manufacturers could live in harmony with one another, and outlined an environmental critique of free trade that had a quite modern ring (see Carter, in this volume): "The argument against Free Trade, or a system of exporting the raw materials of a country, which is to be found

in the exhaustion of her soil, has not been paid sufficient attention to ...
We are accustomed to take too little account of what is due to the earth"
(Buchanan 1864, 75n).[3]

Like other supporters of the National Policy, as well as Carey and
Laing, Buchanan attacked the universal pretensions of English liberal
political economy. As early as 1863, he had criticized the idea that "a
Political Economy suited for Britain ... is equally suited for this young
country" (Buchanan 1864, 229). He went further to argue that a universal science of political economy was impossible and all political economy was nationally context-specific: "I, in fact, deny that political
economy is a science at all! A science is a system of fixed facts; and the
facts of Political Economy can only be circumstances, unless we would
legislate with our eyes shut, and without the least reference to the country in which we legislate" (Buchanan 1864, 229–30; see also 145–6).
Buchanan (1864, 33) preferred to describe his perspective as one of
"Patriotic or Social Economy." Laing had also used the term "social
economy" to describe his preferred approach, which would incorporate the insights of political economy but also examine countries' social
and political institutions and "all that affects social prosperity, and the
well-being, moral and physical, of the individuals composing the social
body of the country" (Laing 1842, 60).

This idea of distinct national approaches to political economy found
supporters not just among Canadian and American protectionist thinkers; it also attracted attention in places as diverse as India, Japan, and
Latin America in the late nineteenth century (Goswami 2004; Helleiner
and Rosales 2017; Metzler 2006). In many countries, the ideas of the
German economic nationalist thinker Friedrich List were particularly
influential. In his widely read book, *The National System of Political Economy*, List ([1841] 1885) had argued that free trade thought was not a
universal science, but merely a British ideology of domination designed
to prevent other countries from industrializing by locking them into a
subordinate position as resource exporters. List's ideas were also cited
by Carey (1858, 2:127), as well as by nineteenth-century Canadian protectionists, including Buchanan (1864, 88–91).

In the context of these challenges to free trade thought, even prominent British liberals began to engage in a debate about the universality

---

3 In addition to trade protectionism, Buchanan had called since the late 1830s for the
Canadian government to issue an inconvertible national currency that would challenge the economy's existing staples-based export orientation even more dramatically.
This aspect of his program did not find a place in the 1879 National Policy (Helleiner
2006, 32–8).

of their approach to political economy. In an important 1876 lecture at the time of the one hundredth anniversary of Smith's *The Wealth of Nations*, Stanley Jevons (1876, 621) noted Laing's comment that "every country has a political economy of its own" when discussing the future of political economy in the context of growing challenges to economic liberalism. In the same year, Walter Bagehot ([1876] 1885, 27) explicitly criticized his liberal colleagues who believed their approach to political economy could be a "universal theory" applicable to all nations and societies. Noting the "revolt" against free trade thinking in many countries, Bagehot argued that liberalism was best described simply as "English political economy" because its tenets were applicable only to "a single kind of society – a society of grown-up competitive commerce, such as we have in England." He continued: "In my judgment, we need not that the authority of our Political Economy should be impugned, but that it should be minimized" (Bagehot ([1876] 1885, 4, 26–7).

Because of the influence of British liberal thought in Canada, these kinds of arguments gave further strength to Canadian thinkers who sought to claim the existence of a distinct "Canadian" approach to political economy that helped to justify the National Policy tariff. This claim to national distinctiveness was complicated, of course, by the fact that they often drew on the ideas of foreign thinkers such as Laing, Carey, and List. In drawing inspiration from foreign thinkers to develop a "Canadian" political economy, however, they set a pattern that would be repeated by Innis in the inter-war years and the NCPE thinkers in the 1970s, as we have seen.

The Strange Neglect of John Rae

At the same time, advocates of a "Canadian" approach to political economy at the time of the National Policy could also cite a local thinker who had pioneered protectionist thought earlier in the nineteenth century. This thinker was John Rae, whose ideas were invoked by Macdonald himself at the time of the debates about the introduction of the National Policy (as well as by other Canadian protectionists) (Canada 1876, 490–1; Goodwin 1961, 52, 57, 126; Heaman 2014, 214; 2017, 139; James 1965, 172; Neill 1991, 58). Rae is rarely mentioned by contemporary CPE scholars, but many historians of economic thought consider him to be the most sophisticated political economist to have emerged from the Canadian context in the nineteenth century (e.g., Hamouda, Lee, and Mair 1998; Neill 1991, 57). This judgment is based on a lengthy book he wrote in 1834 titled *Statement of Some New Principles on the Subject of Political Economy: Exposing the Fallacies of the System of Free Trade and of Some Other Doctrines Maintained in the "Wealth of Nations"* (Rae [1834] 1964).

The book was written while Rae was living in the colony of Upper Canada, and it drew heavily on his Canadian experiences since emigrating from Scotland in 1822 (Dimand 1998, 181–2; Hamouda, Lee, and Mair 1998, 4; James 1965, 30, 146, 154–5, 188; Neill 1991, 58, 65).[4] Although he had been trained in medicine in Scotland, he became increasingly interested in critiquing Adam Smith's ideas in the context of witnessing the contrast between levels of economic development in Canada and in Britain. As is evident from the subtitle of the book, Rae was particularly critical of Smith's endorsement of free trade. Rae felt Smith had overlooked how poorer countries could benefit economically from the introduction of temporary tariffs designed to protect new industries. Temporary protection of this kind, he argued, could promote local industrialization by encouraging two kinds of activity that might otherwise be too expensive and/or difficult for individuals to undertake: local invention and/or the transfer of technology from abroad. Although consumers might experience higher prices in the short term because of the tariffs, the benefits to the country would be large over the longer term as its "productive powers" were enhanced by the growth of manufacturing (Rae [1834] 1964, 70).

Rae was not an opponent of trade in general, and he highlighted the benefits of free trade among products where national advantages were based on natural endowments (Rae [1834] 1964, vii, ix, 362, 366–7; Dimand 1998; James 1965, 197). But he challenged liberal conceptions of a natural and permanent international division of labour. As he put it, "because one country alone now produces particular commodities, we are by no means warranted to conclude that nature intended they should be produced only there" (Rae [1834] 1964, 258). Indeed, in an 1825 article, Rae had detailed Britain's history of borrowing technology from abroad and cultivating industries with various interventionist policies, and had argued that other countries needed to learn from this experience: "While England was gradually raising up that astonishing fabric of manufacturers which now exists, various expedients of a temporary and subsidiary nature were adopted, serving the purpose of ladders, frames and scaffolding, which she can now with safety and advantage thrown down and forget. But the memory of such regulations remains for the instruction

---

4 In 1848, he left Upper Canada and lived in Hawaii for some time before ending up in New York.

of other nations in the commencement of their manufacturing career" (quoted in James 1965, 202).

Although Rae primarily focused on the task of boosting national productivity, he noted that the cultivation of local industry would also generate savings on transportation costs and reduce a country's vulnerability to interruptions of supply from abroad generated by wars and other causes (Rae [1834] 1964, 70). In addition, Rae supported tariffs on luxury imports because these would prevent wasteful spending and generate useful revenue. In his 1825 article, Rae also highlighted broader national security benefits of building up local industry: "In the state of society which has long prevailed in modern times, some particular manufacturers are absolutely necessary to secure the independence of a nation" (quoted in James 1965, 197). At the start of his 1834 book, Rae ([1834] 1964, vii) returned to this issue, arguing that promotion of a country's wealth was needed not just for "internal prosperity," but also "as a means of repelling external aggressions."

Rae's critique of free trade bore some general similarities to Alexander Hamilton's 1791 arguments for infant industry protectionism, arguments with which Rae was familiar (and which Carey and Buchanan would later cite). But Rae's defence of tariffs was more detailed and sophisticated than that of Hamilton. Rae's arguments were also developed before List's well-known 1841 book, which greatly popularized the case for infant industry tariffs in many countries. Indeed, it is interesting to speculate whether List might have drawn on Rae's work. Perhaps the most famous passage in List's book was the idea that Britain, when challenging protectionist policies abroad, "kicks away the ladder" that it had used to become rich (List [1841] 1885, 368). The metaphor was strikingly similar to Rae's 1825 description (quoted above) of Britain's mercantilist policies as "serving the purpose of ladders, frames and scaffolding" that later British free traders had proceeded to "throw down and forget."

The innovative nature of Rae's ideas about trade policy were recognized in the nineteenth century by important political economists outside Canada, including even the liberal John Stuart Mill, who drew on them when he controversially endorsed the case for infant industry tariffs in the late 1840s (James 1965, 167–9). In the twentieth century, other aspects of Rae's thought were also widely praised for anticipating Joseph Schumpeter's work on innovation, Irving Fischer's capital theory, and Thorstein Veblen's views on capital and conspicuous consumption (Hamouda, Lee, and Mair 1998; James 1965; Neill 1991, chap. 4; 1998). When Rae's 1834 book was republished in an edited form in 1905 (under the title *The Sociological Theory of Capital*), it was also reviewed in "almost all the economics journals of the world" (James 1965, 184).

Despite Rae's importance as a pioneer of political economy in the Canadian context, modern CPE scholars and textbooks rarely mention him or his ideas. This strange neglect dates back to the birth of NCPE in the 1970s. Even the influential and very detailed bibliography of existing CPE work that was developed in 1978 by Clement and Drache (1978) includes no reference to this thinker. The lack of recognition of Rae by the pioneers of NCPE was particularly odd given the publication in 1965 – just before NCPE emerged – of an engaging biography of Rae, alongside a reissuing of his 1834 book (James 1965). NCPE scholars were not alone in Canada in overlooking Rae's work at this time: Rae's biographer himself noted of the reissue "that it made barely a ripple in Canadian academic circles" (James 1998, 21–2). Since then, there has been growing awareness of Rae's significance within the economics discipline in Canada, as evidenced by the creation in 1994 of a bi-annual prize in his name for research excellence by the Canadian Economics Association. NCPE scholars, however, have been very slow to follow.

The limited attention given to Rae by NCPE scholars is also odd given the invocation of his ideas at the time of the National Policy, a seminal moment in the political economy of the country (Helleiner 2019). Indeed, historians such as Neill (1991, 65) even argue that Rae's ideas formed "the intellectual foundation of the National Policy." The usefulness of Rae's arguments to Macdonald went beyond the former's defence of infant industry tariffs. Rae's critique of Smith's liberal political economy had also been a methodological one. He had argued forcefully that Smith relied too heavily on deductive argumentation, an approach that he argued was unscientific and inferior to a more inductive, empirical, and historical approach (Hamouda 1998). Macdonald made a similar point when confronting liberal supporters of free trade, noting that the tariff was much more "scientific" than policies informed only by abstract theory unconnected to local empirical conditions (Heaman 2014, 213–16). To reinforce this argument, Macdonald and his supporters also invoked another "Rae-ian" point. The tariff regime in place before the National Policy applied duties more or less equally to all imports. Macdonald emphasized, however, that his new regime would be more scientific in targeting specific products according to criteria such as the availability of raw materials, the prospects for local industry, and whether the products were necessities or luxuries (Heaman 2017, 138, 142–3).

The neglect of Rae by NCPE scholars is also unusual given that he offered an important theoretical rationale and strategy for transcending a staples-based economy in favour of independent industrial development. Rae's emphasis on the need for historical and empirical methodologies also resonates with NCPE scholarship and that of the staples approach. At the same time, however, the parallels to later CPE thought should not be overstated. Like Macdonald's, Rae's politics were much more conservative than the "left" orientation of most NCPE scholars. Rae identified with the merchant class, and was a defender of the British Empire and Crown. Indeed, he was initially prompted to critique Smith's economic liberalism because of his desire to defend Canada's colonial ties to Britain at a time when English liberals were calling into question the economic value of colonies. He was also opposed to those who were sympathetic to new kinds of revolutionary and democratic politics emanating from the United States and Europe, and even fought against the 1837 rebellion in Upper Canada (James 1965, 34, 66, 133–9, 261; Rae [1834] 1964, xi–x).

Rae's writings also included expressions of a Eurocentric settler colonial ideology that praised how the "large extent of the knowledge of the civilized man, compared with that of savage or barbarian, gives him the power of constructing a much greater number of instuments out of the same materials, and enables the European emigrant to convert the soil and forests of America or New Holland, into means of producing a great mass of desirable events, which it was beyond the capacity of the ignorant native to effect" (Rae [1834] 1964, 99; see also Starblanket and Coburn, in this volume). At the same time, when writing about "American Indian," he was very critical of how European settlement had "gradually diminished, or entirely destroyed, the political importance of their tribes, and consequently, the ties binding together the members of each of these communities, and leading them to feel, and to act, in common" (Rae [1834] 1964, 131, 135).

This is not the place to try to explain the unusual neglect of Rae's ideas in NCPE circles. But one relevant factor might be that Rae was also given very little attention by the figure whom many NCPE scholars see as a founder of their tradition: Harold Innis.[5] In some ways, Innis's neglect of Rae was surprising given the former's interest in promoting "Canadian" perspectives on political economy and the fact that some of Rae's interests overlapped his own, such as the focus on technological change, historical and empirical methodologies, and even

---

5 According to Innis specialist Robin Neill (1998, 182), "[t]here is no evidence that John Rae was known to Harold Innis." This statement needs to be qualified slightly by the fact that Rae's biographer, R. Warren James (1965, 174), appears to have called Innis's attention to Rae's work in 1950, near the very end of Innis's life.

institutional rigidities.[6] But Rae's ideas – with their emphasis on an industrially oriented, internally led growth strategy – were also difficult to fit cleanly into Innis's staples-based interpretation of the nineteenth-century Canadian political economy. So too were Buchanan's, another figure who receives little attention either from Innis or from later NCPE thinkers.[7] The fact that the ideas of Rae and Buchanan were politically prominent at the time of the National Policy suggests that this strategy was at least being considered in elite circles, even if support for it might have receded later, when the National Policy became more associated with western expansion and the wheat boom (Neill 1991, 72–3).

Conclusion

In three eras, Canadians have made claims about the existence of a distinctive "Canadian" approach to the study of political economy arising from the study of their own country. The claims made in the inter-war years and the post-1970 period are well known, but claims made in the nineteenth century have been neglected in CPE textbooks and surveys of the field. What is common in CPE thought across these three eras besides the claim of Canadian distinctiveness? In other words, can we speak of a genuine, long-standing CPE intellectual tradition that dates back to the nineteenth century?

If such a tradition exists, the analysis in this chapter suggests that it cannot be defined in ideological terms. Although the New Canadian Political Economy was shaped largely by left-of-centre thought, the staples approach was developed by liberals and nineteenth-century CPE was associated with more conservative thinkers. In other words, ideological diversity, rather than conformity, has characterized CPE thought since the nineteenth century.

At the same time, there are some interesting commonalities across the three periods. One is the relative lack of "parochialism" in the

---

6 For Rae ([1834] 1964, 8) on institutional rigidity: "Institutions and forms very often endure after the circumstances that had originally called them forth have disappeared, and when, consequently, their operation injuriously restrains the movements of some new order of things."

7 Neill (1972, 13–14) mentions Buchanan among a list of nineteenth-century Canadian economic nationalists (including Rae) whose ideas were "largely unknown" to Innis. In one brief mention, Innis ([1937] 1956, 162) even misidentified the main intellectual influence on Buchanan as "William Carey" (instead of Henry Carey).

"Canadian-ness" of the tradition. While proclaiming their desire to develop a Canadian way of thinking, CPE thinkers in each era have been very open to drawing on foreign ideas. For the NCPE thinkers, dependency theory and/or European Marxism provided some inspiration. For both Innis and Mackintosh, Veblen was a key influence. In the nineteenth century, Canadian protectionists drew on the ideas of thinkers in other countries such as Carey, Laing, Hamilton, and List. The "Canadian content" of CPE, in other words, has been interpreted in ways that are open to the international circulation of ideas and global intellectual debates.

Second, CPE thinkers have been consistently interested in studying political economy in a manner that is historically oriented and that draws on many disciplines, not just political science and economics. This wide approach was evident in post-1970 NCPE scholarship and in the inter-war writings of those associated with the staples approach. It was also part of the tradition of nineteenth-century thinkers such as Rae and Buchanan, who reacted against the narrow focus of much British liberal political economy in their era. Neill (1991, 74, 76) describes these two thinkers as leaders of a kind of "Upper Canadian Economics," which had an "empirical and historical" orientation that was committed to seeing humans as more than just "individualistic and selfish."

Finally, CPE thinkers across all three periods showed a consistently strong interest in analysing Canada's place in the broader international political economy (see also McBride, and Fridell, in this volume). This focus was at the centre of much NCPE scholarship, of the staples approach, and of the ideas of nineteenth-century thinkers such as Rae and Buchanan. In the contemporary era, this feature of the CPE tradition has overlapped with the emergence of a separate academic field of international political economy (IPE) in Canada. The links between CPE scholars and IPE scholars have not always been as strong as they could be in recent years. Looking to the future, it is important for them to be strengthened. The two fields have much to learn from each other, particularly at this moment of dramatic upheaval in the global economic order.

2   Dependent Technological Change: The Long Arc of Canadian Innovation and Political Economic Development

BRUCE SMARDON

Introduction

Within capitalist political economies, research and development (R&D) and original innovation are central elements of how processes of accumulation are structured and furthered over time. The development of new products and processes through public sector and private sector organizations is regarded as a key way in which capitalist profits are furthered within existing areas of production and entirely new areas of accumulation are established. In a striking way, these processes of original technological creation have been relatively absent in the Canadian political economy. Beginning in the rapid period of industrialization in the early twentieth century and continuing through both the post-war "Golden Age" of capitalism from the end of 1945 to the early 1970s[1] and the neoliberalism that has characterized capitalist political economic processes since that time, the level of R&D and original innovation in Canadian industry remained at or close to the bottom of the levels in other advanced capitalist economies (Smardon 2014). Recent figures show that this process has accelerated. From 2005 to 2015 there were major overall declines in the areas of R&D and original innovation, and further deterioration in the relative standing of Canadian industry in this area. Significant decreases occurred as measured by a variety of indicators, ranging from business enterprise expenditure on R&D (BERD) as a percentage of gross domestic product (GDP),

---

1 The term "Golden Age" is used to refer to the higher growth rates achieved during the post-war boom years in comparison with both earlier and later periods of capitalist development. Concerning these different growth rates, see Maddison (2001, 125–30).

to business-financed BERD as a percentage of value added in industry, to shares of Canadian industry in triadic patent families – key technological groupings that involve patents filed in the three major economies of the United States, Japan, and the European Union (OECD 2018a, tables 24, 34, 64). R&D spending in Canadian industry fell, while the average was increasing in the wider Organisation for Economic Co-operation and Development (OECD), providing the basis for a major decrease in the ratio of Canadian R&D and innovation spending compared with that of OECD economies overall.

The broad relative decline occurred even with the increase in "tech jobs" and "tech investments" in certain areas of the Canadian economy such as Montreal, Ottawa, Kitchener-Waterloo, and Toronto, a process that has not altered long-standing patterns in Canadian capitalism that have limited the extent of domestic R&D and innovation networks. Reviewing the situation regarding the digital economy and artificial intelligence, Wolfe (2018, 9) notes the continued inability of local Canadian-based capitalists to develop larger companies that are not eventually either sold to US capital or move to the United States: "Promising start-ups all too often end up either moving to the US or being sold to foreign (usually US) investors." Furthermore, as noted by Shopify founder Tobi Lutke, the branch-plant character of the new investments made by transnational tech companies in Canada often means they are not associated with research that is integrated into building up domestic networks, but instead leads to processes where Canadian researchers are plugged into larger US transnational structures that own the intellectual property and are able to appropriate much of the value (Deschamps 2018). The recent announcement by GM, the transnational auto manufacturer, that it is closing its Oshawa plant is an example of this. GM's research operations in Canada are not linked in any way with its production operations in Oshawa.

This chapter examines the long history of how this situation developed. Canadian accumulation processes, particularly in the manufacturing sector, are marked by a systematic reliance on technological borrowing and a dependency on innovation processes in other advanced economies, particularly the United States. Technological dependency has been integrated into the fabric of Canadian capitalist development over time. The chapter traces this pattern by looking at three key periods of development in the Canadian economy that had very different effects on Canada's relative position among the advanced economies: (1) the period of dependent industrialization that was established in the latter part of the nineteenth century and early twentieth century, when Canada, in a way distinct from advanced economies other than the United States, was the first to incorporate the structures and processes of early US Fordism into its political economic processes; (2) the "Golden Age" of expansion after 1945, when Canadian advanced dependent industrialization came under serious pressure from the different Fordisms that were developing in other advanced economies and began to lose its ability to remain at the forefront of key research-intensive capitalist accumulation processes in the manufacturing sector; and (3) the period of neoliberal restructuring that started in the 1970s and continues to the present, in which the processes of dependent technological formation have led to a more restricted space of capital accumulation in the manufacturing sector, with important consequences for the relative standing of the Canadian economy. The chapter will show that, even though patterns of technological borrowing and dependency underpinned the Canadian political economy in all three periods, the consequences of that development varied significantly, particularly in the first and third periods. In the first period, limited technological capacities were combined with rapid development that placed Canada at the forefront of the advanced economies; in the third period, it has led to processes of relative decline.

In making these arguments, I review the extensive literature on the political economy of Canadian development that has focused on the issue of dependency versus Canadian autonomy. Unlike political economy scholarship in other countries, in Canada the question of how technological capacities are organized within specific national spaces and are related to power relations both within and across economies has received a lot of attention. Canadian political economists have debated in an intensive way the structure of the Canadian economy, how it has been constructed to support domestic class interests placed within wider international relations (particularly with Britain and the United States), how that relates to the absence of technological capacities, and whether that absence is significant in defining Canadian accumulation processes. However, while focusing attention on important questions, these writers have missed the specific role of Canadian Fordism in structuring the domestic political economy from the early twentieth century to the post-war Golden Age, and have not sufficiently recognized how the later movement to neoliberalism was informed by the earlier Fordist processes. Canadian political economists also tend to specify their arguments in a dichotomous or either/or fashion, leading to neglect of how Canadian development has had both dependent and advanced features.

Technological Imports, Economic Development, and Dependent Industrialization

The era of the National Policy (1870–1913) was crucial in establishing the pattern of innovation followed by Canadian industry. It was during this era that a unified Canadian economic space was created and important dimensions of the organization of the Canadian economy established. A set of policies, retrospectively given the name "national policy" by W.A. Mackintosh, was pursued at the federal level after Confederation in 1867, centred on three main areas: completion of a transcontinental railway, colonization of the West through the displacement of Indigenous Peoples and support of white settler colonization – a process discussed in greater detail by Starblanket and Coburn, in this volume – and passage of the National Policy tariffs in 1879.[2] A central aspect of development in this period was a deep reliance by Canadian industry on imported technologies. As one historian has noted, "the new products and new techniques came almost exclusively from elsewhere" (Drummond 1987, 132).

Within the approach to Canadian political economy that emphasizes "truncated" or "weak" development in the National Policy period, there are several different interpretations of how this dependent industrialization came about. Writers such as Naylor, Watkins, Williams, and Laxer all emphasize the view that the reliance on imported technologies was symptomatic of a general failure on the part of domestic capital to engage in independent industrial activities. Naylor summarizes this when he states that a "vacuum" existed which was filled by a "reliance on American industrialism, in the form of entrepreneurs, patents or direct investment" (Naylor 1997, 283). Watkins (1997, viii–ix) echoes this view when he states that domestic capitalists followed a "weak" path of industrialization leading to a dependent form of industrialization based on branch plants. Control over the most dynamic areas of capital accumulation was not centred in Canada, and future Canadian development patterns were limited by the branch-plant character of manufacturing activities.

Within this framework, there are differences of interpretation over how this situation arose. Working within what is known as the New Canadian Political Economy (NCPE) framework, Naylor focuses on the commercial/financial orientation of the Canadian business class,

---

2 As Smiley (1975, 41) notes, there were, in fact, three different uses of the term "national policy." See also Brodie (1990, 97–105).

derived from the economic orientation of Canada as a staples-producing hinterland within the British Empire. He argues that domestically controlled commercial/financial capitalists, mainly through their control of Canadian state policies and the banking system, skewed domestic investments away from the more dynamic industrial growth areas. Central to the limitations of commercial/financial capitalist development was "the absence of independent innovative capacity" (Naylor 1997, 283). Similarly, Watkins points to the absence of domestic Canadian innovative activity and the role of the National Policy in encouraging a staples orientation based on banking and railway interests that, through import tariffs, systematically encouraged "the entry of American branch plants into Canada" (Watkins 2006, xviii).

Williams and Laxer come to the same conclusions about the innovative deficiencies of Canadian capitalism, but depart significantly from the Naylor/Watkins perspective in terms of how they understand the sources of low original innovation. Following the NCPE view, they argue, in one way or another, that the failure of state and business elites to support an independent innovative capacity was a serious source of economic limitation, and a key objective of their analysis is to explain how this came about. But, breaking with the NCPE framework, neither Laxer nor Williams agrees that the key source of low innovation was a dichotomy in Canadian capitalism between financial/commercial capitalists and industrial capitalists. For Williams (1994, 50), the source of "an extreme and unchallenged dependency on foreign technology" was the central role of resource exports and the low priority given by state and business elites to establishing a competitive manufacturing sector in the international economy. For Laxer (1989, 150), the source of high levels of "foreign ownership and technological dependence" was the weakness of agrarian populist movements, which, in turn, led to lower support in Canada for nationalist and militarist policies stressing the need for autarkic technological capabilities, lower development of domestic banks providing credit for industrial purposes, and political processes that led to higher levels of wasteful state expenditures on subsidies for railways (for more on the implications of weak agrarian movements for industrial development, see Laxer 1989, 140–51).

Despite their differences, these various writers share a common view linking original innovation with accumulation processes more generally that vitiates their understanding of Canadian political economic development. There is an assumption that Canadian industrialization was limited because of the substantial reliance on technological borrowing in comparison with other economies, such as the US, German, or Swedish. But this Schumpeterian view of the relationship between innovation and growth neglects the fact that there is no simple correlation between technological capacities and levels of relative growth. As shown in the process of Canadian industrialization, particularly in the early twentieth century, Canada experienced higher relative rates of economic expansion despite its almost exclusive reliance on imported technologies. By counterposing original and imported technologies in "strong" and "weak" paths of industrialization, this important dimension of economic development in Canada is missed. The various political economic dimensions that supported rapid capitalist accumulation through borrowed technologies are neglected when it is assumed that the absence of independent technological capacities limited Canadian growth.

The failure to consider adequately the role of imported technologies also leads to a flawed view of the role of the Canadian state in economic development. Various state actions in the National Policy era – the Patent Act of 1872, the pattern of aid to Canadian industry by federal and provincial states, and tariffs – are seen in this framework as aiding and abetting the restrictions on economic development that were created by the failure to follow an autonomous path of industrialization, including an ability to engage in original innovation (Naylor 1997, 38–64; Williams 1994, 33–9). But once it is recognized that Canadian economic development was not restricted in the National Policy era, this view cannot be sustained. The various actions of the state, rather than contributing to restricted growth, promoted a rapid development process.

American Fordist Capitalism

At the core of the rapid accumulation processes in the National Policy era was a set of changes, which started in 1880 and intensified after 1900, through which Canadian industry followed closely the emerging structures of American Fordist capitalism. The new structures involved in this new form of capitalism extended processes of change that had started with the Industrial Revolution in Britain. As Marx noted, the first wave of British innovations, and the new forms of production organization that accompanied them, departed significantly from earlier forms of handicraft and manufacturing production by transforming the relationship of workers to machines and by greatly increasing the scale of production in "Modern Industry" (Marx [1867] 1977, 352–65, see also Rosenberg 1976, 130–5). The American changes continued this process, but moved it to a qualitatively different level with a new order of "cyclopean machines," using Marx's term, in the sphere of production (Marx [1867] 1977, 363). Higher volumes of production had existed from the mid-nineteenth century onwards with the development of the "American system of manufactures," but the advent of truly large-scale production began with the new forms of Fordist capital that were developed in the period from 1880 to the First World War, and provided the foundation for structures of factory production that continued to mark capitalist production processes in the twentieth century (see Burn 1970, 77–98; Nelson 1995; Oliver 1956, 314–448).

The development of Fordist capitalism in the United States involved an interrelated set of changes. The scale and scope economies of large-volume production could be realized only if new managerial hierarchies were established that were capable of governing disparate geographic areas of business operation, coordinating various functional divisions within companies, and instituting the more centralized forms of managerial control over the workplace that accompanied the new methods of production. It was also necessary to create more concentrated industrial structures as, despite the size of the American domestic market, large-volume production could not be supported in a market with numerous firms. As Chandler documents, new large, joint-stock companies were created through mergers and consolidations that provided the foundation for this new approach to organizing production. They applied a range of new technologies, involved extensive managerial hierarchies, operated in concentrated industrial structures, and were based on much larger volumes of production (Chandler 1990, 53–89). These companies also introduced major changes in relations between managers and workers, often in the face of opposition from craft workers (Montgomery 1979). American managers were preoccupied with gaining greater "efficiencies" through combining new technologies with restructured work processes. New forms of centralized managerial control were created, such as cost accounting and measurements of production flows, to monitor the performance of workers and to increase the return from the application of new technologies, which allowed for a greater subdivision of tasks within the production process (Nelson 1995, 5–10). All of these changes were supported by a reorganized American state that provided a legal and institutional basis for the new corporate structures that were emerging (Panitch and Gindin 2012, 30–43).

These changes in the sphere of production were accompanied by the rapid growth of the American domestic market. At the centre of this growth in demand was "a spectacular process of modernization in agriculture" that was part of a broader canvas of change linking owner-operated family farms, construction of railroads connecting dispersed geographic areas, high levels of investment in new producer and consumer goods industries, and overall wage expansion in line with productivity increases (Page and Walker 1991, 296–302; Smardon 2014, 56–8). Along with the structures of gender and racial division that were built into the new forms of "big business" and that informed American progressive movements in a major way (Flanagan 2007), a new structure of Fordist capitalism had been established by the First World War that involved a major break from previous forms of business organization and relied on new forms of mass consumption.

Canadian Industry and American Fordist Capitalism

The US situation provided an essential backdrop to Canadian development as Canadian capital embarked on a general reorganization of industry along lines that paralleled changes in the United States, with the development of the three major dimensions of American Fordist capitalism: joint-stock companies involving new managerial hierarchies governing large enterprises, restructured workplace relations, and levels of market demand capable of supporting large-volume production. These changes allowed the technologies inscribed within the structures of American Fordism to be applied in Canada.

From 1880 to 1910, the joint-stock company became "the dominant industrial form" in Canada, and there was systematic growth of firms with "more impersonal company directorates" and new hierarchies of "career executives" (Acheson 1973, 189). The changes in this area were particularly intense in the first decade of the twentieth century. In that period, "industries on the leading edge of the new industrialism – the highly integrated textile industry, railway suppliers, high-technology manufacturing, and industries associated with the new staples, smelting and pulp and paper – participated fully and rapidly in the managerial revolution" (Craven 1980, 92).

Accompanying these changes was an increase in the number of large firms, particularly with the first great wave of corporate mergers between 1908 and 1913. Very large companies under the control of domestically controlled capital were created out of the merger process, "such as the Steel Company of Canada, Dominion Canners, Canada Cement, Canadian Cottons, and Dominion Glass Company" (Traves 1979, 5; see also Carroll 1986, 49–53). These companies were in addition to the numerous subsidiaries of American corporations that entered Canada with increasing frequency after 1900 (Marshall, Southard, and Taylor 1976, 19–21). Writing from the American perspective, Wilkins (1970, 142) notes that, "[b]y 1914, Canada clearly had more U.S.-controlled manufacturing plants than any other foreign nation." As transnational extensions of American Fordist capitalism, they were based on the same large-volume approach to production, and operated in the industries with the largest growth rates of output, including electrical equipment and supplies, transportation equipment, and chemicals and allied products (Drummond 1987, 393–6; Williams 1994, 38–9). Between 1901 and 1911, the number of large firms (defined as having over $1 million in sales) rose from 39 to 150 and the share of those firms in manufacturing output more than doubled from 15 per cent to 31 per cent. This was part of a longer process in which, by 1921, 410 large firms accounted for 51 per cent of Canadian production (Smardon 2014, 58–68; Traves 1979, 5).

In these companies, there was systematic introduction of the new workplace relations characteristic of Fordist capitalism. Through branch-plant managers, the hiring of American managers by Canadian-controlled companies, and extensive coverage of American production methods in trade journals such as *Industrial Canada*, the new American approaches were transferred to Canada (Craven 1980, 93–100; Palmer 1992, 160–1). As was the case in the United States, the application of these methods was not instantaneous, involved important forms of variation among industries, and often faced resistance from labour (Heron and Storey 1986; Nelson 1995, 119–77). It was not until the 1920s, when the post-war wave of labour struggle was ended by a combination of "severe depression and an employers' anti-union offensive," that the older foundations of craft unionism were "permanently eroded" (Heron and Storey 1986, 16; Palmer 1992, 219–21). Nevertheless, major inroads were made by Fordist capital before the First World War in introducing the new workplace relations, even in the face of labour opposition, through a range of measures, from injunctions against strikes to company welfare plans (Palmer 1979, 216–33). Similar to that in the United States, Canadian Fordism thus involved substantial struggle between workers and managers over restructured work processes, and was not applied in a straightforward way as simply an extension of more "efficient" production methods. Also paralleling the United States, Canadian "big business" relied on structures of gender and racialized difference (Heron and Story 1986, 220–5; Steedman 1986, 156–68), but, in contrast to the American experience, was not confronted by the same resistence to these sources of division within the broader organization of Canadian opposition to Fordist change.[3]

Finally, various changes were made to create appropriate levels of market demand for large-volume production. This was a crucial problem for Canadian manufacturing industry. Even though the level of demand grew rapidly from 1870 to 1913 – fuelled by rising real wages, higher employment, increasing urbanization, further railroad construction, and the expansion of agriculture – the size of the Canadian domestic market was far smaller than the American one and represented a major obstacle to applying the new forms of business, technology, and production (the sources of rising levels of demand are covered in Drummond 1987, chaps. 3, 7, 10, and 13). In 1870 Canadian GDP was $6.4 billion – only 6.5 per cent of the American GDP of $98.4 billion. After the substantial growth that occurred between 1870 and 1913, Canadian GDP levels were still only 6.7 per cent of American levels (Maddison 2001, 184). In a market of this size, the transition to American-style Fordist capitalism could occur only if the limited amount of demand was shared among a small number of companies. In the Canadian context, there was a powerful impetus towards market concentration and control that was in addition to capital's usual desire to manage competition. In his comparison of corporate concentration in Canada and the United States in the 1940s, Rosenbluth (1957, 82–4) noted higher levels of concentration in Canada because firms of similar average size were operating in industries with smaller overall output than in the United States. He pointed out that "the smaller size of the Canadian market typically results in *fewer* firms rather than in smaller firms, compared with the U.S." [emphasis in original]. This pattern, which does not support the argument within the dependency framework that Canadian

---

3 In this regard, the nature of struggle in Canada differed from that in the United States. The US progressive movement and its opposition to "big business" was informed, although with serious divisions within the progressive movement, by the impact of the new forms of business on women and racialized workers. See Flanagan (2007, 51–62, 73–5, 94–7, 107–12, 132–4, and 142–52). The Canadian opposition was not defined as centrally by these issues. It is in this specific sense that I have suggested that "there was no counterpart in Canada to the broad-based movements in the United States" in opposition to the changes that were occurring (Smardon 2014, 71). Contrary to the claims of Heaman (2017, 13), this does not mean that Canada "had no progressive reform movement comparable to other movements elsewhere." Reform movements were in existence, of course, but they were not of the same character as those in the United States – a point that is evident if the substantive part of my claim had not been erased from the quotation Heaman provides of my work (Heaman 2017, 473–4).

firms were inefficient "miniature replicas" of American ones, has its roots in the National Policy era (Levitt 1970, 87).

Large-Volume Production and the National Policy Era

The National Policy era was crucial in two ways in establishing an industrial structure that combined large-volume firms with higher levels of corporate concentration. The first has already been mentioned: from 1880 to the First World War, Canadian capital worked to narrow the field of competition by managing markets through trade associations, consolidations, and mergers (Bliss 1974, 33–54). The drive to concentrate production in this period reached a highpoint between 1908 and 1913, when many of the key companies forming the long-term core of Canadian capitalism were created through "52 important mergers absorbing 229 firms" (Carroll 1986, 52). As the movement towards greater corporate concentration gathered momentum in the twentieth century, reduced competition was justified on the basis that it would lead to greater efficiencies through longer production runs, greater specialization, and rationalized sales forces (Bliss 1974, 49). This echoed claims being made in the United States to justify mergers and the creation of large-volume capitalist firms.

The second method focused on ensuring that the Canadian domestic market was reserved for domestic producers through tariff protection. The relationship between corporate concentration and support for tariff protection could be seen at the end of the 1870s, when the National Policy tariffs were first implemented. The industries that initially supported the tariffs were, for the most part, "characterized by a small number of firms" (Pomfret 1993, 165). This dynamic was reinforced as higher-volume production was developed in the Canadian economy and higher levels of concentration were achieved. The volume of production required by the large companies that were being created in greater numbers after 1900, which included subsidiaries of American branch plants, could be established only if there was no effective American export competition. In this way, there was a unity of interest between Canadian and American-controlled companies in Canada regarding the maintenance of tariffs.[4] Over time, the unity of Canadian

---

4 In their comprehensive survey of Canadian and American-controlled industry in Canada in the 1930s, after the full process of development of Fordist capitalism had been completed, Marshall, Southard, and Taylor (1976, 275) note that "the management of American-owned plants in Canada will be found supporting a protectionist tariff policy."

capital on the issue of protection through tariffs strengthened. The *Monetary Times*, a key voice of Canadian capitalists, moved from an initial position of coolness towards the National Policy tariffs in 1879 to a position of ardent support in 1911 (Bliss 1974, 96). In the reciprocity election of 1911, the Laurier Liberals faced, and were defeated by, a united block of big business interests opposing any removal of tariffs. The impact of the National Policy measures in supporting large-volume production in central Canada was furthered after 1900 by the "wheat boom" in the western region. The intensive growth of owner-operated commercial agriculture in the West fuelled a major rise in investment – accounting for an historic high of 14.6% of domestic capital formation in the period 1901 to 1915 (Buckley 1974, 28). Because the National Policy measures created a captive western market for industry in central Canada, this made a further contribution to the new forms of Fordist capitalism that were being established in that region.

Output, Productivity, and Canadian Fordist Capitalism

Tariff protection was thus an integral part of the process through which advanced forms of American capitalism were brought to Canada. Tariffs were important in contributing to the ability of Canadian manufacturers to control markets and concentrate production, thereby counteracting the effects of the relatively small Canadian domestic market. By furthering the development of a Canadian version of American Fordist capitalism, tariffs also contributed to high rates of productivity, output, and employment growth. In the period from 1900 to 1910, when the development of large-scale capitalism accelerated in the key region of Ontario, "[o]utput grew by 230 percent, more than tripling in a decade; employment doubled" (Drummond 1987, 109–10). By a considerable margin, the highest growth rates of output and output per hour in the National Policy era occurred in the decade of 1900 to 1910 (397), in fact, growth rates of both output and output per capita moved ahead of US rates (Norrie, Owram, and Emery 2002, 191).

The intense growth experienced in the first decade of the twentieth century was central in moving Canada to the forefront of the advanced economies in terms of both productivity and output per capita. As Maddison shows in his comprehensive survey of world productivity and GDP figures, Canadian productivity growth was more rapid than in any of the other leading economies, including the United States. In the period between 1870 and 1913, the rate of growth of GDP per hour worked in Canada was greater than in the United States (2.25 per cent versus 1.92 per cent) and the rest of the advanced economies

(Maddison 2001, 352).[5] The result was that, by 1913, the level of productivity in the Canadian economy was 87 per cent of the US level – surpassing the level of 84 per cent in Britain, which had been the economic and technological leader earlier in the nineteenth century (Maddison 2001, 353).

These figures on the productivity of Canadian industry do not support Panitch's (1991, 276–9) arguments concerning the impact of a "high-wage proletariat" in limiting the competitiveness of indigenous Canadian capital leading to dominance of industrial production by more productive American capital. Canadian-controlled capital did not abandon the manufacturing sector to more productive American capital, but was involved in a systematic process of bringing, along with American-controlled capital, the more advanced, and productive, forms of US capitalism to Canada. The interrelated changes of the period in which domestically controlled capital was an active, even leading, participant cannot be understood in terms of a withdrawal in the face of stronger American capital. Panitch departs from the standard conclusions of the dependency theorists in recognizing that an advanced form of capitalism was developed in Canada through American investment. But he accepted too readily the arguments of the dependency theorists that weaker, domestically controlled capital "lacked the power ... to survive" (1991, 276).

These figures also do not support arguments that the tariffs allowed Canadian capitalists to create weak or inefficient industries behind tariff walls, as is argued in one way or another by various writers in the dependency framework and, in an interesting point of convergence, neoclassical economists.[6] If the tariffs were protecting inefficiency or

---

5 Sharpe (2001, 76) has argued that some caution should be exercised with Maddison's figures because of changes in how the United States calculates its GDP figures, which have resulted in lower productivity levels in the period before 1929–50. However, even if this is the case, it does not remove the high rates of growth shown in the Canadian figures both in relation to future patterns of growth in Canada and in relation to other countries that did not follow the United States in changing their method of calculation. Furthermore, it is highly unlikely that the US figures are so understated that the higher Canadian level in relation to the US level is entirely removed.

6 Neoclassical economists contend that the tariffs were not essential for development, but instead allowed capitalists to charge higher prices and generate higher profits without leading to increases in efficiency (e.g., see Pomfret 1993, 164–8). This echoes the arguments of Naylor (1997, 194) that Canadian capitalists made "monopoly profits" through companies that were weak and vulnerable through excessive "watering" of their stock. Tariffs provided the essential protection that allowed these companies to be sustained. The contention is also echoed by Williams (1994, 50), who argues

uncompetitive production structures, there would have been declining, not rising, relative productivity – particularly in relation to US industries. The image of an economy mired in dependency and limited by inefficient industries is also not supported by the rapid growth of GDP per capita. In the period between 1870 and 1913, GDP per capita in Canada grew at an average annual rate of 2.27 per cent – substantially higher than the US rate of 1.82 per cent and rates in the advanced European economies and Japan (Maddison 2001, 186, 126).

The Role of the Canadian State

The period between 1880 and the First World War, particularly the first decade of the twentieth century, was thus an intensive one for Canadian industry. Although the war did not represent the endpoint of the development of Fordist capitalism, and it was not until the 1920s that the full extent of corporate concentration and workplace reorganization would be realized, the pre-war period nevertheless represented a major break from the organizational approaches of the past. The changes in this period placed the Canadian economy at the forefront of the advanced economies, despite its almost complete reliance on imported technologies.

In understanding how these changes came about, a different view of the role of the state is necessary. In the dependency framework, the state, responding to commercial/financial interests or a framework of elite interests giving priority to resource exports or an environment of weak agrarian interests, allowed more dynamic and competitive American capital to dominate the Canadian manufacturing sector. A separation is created between a weak form of domestically controlled capital and a strong form of American transnational capital, both of which were accommodated by state policies.

But this division between Canadian- and American-controlled capital is invalid. Rather, *both* forms of capital were involved in a project of Fordist capitalism that led to a common set of interests around tariff protection, workplace reorganization, and competition policy, and formed an important basis for the actions of the state. Tariff protection

---

that an uncompetitive manufacturing sector was established because of the emphasis placed on import substitution behind protective tariffs. Laxer (1989, 159) points in the same direction with his claims about deficient investment by domestic capitalists in industrial activities because of the defeat of free banking, delayed prairie settlement, and wasteful expenditures on railways, although he does not rely to the same extent on the protective impact of tariffs.

was maintained by the state as an integral part of a broad process of development of advanced capitalism in Canada, not as part of a process in which weak, domestically controlled capital and a compliant federal state accepted domination of the manufacturing sector by stronger American capital. Similarly, throughout the period after 1900, the federal state took on a more active role in labour relations through forms of both regulation and repression to moderate the conflicts between capital and labour in the new industrial environment.[7] In these actions, the state was not promoting a dependent economy with weak forms of industrialization, but intervening intensively to support the workplace relations associated with advanced forms of capitalist production. Finally, the state adopted a hands-off approach to mergers and other forms of corporate concentration.[8] William Lyon Mackenzie King, a key member of the ruling Liberal Party, "fully accepted the argument that most mergers promoted economic efficiency" (Bliss 1973, 185). The importance of this policy in relation to large-volume capital cannot be understood if Canadian industry is seen only as an American-dominated, miniature version of capital in the United States.

By taking seriously the role of Fordist capitalism in the Canadian economy, a different view of the actions of the state in supporting technological dependency is also possible. In the usual way of understanding the role of the state, various state actions, such as the Patent Act and the National Policy tariffs, encouraged American investment in branch plants, leading to a reliance on transfers of technology from US parent corporations (e.g., see Niosi 1985, 33–40). However, as noted by Panitch (1991, 280–1), the incentives provided by these state policies would have had little effect without the attraction for American investment that was provided by the size of the Canadian domestic market. In this respect, the impact of the tariffs in allowing Canadian manufacturers to exclude imports and to develop more concentrated production was more important to the growth of American branch plants, and imported technologies, than the incentive they provided for American capital to "jump over the tariff wall." Other economies had substantial levels of

---

7 The state-managed labour relations framework involved periods when the state was able to shift outcomes in favour of capital, such as in 1907 and 1908, periods when state-managed outcomes favoured labour, such as in 1911 and 1912, and periods when capital "had unquestionably gained the upper hand," such as after 1912. The role of the state in this respect was not monolithic (Russell 1990, 57–152). See also Craven (1980, 230–352); and Kealey (1995, 423–33).

8 Bliss (1973, 177) observes that "Canadian anti-combines legislation … was insignificant and ineffectual."

protection, but did not experience the same increases in American direct investment in the period before 1914 (see Hansen 2001, 162–6).

The Distinctiveness of the Canadian Case

My arguments against the writers who emphasize a weak dependent economy would seem to agree with those who claim that Canadian economic development was not distinguished in any fundamental way from that of other advanced economies. They would seem to support the argument of Carroll (1986, 52) that, by the second decade of the twentieth century, "an advanced form of capitalist production, circulation, and finance was in place in Canada" that, in its fundamentals, was no different than the forms of "finance capital" in other economies. But the ability of manufacturing capital to generate intensive growth by developing a Canadian version of American Fordist capitalism led to several distinctive characteristics relative to other advanced economies. There is not sufficient space to provide a detailed analysis of this point, but one can offer an outline of some key differences.

In the first place, the development of Canadian Fordism was associated with a process of industrialization that focused almost entirely on the domestic market. The rapid growth in manufacturing production in the key area of Ontario was not generated by exports, but through rising internal demand. The American market was closed for the most part through extensive protectionist measures, and thus could not have provided the key source of growth even if it had been needed (Drummond 1987, 110). Because of the rapidly growing domestic market, which was channelled to a small number of firms through processes of concentration and tariff protection, Canadian manufacturers were able to develop large-volume production in a greater range of sectors, and were therefore able to integrate American innovations into production in a more extensive way than in other economies. The more limited size of domestic markets in other leading economies, including the largest European economies of Germany and Britain, meant that plants with sufficient volumes of production could not be established, which represented a continuous obstacle to the transfer of American technologies (concerning the reasons for this situation in the other leading economies, see Smardon 2014, 78–81).

Referring to the situation in the period before 1914, Milward and Saul (1977, 40) note that "[t]he insufficient size even of a market as large as that of Germany was a persistent obstacle throughout the period to the advance of engineering technology." The German economy continued to rely on American imports in a range of areas – including agricultural implements, typewriters, cash registers, and machine tools in areas of lighter industry. Such reliance reflected a general failure to develop Fordist capital in the industries producing goods for mass markets. The large German companies that developed in the period between 1870 and the First World War, while in technologically advanced areas, were not oriented towards mass production. In his comparison of German and American firms in the first decade of the twentieth century, Kocka (1980, 99) observes that "[m]ost of the large United States firms – but not those in Germany – produced goods for the mass or high-volume market." The development of large-scale capitalism in Germany was largely confined to producer-goods industries and, within this area, there was greater emphasis on "heavier equipment, usually to customer specifications" (Kocka 1980, 99), rather than the lighter, more mass-oriented forms of machinery production – a pattern shared in the Japanese economy (Odagiri and Goto 1993, 80–1). The British economy also exhibited a more limited pattern of development of Fordist capitalism. In that case, large-scale enterprises were concentrated in consumer-goods industries serving the large number of people living within the "small quadrangle bounded by London, Cardiff, Glasgow and Edinburgh" (Chandler 1990, 251). However, these consumer-goods industries were not located, for the most part, in the "new, technologically-advanced, growth industries," and were generally "smaller than their American counterparts" (239–40). British industry failed to develop a substantial number of large-volume firms in the technologically advanced areas of innovation and production (see Hobsbawm 1969, 172–93).

The burst of development in Canada before 1914 thus placed Canadian industry in a unique position within the advanced capitalist world. In a manner unlike any other leading economy outside the United States, it was able to incorporate large-volume production in technologically advanced areas into the domestic economy. This situation had some important consequences. The relatively high growth rates of productivity and output per capita that occurred in Canada on this basis meant that there was no need to develop autonomous technological capacities. A structure of intensive accumulation could be established that was based almost entirely on imported technologies. In this respect, there was an unusual quality to Canadian industrialization that was not shared by leading economies such as the United States or Germany, which had begun to industrialize earlier in the nineteenth century, or those such as Sweden and Japan, which industrialized at the same time as Canada. In these other countries, with the differences that have just been discussed, the development of capital-goods industries and of manufacturing was premised on varying degrees of original innovation, ranging from a substantive capacity in the case of Germany, the United States, and Sweden to a more limited capacity in the case of Japan (see Nelson 1993).[9]

The absence of original innovation in the approach of Canadian industry, in combination with the ability to rely heavily on the Canadian domestic market, had a further effect: there was less development of transnational capital in the manufacturing area. As Wilkins (1988, 23) notes, in the period before 1914, "[i]t was often in the newest and most technologically advanced products that German and US businesses invested abroad." By expanding their foreign investments in these areas, German and US firms were able to capitalize on the advantages created by the initial development of new technologies. Because Canadian industry did not develop an original innovative capacity, this motivation for foreign investment was removed.

Thus, several distinctive features of Canadian development in the period before 1914 marked it off from other advanced economies in crucial ways. Canadian capital, in a manner unlike capital in these other economies, never developed a broad capacity to engage in original innovative activities. Furthermore, in a range of important industries, such as auto manufacturing, electrical appliances, chemicals, and rubber, American transnational capital organized production and treated the Canadian market as one part of its overall approach to spreading the overhead costs of R&D and innovation over larger production volumes. Unlike the European and Japanese states and the different blocks of domestically controlled capital in those countries, both the Canadian state and Canadian-controlled capital accepted that Canadian industrialization was uniformly integrated into foreign (primarily US) sources of technology and that important sectors of the Canadian economy were controlled by transnational capital (primarily US) using technologies developed in other countries. In contrast to the orientation of transnational capital in other countries, which was actively using original technological capacities to further its ability to organize markets both domestically and internationally, Canadian manufacturing capital, both Canadian and foreign controlled, remained divorced from these wider processes.

Neither of the interpretations on either side of the dependency/autonomy divide adequately account for this situation. Contrary to the

---

9 Even though Japan used imported technology extensively in the three decades between 1885 and 1914, it still had original innovative capabilities in the important textile and iron and steel industries.

arguments of the theorists stressing truncated development, the emphasis on non-original innovation did not arise from an incomplete industrialization process.[10] The key reason for the lack of original innovation was not, following Williams, the low priority placed on this type of innovation in a staples-based economy that was exporting resources in exchange for imports of finished manufactured goods and that developed only a limited manufacturing sector through import-substitution industrialization.[11] Neither did it result, following the NCPE perspective, from an excessive fixation by Canadian domestic capital on commercial/financial activities, leaving the manufacturing sector open to domination by American capital (Robert 1998, 31). Rather, it resulted from the various political economic conditions in Canada that allowed transferred or borrowed technologies to be used by both Canadian-controlled and foreign-controlled companies in a rapid process of growth and accumulation that placed the Canadian economy at the forefront of the advanced economies.

On the other hand, contrary to the theorists arguing for a nationally based autonomous Canadian capitalism, the reliance on technology imports created a form of dependency that was deeper than in any other advanced capitalist economy in the period before 1914. Technological dependency was built into how Canadian capital absorbed the new forms of US factory organization and technologies. Canadian capitalists followed an approach to accumulation in which they were able to avoid all of the expenditures and investments involved in researching and developing new products and processes of production, while at the same time gaining the profits from establishing a range of advanced manufacturing processes with much higher levels of productivity within a protected domestic market, and selling those products in highly concentrated oligopolistic mass market structures. New mass production techniques (exemplified by Henry Ford's new auto assembly operations in Highland Park in 1913, which were introduced into Ontario in 1914) and new levels of mass consumption (exemplified by the new massive retail complex established by Eaton's in Toronto at the

---

10 According to Laxer (1989, 15), "[t]he National Policy, an import-substitution strategy, was not compatible in the long run with full industrialization."

11 Williams (1994, 50) argues that building a competitive economy capable of exporting manufactured goods through developing original technological capabilities was not given priority because "maximum energy and investment" was placed on "building a staples economy based on the production of western wheat ... An extreme and unchallenged dependency on foreign technology" was allowed because manufacturing was only "a supplement to the resource export economy."

beginning of the First World War) were introduced that paralleled the kinds of highly profitable industrial and mass-marketing organizations that were being established south of the border (Colvin 1998; Monad 1996, 120, 146; Traves 1987, 214–15). The contours of Canadian development before 1914 laid the foundation for a systematic absence of domestic technological capacities that would remain an underlying dimension of Canadian capitalism in subsequent periods. As the next sections of the chapter show, both the post-war Golden Age of Fordist expansion and the neoliberal restructuring period that followed it were informed in major ways by the structures of advanced dependent accumulation established in the early twentieth century.

Technological Dependency and the Golden Age

The next intensive era of accumulation in the Canadian economy, the Golden Age from 1945 to the first oil shock in 1973, continued the pattern established in the earlier Fordist period. Once again, Canadian industry was able to combine a heavy reliance on technologies primarily imported from the United States with levels of productivity and income that were second only to those of the United States in the world economy (Maddison 2001, 185). The United States emerged from the Second World War as the dominant technological leader in a range of research-intensive industries, and this leadership expanded in the immediate post-war period of the 1950s and 1960s (Mowery and Nelson 1999). As is well documented by the writers arguing for limited development in Canada, a central way in which these technologies were transferred to Canadian industry was through foreign direct investment (FDI). The rise of FDI over the 1950s and into the early 1960s reinforced previous patterns that started in the early twentieth century, particularly after the First World War, when American capital entered in a major way into key growth areas of manufacturing: automobiles, chemicals, and electrical products. Canadian subsidiaries were given limited responsibilities for research and product development, relying instead on technology transfers from their parent corporations (e.g., see Cordell 1972, 29; Cordell and Gilmour 1976, 36–48; Hymer 1966, 191–202; Williams 1994, 117–18).

The technology transfers from parent corporations were in addition to continuing high levels of imports of machinery and equipment, by both domestically and foreign-controlled capital. At the end of the Golden Age in the early 1970s, 60 per cent of machinery requirements were imported (Williams 1994, 117), comparable to import levels during the boom years of the earlier era. Finally, there was extensive reliance on licensing agreements by Canadian capital, once again both domestic and foreign controlled. This can be seen by comparing Canadian levels with those in Japan, a country seen as relying extensively on imported technology in the post-war period. In the latter country, the ratio of payments for licences and technological know-how to R&D fell gradually over the 1960s from its peak level of 18.5 per cent in 1960 and then rapidly in the 1970s (Minami et al. 1995, 8–9). This contrasts with the Canadian trend where, in 1972, the ratio of payments for licensing agreements to R&D amounted to 25.7 per cent, significantly above the Japanese peak (Statistics Canada 1973, 17; 1991, 4).

Contrary to writers who emphasize a limited Canadian capitalism, however, the extensive reliance on imported technology – through transfers to Canadian subsidiaries, licensing agreements with domestic companies, and imports of machinery – did not reflect acceptance by Canadian political and economic elites of a less robust form of capitalism in which the post-war reliance on American capital led to a restricted space of accumulation relative to other economies (Heintzman 1979, 145; Kent 1988, 22–3; Phillips 1979, 12).[12] Instead, as noted, the reliance on imported technology was incorporated into a context of growth in the home market that allowed non-original innovation to be combined with relative levels of productivity and income that were among the highest among the advanced economies. On the other hand, this time contrary to writers who argue for an autonomous, nationally based capitalism that can be analysed outside of dependent relations with other economies, the extensive reliance on borrowed technologies underpinned the growing inability of Canadian manufacturing capital to sustain its position at the forefront of leading sectors of accumulation. This was a process that started with the post-war Golden Age era and accelerated in the following period of neoliberal restructuring.

The specific organization of advanced dependent development in the Canadian economy began to face some serious headwinds in the 1950s and 1960s, when international changes in the organization of Fordism undermined the integrity of the previous strategy of accumulation based on the home market. The reliance on the domestic market that had underpinned Canadian advanced manufacturing from the early part of the twentieth century faced a growing problem in the post-war Golden Age. The Canadian domestic market was no longer large

---

12 According to Phillips (1979), the reliance on American capital for development was part of a long-term failure to develop a national economic strategy after the previous National Policy framework ceased to have much effect by the 1920s.

enough to support the high levels of relative efficiency that had existed in the earlier part of the twentieth century or to allow Canadian capital to justify the increasing size of investments necessary to support large-scale manufacturing. This was especially the case when Canadian productive capacities were considered in relation to the ongoing expansion of US capacities, the new Fordist plant capacities that were being built in western Europe with the US-led reconstruction of those economies under the Marshall Plan and the explicit sharing of American technological information through productivity councils in Europe, and the post-war "leap forward" of the Japanese economy (Smardon 2014, 88–92). The post-war expansion of income and demand under Canadian Fordism paled in comparison with the levels that were being experienced in the western European and Japanese economies as they rapidly developed under post-war reconstruction – leading to a pattern of "convergence of productivity" among those economies and the United States (Abramovitz 1994, 89–108; Glyn 2006, 9). The changes made with the Auto Pact in 1965 reflected these pressures. Under its provisions, domestic auto production – which was based to a greater degree in the 1950s and early 1960s on the Canadian domestic market – was restructured so that Canadian subsidiaries of US auto manufacturers were now producing for export markets in the United States (Holmes 1983, 258–60).

But the Auto Pact, while foreshadowing the broader changes to come, still was limited to one sector of the Canadian economy, and thus did not solve the wider problem of how to place capital accumulation on a stronger footing. Canadian capital had not yet made a decisive move to abandon its reliance on the Canadian domestic market. All of this changed as the political economy of Canada increasingly was defined by neoliberal restructuring starting in the 1970s. Along with other advanced economies, the Canadian political economy in the 1970s faced growing stagflation (higher inflation and stagnant economic growth) in which the forces that had underpinned the post-war growth boom were undermined by the profit and productivity squeeze brought on from various sources: the growing strength of labour vis-à-vis capital in full-employment economies; the growing disintegration of the fixed-exchange-rate system of international trade and investment; the limitations arising from Fordist sources of growth reaching a point of diminishing returns; the instabilities introduced by rising commodity prices; and the greater uncertainty of capitalists in a context where capital's control over economic relations was being challenged by various left movements (Glyn 2006, 1–23). The difficulties experienced by capitalists in this situation led to a systematic campaign of neoliberal change – led by the US state – to restore the foundations of capital accumulation across the advanced economies (Panitch and Gindin 2012).

Trade, Technology, and Neoliberal Restructuring

In Canada, a core part of this restoration centred on a mobilization of capitalist forces around free trade, particularly through the Business Council on National Issues (BCNI, now known as the Business Council of Canada) formed in 1976. The key thrust of its actions was to mobilize a range of capitalist interests across both foreign-controlled and domestically controlled capital in a systematic campaign to further the "international competitiveness" of the Canadian economy through placing a greater reliance on "market-based forces" at the core of federal policy making (Langille 1987, 58–9). By the early 1980s, the efforts of the BCNI in this direction were concentrated on gaining greater unanimity of support across various business associations representing different segments of capital in Canada for a comprehensive trade deal with the United States, and selling the merits of this type of arrangement to the federal state. The Tokyo Round of negotiations under the General Agreement on Tariffs and Trade in 1979 had led to major reductions of tariffs, but this more narrowly focused set of measures did not provide the comprehensive set of changes that were being promoted in the BCNI's campaign. The BCNI launched its neoliberal project of trade restructuring for several reasons: the stagflation of the 1970s had further reduced the ability of the Canadian domestic market to provide an adequate basis for accumulation in the manufacturing sector; Canadian per unit labour costs were rising relative to those in the United States as Canadian organized labour demonstrated greater strength in the 1970s; the rise of protectionist sentiment in the United States with the recession of the early 1980s raised fears that the US market might be closed off to a greater extent, thus challenging a core objective of Canadian capital to expand into that market; and, finally, Canadian capital wanted to avoid any repeat of the nationalist measures in the National Energy Program (NEP) that the Trudeau Liberals had implemented in the early 1980s (see Doern and Tomlin 1991, 19–20; Hart 1994, 76–8; Roman and Velasco Arregui 2015, 19–22; Smardon 2014, 101–2).

The BCNI campaign, in conjunction with other forces – such as the recommendations of the Royal Commission on the Economic Union and Development Prospects for Canada, the decline of legitimacy surrounding the Keynesian welfare state, the greater level of public support for neoliberal projects, and the need for a unifying agenda by the governing Mulroney Tories – was successful (Smardon 2014, 312–19). By 1985 there was widespread agreement across the different segments of capital that a trade deal was necessary, and the Mulroney government announced it would negotiate an agreement with the United States, which was reached in 1987. By codifying neoliberal norms of trade, investment, and production, the trade deal was part of the process through which a foundation for capital accumulation was reconstructed after the intertwined problems of the 1970s. This happened in several ways: the agreement provided greater certainty to Canadian capital that it could pursue its expansion plans in the US market without facing US protectionist measures (although the agreement was flawed in that the United States was not willing to give up final control over passing protectionist legislation); it restricted the ability of the Canadian federal state to use tariffs or other protectionist measures designed to develop domestically centred accumulation bases, particularly through nationalist measures that violated "national treatment" provisions, thus ruling out any future legislation similar to the NEP; and it increased the ability of Canadian capital to demand concessions from workers through strengthening the ability of capital to move to other locations (concerning how trade deals limit the actions of states, see Grinspun and Kreklewich 1994, 33–61). The implementation of the North American Free Trade Agreement in 1994 furthered this process, and created an even larger space for extracting concessions from workers by including Mexico, with its much lower wages, within the free trade zone. In this new environment of strengthened capital, concessionary bargaining for unionized workers became commonplace, and new forms of precarious employment became the standard throughout the North American zone, with the highest concentrations located among gendered and racialized workers (Caulfield 2010, 90–141; Vosko 2006a, 18–33).

It is easy to conclude from all of this that, in Canada, the trade deal reflected an autonomous, nationally based set of class interests that was mobilized through the BCNI, and allowed a "more concentrated and more transnational" Canadian capitalist class to assert a changed set of strategic goals on an international basis (Roman and Velasco Arregui 2015, 18). But this view, despite recognizing the important ways in which Canadian capitalists were organized nationally to respond to the previous obstacles to accumulation, neglects the constraints that were created by the legacies of previous eras of accumulation and the technological dependencies that were created. Because of these limitations, Canadian capital was not able to create or sustain technological capacities that would allow it to remain at the forefront of a range of key new areas of capitalist growth and accumulation. Contrary to the expectations of the proponents of free trade who argued that greater competition from reduced tariffs would lead to expanded R&D and original innovation, Canadian capital avoided making the major investments in these areas that would close the gap with other advanced economies. These other economies – continuing patterns established in the earlier period of industrialization before 1914 – relied to a greater extent on domestic technological capacities in their post-war Golden Age expansion. This was especially so in the United States, the leading country in terms of the level of R&D and original innovation and the market Canadian capital was targeting in terms of its expansion plans (Smardon 2014, 92–5).

Instead, the focus of domestic Canadian capitalists shifted in important ways to resource-related investments in areas such as pulp and paper, petroleum and natural gas, smelting and refining of non-ferrous metals, and other mining (see also Carter, and Brownlee, in this volume). The reduction of foreign ownership in the Canadian economy over the 1970s and 1980s was in these resource-related areas, not in research-intensive manufacturing production (Smardon 2014, 274). Similarly, reflecting the weak basis of domestic technological capacities, imports of high-tech products into the Canadian economy grew substantially to over 73 per cent of overall consumption – a level that was not approached by any other advanced economy in the 1990s (Smardon 2014, 116). As the figures presented at the beginning of the chapter show, Canadian capital has not changed its orientation in the twenty-first century. R&D spending by Canadian capital as a proportion of GDP declined considerably from 2005 to 2015, and trade balances in a range of high-tech areas deteriorated as well. These patterns were the result of a long-term process throughout the neoliberal era of restructuring from the 1970s onwards, in which Canadian domestic capital either did not emphasize emerging research-intensive areas of production in the machinery and fabricated metals products sector (for example, information and communications technologies), or did not challenge the dominance of foreign transnational capital in research-intensive areas (for example, automobile production), which continued to rely on branch-plant operations using technologies developed by parent companies in other countries, particularly the United States.[13]

---

13 This pattern was particularly evident in the relative lack of development of domestically centred innovation clusters in the Canadian economy and in various patterns, including falling trade shares in research products; a growing divergence in the relative size of R&D expenditures in the Canadian economy, especially in comparison with the US economy; rising trade deficits in technology services; falling relative productivity; and reduced autonomy for the Canadian affiliates of US-based corporations in high-tech sectors (see Smardon 2014, 103–31).

In turn, this pattern is important in explaining why Canadian capitalism was defined by relatively low levels of R&D and original innovation, and why Canadian capitalist interests were so resistant to a broad expansion of domestic technological capacities. Because of the specific trajectory of Canadian development, major investments in domestic R&D and original innovation were not part of how Canadian manufacturing capital defined its overall growth strategies over time – either in the initial Fordist period of expansion in the early twentieth century, the post-war Golden Age, or the period of neoliberal restructuring afterwards. Although there were specific areas of R&D and innovation strength, such as in the aerospace industry with Bombardier, the software computer technology industry with Research in Motion (now known as Blackberry), or the telecommunications sector with now-defunct Nortel, these were exceptional instances that did not reflect the overall pattern. The extensive federal state initiatives to promote R&D and original innovation from the 1960s onward through giving tax incentives or promoting greater research partnerships between the federal state, the universities, and Canadian capital came up against this reality. Far from promoting a sustained increase in domestically centred R&D and original innovation in Canadian industry, these initiatives could not prevent a sustained decline in this key area in the twenty-first century (Smardon 2014, 360–74).

Conclusion

The Canadian economy has gone through several different eras of economic development. Underlying all of them has been a reliance on non-original innovation by Canadian industry. The consequences of this reliance have differed considerably. In contrast to the National Policy era and the post-war Golden Age, the ability of Canadian industry to maintain a presence in leading areas of technological change and accumulation has eroded in the era of neoliberal restructuring. Canadian manufacturing capital is caught in a situation where the legacy of technological dependency has restricted its ability to enter key growth industries in the twenty-first century. The absence of these sources of growth has reinforced the reliance of Canadian capital on resource-related extractive activities, often in raw or near-raw form, with a specific set of consequences in terms of poor employment creation; growing polarization of income in regions relying heavily on resource extraction between the owners of capital, on the one hand, and workers, on the other; and declining taxes paid by corporate capital arising from the low rates of tax assessed by the "extractive" provinces on their resource sectors (concerning these trends, see Fast 2014, 45–53). The pattern of neoliberal growth in Canada thus has taken a particular turn that has major implications for how employment, income distribution, and taxation are being determined. But it cannot be understood simply as the result of a linear trajectory of truncation or processes of economic restructuring common to all the advanced economies. The variability of economic development in Canada arising from the reliance on non-original innovation cannot be fitted into either of these two conceptual boxes.

3 Canada's Continental Political Economy

Introduction

This chapter traces Canada's experience as a capitalist, liberal-democratic nation-state that has been dependent for its prosperity on functioning effectively within a hierarchical international political economy. Much of its success (or failure) depends on the Canadian state's management of its relationship with hegemonic powers, particularly, for most of the past century, with the much bigger capitalist, liberal-democratic state to the south.

Although rooted in a class analysis, the focus of this chapter is on the state, in both senses of the word: a territory and population, and a system of power ruling over them. In particular it focuses on the broad strategies the state (system of power) has followed to deal with the challenges posed by Canada's historically subordinate insertion into the global economy. A number of national strategies are noted. Which ones were used at various times depended on external constraints and pressures and the preferences of powerful domestic actors, notably business interests. The transition from one strategy to another was generally provoked by some kind of crisis, with conflicts over posited solutions preceding the construction of a new strategy. However, while crises have preceded change, not all crises have produced changes.[2]

---

1 I would like to thank Mohammad Ferdosi and James Watson for valuable research assistance in the preparation of this chapter. Portions of it draw upon previously published work in McBride (1996, 2003, 2005, 2006, 2012) and Bowles et al. (2008).
2 The deep financial and economic crisis of 2007/8, for example, did not result in the abandonment of the neoliberal accumulation strategy in place since the mid-1970s, nor in the free trade regime implemented from the 1980s onwards.

We are dealing therefore with the political economy of one nation-state's interactions with its international or global context. All nation-states exhibit different characteristics. In Canada's case, some of its characteristics have led, within the Canadian political economy tradition, to intense debates about how to categorize or locate Canada within the global political economy and about what practical consequences flow from particular analytic positions. Within Canadian political economy, various positions occupy a spectrum from what is sometimes termed "left nationalism" – in which Canada is viewed as a dependency of successive economic hegemons, notably the United States – through a perspective that views Canada as a "semi-peripheral" country,[3] rich but not powerful in the international order, to views that it is a fully imperial power in its own right (among others on these issues, see Bowles et al. 2008; Clarkson 1968; Klassen 2014; Laxer 1973; Russell 1966).[4]

These debates are connected to others about the nature of Canada's capitalist class – whether it is a weak and dependent entity in thrall to that of the United States (or previously to that of the United Kingdom), or whether it represents a mature and normal example of such a class in Western societies and, if so, when it achieved this status (Carroll 1986; Clement 1975; Naylor 1972; Ryerson 1973; see also Smardon, and Brownlee, in this volume). No resolution of these positions can be attempted here, but it might be helpful to the reader to indicate where, among these controversies, the analysis in this chapter can be located.

Broadly speaking, it takes the position that Canada was founded and its early policies shaped by the interests of a nascent industrial bourgeoisie, not a commercial one (Ryerson rather than Naylor), and that it matured into a normal class, rather than a comprador one (Carroll rather than Clement). Its strategies for the Canadian state led, over time, to a degree of autonomy from the hegemons with which it was inevitably entangled. However, even if it functioned as an imperial state within the imperial bloc (Klassen), it did so in a subordinate position, and never achieved a "core" position within the global economy (contrary to Kellogg) and, since the adoption of neoliberalism and a

---

3 The term "semi-periphery" is used variously in the political economy literature, perhaps most notably in world systems theory. This chapter, however, does not employ the concept in the that way, preferring instead the usage of Bowles et al. (2008), in which semi-peripherality refers to the paradox of economic relative affluence combined with structural weakness, with a related political subordination in international affairs.

4 For a critique of many of these views, see Kellogg (2015).

determinedly free trade posture, has shown signs of regression to the semi-peripheral position from which it had never completely escaped (Bowles et al. 2008).[5]

Canada's Location in the International Political Economy and Its National Policy Strategies

The modern Canadian state was the successor to a number of British colonies in North America, and was founded for a mixture of domestic and international reasons. Domestic elites interested in the economic development opportunities offered by the vast territory and its natural resources needed a way to bypass the deadlock in French-English relations. Additionally, they needed to overcome the limited investment and credit possibilities available to the existing colonies by establishing a more creditworthy political vehicle (Dubuc 1966). And, for these domestic elites, as well as for Britain, there was a perception of external threat: the US Civil War was ending, leaving the Americans in possession of a powerful military machine should they choose to use it; a number of border incidents involving Irish republicans (Fenians) from the United States had occurred; and the doctrine of the God-given "manifest destiny" of the United States to establish its rule over all of North America was popular in that country. In a context of anticipated US expansionism, it was in Britain's interests to establish a more coherent and defensible polity in the northern part of North America. Much of the subsequent political history of Canada since its foundation in 1867 consists of attempts to manage these three issues: French-English relations, the economic development of a former colony heavily integrated into an international economy over which it exerted little or no control; and, the focus of this chapter, its relationship with its far-stronger southern neighbour.

The territory that became Canada had been colonized by European powers in pursuit of natural resources for shipment to home markets. Its economic development became dependent on a succession of resource staple products – fur, fish, timber, wheat, minerals – and the new country was unusually subject to the ebb and flow of demand for these products abroad. Canada occupied a semi-peripheral position[6]

---

5 One example of this might be Canada's continued technological dependence and decreasing effectiveness (from an already low base) in research and development – see Smardon, in this volume.

6 Defined as a relatively affluent but structurally weak country exhibiting a truncated form of economic development and a resulting subordinate political and military relationship with the hegemonic power.

within the international economy. Continuing to take advantage of international markets, but insulating the country somewhat from their volatility, was an ongoing objective of state policy.

For many years Canada's economic relations were heavily concentrated on the former colonial power, Britain. Over time, the north-south pull of geography and the displacement of Britain by the United States as the world's dominant power led to increased dependence on that country for trade and investment and military cooperation. By the mid-1920s, US investment in Canada surpassed that of Britain, and after the Second World War, the United States assumed far greater importance than Britain as a destination for Canadian exports. The fact that Canada exchanged one dominant economic partner for another equally dominant or more so, with associated political and strategic relationships, led to depictions of Canada's transition as being one of "colony to nation to colony" (Grant 1965; Lower 1946).

Yet distinctive regional and local factors apart, Canada's efforts to manage its political economy within a hierarchical international context followed a similar pattern to that pursued by other semi-peripheral countries. Senghaas (1985, 27) has identified two broad strategic responses by such countries in their dealings with hegemons. The first consists of "adapting to the superior economy through division of labour. This amounts to the free trade position." The second involves "attempting to develop the domestic economic potential in the shelter of more or less far-reaching protectionist measures, international competitiveness *not* being the guiding criterion for development promotion" (ibid). Senghaas notes (1985, 40) that consistent pursuit of the free trade option was the exception rather than the rule for those countries that achieved development successfully. In most, including Canada, "a non free trade posture played a major part in the broadening and deepening of the industrialization process" (ibid). These countries followed what Senghaas terms an *associative-dissociative* sequence of development. This means that their development

> began with an upswing in export growth (a predominantly associative phase), the agricultural, silvicultural and mineral resources of the societies in question being devoted mainly to exports. In a later phase, a dissociative development policy was pursued, corresponding with the well-known pattern of industrialization through import substitution: the substitution by local products of, at first, formerly imported consumer goods, and later, of basic, capital and engineering goods. In the long-term, development of this kind led to a comprehensively associative free-trade posture, which, however, was not adopted until decades after the start of

modern development, for the most part not until decades after the Second World War. (Senghaas 1985, 32)

In the years since Seghaas wrote, with the multiple trade and investment agreements that have been signed, one might amend his sequencing as applied to Canada to *associative-dissociative-reassociative*. Concerns have been expressed that adopting the free trade posture, even at a later stage of development, might return some of these semi-peripheral countries to their original role and heavy dependence on natural resources (Bowles et al 2008; Stanford 2008).

The fear that Canada could not escape its resource dependency (the "staples trap") has been a long-running theme in Canadian political economy (Drache 1991; Innis 1975; Watkins 1989; cf. Carter, in this volume), although a more optimistic version of staples theory, associated with W.A. Mackintosh, rather than with Harold Innis, suggests that more rounded economic development eventually would occur (see McBride 1996). Efforts to escape the staples trap were intertwined with resistance to the continental pull of the United States and an emphasis on "*control* of the processes of national development, the element of the collective will of the dominant class expressed through the public institutions of the state ... [which] was crucially relevant to a thinly settled frontier colony struggling on the fringes of a growing economic and political power to the south" (Whitaker 1977, 38). Conservative nationalists in Canada supported a degree of state activism even if the state was a client of business (Nelles 1974). For Stanley Ryerson (1973, 309), Confederation itself resulted from "the growth of a native, capitalist industry, with railway transport as its backbone, and expansion of the home market as the prime motive for creating a unified and autonomous state."[7] The term "national policy" has been defined as "overarching federal development strategies for achieving economic growth and social cohesion within the Canadian political community" (Bradford 1998, 3) and, if Ryerson's argument is accepted, it was as much a class policy as a national one. The first national policy, implicit in the Confederation agreement and taking definite shape with John A. Macdonald's conservative nationalist initiative in 1879, consisted of creating the transportation link for a national, east-west economy through

---

7 The other pressure sprang from "an imperial strategy that required unification not only in order to preserve the colonies from United States absorption, but also to strengthen a link of Empire reaching to the Pacific and hence to the approaches of Asia" (Ryerson 1973, 309). This account should remind us that, although we might be living in an age of globalization, there have been others.

railway building – projects that also served as a stimulus to the manufacturing industries of central Canada. High tariff barriers on imports served as a further aid to manufacturing and industrialization. As Eric Helleiner's chapter in this volume makes clear, such protectionist initiatives found a theoretical rationale in the works of Canadian political economists of the day such as Isaac Buchanan and John Rae. Finally, the government pursued an active immigration policy for agricultural settlement in the West and to provide some of the labour power necessary in the new manufacturing industries.

This national policy was depicted as "nation building" and the gradual emergence of Canada from colonial status. Such representations mostly ignored the fact that it was built upon the internal colonization of Indigenous Peoples, who were dispossessed of their lands and reduced to subordinate status (Green 2003; see also Starblanket and Coburn, in this volume). In terms of Canada's status within the global order, these policies implied and delivered greater autonomy.

A second national policy (Neill 1991, 173) was articulated following the Second World War. In domestic terms, it was a liberal or even social democratic Keynesian demand-management economic strategy, complemented by the construction of a social welfare state (Brodie and Jenson 1988, 293; Smiley 1975, 47–8). Arguably, as a result, Canada was a more equal place, in terms of distribution of income, than it had been previously or than it subsequently was to become (Veall 2012); its level of social provision was generally considered superior to that of the United States. But inequalities certainly remained: the Keynesian labour market, the centrepiece of the new national policy, was a gendered and racialized one. The new approach went along with the active pursuit of a liberalized international trading system (see Eden and Molot 1993, 235–40). Ultimately the expansion of that trading system helped undermine the Keynesian welfare state, and was succeeded by the era of neoliberalism and free trade.

Thus Canadian economic development was shaped by "national policies" that succeeded one another, with overlaps, as the guiding principles for detailed public policy (see, for example, Brodie 1990; Eden and Molot 1993; Leslie 1987). Notwithstanding these broad policy approaches, the long-run structural trend was one of ever-increasing economic integration with the United States.

Yet, until the 1980s there were moments of assertion against that trend. These included initiatives such as the Foreign Investment Review Agency (1973) and the creation of the state oil company, Petro-Canada (1975), both undertaken in the aftermath of the Watkins (Task Force on the Structure of Canadian Industry 1968) and Gray (1971) reports that flagged the dangers of US direct investment in Canada. The reports led to an increase of national consciousness in Canada and, in the belief of some astute observers (Smiley 1975), there were real prospects for a new national policy based on repatriating control of the Canadian economy. A statist industrial strategy would form a central component of such a policy. The historical alternative to an industrial strategy was to embrace free trade and further economic integration with the United States. Ultimately it was that option which was to prevail, despite the set of policies taken up by the Liberal governments of Pierre Trudeau in the early 1980s. These policies represented an embryonic state-directed industrial strategy, with a highly interventionist role reserved for the federal government (Leslie 1987, 8), and would have amounted to a third national policy. The National Energy Program and various mega-projects aimed to consolidate Canadian ownership in the energy sector and to use the sector as the cutting edge of an economic development strategy. Thus the new industrial and national policy would have been "staples based," but intended to link that sector to more ambitious industrial projects. It was partly a response to a nationalist agenda created by the revival of academic political economy in the 1960s (Clarkson 1985, chap. 4).

This attempted third national policy failed, for two reasons. First, it was dependent upon prices in the volatile international commodities market. To sustain the strategy and support the energy megaprojects, oil prices had to keep rising. Instead, they dropped. Second, the initiative ran into major opposition from the US state, American business interests, and Canadian business. The pressures emanating from these sources were accentuated by structural factors. Increased Canada-US trade had made the economy vulnerable to US policy and threats. US-based capital successfully encouraged its state to pressure Canada to abandon its new national policy. And Canadian business generally, both domestic and foreign owned, became increasingly nervous about the degree of state interventionism inherent in the Liberal strategy. Its commitment to Canadian state autonomy diminished. Such concerns had already prompted business to reorganize its representative capacity – hence the earlier formation of the Business Council on National Issues in 1975 (Langille 1987).

The collapse of the Trudeau Liberals' attempt at a new national policy opened the door for the Progressive Conservative Party's election victory in 1984 and the gradual implementation of a neoliberal economic agenda based on free market principles, a trajectory followed enthusiastically by Liberal governments once that party returned to office in the 1990s. This meant abandoning a national policy (energy or otherwise) in favour of the continentalist approach, eventually embodied in the North American Free Trade Agreement (NAFTA). The provisions of that agreement continentalized the disposition of Canadian energy and led to closer integration of the two economies generally. The scope for autonomous action by the state was reduced (McBride 2003).

This sharp change of direction was intimately associated with the shift from Keynesianism to neoliberalism and the implications of that change for Canada as a trading nation. With the abandonment of Keynesianism after 1975 came a resurgence of interest in export-led (see Cohen 1991) and market-driven economic growth, a sharp contrast to the Keynesian tilt towards economic growth based on a degree of domestic economic management by the state.

The pivotal domestic political event was the embrace of free trade by Canadian business (Doern and Tomlin 1991, 40). The mature, highly centralized, politically well-organized, and increasingly internationally oriented Canadian business sector saw free trade with the United States as in its interests for three commonly advanced reasons: security of access to the US market; improved competitiveness through an increased ability to achieve increased productivity, economies of scale, and access to state-of-the-art technology;[8] and as a spur to domestic economic reform (Carroll 1986, 1989; Richardson 1992).

Business's preferences were a product of its growing strength. The push to free trade would serve both the material interests of the Canadian capitalist class and its political ambitions to refashion Canada along explicitly pro-market lines.[9] The increasing interest of Canadian capital in external markets was due only partly to a defensive concern about protectionism in the United States; it also reflected the new multinational aspirations of Canadian capital itself. By the early 1980s, "Canadian firms with global operations were increasingly coming to share the view of their US counterparts that nationalistic restrictions only impeded their worldwide growth" (McQuaig 1991, 82).

The rationale for the policy shift was provided by the report of the Royal Commission on the Economic Union and Development Prospects for Canada in September 1985. Its message was unambiguous:

---

8 See Smardon, in this volume, for an account of Canadian business's deficiencies in innovation and research and development, a situation that somewhat qualifies the picture of a mature and self-confident capitalist class.

9 Linda McQuaig (1991) develops a compelling account of how Canadian business leaders saw free trade in part as a vehicle by which they might achieve a massive overhaul of Canadian society.

"Market liberalization, social adjustment, and limited government" (Bradford 1998, 113). It followed that free trade with the United States was essential to any Canadian economic strategy. The commissioners argued: "Our basic international stance complements our domestic stance. We must seek an end to those patterns of government involvement in the economy which may generate disincentives, retard flexibility, and work against the desired allocation of resources" (quoted in Bradford 1998, 114). Clearly, the domestic implications of this stance were as important as the international factors.

The strategy was underpinned by an implicit theory of export-led growth to replace the domestic demand growth of the Keynesian era. Hence the route to sustainable economic growth lay through encouraging exports, rather than, as in the Keynesian period, attempting to sustain the level of aggregate demand by a variety of domestically focused measures. Its attractiveness to business included claims that it would it enhance competitiveness and encourage restructuring, as less efficient producers would not be able to compete. Upward wage pressure would be discouraged – exports needed to be competitive, and lower wage costs was one means of achieving this; and domestic demand achieved by high wages was no longer a priority (Cohen 1991).

Security Dimensions of a Semi-Peripheral State

Side-by-side with economic integration went enhanced collaboration in military matters. Until the Second World War, Canada functioned as a strategic ally, or perhaps dependant, of Britain, loyally participating from the outset of both world wars while the United States only joined at later dates. However, even before the US entry into the Second World War, there was increasing Canadian military cooperation and consultation with the United States. Then, in 1940, the Ogdensburg Agreement created a Permanent Joint Board of Defence between the two countries, and subsequent joint policy declarations, notably the Hyde Park Declaration in 1941, left no doubt that a complete integration of North American resources and facilities was the common aim.

After the war, in the foreign policy arena Canada was clearly and enthusiastically a member of the multilateral Western alliance, and accepted US leadership of it while simultaneously pursuing extensive bilateral military initiatives with the United States. Canada supported the NATO alliance, contributed troops to the Korean War, joined NORAD (a bilateral air defence agreement with the United States), and stationed armed forces in Europe. The number of bilateral agreements between Canada and the United States expanded dramatically: by 2016 there were 223 in effect covering a wide range of subjects, with the largest number (56) defence related (United States 2016). These formal agreements led to tight integration of the two militaries through provisions for interoperability, exchanges of personnel, procurement of equipment, joint training exercises, and much more.

Canada's geographic location between the United States and the USSR meant that Canadian airspace and the Arctic Ocean were crucial to US military strategy (see Thompson 2014, 38–40; 43–51). The US position found expression in official documents such as a statement that "our commitments and risks are so extensive and important that Canada in a military sense must be considered as if it were an integral part of the United States" (US State Department, cited in Thompson 2014, 39). During the Cold War, radar stations were constructed in northern Canada, largely staffed by US military personnel. The bilateral NORAD agreement complemented joint defence efforts through multilateral NATO. The case for compliance with the American interests has been articulated by historians like J.L. Granatstein, whose notion is that Canadian sovereignty consists of recognizing the inevitable, or the necessary: "Canada's links with the United States are key to our survival as an independent and sovereign state ... Washington's capacity to inflict pain and enforce compliance on Canada is boundless. Canadian policy must be devoted to keeping the elephant well fed and happy" (Granatstein 2002, 15). For the most part, Canadian policy has adopted this stance.

There were tensions along the way. In 1959 Prime Minister John Diefenbaker retracted a previous undertaking to arm Bomarc missiles stationed in Canada with nuclear warheads. During the Cuban missile crisis, Diefenbaker refused an American request to place Canada's armed forces on the same level of alert as US forces until the cabinet had had a chance to deliberate. The Canadian armed forces, however, complied with the American request, and ignored its own government (see Lennox 2009). American displeasure at the government's delay (cabinet subsequently approved moving to a higher alert level) led to US interference (meddling, in today's parlance) in the 1963 Canadian election. This contributed to the defeat of Diefenbaker and the election of the Pearson Liberals, who accepted nuclear weapons in line with American preferences (Bourque and Martin 2013).

Still, by participating in peace building and campaigning to outlaw anti-personnel land mines, promoting the concept of human security, and advocating a UN-sponsored International Criminal Court, Canadian foreign policy demonstrated its aspirations to a distinctive middle-power role (David and Roussel 1998, 131). Yet Canada's involvement in many multilateral regimes has been depicted as primarily designed to support US preferences and policies: "Multilateralism was always first and foremost a product of American hegemony" (Black and Sjolander 1996, 27). In sum, Canada's multilateral involvement "provides direct reinforcement for United States foreign policy doctrines and limits [Canada's] dissent from US positions to marginal aspects. Bilaterally [Canada] assigns the highest importance to themes of harmony and commonality in the 'special relationship' ... and encourages a flow of transaction from the United States into Canada" (Dewitt and Kirton 1983, 28).

The most notable exception was Canada's refusal to contribute troops to the US-led war against Iraq. However, perhaps to placate the United States, Canada sent troops to Afghanistan, participated in the attacks on Libya, and aligned itself with the United States in Syria. The Iraq case was very much an aberration. Before Iraq, Canada had been an enthusiastic participant in US-organized military ventures such as the Gulf War and Kosovo (Allen 1999; Phillips 1999) and operated very much as a junior partner of US foreign policy. In the process, the country transitioned from peacekeeper to combatant, from an advocate of the UN's centrality in international security to viewing NATO or "coalitions of the willing" (Keating and Murray 2014) as an adequate substitute. The changing stance should not be attributed solely or even mainly to US pressures. For the most part, Canadian leaders share a common world view with their American counterparts – sometimes exacerbated, as in the case of Canada's particularly tough stance against Russia over the Ukraine issue, by political calculations or loyalties (see Popeski 2015; Pugliese 2017; Walkom 2018).

Back to Continental Political Economy

The ratification of the Canada-US Free Trade Agreement and subsequently NAFTA brought much closer continental economic integration, and marked a reversal of the various and mildly nationalist strategies or national policies that had been in place periodically since Confederation. Opponents of the ostensibly economic deal argued that loss of political autonomy and national and cultural identity would follow (see Ayres 1998, chap. 2). They also pointed out that most of the posited economic gains – increased productivity and competitiveness, and guaranteed access to the US market leading to greater diversification of the economy – did not materialize (see Fridell, in this volume). Even the vast increase in trade between the two countries can be exaggerated: Canada's share of US merchandise imports actually declined in the post-NAFTA period. Defenders of the agreement could argue that the situation would have been worse without it. It is not really possible to assess a counterfactual argument of this type, but it seems that previous progress towards escaping the staples trap and achieving a more balanced economic structure was reversed. As a result of a variety of political interventions and policies over a lengthy period, Canada had achieved an intermediate position in the global economy: "neither a simplistic staples model nor ... a fully-fledged and independent capitalist power in its own right" (Stanford 2008, 10). Partly for structural reasons, but certainly enhanced by the hands-off neoliberal approach and by the comparative advantage logic built into trade agreements such as NAFTA, a reversion to dependency on resource-based industries and a concomitant relative decline in manufacturing occurred from the mid-1990s (Stanford 2008).

Of course, in the case of trade, Canadian-US relations are not always harmonious. Canada's heavy reliance on the United States as an export market, combined with the two free trade deals, put Canada in a vulnerable position vis-à-vis its trade partner. Nonetheless Canada has engaged vigorously in numerous trade disputes with the United States through both the World Trade Organization and NAFTA. The ongoing softwood lumber dispute is perhaps the best known of these disputes, but many others have taken place in areas surrounding agriculture, steel, fisheries, and magazines. These, however, are disputes over specific applications of the internationally agreed rules. On the need for a rules-based system and the content of these rules, Canada bought completely into the position favoured by the United States until 2016.[10]

NAFTA's objectives included eliminating barriers to trade, encouraging the cross-border movement of goods and services,[11] increasing investment opportunities, protecting intellectual property rights, and creating an effective framework for dispute resolution (Article 102). NAFTA imposed a variety of obligations that operated to reduce the parties' discretion to discriminate in favour of domestic industries. The agreement's Chapter 11 covered all forms of investment interests, and prohibited a wide range of performance requirements that states might impose on foreign investors. It also created investor

---

10 As reflected in enthusiasm for the Trans-Pacific Partnership, the Comprehensive and Progressive Agreement for Trans-Pacific Partnership (CPTPP), the Canada-EU Comprehensive and Economic Trade Agreement (CETA), and various bilateral trade agreements.

11 The NAFTA text can be found in CCH 1994.

rights in dispute resolution. The restrictions on performance requirements made it difficult to use investment for long-term reasons of
national or regional industrial strategy (Stanford 1993, 166–7). As a
result, investors were likely to focus on areas of "natural" comparative advantage – in Canada's case, natural resources. The type of
regime NAFTA created was far more consistent with traditional US
approaches to economic policy than with either Canadian or Mexican
traditions. Similarly the inclusion of intellectual property rights in
NAFTA represented a victory for US policies and US multinational
corporations in research-intensive areas such as computer software
and pharmaceuticals.

For Canada a putative gain in the original free trade agreement
between the two countries, and carried forward into NAFTA, was the
Chapter 19 special dispute-settlement mechanism covering allegations
of dumping and subsidization. Retaining this mechanism in NAFTA
became a major priority of the Canadian side, even though the provision had proved unsatisfactory due to US hostility (McBride 2012; see
also Sinclair 2018b).

On energy, NAFTA Article 605 provided that any restrictions applied
to energy exports did "not reduce the proportion of the total export
shipments of the specific energy or basic petrochemical good made
available to that other Party relative to the total supply of that good of
the Party maintaining the restriction as compared to the proportion
prevailing in the most recent 36-month period." For the Americans, it
locked in supplies of Canadian energy and provided security of supply.
For Canadian business, it was an important limitation on the interventionist powers of the Canadian state and a "desirable loss of sovereignty" (Doern and Tomlin 1991, 258). Yet, in 2018, at US insistence it
was excluded from the new United States-Mexico-Canada Agreement
(USMCA).

Multinational corporations (private actors) acquired rights that
strengthened their hand vis-à-vis public actors (states), giving them, for
certain purposes, equal status with states. There was no reciprocal
imposition of obligations. Critics considered that the procedures
impinged on the sovereignty of states through granting (foreign) investors the right to challenge national (and provincial) legislation and regulations before a private arbitration tribunal. Canada has been much
sued under Chapter 11, especially with regard to environmental regulations, and its losses in cases have been both financially costly and, arguably, have exerted a chilling effect on its willingness to engage in
regulation in the public interest (Sinclair 2018a). Given Canada's continued commitment to investor-state dispute mechanisms in

international agreements, one can conclude that the regulatory chill effect is not unwelcome. In the negotiations that led to the USMCA the United States, for national sovereignty reasons, demanded and won the removal of the investor-state dispute provisions with Canada.[12] The energy proportionality and investor-state dispute clauses had been viewed as significant intrusions on Canadian sovereignty (McBride 2006), so their removal, although not instigated by the Canadian government, represented a gain for those wishing to enhance the country's autonomy and policy capacity. Other clauses in the USMCA, however, more than offset their removal.[13]

Under USMCA Chapter 32.10, notice must be given of intention to negotiate a free trade agreement with a non-market economy, widely interpreted to mean China. The USMCA member must supply all details of the negotiations and the final full text of the agreement to its partners, which have the right to terminate the USMCA if not satisfied. Essentially it gives them a veto power, and was condemned by the Chinese government: "[it] blatantly interferes with another country's sovereignty. We feel sad for the harm of economic autonomy inflicted on the relevant country" (Chase, Fife, and Stone 2018). Canadian commentators were hardly kinder. For Wenran Jiang (2018), the clause was the equivalent of colonial-era unequal treaties; Hugh Stephens (2018) considered it a major setback to trade diversification; and Paul Evans (2018) found it "astonishing … a severe restriction on Canadian independence and capability," as well as putting Canada in the American camp in its trade war with China. China is Canada's second-largest export market, but the clause sigificantly reduces Canada's latitude to build on that connection.

Further, Chapter 33 has the potential to reduce autonomy in macroeconomic policy making. It establishes a Macroeconomic Committee

---

12 Back-door routes to the use of investor-state dispute settlement mechanisms by US investors remained. Canada is a member of two multilateral trade agreements – the CPTTP and CETA – that retain these mechanisms in very similar form to those in NAFTA. So a potential US investor in Canada, wishing to retain these rights, could make the investment from a subsidiary in one of the countries that is a signatory to those agreements.

13 This is not the place for a detailed examination of the USMCA. In some areas – such as the dairy industry, data protection, and pharmaceuticals – and in failing, so far, to have tariffs on steel and aluminum removed that President Trump had imposed on "national security" grounds, Canada clearly lost ground; in others, such as automobiles, it made gains. For the purposes of this chapter, though, it is the institutional provisions that are the focus.

to conduct annual reviews of this policy area, including exchange rates. This opens the door for US pressure, in particular, should that country feel its trade is being adversely affected by policies designed to produce a weak currency in either of its partners. This does not entirely remove a policy instrument – de facto currency devaluation – that has been used to support exporters, but it does open it up to more scrutiny and pressure. Similarly, Chapter 26, establishing a North American Competitiveness Committee, and Chapter 28, on Good Regulatory Practices, are designed to enhance policy coordination in these areas.

Finally, the US proposal for a "sunset clause" terminating the agreement after five years unless expressly renewed was not included. However, Article 34.7 provides for a joint review of the agreement after six years in which the parties will confirm, or not, their wish to extend the agreement by sixteen years, but with a six-year review within each sixteen-year period. This undermines the certainty that an ongoing agreement supposedly provides investors and others, and exposes the less powerful partners to a potentially endless series of pressures as issues arise.

Conclusions: The Constitutionalization of a Continental Political Economy

There is little doubt that NAFTA produced closer economic integration between Canada and the United States. Institutionally, NAFTA set up no powerful institutions to rule over North American economic space. Rather, it established a set of rules that diminished the role that state institutions, especially those of Canada and Mexico, had used to shape their economies and preserve their sovereignty. NAFTA thus served "as a conditioning institutional framework that promotes and consolidates neo-liberal restructuring" (Grinspun and Kreklewich 1994, 33) or as a form of "constitutionalism." Stephen Clarkson (1993) was among the first to take seriously the view that the Canada–US Free Trade Agreement could be understood, in Ronald Reagan's phrase, as "a new economic constitution for North America." In Clarkson's view, this constitution was asymmetrical: it constrained the exercise of autonomy in Canada – and, since NAFTA, in Mexico as well – far more than in the United States (see also Gill 1995; McBride 2003; 2006). The USMCA has removed some of the constraints but added others, so the problem remains of structural pressures towards integration being reinforced by quasi-constituional measures that reduce the options of the weaker North American states.

Notwithstanding the impressive, although unsuccessful, display of opposition to free trade with the United States in the 1980s,[14] free trade and close economic integration with the United States has become uncontroversial in Canada. Donald Macdonald, chair of the Royal Commission that recommended free trade with the United States, had invited Canadians to take a "leap of faith" on the issue. Enormous controversy surrounded it, and in the 1988 election a majority of voters supported parties opposed to free trade, but the first-past-the-post election system delivered victory to the party supporting it. At the elite level, there is no evidence that, having taken the leap of faith, there has been any desire to revisit it. At the mass level, it seems the Canadian public eventually became habituated to free trade as part of a new reality, and one not seen as problematic. In polling conducted for Unifor in 2017, 29 per cent of respondents felt they had benefited from NAFTA, 14 per cent said they had been hurt by the agreement, and fully 57 per cent believed it had made no difference to them personally (Environics Unifor 2017). Even the opportunity presented by the unattractive Trump administration to terminate the agreement occasioned no rallying of significant forces willing to take advantage of the offer.[15] In official discourse this is explained by presenting North American economic integration as a success story that produced widespread benefits, including millions of trade-dependent jobs (see also Fridell, in this volume).

Yet the official narrative is hardly sustained by NAFTA's actual record or by estimates of the costs of termination of the agreement. A Bank of Montreal study considered that, over a five-year period, Canada's gross domestic product could be 1 per cent less than it otherwise might have been: "a relatively moderate impact on an economy that is expected to expand by close to 9 percent over that period" (Porter 2017, 2). By the same token, if the costs of termination are moderate, the economic benefits of participation must be modest. In terms of the original claims of NAFTA proponents – for example, that it would secure access to the US market and thus guarantee jobs in export-based industries and that it would increase productivity and hence competitiveness – the record is unconvincing. Canada's productivity continues to lag that of the United States, its share of total US imports has actually declined,

---

14 An opposition that reflected an earlier rejection of free trade in the 1911 election and Mackenzie King's suppression of the idea in the immediate post-war period.

15 Similarly, opposition to US military adventures around the world seemed to atrophy after the large demonstrations against the Iraq war in the early 2000s.

and continuous US threats or actual trade sanctions mean that access to the US market is far from guaranteed.

The degree to which tight economic integration has become an unconsidered part of the political landscape testifies to the effectiveness of NAFTA as a conditioning framework and, much more broadly, neo-liberal constructions of the proper relationships among state, economy, and society. These notions seem now to be hegemonic, and the less-than-impressive actual results of the agreement and neoliberalism generally seem so far to have had little impact on public opinion or political activism.

4 "This country has another story": Colonial Crisis, Treaty Relationships, and Indigenous Women's Futurities

GINA STARBLANKET AND ELAINE COBURN[1]

Introduction

This country has another story

– Katherena Vermette

This line is from a poem by Katherena Vermette (2018), a Métis writer and poet from Treaty One territory. Without taking away from other readings of these lines, we might offer one possible interpretation of them as an introduction to thinking through the conversations between Canadian political economy and Indigenous feminist scholarship and struggles. Specifically, Vermette troubles mainstream stories about Canada, and recalls alternate, relational narratives of life in these lands. This is because, for many, perhaps most, Indigenous Peoples, Canada is a violent imposition, a way of naming and claiming Indigenous lands by and for the colonizer. Far from being self-evident, much less self-evidently desirable, the settler colonial project that is currently called "Canada" is part of the deliberate erasure of layers of Indigenous names and relationships with Creation. For, as Kwakwaka'wakw scholar Sarah Hunt (2013) observes, Indigenous names for themselves and their territories are much more than a form of identification. They represent complex overlapping networks of relationships, including rich and ongoing cultural, political, spiritual, ceremonial, and legal relations.

Informed by such insights, we might interpret Vermette's statement, "this country has another story," as an opening that invites the reader

---

1 The co-authorship was undertaken cooperatively and reflects shared insights and labour.

to think otherwise about the stories that they hold relative to the geographies they inhabit. Here, the land does not signify an object that is merely taken away, returned, and repossessed. Rather, for many Indigenous Peoples, the land represents a web of living, constitutive relations, the nature of which has been irrevocably altered through colonialism. As exploitative, capitalist structures and colonial settlement have confined Indigenous relations to the land within imposed and often alien terms, so too have heteronormative identity constructions functioned to misrecognize, deny, or preclude Indigenous subjectivities.

We might also extend our understanding of the line "This country has another story" as invoking the need to unearth and centre Indigenous relationships with Creation, taking seriously their various forms and implications. In a modest way, we seek to do the latter here by foregrounding Indigenous analyses of the colonial present and imaginings of Indigenous futures. We begin with a broad overview of the interrelated social, political, and economic logics of colonialism. In particular, we explore these dynamics through contested interpretations of treaties, contrasting colonial understanding of treaties as transactions sealing land cessions with critical Indigenous interpretations of treaties as about ongoing relational responsibilities. From these, we draw out alternate ideas of political economy grounded in treaties. We then foreground Indigenous women's voices as offering vital insights into Indigenous relationality with Creation, in and beyond treaties. These are the starting pointing for conversations about Indigenous feminist futurities beyond the colonial present.

"Canada" as the Foundational Crisis for Indigenous Peoples

It is an illuminating irony that "Canada" is commonly represented as having derived from an Iroquois word, evidence of the long-standing nature of the settler state's drive to engage selectively with Indigenous relations – denying the existence of Indigenous laws, governance, and jurisdiction, while simultaneously appropriating Indigeneity for its own purposes.[2] The symbolic incorporation of Indigenous contributions in the naming of the Canadian state stands in stark contrast to

---

2 As Wolfe (2006, 388) writes, settler colonialism's eliminatory logic involves much more than the "summary liquidation" of all Indigenous people; it also involves the creation of new colonial societies that, in some contexts, symbolically appropriate elements of Indigenous languages, imagery, and motifs to construct their own national identity.

material forms of violence and dispossession Indigenous Peoples face in Canada's collective name. The foundations of the Canadian state rely on the simultaneous continuity *and* containment of Indigenous relationships to the land – that is, continuity of Indigenous "consent" to share the land and containment of forms of relationship that interfere with the state's exercise of perfect territorial sovereignty. This echoes contradictory movements to erase Indigenous worldviews and practices, while selectively recalling Indigenous presence to legitimate state claims.

The first movement of Canada's colonial history is well known, if strategically forgotten or intentionally disavowed.[3] This movement is the systematic eradication of Indigenous Peoples and their ways of knowing and being. This has been the conscious, explicit aim of much colonial policy, including through genocide and forced relocations. Infamously, Canada's first prime minister, John A. Macdonald, spoke openly about keeping Indigenous Peoples "on the verge of actual starvation," and directed federal officials to deny them food to force them off their lands and into submission to the colonial state (Daschuk 2013). Diverse Indigenous Peoples have been contained to small, sharply defined territories through the reserve system or, for the Métis, the road allowances.[4] The forced relocations of the Inuit throughout the post-war period participated in these broader colonial strategies of containment and resettlement of Indigenous peoples, including for military purposes (Tester and Kulchyski 2011). The removal and containment of diverse Indigenous Peoples was and is motivated by – and makes possible – the conversion of Indigenous lands, waters, and the natural world into private property. As private property, Indigenous lands become available for corporations and for settlement. In other cases, they are set aside for the creation of Crown parklands (Corntassel 2012, 93).

Operating over more than a century, the residential school system murdered more than 5,000 Indigenous children through physical abuse, starvation, and neglect, while forcibly assimilating others into a servant class and later as badly paid, expendable unskilled labour (Coulthard 2014; Truth and Reconciliation Commission of Canada 2015). The "sixties scoop" removed Indigenous children from their

---

3 We recall Prime Minister Stephen Harper's assertion to a G20 summit that Canada has no colonial history (Dolha 2009).
4 The road allowances were parcels of land set aside by the federal government for the future railway. This meant the Métis could be and often were forced off this land claimed by the Crown.

communities, placing them with white adopted families (Fournier and Crey 1997; Johnston 1983). Today there are more Indigenous children "in care" than were in the residential school system at its height (Bennett, Blackstock, and De La Ronde 2005, 18–21). Indigenous children are routinely schooled in colonial languages, in underfunded schools. This compounds the legacies of residential school systems and child "welfare" programs that purposefully or institutionally prevent intergenerational transmission of language, knowledge, culture, law, and spirituality (Bennett, Blackstock, and De La Ronde 2005). Indigenous people, both men and women, are overrepresented in the federal prison system and suffer from far higher rates of violence than do non-Indigenous people (Sapers 2016; Truth and Reconciliation Commission of Canada 2015). Taken together, these appear as contemporary strategies of containment and assimilation, in new forms, despite quite different political rhetoric today compared to one hundred or even fifty or twenty years ago.

On lands claimed by the Canadian state, the history of colonialism is thus one of the violent sundering of Indigenous relationships and the systematic suppression of Indigenous knowledges, economies, laws, and political orders. From the perspective of many Indigenous Peoples and actors, this colonial rupturing of Indigenous relationships is the foundational crisis at the heart of the Canadian political project. Yet, in a second movement, the colonial state also draws selectively on Indigenous relationships with the land to legitimate its ongoing presence, since the forcible dispossession of Indigenous Peoples is still practised, but less politically acceptable, given centuries of Indigenous struggles to reassert their humanity, responsibilities, and rights. Too often, however, mobilization of Indigenous political practices, including treaties, enables the state to recognize Indigenous worldviews, only to radically denature them by reincorporating them into existing capitalist economic relationships under the authority of the colonial state (Atleo 2015; Coulthard 2014; Kuokkanen 2011). It is to these contradictory logics of colonialism, and the complex ways they manifest, at once economically, socially, and politically, that we turn next.

Settler Colonial Logics of Dispossession

Colonialism, with its contradictory movements, is not reducible to any singular act or set of challenges. We have already pointed to contradictory colonial impulses of erasure, containment, and appropriation. As Shalene Jobin (2015) has argued, moreover, settler colonialism is grounded upon interconnected logics, at once economic, political, and social. She aptly notes that analyses of any one of these on its own can result in a failure to understand adequately the comprehensive inner workings of the structure of colonialism, and so can function inadvertently to reproduce settler colonial domination by perpetuating aspects of its logic. Attempts to address the political and social dimensions of domination, for instance, without attending to the economic aspects of settler colonialism are inherently limited. They lead to resistance strategies that pursue the political liberation of Indigenous communities, all while reproducing capitalist logics that undermine the desired political transformation by reincorporating Indigenous polities into capitalist relationships and under corporate power (Coulthard 2014; Kuokkanen 2011). The same limitations mark attempts to reconcile social relations between Indigenous and non-Indigenous people that do not account for the political and economic requirements of reconciliation (Green 2015). Such efforts reduce reconciliation to folkloric displays of "culture" disconnected from meaningful Indigenous self-determination.

An important feature of contemporary colonial governance lies precisely in practices of splitting apart these different, integrated aspects of the colonial relationship and of Indigenous ways of being. Not least, political dimensions of Indigenous power are formally split from economic concerns, in a classically liberal juridical move. Characteristically, the federal government began conceding limited powers of self-governance to Indigenous Peoples in the 1970s, while considering land claims separately from questions of formal political self-governance. Yet even then, the colonial state offered only very limited recognition for self-governance, ensuring sharply circumscribed Indigenous jurisdiction over the lands, waterways, and resources that is always lesser than the form of title enjoyed by the federal government, and thus can be infringed upon in the name of the "national interest." In the 1997 *Delgamuukw vs. British Columbia*[5] decision, notably, the Supreme Court of Canada, in a groundbreaking legal judgment, recognized contemporary Indigenous land title. This was then nearly entirely undercut by specifying that the colonial state could override the Indigenous jurisdiction, just granted, for the purposes of "the development of agriculture, forestry, mining, and hydroelectric power, the general economic development of the interior of British Columbia, protection of the environment or endangered species, the building of infrastructure and the settlement of foreign populations to support those aims, [these]

---

5 *Delgamuukw v. British Columbia*, [1997] 3 S.C.R. 1010.

are the kinds of objectives that … in principle, can justify the infringement of aboriginal title" (cited in Atleo 2008, 12).

In recent decades, the grounds for justifiable infringement have gradually become wider in scope and more formulaic for Crown governments (see *Tsilhqot'in*[6] and *Grassy Narrows*).[7] Thus, not only is the
colonial state both party and judge, but legal "recognition" of Indigenous relationships to the land is highly circumscribed by colonial political and economic self-interest. In these decisions, the colonial state
does not act on behalf of a Canadian citizenry, but rather in the interests
of capitalist enterprises seeking to exploit resources. Increasingly, it has
allowed local (provincial) governments, which are the closest to and
have the most to gain from Indigenous lands, to justify infringements
of Indigenous rights and title (Borrows 2017, 30). In other instances, the
state claims the right to override Indigenous jurisdiction in the name of
the "protection of the environment," a caveat that implicitly positions
Indigenous Peoples as dangerous to the natural world and colonizers
as protectors of this relationship.[8] Through such legal interpretations
and decisions, the colonial state offers limited forms of delegated political independence, while perpetuating Indigenous Peoples' social and
economic assimilation under the auspices of federal and provincial
governments.

Similar colonial logics of dispossession are expressed through contemporary understanding of treaties.[9] Many non-Indigenous polities
and individuals – and some contemporary Indigenous polities and
individual Indigenous persons – understand treaties as transactional
documents. In this view, treaties are contracts that formalize the permanent transfer of land ownership from one party to another. Although
there is new colonial recognition of Indigenous interpretive principles

---

6 *Tsilhqot'in Nation v. British Columbia*, 2014 SCC 44 (CanLII).
7 *Grassy Narrows First Nation v. Ontario (Natural Resources)*, 2014 SCC 48 (CanLII).
8 We do not want to position Indigenous Peoples, romantically, as always-already
   contemporary eco-warriors. On the contrary, we seek to recognize the full range of
   Indigenous political positions, some of which see profit sharing in resource extraction
   as politically and economically desirable or at least pragmatically necessary given the
   realities of poverty in too many Indigenous nations.
9 Not all Indigenous Peoples understand their relationships through treaties. Without
   collapsing diverse Indigenous polities into a pan-Indigenous paradigm, we would
   suggest the relationship to the land, formalized in treaties, bears a family resemblance
   to non-treaty Indigenous understandings of the critical spiritual, political, economic,
   and social importance of reciprocal relationships of respect with the land, seas, and
   water.

surrounding treaties, aimed at integrating Indigenous understandings of their spirit and intent, such efforts have been dedicated to detecting Indigenous understandings of specific clauses (Stark 2017, 273), and thus have failed to affect a substantial transformation in understandings surrounding the nature of treaties themselves. Consequently, treaties are still interpreted in Canadian discourses and institutions to mean that land has been ceded and surrendered in exchange for set terms. Such readings confirm, rather than subvert, narrowly juridical and, ultimately, capitalist readings of treaties within a broader worldview that construes land as a commodity like any other, which may be bought and sold for profit. In the case of treaties signed prior to the contemporary era, these have become historical acts, legitimating the permanent land transfer from Indigenous Peoples to the colonial state (for an important challenge to such interpretations, see Kovach 2013).

Treaties: Changing and Conflicting Perspectives

Such transactional understandings of treaty might be widely held across both colonial and Indigenous nations. Consider the ways in which the importance of treaty implementation is contextualized by the Saskatchewan Office of the Treaty Commissioner: "we must also recognize the importance to Canadian society of having First Nations people enter the modern economy and actively seek to foster their socio-economic inclusion, so that the livelihood promises in the treaties are fully implemented" (Arnot 1998, 58). From this perspective, treaty implementation is about Indigenous economic development and participatory inclusion in the capitalist economy (Poelzer and Coates 2015, 263). Similarly, extinguishment is necessary for "resource sharing," including a percentage of profits from projects such as the trans-Canada pipeline. Such approaches might be embraced enthusiastically as symptomatic of a new Indigenous entrepreneurial business acumen (Newhouse 2000; for a critique, see Atleo 2015), or with pragmatic reluctance as complex trade-offs that might provide a means of addressing poverty within resource-starved Indigenous communities.

Indigenous Peoples' livelihoods and survival are certainly part of the intent of treaties. Nonetheless, following many Indigenous knowledge holders and scholars (Altamirano-Jiménez 2004; Green 2003; Kuokkanen 2011; Stewart-Harawira 2005), we reject the logics that underlie the "economic development" approach to treaty implementation. Not least, this perspective splits culture, as a "way of life," from economics and politics, reducing treaties from political frameworks to "cultural" claims (see Starblanket 2019). In this view, protecting diverse Indigenous ways of life is interpreted as Indigenous abilities to hunt, gather, and harvest – but only as long as these do not interfere with resource extraction or the sanctity of Crown parklands. At best, cultural rights are interpreted as embodying a limited spectrum of self-government responsibilities, akin to those of a municipality. The consequence is that Indigenous Peoples' survival, as such, is narrowly construed and always in ways compatible with the continued informal but powerful economic authority of corporate actors and the formal political authority of the colonial state.

In contrast, we maintain that treaties sought to ensure Indigenous survival through the maintenance of distinct legal, political, and social structures within Indigenous nations, polities, and communities. In other words, while treaties were intended to provide assistance in times of need, the desire to enter into relations where Indigenous and non-Indigenous people might learn from each other and depend upon each other at times did not equate to a will to enter into relations of subordination (Asch 2014). A nation-to-nation relationship was not intended to facilitate economic wellness as something given or endowed by settlers, but as something to be maintained through Indigenous Peoples' ongoing ability to make a living and ensure their survival by learning new ways without relinquishing existing ones. In short, Indigenous Peoples made treaties to ensure the continuity of their ways of life, while agreeing to share the land with newcomers.

The proper foundations, function, and exercise of Indigenous communities are not rooted in corporate or colonial authority and power. Instead, as the late Elder Gordon Oakes (Nekaneet First Nation) explained, governance arose from Indigenous Peoples' relations with Creation. At a 1997 Treaty Four Elders Forum, he stated that Indigenous Peoples "had self-government before the coming of the white man. The buffalo provided every need that a nation would require and that was our self-government flowing from there. Today we have no land base to sustain ourselves" (quoted in Oakes 1997, 76). In short, self-government is inherent in sustaining relationships with the natural world; it does not emerge from "recognition" by an implicitly superior colonial body (Coulthard 2014). Central to the maintenance of Indigenous ways of life is the need for the relations that sustain us, which also requires a vibrant and healthy land base that can sustain the life of animals and other living beings as well. Neoliberal imperatives of economic participation and restructuring eclipse the unique nature of the treaty relationship, where authority is derived from moral, political, and spiritual relationships to the land. They distort and displace the focus of treaty dialogue today, transforming this into a legally binding narrative of land cession and profit sharing, even as it destroys the sustainable land base for Indigenous survival on Indigenous terms.

Gendered Dispossessions in Colonial Canada

In this exploration of colonial dispossession, notably through transactional understandings of treaties, we have so far written as if gender is not salient. Certainly, colonialism has had devastating effects upon all Indigenous Peoples. Nonetheless, Canada's economic interests, especially those of elites, both historically and today, require the exploitation and strategic managing of Indigenous relationships with Creation – and both these relationships and colonial efforts to eliminate them are gendered. In familiar dynamics, these gendered relationships have been selectively mobilized for the purposes of exploitation. In other cases, they have been destroyed as inimical to colonial political economy and governance.

Many Indigenous scholars have argued that Indigenous women are intimately responsible to and associated with Creation (e.g., Anderson 2000). As such, Indigenous women have been central targets in colonial processes, albeit in different ways in shifting socio-economic contexts. The fur trade economy, for instance, depended upon the maintenance of Indigenous women's relations to the land to help establish kinship and share knowledge of local geographies (Kuokkanen 2011). Later, the shift from mercantile to industrial capitalism required the separation of Indigenous Peoples from the land and its conversion to private property, to make it available for settlement, further development, and new forms of exploitation. Under these circumstances, Indigenous women's power, authority, and relationships were targeted for elimination. Put simply, although the drive to sever or repress Indigenous relationships with the land certainly affected all Indigenous Peoples, Indigenous women's power and centrality within communities constituted a particular threat to settler governance, as they represented a fundamentally different form of political organization (A. Simpson 2016; L.B. Simpson 2017).

The role of women in treaty making is one example of Indigenous women's traditionally important political role within many Indigenous polities. As the late Elder Noel Starblanket (Star Blanket Cree Nation) observed, regarding women's role in negotiating Treaty 4 on lands now claimed by Saskatchewan and the federal government: "The Chiefs would go back and talk to the Old Ladies. They went back to their homes, and they talked to the women. They were the ones who told the men the astonishing concepts of as long as the grass grows, as long as the sun shines. The Treaties were understood as existing in perpetuity, just like the things that they were referring to. For four nights, they went back to talk to the Old Ladies. The Old Ladies told them to think of the future, and of the children yet unborn" (McLeod and Starblanket, 2014, 38). Here, Starblanket suggested that it is women who developed the languages later enshrined in treaties, which were not imagined as one-time transactions but were meant to hold in perpetuity "as long as the grass grows, as long as the sun shines." The Old Ladies were critical in framing the temporality of treaties with respect to the rhythms of the natural world, but also with specific regard for future generations.

Of course, not all Indigenous polities and societies necessarily had or have a similar gendered division of spiritual, political, and epistemological labour. Moreover, the institution of all-male chiefs, in the instance just described, might suggest unequal and not only complementary gendered social realities (LaRocque 2017, 125); this might also reflect a colonial refusal to negotiate with women representatives. In any event, such recollections clearly situate these Indigenous women, the Old Ladies, as powerful, respected (spiritual) knowers within their own polities and societies. Despite such political, social, and spiritual expressions of Indigenous women's authority, early European newcomers failed to acknowledge Indigenous women's jurisdictions and importance within their communities. Indigenous scholars have argued that this was driven by the social norms and values of Europe at the time, but it also reflected distinctly political aims. The extension of settler political authority over Indigenous Peoples required the removal or erasure of Indigenous polities, and particularly those aspects of Indigenous political orders that called into question settler claims to sovereignty. This included the specific powers of Indigenous women.

Here, narrow interpretations of treaties as transactions coexisted alongside other colonial instruments that specifically dispossessed Indigenous women. Notoriously, provisions of the 1876 Indian Act stripped Indigenous women and their descendants of Indian status when they out-married – that is, when they married men without Indian status, as defined by the colonial state (Lawrence and Anderson 2005, 2). The same, patriarchal, racialized legal measures granted non-Indigenous women Indian status when they married "status Indian" men. As Simpson (2008) observes, this movement was asymmetrical. Indigenous women and their children were dispossessed of relationships in their communities, including through forcible exile from reserves. In contrast, white women who married Indigenous men maintained relationships with their home communities, while also gaining entry into their spouse's Indigenous community. This legal manoeuvre juridically "disappeared" Indigenous women and their descendants into the Canadian polity, while Indigenous communities were correspondingly "whitened" through the entry of non-Indigenous women onto reserves.[10] The sexist provisions of the Indian Act were ended only in 1985 as a consequence of Indigenous women's legal challenges to the colonial state. Ironically, Indigenous women were forced to pursue this remediation through colonial courts that were at once both party and judge, since the colonial state does not recognize Indigenous systems of justice.

Such legal struggles are symptomatic of, and participate in, much broader struggles by Indigenous women, both status and non-status, to retain, reassert, but also reinvent their relationships with their lands and nations (Green 2017; Lawrence and Anderson 2003; Suzack et al. 2011). Although often interpreted in narrow, instrumental ways by non-Indigenous people, these struggles are not about Indigenous abilities to "access" land for traditional practices, nor are they about reconciling Indigenous rights with competing federal, provincial, and municipal claims. Rather, this is about Indigenous women drawing attention to gendered patterns of dispossession – land theft – while highlighting responsibilities towards the land, in contrast to a liberal colonial emphasis on "rights" to "use" the land, understood primarily as a potentially profitable resource. If now formally ended, Canada's long-lasting policies remain a stark reminder of the gendered nature of institutionalized forms of colonial dispossession.

"Girl go this way, boy go this way": The "Anomalous" Indigenous Body

Establishing settler political authority demanded the forcible erasure of other Indigenous political and social relationships, including practices that disrupted colonial legal, political, and social norms. Following Alex Wilson of the Opaskwayak Cree Nation, for instance, we recall the apparently banal observation of a residential school survivor, who described her introduction to the establishment this way: "The first thing they did was divide us by boy/girl. Girl go this way, boy go this way. Girl wear pinafores. Boy wear pants" (Wilson 2008, 194–5). From

---

10 As Arvin, Tuck, and Morrill (2013, 12) might observe, this recalls Sherman Alexie's warning of a (North) American future, in which "all of the white people will be Indians and all of the Indians will be ghosts." This is one variant of the tenacious colonial myth that Indigenous Peoples are destined to disappear, persisting only as an appropriated (white) identity.

the perspective of both historical and, to a significant extent, contemporary colonial culture, such social divisions, rooted in gendered binaries, appear natural, if increasingly challenged. In contrast, from the perspective of the child so socially "sorted," this was a confusing and in many respects devastating social division, with respect to the child's own everyday gendered embodiment, which did not fit colonial binary gender norms and stereotypes, and because this practice of gender segregation separated the child from siblings. As Billy-Ray Belcourt of the Driftpile Cree Nation describes, such seemingly minor acts are part of the colonial "history of eliminating recalcitrant indigeneities incompatible within a supposedly hygienic social" (Belcourt 2016, 22). Through the everyday, here forcible institutionalization of their own taken-for-granted social relations, colonial practices such as these erased "anomalous" Indigenous social relationships, familial and political, including diverse forms of Indigenous gender embodiment.[11]

The colonial legal institution of two binary genders in legal documents and, until the 1970s, laws against same-gender sexual relationships likewise functioned to suppress Indigenous political, social, and cultural forms that challenged colonial heteropatriarchy. Christian religious strictures against same-gender love and sexual expressions are another source of disciplining biocolonial power over Indigenous bodies (Driskill 2004). Today, these are "indigenized" among (some) Christians within Indigenous communities and institutionalized more or less autonomously by (some) Indigenous polities (Justice 2010) that reify heterosexual relationships, especially through formal marriages. Such practices join popular gendered stereotypes about Indigenous women, often with dangerous consequences. The myth of the Indian princess, infatuated with (white) male settlers, and the sexually available "squaw" both situate Indigenous women as the natural sexual objects of (white) male colonizers (Acoose-Miswonigeesikokwe 2016). They also denaturalize Indigenous women, today including LGBTQ2S-identified women who do not conform to colonial stereotypes. The repression of Indigenous women's roles and political authority and the "anomalous" sexual and gender queer Indigenous body (see also Justice 2010), in both historical and contemporary Indigenous contexts, is not separate from, but part of, broader colonial practices of biodisciplining power over Indigenous Peoples. Violence against Indigenous women, not least LGBTQ2S women, is part of broader colonial practices of political repression.

---

11 This analysis is partly drawn from a French-language essay (Coburn 2017).

Against Commodification and for Indigenous Feminist Creations

For colonial state and religious authorities, the very presence of Indigenous women in the political life of their communities signified a threat to the settler colonial project, which historically allowed no such role for women. So, too, did those who held social and sometimes political or spiritual positions beyond colonial gender binaries and heteronormative sexualities. Their political authority, and the relationships of responsibility they represented, recalled the continuity of a political order that was not only different, but served to challenge settler claims to jurisdiction. For these reasons, the colonial state sought to erase Indigenous women. Yet they have survived, they have resisted, and more than this, they have continued to exercise their diverse ways of being, knowledges, and practices.

Among them, many Indigenous women and feminists have argued that neoliberal economic ideas and structures distract from the culturally grounded ideas and practices of relationality that have sustained Indigenous livelihood for hundreds of years. These Indigenous women challenge a positive association between capital accumulation and Indigenous visions of decolonization, freedom, and relationships of reciprocal responsibility. Saami scholar Rauna Kuokkanen (2011, 286), for instance, questions presumptions about "the compatibility of Indigenous self-determination and free-market ideologies," suggesting there are "deep-seated ontological differences between neoliberal ideologies and Indigenous philosophies based on a close interaction with the land and emphasizing individual and collective responsibilities of taking care of the land." Not only are many economic development proposals incompatible with Indigenous visions of relationality, they might be counterproductive to the liberatory and (re)conciliatory possibilities that capitalist ventures claim to offer. As Joyce Green (2019) writes, Indigenous self-determination cannot be achieved through political and social assimilation into the Canadian status quo, but requires dismantling of the many related forms of domination (including patriarchal, capitalist ones) that structure relations of colonialism. Further, she argues that incorporation into the neoliberal economy cannot be situated as a prerequisite for the amends and relational possibilities inherent in reconciliation, calling instead for "a concrete set of acceptable liberatory alternatives" directed by Indigenous people, even if such alternatives negatively affect "corporate ambitions and expectations of profitability" (Green 2019, 249). In the academy, Maori intellectual Makere Stewart-Harawira (2013) has warned against the capture of (some) Indigenous knowledges by capital within universities that now promote public-private partnerships, including with Indigenous knowledge holders. In such "partnerships," Indigenous knowledges and practices, like Indigenous lands, become commodified as private (intellectual) property.

More than this, Indigenous women remind us of the many ways in which Indigenous Peoples traditionally have maintained relationships with and responsibilities to Creation in the face of efforts to commodify it (Jobin 2015; Simpson 2017). For some, this might mean essentialist articulations of Indigenous womanhood. Such approaches emphasize Indigenous women's inherent connections with Creation and special powers for women, especially linked to mothering and nurturing – for instance, as Aunties – whether this role is biological or social (e.g., Anderson 2000). For others, more promising approaches are those developed by Indigenous feminists who highlight the biopolitics of resistance, arguing that self-determination does not just mean collective governing rights, but the right of individual people to be self-determining in terms of their own bodies and to choose how to honour the many relations they inhabit (Bear 2016; Hunt 2015; LaRocque 2017). This is a feminist commitment, but it might be understood simultaneously as a basic affirmation of Indigenous women's humanity, since all human beings are moral agents with the capacity to make choices for themselves in relationships with others. Not least, this is true with respect to Indigenous women's own bodies, including their own embodied gender expression, sexuality, and love relationships (LaRocque 2017).

For this perspective, Indigenous women and, in particular, Indigenous feminists are sometimes critiqued for focusing on "individual rights" at the expense of collective concerns and relational responsibilities (Starblanket 2017). Similarly, Indigenous feminist anti-essentialist critiques have been depicted as narrow sighted for their failure to account for the intersecting and structural forms of oppression that condition Indigenous patriarchy and for undermining the potential for essentialist constructions to advance national liberation (see Coulthard 2014, 83–102, although he affirms the necessity of gender equity within Indigenous political organizing).

If Indigenous women reject the idea of the land as a commodity that can be individually owned, elsewhere they challenge any easy distinction between individual and collective justice. Rather, as Sarah Hunt (2015, 4) has argued, they have worked to collapse the "scalar division" between micro and macro levels of colonial violence. In her important intervention, Hunt problematizes the supposed distinction between broader structural issues such as land, resources, and jurisdiction, and the everyday, intimate iterations of colonial violence. She calls on Indigenous Peoples to confront masculinist conceptions of what is politically significant in activist and scholarly works, emphasizing the need to take seriously the interconnected and co-productive nature of micro and macro scales of colonial violence.

Indeed, many Indigenous women have challenged the notion that justice is to be found either through large-scale collective actions, or through individual resilience and healing (De Finney 2017: Goeman 2017; Million 2013), showing instead how responses to violence in fact are to be found between and beyond these parameters. For Hunt (2015, 8), Indigenous resurgence involves not just a *scaling up* of localized, on-the-ground practices aimed at transforming the colonial economy, but also a scaling of resurgent actions down to the intimate level of everyday relations. To this end, she argues that Indigenous law and jurisdictional power should inform not just the purportedly broader terrain of political struggles over homelands, but the narrower struggle over bodies as well, asking: "what would happen if every time an Indigenous woman had her personal boundaries crossed without consent, we were moved to act in the same way as we've seen to the threat of a pipeline in our territories – the nonconsensual crossing of territorial boundaries?" (Hunt 2015, 8–9).

"This country has another story": Indigenous Feminist Futures

This question might prompt us to circle back to Vermette's poem, which points to the significance of possible ways of thinking and being in this country, reminding us of the existence of multiple storied narratives, including ones that are too often left unheard. As Tonawanda Seneca scholar Mishuana Goeman (2013) explains, settler models of gender, territory, jurisdiction, and race can be challenged not just by invoking relations with Creation, but also by revisiting how it is we name and understand these relations and imagining alternative futures on that basis. Through analyses of discursive techniques and literary/oral traditions, Goeman explains how Indigenous women's writings unsettle colonial naming and organizing of land, bodies, and social and political landscapes. And as Indigenous women resist colonial efforts to narrate Indigenous histories and relationships to territories, Goeman highlights how they foreground Indigenous naming, and so conceptions of space, relationships, and autonomy in their place. These ways of thinking and being in active defiance of the ontologies that are imposed upon Indigenous Peoples are, in our view, where the most truly transformative possibilities lie.

Here we can gesture to just a few of the many ways Indigenous feminists are broadening the spaces where Indigeneity can be understood to thrive. Some renew treaty relationships. Heidi Kiiwetinepinesiik Stark (2012, 122), Turtle Mountain Ojibwe, suggests that treaties are about active dialogue, and that this is fundamental to nation building, "both real and envisioned, what nations were and what they hoped to become." That is, for Stark, treaties are a source of factual insight into how a nation "is" in relationships with other nations, including human, animal, and plant nations, among others. Further, treaties are political aspirations, suggestive of how relations among nations might be in a more just world. They have simultaneously both a political and a moral dimension. As Starblanket and Stark (2018, 193) observe, moral obligations are renewed through everyday and ceremonial practices: "We offer tobacco to the water beings before we enter our canoes, we petition the plants and animals in recognition of their agency and our relationships with these beings." Water walks that draw attention to the damage pollution causes to waterways, by literally walking along and so tracing the edges of lakes and rivers, are another way of honouring treaty relationships. Likewise, protest against the trans-Canada pipeline might be another way of refusing infrastructure that violates the reciprocal relationships among humans, animals, and water beings that treaties seek to honour. Such actions of recognition support ways of living together within shared spaces that make possible the survival and wellness of both human and non-human beings.

In her writing, Alex Wilson considers feminist reinvention for those who identify as two-spirit. Wilson (2008) suggests that two-spirit identity is about a creative, but deeply grounded politics. She contrasts LGBTQ "coming out" stories in settler colonial contexts with what she calls "coming in" stories as a grounded, creative, spiritual and political movement. She writes that, "[t]wo-spirit identity is about circling back to where we belong, reclaiming, reinventing, and redefining our beginnings, our roots, our communities, our support systems, and our collective and individual selves" (Wilson 2008, 98) Others, like Sarah Hunt and settler co-author Cindy Holmes (Hunt and Holmes 2015), write about decolonizing queer practices in everyday life through dialogues within the home that might crosscut Indigenous-settler relationships, as well as through more extraordinary political actions, from petitions to marches to direct action. Here the aim is to "see, hear, think and act differently" (Jeanette Armstrong, quoted in Hunt and Holmes 2015, 169) to foster relationships that are at once both queer and decolonizing.

Importantly, Indigenous women are employing a range of means and ways of conceptualizing futures that defy essentialist conceptualizations of Indigenous life, unsettling notions of Indigeneity as bounded to particular tracts of land. For instance, urban Cree scholar Karyn Recollet (2015) uses the concept of "multi-plexed geographies of Indigenous resistance" to examine the transformative potential of Indigenous Peoples' artistic and creative initiatives within urban spaces. She argues that Indigenous Peoples are actively engaged in forms of "spatial tagging" in urban centres that constitute a rupture from normative categories and practices, and generate new modes of identity, knowledge production, and ways of being in the world. For instance, she describes the urban flash mob round dance as creating both forms of solidarity and resistance to "the multiple layers of occupation and representational practices" that produce an urban centre such as Toronto as a site of capital accumulation and exploitation, rather than as an Indigenous territorial homeland and sovereign space (Recollet 2015) Her analysis emphasizes Indigenous Peoples' vibrant and generative engagements within urban spaces, among other in-between spaces, as acts of Creation and resistance wherein Indigenous women enact forms of community and relationality.

Here we might end with an all-too-familiar metaphor. If one is attached to the association between Indigenous women and Creation, perhaps this association might be repurposed in such a way as to frame our central claims. To be clear, the metaphor we are referring to is that of Indigenous women as the givers of life, which commonly associates Indigenous women with the land and Creation due to the intimate association with the creator that arises from the biological ability to bring forth life. But what if we think of "life" in broader terms? Here life might lie outside the boundaries created both by colonial worlds and by traditionalist, essentialist Indigenous approaches, and instead be understood as the ways in which Indigenous feminists are creating open-ended yet relationally grounded possibilities for existing – for "being Indigenous" now and into future generations.

5   Canadian Ecological Political Economy

ANGELA V. CARTER[1]

Introduction

Ecological thought offers political economy a blueprint for a radically transformed model of development ... Indeed, no other body of thought has offered a comparable opportunity to left political economy to renew itself as a
counterhegemonic discourse with enormous transformative potential. (Adkin
2003, 393)

Some of Canada's most difficult contemporary political-economic
dilemmas are in essence ecological: they express intractable conflicts
between historical economic imperatives to extract natural resources
and the local-to-global social and environmental consequences of that
mode of development. This tension surfaces across the country now
more than ever. Today the governments of Alberta and Saskatchewan,
alongside oil firms and associations, are pushing for new pipelines to
bring oil to non-US markets. They are met by an unprecedented wall
of opposition from Indigenous communities, environmental organizations, the governments of British Columbia and Quebec, and municipalities along pipeline routes concerned about the environmental
impacts of expanding oil development. Meanwhile the Trudeau government, while ostensibly committed to Indigenous reconciliation and
to dramatically reducing greenhouse gas emissions that are causing

1 I thank Laurie Adkin, Angele Alook, Bill Carroll, Simon Dalby, Nadine Fladd, Peter
  Graefe, Eric Helleiner, Ian Hussey, Leigh McDougall, and Heather Whiteside for
  advice and assistance, and I acknowledge support received from the University of
  Waterloo for a Social Sciences and Humanities Research Council of Canada travel
  grant to present this work at a 2018 Canadian Political Science Association workshop.

the global climate crisis – desperately wants expanded oil development. Perhaps the most egregious demonstration of this occurred in 2018, when Kinder Morgan threatened to withdraw its proposal for the Trans Mountain pipeline expansion project (intended to triple the line's capacity to carry Albertan bitumen to the west coast), and the federal government responded by purchasing the existing pipeline and vowing to build its expansion.

Debates around Canada's energy and climate future have triggered an unprecedented range of political conflict: civil disobedience against the Trans Mountain pipeline expansion, leading to mass arrests on British Columbia's Burnaby Mountain, alongside a "wine war" when Alberta banned BC wine imports to protest that government's opposition to the project; broad-based protests across Quebec in response to risks to waterways posed by the Energy East pipeline proposal; and constitutional challenges by Ontario and Saskatchewan to the federal carbon price. Indigenous communities have played a lead role, increasingly contesting the neocolonial nature of Canada's oil economy and its ecological consequences across the country, as seen in resistance to fracking in western Newfoundland, oil and gas exploration in Lancaster Sound, Nunavut, and petrochemical refining in Sarnia, Ontario. Decisions on energy and climate are now among the most fractious political economy controversies of our time, in great part due to the ecological stakes.

Given the ecological roots of these disputes, understanding and resolving them requires an analytical approach that moves beyond conceptions of the environment as mere "natural resources" to fuel extractive-based development. Yet this has been the long-held view of the environment in the field of Canadian political economy (CPE). Ecological political economy (EPE), a burgeoning subfield of CPE, provides a corrective to this limited view.[2] EPE is aligned with CPE's commitment to analysing structural power and redistribution. However, it also offers a more dynamic theorization of capitalism's consequences, given its focus on ecological degradation and social injustice and on fostering new modes of production that are socially and environmentally sustainable. EPE is well equipped to confront our complex eco-political-economic moment, and students of political economy

---

2 This parallels the foregrounding of EPE in Canadian international political economy scholars, recently advanced by Katz-Rosene and Paterson (2018), with roots in early analyses of free trade agreements, for example in Phillips (1991), Shrybman (1993), and Tester (1991).

will find it valuable to foreground EPE's theoretical approaches and analytical practices.

This chapter first describes CPE's original notion of the environment as natural resources, as seen in the staples tradition. It then traces out the origins and development of EPE, focusing on its major currents of theory and practice. Next, it illustrates how the EPE approach is being effectively applied in analyses of the socio-ecological consequences of Canada's oil sector.

Canadian Political Economy's Ecological Blindspot

Canada emerged as a political entity with boundaries largely determined by the fur trade. These boundaries included a vast north temperate land area extending from the Atlantic to the Pacific and dominated by the Canadian Shield. The present Dominion emerged not in spite of geography but because of it. (Innis 1930, 393)

Since the earliest contributions to CPE, our discipline has acknowledged that the lands we came to call Canada were defined by the natural resources and geography that were integral to settler Canadians' economic development. Even so, the environment in this field has long been narrowly conceived – imagined merely as an obstacle to be overcome or as raw inputs to fuel development.

This view is evident in CPE's enduring focus on staples theory. Staples literature, originating in the 1930s with the early work of Innis (1930, 1940) and Mackintosh (1934), identifies a specific form of political economic development, one dependent on massive resource extraction for export (fur, fish, timber, minerals, and/or agricultural products, and later hydroelectric power), typically driven by foreign investment. Writing in this vein argues that staples economy is marked by a core-periphery dichotomy, with industrial centres managing extraction in hinterlands that provide raw resources for economic growth. Although staples states are considered highly vulnerable to inevitable commodity price volatility and eventual resource depletion, it is difficult for these states to develop more mature and diverse economies with strong manufacturing and knowledge-based sectors due to key structural barriers.[3] Staples literature identifies extractive corporations as highly committed to continued extraction, given the high profit potential,

---

3 Watkins (1963), however, argued that governments could use rents from the extraction and export of resources to diversify from staples sectors.

especially when accessing resources with high commodity prices, while the state, dependent on extractive-based revenues, facilitates extraction by offering financial and regulatory incentives.

While the staples literature observes how massive extractive activity exhausts natural resources and requires shifting extraction to new regions or focusing on new staples (Keil et al. 1998), the field traditionally focused on territorial relationships (between regions, between Canada and the United States) and on the social and economic implications of resource extraction – not on the ecological consequences of this logic of development. In this way, CPE's historical approach to the environment was primarily one of "resourcism": interpreting the environment as outside of individuals, communities, and their political-economic institutions, as a tool to be used for human development (Adkin 1994, 150).

This narrow conception of the environment continued into the late 1980s, even after environmental movements and Indigenous communities in Canada had begun objecting vociferously to industrialization's intensifying socio-environmental repercussions. As demonstrated in Clement and Williams' landmark 1989 survey of the revival of CPE, while the field had begun to engage with issues around gender and Indigenous Peoples, it continued to avoid discussions of the environment as more than natural resources fuelling Canada's export-led growth and to ignore the ecological impacts of production (Clement and Williams 1989b). Three years later, Williams noted that "there has been remarkably little written within the Canadian political economy tradition that directly addresses the degradation of our environment" (Williams 1992, 5). He critiqued the field for focusing primarily on issues of class disparities and Canada's relationship of dependence to the United States – on "*distribution* at the expense of addressing the ecological consequences of *production*" (21, emphasis in original). The field continued to have an "environmental blind spot, Williams argued (5) – one that he and others set out to illuminate via an EPE approach.

Defining Canadian Ecological Political Economy

Williams's piece was among the first of a wave of work in CPE that foregrounded social injustices bound up in ecological degradation resulting from economic activity. This body of research, notably developed by Adkin (1994), Wallace and Shields (1997), Keil et al. (1998), Gale and M'Gonigle (2000), Biro and Keil (2000), Dalby and Keil (2003), and Adkin (2003), collectively established a unique theoretical terrain and line of inquiry – four distinct contributions elaborated below – that define EPE.

Capitalism is inherently "eco-hostile"

Canadian EPE theorizes ecological crises as rooted in capitalism, our dominant economic system. Capitalism is inherently "eco-hostile" (Williams 1992, 17), given its requirement for continuous growth based on ever-expanding natural resource commodification and extraction (Polanyi [1944] 2001) and its interpretation of the environment as "an almost unlimited storehouse of *resources*" (Wallace and Shields 1997, 386, emphasis in original) to be purchased, taken for free as inputs for production, or used as dumping areas for production's waste. Ecological degradation is understood as "an integral feature" of the capitalist production system (Williams 1992, 19) that EPE critically assesses.

Canada's historical staples-based economic development since European settlement is interpreted in EPE as a particularly acute variant of eco-hostile capitalism. Researchers in this vein document how staples dependence accelerated in the post-war boom period as the extraction of minerals, forest and fishery products, and energy (oil, gas, and hydroelectrical) intensified across Canada. In its wake this process left a distressing catalogue of environmental catastrophes: depleted fish stocks on both coasts, clear-cut old-growth forests, exhausted prairie soils, land and water systems contaminated by toxic spills, pollution, and acid rain (Wallace and Shields 1997).

Capitalism's eco-hostility necessarily results in multiple forms of social injustice

The EPE approach challenges capitalism with insights from ecology, underscoring the need to reject unlimited growth and consumption and instead focus on living within ecological limits. However – and importantly – EPE joins an analysis of capitalism's ecological consequences with an assessment of social injustices intertwined with environmental degradation. EPE understands capitalism as intensifying environmental degradation that causes or exacerbates inequity across a range of social divides such as class, race, and gender. It is attuned to the distributional impact of economy-environment interactions – that is, who is burdened with ecological, community, health, economic, and other costs of capitalist extraction.

Environmentally degrading and socially unjust economic development is sustained and extended by those benefiting most from the activity, both state and industry actors

Although attuned to the social injustice of extraction, EPE also analyses who primarily benefits from extracting, transporting, and consuming "resources." It assesses how environmental degradation benefits both state and private actors and how they then protect or attempt to extend status quo extraction. Here federal and provincial governments are not interpreted as neutral arbiters of stakeholders involved in economy-environment interactions. Rather, state actors are seen as claiming resource ownership and encouraging private firms to extract for structural reasons: governments depend on revenue from extraction or on revenue received from firms doing extractive work, and they are heavily influenced by politically powerful firms and associations that seek to profit from resource extraction.

EPE examines how capitalism's eco-hostile tendencies have intensified during the deepening of neoliberalism since the 1980s. EPE research has documented how the state over this period has been a "significant 'extra-economic' actor, enabling resource mobilization and capital accumulation" (Bridge 2014, 118), either through rolling back state constraints on extraction and production or by extending support for markets and extraction (Heynen et al. 2007).

Systemic change – led by social mobilization efforts – is required to address the socio-ecological consequences of capitalism

Although EPE is critical of capitalism's ecological and social consequences, and focuses on discerning the power holders that entrench this system, the field is also reconstructive. It ultimately works towards alternatives to capitalism, seeking models of development that are both socially just and environmentally sustainable. Biro and Keil (2000, 84) propose ecological socialism as an alternative model, where relationships are "based on reciprocal, symmetrical, and participatory interaction – which challenge forces of exploitation, domination, and objectification both within human communities and between humans and the rest of nature." This alternative to capitalism must ensure everyone has enough income, and that production and consumption are environmentally sustainable, with all environmental costs internalized.

Given capitalism's entrenched supporters, implementing alternative models of development necessarily requires authentic democratic practices and broad-based collective action. Responding to capitalism's socio-ecological destruction, therefore, is fundamentally a project of democratization. With this in mind, EPE research understands social movements – social justice and environmental coalitions – as fertile sources of ecological critique and resistance, and studies them seriously (Adkin 1994).

So how do we "do" Canadian ecological political economy?

These theoretical and normative orientations of EPE research help researchers understand, and account for, the intertwined social and ecological effects of economic activity. In practice, "doing" EPE involves identifying who is considered to own "resources" and why, and how access to them is organized. EPE researchers ask: who gets to use or extract "resources," and through what institutional structures? The subfield maps how and where profits of environmental extraction accumulate and who experiences the most direct impact of environmental degradation. Meanwhile it pays attention to who is harmed by the extractive process, or largely left out of its benefits, relegated to lower-paying extractive work or contributing unpaid work essential for extraction. Importantly, the Canadian EPE approach confronts the neo-colonial character of economy-environmental interactions, recognizing that the land rights of Indigenous Peoples have been and continue to be trampled by settler governments, and acknowledging how Indigenous communities continually bear the worst impacts of settler environmental extraction (see Starblanket and Coburn, in this volume). Moreover the subfield is attuned to disparity across space. EPE underlines how the ecological costs of economic activity are borne by vulnerable populations concentrated in rural communities, pockets of urban areas, poorer provinces, or developing nations that are not primarily benefiting from the economic activity. The approach also underscores how costs are simply left for future generations – a matter of intergeneration injustice. Finally, work in EPE is concerned with resistance arising in response to these multilayered ecological and social inequities and how social mobilization is fostering the creation of alternatives to capitalist extraction.

Put simply, Canadian EPE centres on capitalism's environmental impacts, analysing the unequal relations of power resulting from our dominant economic system and its interactions with the environment and the communities it supports. Meanwhile, Canadian EPE is attuned to the institutional and value systems that sustain this system – both of which are resisted by those reclaiming power and forwarding alternatives. Below, to provide working examples of research this sub-field, I illustrate how EPE researchers have used this approach to understand critical issues surrounding Canadian oil extraction.

Ecological Political Economy at Work: Confronting Oil Extractivism

As signalled at the outset of this chapter, oil development entails some of the toughest environmental, political, and economic quandaries facing our country. Surveying EPE research on this issue demonstrates the unique terrain and scope of the subfield and how it can be usefully applied to reveal and confront complex tensions. Below I survey EPE research on Canadian oil development across the subfield's four distinctive contributions: (1) theorizing ecological degradation as a function of capitalism; (2) analysing the multilayered injustices of oil development across class, race, and gender; (3) assessing power structures that maintain status quo extraction using a range of strategies, including discursive legitimation; and (4) exploring resistance to fossil extractivism and advancing alternatives.

Petro-capitalism is inherently ecologically degrading

EPE work draws attention to environmental degradation left by oil extraction, transportation, and consumption, but understands this degradation as a necessary result of our dominant capitalist system. Altvater's (2006) chapter in Panitch and Leys' *Coming to Terms with Nature* Socialist Register volume was a landmark contribution to this line of thinking. Altvater's notion of fossil-capitalism underscores both capitalism's "inherent and unavoidable dependence on fossil fuels" (2006, 39) as well as the "ecological destruction" (45) inevitably flowing from that system, given industrial capitalism's need for infinite economic growth and ever-expanding consumption based on extraction from the natural world. These environmental demands of capitalism undermine the very basis of human life (and economic activity along the way), notably by causing emissions that make earth uninhabitable for humans. This concept has continued to inspire EPE research, more recently Adkin's (2016) comprehensive ecological political-economic study of the Alberta tar sands. The edited volume documents the ecological consequences (air, water, land impacts – from community to global levels) of Canada's largest oil extraction region, many contributors understand these impacts as characteristic of capitalism. New theoretical work continues to deepen this analytical approach. For example, Pineault (2018, 4) theorizes the critical tension of our "era of extreme oil," which is torn between the "capitalist imperative to extract and burn" oil reserves and the "ecological imperative of transition," which, given the climate crisis, requires leaving fossil fuels in the ground. A "specifically capitalist logic" (Pineault (2018, 2) is the basis for Canada's fossil extractivism and its myriad socio-ecological consequences. Theoretical contributions such as these on the structural origins of ecological destruction and political-economic struggles have provided a foundation for EPE research on inequity, power, and resistance, treated in turn below.

Oil development generates multilayered social injustices

EPE research on Canada's oil sector also emphasizes how the burden of development has been unequally shouldered across society. EPE literature continues to treat traditional questions of CPE relating to class inequities. Shaffer's (1980) contribution to the *Oil and Class Struggle* volume is an early example of analysis highlighting the class implications of the tar sands boom – it created conflict between a rising bourgeoisie benefiting from oil development and non-oil workers or farmers – alongside rising environmental degradation. This approach has been deepened and extended in contemporary research on Alberta, notably by the Parkland Institute (see, e.g., Flanagan 2015; Hussey 2020), as well as in work on other petro-provinces. For example, Cadigan (2014) traces how the benefits of Newfoundland and Labrador's oil boom have accrued predominantly to an elite class of professionals in the capital, as well as to specific groups of unionized construction workers employed in the sector. Few benefits, however, have flowed to the rest of the workforce, particularly those in rural regions working in declining extractive sectors (fisheries and forestry). Warnock (2004) notes similar rising class disparity as Saskatchewan became a major oil producer.

In addition to these familiar political economy concerns, however, perhaps EPE's more profound contribution is to research the racial and gender inequities arising from Canadian oil extraction. The impact on Indigenous communities is a primary racial disparity inherent in Canadian oil development treated in this research. Often ignored in mainstream discussions, EPE analysis understands oil development as predicated on settler governments' historical and contemporary dispossession of Indigenous communities. Although tar sands development motivated the resolution of land claims and resulted in employment and business development benefits for some, research in this vein emphasizes how the intense growth of the industry, particularly since 2005, has resulted in significant negative impacts on Indigenous communities.

Parlee (2016, 329), for example, discusses how the economic, social, and ecological impact of Alberta's extractivism-as-development model "has arguably unsettled, undermined, and transformed the circumstances of Indigenous communities more than it has those of any other peoples in the province." Parlee argues that, given their important cultural, spiritual, social, and economic connections to ecosystems in the region, First Nations and Métis have "suffered disproportionately from loss of access to land and from degradation of the environment" (2016, 331). The ecological impact is direct and significant for Indigenous Peoples in the tar sands region: downstream communities fear drinking water or eating fish from, or allowing their children to swim in, the rivers; animal populations important for subsistence hunting have declined; and Indigenous communities experience unusually high cancer rates and other health impacts from exposure to toxic pollution (Hussey, Hill, and Alook 2017). These communities also cope with severe cultural, community, and family disruptions related to the expanding tar sands industry (Parlee 2016; Slowey and Stefanick 2015). Meanwhile, they experience fewer economic benefits of the sector. Rather than "democratizing" employment opportunities, labour market policies surrounding the tar sands boom in northern Alberta extended colonial power dynamics (Friedel and Taylor 2011, 30), with Indigenous workers typically relegated to low-paying, insecure jobs.

EPE analysis reveals another form of racial inequality in Canada's oil economy, relating to the treatment of racialized new immigrants and foreign workers – again, most evident in Alberta's tar sands. The sector's demand for labour drove a rapid increase in temporary foreign workers – approximately 165,000 during the 2006–10 boom years – predominantly in the accommodation and food services sector (Foster and Barnetson 2015, 254). These workers face multiple vulnerabilities, including precarious, low-paying work and a lack of full citizenship and employment rights (Alook, Hill, and Hussey 2017; Hill, Alook, and Hussey 2017).

EPE research has also contributed to our understanding of the gender inequalities resulting from Canada's oil extractive development. As men leave their communities to work in remote camps, women who stay behind take on ever-more unpaid work at home and in local communities. Women living near extractive sites also support male employment with unpaid social reproduction work, caring for children, families, and communities, all while experiencing striking wage disparity if they work outside the home – the vast majority of high-paying oil jobs go to men, while women are concentrated in lower-paying precarious services sector work (Alook, Hill, and Hussey 2017). Thus Dorow (2015) has described tar sands extraction and accumulation as hypermasculine: 90 per cent of extractive work is done by men who are supported by women in precarious and underpaid jobs in the services, retail, and care sectors. Comparing full-year, full-time jobs, men's median earnings were more than double women's earnings in Fort McMurray. Mothers in Fort McMurray face particularly difficult choices as child care shortages force them to leave full-time employment for more "flexible" jobs.

Here again, the gendered inequities emanating from Canada's oil extractive economy are not limited to Alberta's tar sands. Ecological political economists note the disparities experienced by women working in this sector, or in support of it, across the country. For example, Cadigan found that the employment benefits of Newfoundland and Labrador's oil sector were limited to the growth of low-paying jobs for women in the retail, food, and accommodations sector. Rather than a boom, "the reality for many Newfoundland workers over the past decade has been a continuing struggle with low-wage work, growing job insecurity and the simple lack of permanent jobs in the province" (Cadigan (2014, 68) – and these precarious jobs have been disproportionately held by women who experience deep wage disparity compared to men.

EPE analysis is particularly apt to reveal the complex, multilayered social injustices in Canadian oil extraction. In Alberta's tar sands, women and visible minorities, including refugees, immigrants, and temporary foreign workers, are concentrated in lower-paid, precarious jobs in the retail, services, and hospitality sectors – "the commodified reproductive work of keeping industry workers fed, housed, groomed, and entertained" (Dorow 2015, 287). New research, however, documents how wage disparity and employment precarity is particularly prevalent in female visible minority populations (Alook, Hill, and Hussey 2017, 2019; O'Shaughnessy and Doğu 2016). Meanwhile racialized female immigrants face more discrimination as they seek employment in the extractive sector. Moreover, women, especially Indigenous women, in economically vulnerable situations at the margins of the tar sands economy are at risk of domestic abuse and sexual exploitation (O'Shaughnessy and Doğu 2016). Bagelman and Wiebe, building from Wiebe (2016), add another harrowing dimension to the gendered-racialized impacts of Canada's oil sector in their study of "Chemical Valley" in the Aamjiwnaang First Nation in Sarnia, Ontario. They discuss the "intimate and everyday" ways the fossil fuel–based chemical industry in the region impacts Indigenous women's bodies: exposure to toxins has been linked to declining male birth rates in communities near the petrochemical plants (Bagelman and Wiebe 2017, 76).

Power structures maintain fossil extractivism

As EPE research reveals the environmental destruction in petro-capitalism as well as the multilayered social inequities it exacerbates, it also unpacks how states and firms maintain fossil extractivism and lend legitimacy to its undesirable environmental and social outcomes.

Focusing on the state, Carter and Zalik (2016) redefine Alberta as a rentier state, where dependence on oil revenues instead of income taxation breaks the tie of accountability between citizens and the government, which is now beholden to oil companies. Given these constraints, even when pressured by a growing environmental movement, Haley (2011) anticipates that governments dependent on fossil fuel production would "decline to heed calls for policy intervention that would penalize the industry for its pollution," and instead protect the sector.

EPE work has also analysed this process at the provincial level, particularly over the most recent oil boom period (spanning roughly 2005–15), noting how the governments of Alberta, Saskatchewan, and Newfoundland and Labrador actively defended and promoted the oil sector for its perceived economic value. Alberta led the way, mounting a domestic and international public relations campaign to respond to growing critiques of the tar sands and to protect the province's exports from US and European regulations that would have marked bitumen as particularly emissions intensive. Meanwhile Alberta implemented a new form of public consultation that gave the illusion of improving regulation through public participation, while serving to control the message and public expectations in the interests of continued extraction. At the same time, each of these petro-provinces retooled environmental policy to facilitate oil extraction, or simply let it erode as oil extraction intensified.[4]

At the federal level of analysis, EPE research has noted how, over the boom period, the government led by Prime Minister Stephen Harper obstructed environmental research on the impact of the oil industry,

---

4 These trends and literature are summarized in Carter (2018, 2020) and Carter, Fraser, and Zalik (2017).

retrenched environmental policy to remove obstacles to the sector, and suppressed or criminalized dissent (Carter 2016). This neoliberal roll-back of environmental regulation facilitated "aggressive resource culti-vation" (MacNeil 2014, 81). Although Prime Minister Justin Trudeau redressed some of this policy retrenchment, federal support for the oil sector continues, as demonstrated in the Trudeau government's pur-chase of the Trans Mountain pipeline and continued subsidies to the fossil fuel sector.

EPE literature has also noted corporate actors' role in securing con-sent for continued extraction. Carroll (2017) documents the dense cor-porate connections underpinning the hegemonic fossil extractive order in Canada – between companies involved in extracting, transporting, and processing fossil fuels, as well as those financing these activities – locating concentrated economic power among a few large corporations. Carroll also provides insight on how national and transnational corpo-rate power is articulated through the state, resulting in an "entrenched oligarchy" (2017, 254) committed to carbon-intensive extractive development.

Meanwhile Eaton and Enoch (2018) provide on-the-ground analysis of how oil industry actors' social responsibility activities in oil-produc-ing communities foster "psychological identification" with oil among citizens. These interventions – donations for essential services such as firefighting and other forms of community engagement, including pro-viding "energy and environmental literacy" programs to rural elemen-tary schools – quell community opposition to the negative social and environmental consequences of extraction. Urquhart (2018, 130, 140) details how firms have leveraged profits to mount a formidable lobby-ing force, undercutting opposition through a "counter, coopt, and com-promise" strategy. This has included attempts to silence or "temper" First Nations resistance by negotiating confidential impact and benefit agreements, and helping create Indigenous oil corporations that now have a stake in extraction.

New work is also charting how oil sector representatives gain access to governments via donations to political parties (Enoch 2012), and intervene in government regulatory processes, such as policy delibera-tions on climate change and emissions policy, that would constrain their operations (Daub and Yunker 2017).

Resistance to fossil extractivism is rising, alongside post-oil alternatives

EPE analysis of how state and private actors that benefit from the oil sector institutionalize oil development or sustain community consent is paralleled by studies of how civil society mobilizes to resist oil extraction and promote just, sustainable alternatives. Recent literature has begun to document the significant barriers to community mobilization against fossil fuel extraction in Canada, such as the economic and psychological dependence on the sector developed within communities by industry and government (Eaton and Kinchy 2016) and the marked democratic deficit in oil-dependent jurisdictions (Shrivastava and Stefanick 2015). Yet, against these formidable barriers, increasingly successful "blockadia" movements (Klein 2014) – often Indigenous-led – have arisen across Canada over the past decade.

Social movements have developed particularly in reaction to the tar sands industry. That industry's dual affront to ecological integrity and the sovereignty of Indigenous communities (Black et al. 2014) has ignited some of the most vigorous environmental activism in Canadian history. Haluza-Delay and Carter (2016), for example, assess the material-political as well as the discursive power of social movements spanning labour, Indigenous, religious, and environmental organizations that contest the tar sands, scaling up from local struggles to bring the debate around the tar sands to transnational actors and global institutions. Bowles and Veltmeyer (2014) also document the growth and efficacy of opposition by Indigenous, community, and environmental non-governmental organizations along the path of Enbridge's proposed Northern Gateway pipeline from the tar sands to the west coast. The empowerment and solidarity built across these diverse groups were used to contest the Trans Mountain pipeline. EPE researchers are also analysing instances of blockadia against multiple forms of fossil fuel extraction taking place across the country, from northeast British Columbia (Garvie and Shaw 2016) to western Newfoundland (Carter and Fusco 2017), from the Yukon (Neville and Weinthal 2016) to southwestern Ontario (Black 2014).

The role of Indigenous communities in these resistance efforts is often central, as seen in Parlee's (2016) study of how the Mikisew Cree First Nation and Athabasca Chipewyan First Nation of Fort Chipewyan challenged tar sands development using a range of strategies from very institutional measures (participating in government-led multistakeholder bodies and consultations; using the courts to protect their rights), to strategies that are more independent of the state, or even adversarial to it (leading community-based environmental monitoring efforts; bringing their concerns to the international arena of the United Nations to draw global attention to human rights violations and climate consequences associated with the tar sands) (see also Slowey and Stefanick (2015). Meanwhile, Bagelman and Wiebe's (2017) analysis of "Chemical Valley" in the Aamjiwn-aang First Nation in Sarnia, Ontario, has captured how Indigenous women lead creative resistance to the fossil fuel industry far beyond the tar sands extraction site, raising awareness about the pollution through giving "toxic tours," participating in health and environmental monitoring to track the impacts of the pollution, and chaining themselves to pipelines to draw attention to proposals to transport tar sands bitumen into the community.

EPE work on resistance to Canada's oil economy is accompanied by research on alternatives. Canadian ecological political economists propose bold futures of decolonizing and phasing out the oil industry, redressing environmental degradation, and transitioning to climate-safe energy. Laxer (2015), for example, has presented an "eco-energy security plan" whereby governments take a strong lead in declining unconventional fossil fuel production such as the tar sands, and then using conventional oil and natural gas to transition to low-carbon-energy systems. In Saskatchewan, Eaton and Gray-Donald (2018) have advocated a public oil sector oriented towards winding down production, implementing a just transition to a low-carbon economy, cleaning up the environmental degradation left from the oil sector, and repatriating land to Indigenous Peoples. In Newfoundland and Labrador, Gibson et al. (2016) and Ommer, Neis, and Brake (2017) similarly imagine pathways to a new green economy.

Thanks to this work, we now have clearer models for how to implement a "just transition" that would see governments taking a lead role in investing in Canada's transformation to a decarbonized energy system while supporting communities and workers currently reliant on the fossil fuel sector to transition away from carbon extraction (see, for example, Mertins-Kirkwood 2018). More of this reconstructive EPE work continues to emerge – for example, via the "Feminist Energy Futures" project, which confronts the patriarchal, colonial, environmentally degrading character of Canada's oil economy, and outlines possibilities for "just and sustainable energy and social futures" (Wilson 2018).

EPE research indicates that we have reached, to use Adkin's (2017) metaphor, a crossroads of "climate capitalism" and "ecological democracy." Following a climate-capitalist path would mean continuing "neoliberal environmentalism," in which solutions to the climate crisis are primarily market based and dependent on technological innovation (Sapinski 2016, 89–90). This corporate-led approach poses no threat to growth, consumption, or fossil fuel production, and does little to address social injustice; it also offers only limited decarbonization potential. In contrast, turning towards "ecological democracy" would have governments – responding to citizens who are fully participating in democratic decision making – confront corporate power and build public renewable energy systems that meet "democratically-determined social needs" (Adkin 2017, 8). For Adkin and others working in the EPE terrain, this is the only hope for the deep decarbonization required to confront the global climate crisis.

Surveying EPE research on Canada's oil sector illustrates the dynamic contribution of this approach to the broader field of Canadian political economy. As demonstrated above, EPE theorizes how our dominant petro-capitalist system forwards extraction that undermines the environment and heightens social inequities. It also reveals how this fundamentally environmentally degrading and socially divisive mode of development is entrenched by governments and private actors alike – and vigorously contested by those offering ecologically sustainable and socially just development alternatives. EPE offers a unique theory and practice for unpacking the environmental consequences, power relations, and possibilities for change in CPE debates.

Foregrounding EPE to Renew Canadian Political Economy

By the end of the 2000s, an EPE approach had been articulated to challenge CPE's historical "resourcism." This new approach took a more nuanced view of the environment: rather than interpreting the environment as mere natural resources for exploitation, this new subfield saw it as nature or ecology that sustains our communities while being threatened by a dominant mode of economic development that must be resisted and replaced. In so doing, EPE has long held great promise for renewing the field of political economy. Over fifteen years ago, Dalby and Keil (2003) – echoing calls made a decade earlier by Williams (1992) and Adkin (1994) – urged CPE to put ecology and justice at the forefront in analysing the fallout of capitalism. "[T]he ecological," they argued, "has become an important political battleground over the future of capitalist expansion, ecological modernization and environmental justice" (Dalby and Keil 2003, 6), and therefore integral to CPE's development. This is all the more true today. The subfield returns to the original commitments of CPE by assessing power relations and structural inequality and examining the fallout of our dominant economic mode. Yet it does so with attention to urgent ecological crises, as well as understudied social ones, with particular attention to race and gender inequity.

The EPE approach, however, is by no means central in the broader field of political economy; rather, it continues to sit uneasily within it. Most pressing is the difficulty in bringing ecology to the centre of a field that has been historically committed to extractive-based growth – albeit undertaken for the purpose of growing the economy to meet collective needs. An ecologically centred perspective, by contrast, questions whether this form of growth is sustainable, and argues for circular, steady-state economies. Another difficulty surrounds the question of where to situate labour within an EPE approach. Is not labour complicit in undermining the environment, demanding eco-hostile development for the sake of jobs and community sustainability? Or are workers in extractive sectors – given they are among the first and worst exposed to the environmental degradation (Adaman and öZkaynak 2002) – central actors in the critical transition work ahead? The role of workers – central in traditional CPE analyses – is more complex in EPE research.

Irrespective of its place within the field of political economy, Canadian EPE faces numerous pressing theoretical and empirical challenges, perhaps the most daunting being the implementation of an alternative social and ecological vision that avoids capitalism's dual crises. What society do we build to cope with compounded eco-socio-political-economic crises as we surpass multiple planetary boundaries, not least of all the greenhouse gas emissions that are causing the global climate crisis?

Ecological political economists articulate an ecological-socialist alternative, a political economic system that is egalitarian, oriented towards caring for the collective (as opposed to driven by individualist competition), ecologically sustainable and restorative, and democratic – that is, based on collective planning, with equity at the forefront. But from where does egalitarian and environmentally sustainable democratic planning come? As we have seen with the current federal government, even governments vowing to address climate change can be as committed to extractive development as extractive firms themselves (Dalby 2019) – insisting on financing infrastructure that perpetuates colonialism and locks the country into additional decades of tar sands extraction and extensive carbon emissions. Those sceptical of both centralized state and corporate leadership and who emphasize the need for decentralized, community-based political organizing provide another option. Yet eco-localism is also fraught (Albo 2006), especially for communities deeply dependent on, and even psychologically identifying with, extractive industries.

Envisioning how to reroute Canada from a path of increasingly unjust and environmentally corrosive capitalism to a socially equitable and environmentally sustainable political economic system is the paramount challenge of EPE. It is also an area of research and activism that urgently needs the attention of new Canadian political economy students.

SECTION 2

Agents in Canadian Political Economy

6 The Politics of Public Administration: Constructing the Neoliberal State

BRYAN EVANS

Introduction

Public administration, in Canada and as it is practised and taught, tends to understand itself as a technocratic and managerial discipline. That is understandable given the focus on the management of state organizations, production and delivery of public services, and, of course, the development of public policy. The more explicitly political and ideological aspects of public administration, specifically the array of forces which shape the structure and policy work of the administrative state, are provided less consideration. This close relationship between academic study and the actual operations of the state privileges a very pragmatic approach. In this sense, pragmatic means an acceptance of the broader structural context as an immutable given. Public administration and policy are, in this respect, concerned with the "art of the possible" within all the constraints imposed by the unequal distribution of power and resources that characterizes liberal democratic capitalism. Given this pragmatic bent, the application of a political economy lens to the study of public administration yields important insights into the work of the state not as an "impartial umpire" (Craven 1980) standing above the fray, but rather as itself the organizational distillation and expression of political and economic forces.

A central aspect of this contestation is the inherent contradiction between production for the market as central to the process of commodification, including that of waged labour, and social reproduction entailing the paid and, importantly, unpaid work necessary to sustain the labour force (Findlay 2018, 213). The state, and the public services it produces and delivers, is a key component in supporting social reproduction, insofar as social reproduction is concerned with "maintaining and reproducing people, specifically the labour population, and their labour power, on a daily and generational basis. It involves the provision of food, clothing, shelter, basic safety, health care, along with the transmission of knowledge" (Bezanson and Luxton 2006, 3). In the Canadian context, state funding and delivery of critical public goods and services, uneven and modest as they may be – encompassing health care, education, labour standards, occupational safety, and law enforcement, whether through the court or policing – are important foundations of capitalist reproduction. Consequently the neoliberal obsession with reducing certain forms of public expenditure and public provision of the services most necessary to sustainable social reproduction puts in motion a war of position between labour and capital.

Understanding political economy as the "the ontological interconnection between politics and economics in society" (Whiteside, Introduction, in this volume) has important implications for understanding the role of the Canadian state and the administration of that state in capitalist development. Unlike standard approaches to public administration, the application of a political economy lens creates conceptual space to situate developments within the state – more specifically, the public sector and public service – in the larger context of contestation between and among political and economic forces. The process of building neoliberalism is a global phenomenon characterized by common features such as the centralization of power, the politicization of the policy process, and the application of New Public Management (NPM). Canada is not unique in this regard, and in the discussion below the processes and expressions of neoliberalization in Canadian public administration can also be seen at work in the other Anglo-American liberal capitalist democracies – specifically the United Kingdom, Australia, New Zealand, and the United States. The Ontario case of the 1995–99 "Common Sense Revolution," drawn upon here, captures these overarching tactics and strategies of neoliberal restructuring of the cultural norms and processes of public administration in the capitalist state.

The late twentieth century experienced a historical paradigm shift as the post-war order that gave rise to the welfare state in the liberal democratic West was challenged by a different set of ideological, theoretical, and political frameworks and agendas. The administrative state, expressing the compromises and orthodoxies of the post-war era, was, as a result, set on a course to reinvent itself as it adjusted to the new realities of liberalized trade, investment, and production. The result is a distinct neoliberal public administration (NLPA) linked to the neoliberal political project. It is the means by which that project is operationalized through policy, law, regulations, and new modes of production for public goods and services. This transition is, at its fundamental base, a political economy story of structural forces engaged in a battle over which of those forces determines how resources will be produced, distributed, and redistributed. That "how" comes down in simplistic terms to the roles of the state and the market.

As a site of political contestation, the Canadian state is an active participant in writing its own history (see McBride, in this volume). The industrial democracies began the turn towards neoliberalism in the mid-1970s, before we even had the term. The times were "a-changin'" as Bob Dylan sung a few years prior, but not exactly in the way he had envisioned. Canada was no exception. Just as the Canadian state played a critical role in stitching together the far-flung nineteenth-century territories of British North America, so too did that same state play a role in facilitating the shift from the broadly Keynesian post-war consensus towards neoliberalism. C.B. Macpherson, writing in 1957, noted that "one of the main achievements of Canadian economics has been to show in more detail the close interdependence of political and economic structure. The constitutional structure of Canada has been to a large extent determined by the need to secure capital at favourable rates of interest and to promote the expansion of the economy" (Macpherson 1957, 200–1). The point is simple and direct. The Canadian state historically has played an important role in the economic development of Canada (see Smardon, in this volume). In the era of neoliberalism, the state would not withdraw from intervention to enable economic development and capital accumulation, but rather would change the nature of that intervention. Neoliberalism is conflated with reducing state intervention. The reality is that it rolls out a "different kind of intervention," where intervention in the interests of workers or that constrains the freedom of capital and profit making – the characteristic that marked the Keynesian welfare state – is reduced (Brownlee 2005, 27). This speaks to a certain definition of neoliberalism whereby the objective is to establish the "conditions for profitable capital accumulation on the part of both domestic and foreign capital" (Harvey 2005a, 7). Based on the principles of competition, laissez-faire, efficiency, productivity, profitability, and individual responsibility, neoliberalism comes to be expressed in policy forms such as liberalization, deregulation, and privatization (Larner 2000). Since the 2008 global financial crisis, there has been a reconceptualization of neoliberalism that has taken an authoritarian turn. This "authoritarian neoliberalism" is described as "the reconfiguring of state and institutional power in an attempt to insulate certain policies and institutional practices from social and political dissent" (Bruff 2014, 115). Both politicization and centralization of power within the state apparatus, a phenomenon explored below, serve this objective of insulation.

What follows is a historical and theoretical exploration of the construction of neoliberal public administration in theory and practice. This chapter is organized to address the following key themes: a short history of the transition from the Keynesian welfare state era to neoliberalism; a theoretical discussion of neoliberal public administration, including the centralization of power and the increasing politicization of policy work; the creation of public policy, the most unique aspect of public administration, and how the scope of policy alternatives is constrained; and, finally, a case study of the province of Ontario through its Common Sense Revolution of 1995–99.

From Post-war Keynesian Welfare State to Neoliberal Lean State

The end of the Second World War witnessed the high-water mark of the construction of the Canadian welfare state. The provinces, through federal cost-sharing arrangements, led much of this transformation in the public economy, given their constitutional responsibility for key policy areas (see Graefe, and Smardon, in this volume). Although it was not the original intent of the nineteenth-century framers of the Canadian Constitution to create strong provinces, the powers conferred upon them, directly and inadvertently, evolved into significant policy fields, such as health, education, transportation, resources development, and labour, to name but a few. Over time, and particularly in the twentieth century, these areas "have become increasingly important," and "that they are separate political entities has given them the institutional and political legitimacy to seek further powers" (Brownsey and Howlett 2001, 13). The expansion of the post-war public sector saw total provincial government spending rise from 6.4 per cent of gross national product in 1955 to 16 per cent in 1974 (Stevenson 1977, 80). These decades were certainly the golden age of Canadian welfare state building, and with it an expansion of the administrative and policy capacity to produce and manage those public services and programs.

That paradigm wobbled in the 1970s as stagflation, a heretofore unheard of combination of double-digit inflation and high unemployment, took its toll on the economy, workers, and the mixed economy model that had emerged in the decades following the end of the Second World War. The provinces, given the program fields for which they are responsible, would become sites of struggle and contestation. The federal structure of Canada, together with its highly regionalized economy, ensured this historic turn would be as uneven, jurisdiction to jurisdiction, as the geography of the country. As the economy came under increasing stress as a consequence of stagflation, the ideas and policy prescriptions derived from Keynesian economics came under political and theoretical challenge. The dominant and official state economic ideology of the post-war era began to ebb in the wake of a declining growth paradigm. The history of this period of paradigm shift is succinctly expressed by Rea (1985, 12): "the beginning of the 1940s was marked by growing acceptance of government intervention in economic life and intense interest in the mechanics of economic control. Thirty-five years later, in the mid-1970s, confidence in intervention was on the wane and the intellectual systems that had inspired it were under severe attack." The need for public sector "reform" or "modernization" has since been linked to "building states better suited to remaking societies" in an era of economic globalization and lean production (Camfield 2007, 288).

Neoliberalism emerged as an alternative to the post-war order, proposing "the restructuring of capitalism ... to provide a means by which capital could begin to disengage from many of the positions and commitments which had been taken up during the Keynesian era" (Gamble 2001, 131). Existing neoliberalism is, in fact, a paradox: the "state is to be simultaneously rolled back and rolled forward. Non-interventionist and decentralised in some areas, the state is to be highly interventionist and centralised in others" (Gamble 1988, 28). It is necessary to shrink the state while simultaneously centralizing power in order to dismantle state-provided social protections, and to use state power to advance the neoliberal project. In short, building the neoliberal state requires that the state be captured and reorganized as an active instrument in constructing neoliberalism (Gamble 2006, 21–2).

Theorizing the Construction of Neoliberal Public Administration

Neoliberal public administration is a composite of theory and praxis serving to align public management with the neoliberal political project. A number of ideological and theoretical streams – notably, managerialism, public choice, neo-institutional economics, monetarism, and supply-side economics – inform New Public Management and are linked through a common critique of the Keynesian welfare state. NPM is not a coherent doctrine, but rather a "label under which private sector disciplines can be introduced to the public services, political control can be strengthened, budgets trimmed, professional autonomy reduced, public service unions weakened [see Smith, in this volume] and a

quasi-competitive framework erected to flush out the natural ineffi-
ciencies of bureaucracy" (Pollitt 1990, 49). In this respect, NPM, as the
"domesticated, depoliticized version of the New Right or market liberal policy analysis, made somewhat more technical, consensual and
generic," offers policy and organizational solutions based on disaggre-
gation, competition, and incentivization (Dunleavy 1997, 17).

Concrete expressions of such approaches serve to advance a public
sector productivity revolution through decentralization and disaggre-
gation – including resort to quasi-governmental agencies set up to
engage in very specific tasks and employing a variety of methods aimed
at increasing public sector productivity, such as decoupling policy from
delivery, splitting purchasers from providers, competitive tendering,
and deprivileging professions (Dunleavy 1997, 20–3). The result is that
citizens come to interact not with the state, but with non-state service
providers as the "dichotomy between formally public and formally private spheres becomes blurred" (41). The separation of policy from
delivery by creating special purchasing authorities and establishing a
quasi-market for service delivery is central to this objective. This agenda
constitutes something rather more than mere managerial tinkering.
Hood (1991, 3) – who first coined the term "New Public Management"
to capture what he observed as a general trend within the theory and
praxis of public administration through the 1980s – saw this as intimately linked to neoliberal policy objectives to "slow down or reverse
government growth." There is within NPM a conviction that private
sector management is superior to public administration. The solution,
therefore, is to transfer government activities to the private sector,
including the non-profit sector (see Joy and Shields, in this volume),
through privatization and contracting out.

Driving the public management reform was a political framing where
the Keynesian welfare state could no longer respond adequately to the
challenges presented by the new policy priorities accorded to the reduction of public debt and deficits, declining public confidence in the
problem-solving efficacy of public policy, the eroding quality of public
services, and the impact of globalization upon state sovereignty (Aucoin
1995a, 2). The parameters of intervention have been shrunk by fiscal
considerations and power redistributed upward within the state under
the guise of "priority setting" (Hart 1990, 250). Paradoxically the neoliberal state has not withered away, and governance without government has not emerged in any absolute sense. The neoliberal state is still
an important construction despite the assaults and restructuring. To the
point, Table 6.1 presents total public sector employment in Canada and
within individual provinces over the 1995–2017 period. Through nearly

Table 6.1. Public Sector Employees as a Percentage of Total Workforce, excluding Self-employed Workers, Canada and Provinces, 1995–2017

	1995–99	2000–04	2005–09	2010–14	2015–17
	(per cent, condensed multiyear average)				
Canada	23	22	23	24	24
Newfoundland and Labrador	34	32	31	32	29
Prince Edward Island	32	31	31	33	32
Nova Scotia	29	26	28	28	29
New Brunswick	28	27	28	27	27
Quebec	25	24	24	25	25
Ontario	21	20	22	23	22
Manitoba	29	29	30	30	29
Saskatchewan	30	31	31	30	30
Alberta	22	20	21	20	22
British Columbia	23	22	22	23	22

Note: Public sector employees are defined as those who work for a local, provincial, or federal government, for a government service or agency, a Crown corporation, or a government-funded establishment such as a school (including universities) or hospital.

Source: Statistics Canada, "Employment by class of worker, annual (x 1,000)," table 14-10-0027-01 (formerly CANSIM table 282-0012).

a quarter-century, the relative proportion of the labour force employed in the public sector has remained stable.

In the post-war period, the construction of the Keynesian welfare state made use of the existing pre-war public administrative structures and simply expanded and improvised upon that legacy. In contrast the neoliberal project is to dismantle the institutional and ideological arrangements that operationalized the Keynesian welfare state and replace these with new models, processes, and understandings of public administration and the role of the public sector. The key method for overcoming this historical legacy is to centralize political and administrative power.

A defining characteristic of NLPA is its explicit political dimension. This is expressed by a trend towards the centralization of power over decision making, particularly with respect to policy matters, resulting in a much more circumscribed role for the public service in policy development. The Ontario case below provides some explicit elaboration on this point, drawing on that province's experience through the government of Mike Harris and the Common Sense Revolution. The public service's role is not to provide a range of options, but to implement political directives. Given the political challenges inherent in the restructuring and marketization project, this is a necessary tactic. To hollow the state, it has been necessary to construct a strong state (particularly at the strategic centre) capable of marshalling the political/managerial resources to overcome political and sectional opposition.

The doctrine of the political-administrative dichotomy notwithstanding, the relationship of senior public servants to elected politicians was destined to be problematic, given the role public servants played in developing and shaping policy in the post-war period. However, as long as a broadly accepted consensus prevailed on the most pressing questions of policy, the integrity of the Keynesian paradigm, and the central role of a professional public service within that framework, was not contested. although politicians occasionally might have resented their limited control over public servants' role in the policy process and in administration generally, the continuity and stability provided ensured that political interests were served (Aucoin 1995b, 117).

Through the 1980s, neoliberal-led governments seized "power over strategic decisions, especially expenditure budgets, [and they] became inexorably concentrated at the centre, that is, in the offices of the prime ministers and presidents, and in treasury or finance departments" (Aucoin 1996, 647). Along with centralization, paradoxically, "decision-making authority over the management of multiple government operations was increasingly delegated, deregulated and decentralized" (647). This process of "simultaneous centralization and decentralization in government structures has constituted a central feature of the new public management" (648), and allows government to manage from a distance. That is to say, greater managerial autonomy is granted with respect to operational (as opposed to policy) decisions, and the instruments for this steering from a distance are typically arm's-length agencies or contracts.

The public service was seen as integrally allied with an ineffective model, which led critical politicians "to question the value of a career public service to good government" and consequently to "challenge their public services directly" (Aucoin 1995b, 117). Resurrecting the political-administrative dichotomy, where managers are concerned with implementation and governors are concerned with governing – that is, with setting policy and priorities – became an important dimension of Rhodes's hollowed state thesis. This is not so much about greater managerial autonomy as about a means of exerting greater control over state managers by "limiting the discretion of public servants through the new public management, with its emphasis on managerial account-ability, and clearer political control through a sharper distinction between politics and administration" (Rhodes 1994, 139).

With respect to the public service, NLPA set as its objectives the reduction of the influence of permanent officials on policy and the policy process and the increased capacity of government officials to manage. The role of the senior bureaucracy has been redefined to emphasize management, rather than policy functions. Fundamentally this is a revival of the doctrine of the political-administrative dichot-omy, and in part might be operationalized through the appointment of non-career public servants to key positions (Savoie 1995, 93). Such reforms communicate a clear and negative signal to the public service that their political masters possess little faith in the neutrality of the bureaucracy. As a consequence, the public policy expertise upon which governments rely is increasingly centred outside the civil ser-vice. Public policy expertise becomes increasingly politicized as work that had been the purview of the public service is "turned over to ... partisan policy advisors, to think tanks and to lobby firms for advice" (Savoie 1993, 21–2).

This politicization of public administration challenges the traditional doctrine of the political-administrative dichotomy, where there is a clear division, at least conceptually, between the roles of politicians and their staff and that of the permanent public service (Peters and Wright 1996, 636). It is, in part, a response by political leaders who perceive a loss of their own power to direct government, and blame "aggressive" senior public officials who have been too successful in influencing, shaping, and undermining political priorities and objectives (Peters 1991). Politicization is not to be conflated with partisanship, as party association is much less important than the sharing of values and an overall orientation of being "one of us," as Margaret Thatcher would query of senior public servants. That is, a key job qualification is the possession of a shared ideological conviction respecting the need for public sector restructuring (Peters and Pierre 2004, 2). With the central-ization of decision making at the apex of the administrative state, that is where the politics over policy choices is contested, and public service advisors are either shunted aside or recruited for their "political" fit. For Whitehall scholar Peter Hennessey, the expanding role of external policy advice has produced "an era when the Armani-clad minds in the penumbra of fad-and-fashion prone private think tanks can be pre-ferred (especially if their advice comes gift-wrapped and suitably polit-ically tinted) to that more sober, sometimes inconvenient fare served up by the tweed-clad minds in the career bureaucracy" (1997, 4–5).

These conjoined tendencies towards the centralization of power and the politicization of administration are not intended to diminish the power of the state, but rather to reshape it. The result is a further paradox, which lies at the heart of NLPA: "Managerial reform calls for a significant deregulation of central administrative controls over the management of government as well as an organizational decentralization of decision-making authority within government. These requirements are obviously at odds with the centralizing pressures and tendencies inherent in the politicization of public administration for the purposes of state contraction" (Aucoin 1988, 144). Leading change necessitates an enabled centre of government. As noted, a "strong state" is the necessary midwife to a different kind of state. At this historic juncture, the administration of the status quo must give way to the management of transition. To accomplish this successfully, "political leaders require partisan-political assistance in managing the state ... Political leaders now require a strengthening of the political arm of government if they are to cope with the demands of the transformed political systems that they must govern" (Aucoin 1988, 126).

The resurrection of the political-administrative dichotomy obscures the fundamentally political nature of these changes through the discourse of efficiency and productivity. Keynesianism's technocratic impulse to engage has been displaced by a new-wave perspective focusing on the micromanagement of resources. The continuity of policy and process that characterized the Keynesian paradigm, and the role of the professional public service within that framework, is thus transformed.

Manufacturing Policy Advice in the Neoliberal State

The public services and programs produced by the state are themselves the outcome of policy work – research, analysis, consideration of alternative options – conducted by both public service policy analysts and policy staff working directly for ministers or the head of government. In addition, advisors external to government in the form of lawyers, management and policy consultants, think tank analysts, and academics may participate in the work of manufacturing the substantive elements of public policy (Craft 2015). Policy work is a unique and most important aspect of government, since only government has the legal authority and capacity to write, implement, and enforce legislation and regulations.

The process of policy work takes place within a policy advisory system: "the interlocking set of actors and organizations with unique configurations in each sector and jurisdiction that provides recommendations for action to policy-makers" (Craft and Halligan 2017, 48). In Canada, as in most countries with a Westminster-style government, through the golden age of the Keynesian welfare state so-called government line departments – departments responsible for program delivery and/or regulatory enforcement – played key roles in conducting policy research and development. Policy proposals generally moved "upward" through the line ministries to cabinet committees for political consideration and decision. The sources informing policy proposals were varied: stakeholders, and issues identified by front-line field offices, collaboratively developed with other departments, and politically directed by the executive. Policy advocacy for redistribution was robust, and supported by influential cabinet ministers and knowledgeable senior-ranking state managers supported in turn by public service–led policy analysis (Good 2003, 213). Given the policy activism of the public service and the inherently political nature of all policy work, this role contradicted the doctrine of the political-administrative dichotomy, and was an area of significant concern for neoliberals.

The political arm of government now has become more robust through the centralization of power in the executive. Expanding numbers of political staff provide an alternative source of analysis and advice to ministers, and thus contribute to shifting power and influence away from the line departments and towards the political arm of government (White 2001, 21). This expansion of capacity, the consequent shifting of power towards ministers' offices, and the increase in the role of the centre of government – the finance ministry, executive leadership, such as the Prime Minister's Office – are said to constitute the emergence of a "new political governance" (Aucoin 2010, 64). Finance departments in particular have taken on a commanding role in gatekeeping – blocking policy innovation deemed out of step with economic policy objectives. Moreover, they have become the overarching policy designer for the entire government. The result is a significant shift in power within the state, where the "most critical issues of policy direction, resources, and program design are being handled directly and exclusively by the central players ... the policy advice of deputy ministers is becoming guarded, provided in a complaint fashion to address predetermined priorities" (Good 2003, 215–16).

One concern stemming from the centralization of power and decision making within government is the more explicit politicization of policy work, as the discussion above suggests. "Politicization" here refers to the diminishing distance between the provision of policy advice by the professional public service, based on the best information and analysis available, and the partisan concerns of their elected counterparts (or their staff) in the policy advisory system (Mulgan 2007, 570). Moreover, there is a human resources aspect to politicization whereby political criteria displace merit-based guages in the selection, retention, and promotion of public servants (Peters and Pierre 2004, 2).

The 1990s was a pivotal period in the transformation of the policy advisory system in Canada. The managerial, economic, and political reforms of that decade brought about new performance and quality expectations for policy advice in the public service as well as the reduction of internal policy capacity through the reduction of "in-house" policy units. Politicians placed greater demands on bureaucrats to ensure that policy "products" reflected government needs. Consequently the structured-stages approach to analysing problems and proposing solutions to decision makers – an approach emphasizing "structuring of the problem, information gathering, analysis, formulation of options, and communication of results" – gave way to "political advice" (Halligan 1995, 138–9).

A further consideration with respect to the policy process and policy work is, who actually informs the making of public policy? New Public Governance (NPG) is a theoretical perspective that proposes a more open policy process, one that allows for greater collaboration and deliberation between government and non-government policy actors. Phillips (2007, 497) asks: "Are policy processes in Canada actually as open and as participatory as this model of 'governance' suggests?" A survey of Canadian non-government organizations found that approximately 30 per cent had never been invited to engage with their provincial government on a policy matter, and nearly a quarter indicated they would have no more than one such encounter with government in any given year (Evans and Sapeha 2015, 258). Even long0standing non-government institutions such as trade unions fared no better. Nearly 34 per cent responded that they had never been invited by their provincial government to provide input on policy questions, and of those who had been 45 per cent indicated that this had taken place only after key policy design issues had been determined (Evans and Ross 2018, 338).

It was also during this period that the evidence-based policy-making movement arose, arguably as an alternative to the ideologically driven policy of the past (Head 2008, 2). Despite the claim that evidence-based policy making has no universal definition, it is largely agreed that it represents an effort to improve the likelihood of policy success by broadening the amount and type of information used in public policy making (Howlett 2009). Its ascent was seen as a means by which government policies could be made more transparent, efficient, effective, and accountable, by using "evidence" – a decidedly broad term – to inform decision-making processes and to evaluate the success and impact of policies and programs. The possibility of policy based purely on scientific evidence is highly contested. Knowledge and expertise are not found in a power vacuum – especially with respect to economic and social policy. The hierarchy of knowledge and expertise – what is understood as legitimate and credible – forces one to ask: "who decides what constitutes 'valid evidence'? Who has the power over these choices?; and evidence is not equally available to everyone who wants to influence policy-making; more powerful and resourceful groups can produce evidence more readily than those with less power and fewer resources" (Gauthier 2016, 4).

It might be that evidence-based policy making serves to corral policy debate in the sense that "the use of technical methods suppress[es] alternative points of view in order to maintain the ideological paradigms of the dominant status quo" (Newman, Cherney, and Head 2017, 159). The use of such methods has resulted in a reframing of the concept as "policy-based evidence making," or the manipulation of evidence to fit predetermined policy choices (Lowndes 2016, 103). One study focused on senior policy officials in the United Kingdom and New Zealand during the 2012–14 period found that officials would often use evidence in the policy-making process "as window dressing rather than as the decisive factor in decision-making" (Stoker and Evans 2016, 16). Similar conclusions have been arrived at with respect to policy work in North American jurisdictions (Jesuit and Williams 2018, 224).

The contested turn to a more evidence-based approach to policy work has been accompanied by a trend towards the externalization, or contracting out, of that work to non-government actors. One study of Canadian federal government expenditures on "other professional services," largely composed of consulting services, found these had grown dramatically since the 1980s, with expenditures exceeding $1.5 billion by 2000 (Perl and White 2002), and still growing (Howlett 2009). One conclusion regarding this development is that outsourcing of policy advice has contributed to the politicization of policy advice (Howlett and Migone 2013a).

The shift to outsourcing and/or privatizing policy advice was one of the key characteristics of NPM (Osborne and Gaebler 1992). Both the UK and Canadian government, in particular, hired consultants to support the diffusion of NPM ideas, and both countries' finance ministries issued directives encouraging the public service to employ the "expertise" of private consultants (Canada 1991; United Kingdom 1990). Not surprisingly, this externalization of policy advice has been encouraged by the rhetoric of fiscal austerity, which seeks to reduce the size and functions of government. One outcome has been that the public service is required to "play an increasingly political role" in selecting from the range of solicited and unsolicited advice it receives from external sources (Halligan 1995, 160–1). Externalization has also been explained as a mechanism elected politicians use to "secure greater political control" of the policy process, because it is believed that the public service does not have the capacity to address these issues (Craft and Howlett 2013, 190).

The new role that private consultants were taking up in government was termed "consultocracy" (Hood and Jackson 1991). One critique of this development contends that consultants are "rational actors who – because they work for profit-based organizations – have deeply vested interested and important financial stakes in pushing for the implementation of more and more NPM policies within the state" (Saint-Martin 1999, 83). Thus the ascent of NPM alone does not fully explain the rise of contracting out and/or privatizing policy advice. The influence of consultants has been explained as mostly determined by institutional and political processes where "the role of consultants has been more important when they have served the knowledge needs of those who hold positions of political power within the state apparatus" (Saint-Martin 1998, 348).

Little attention has been given, however, to the ways in which the outsourcing of policy advice has contributed to hollowing out the centre of government (Speers 2007). The awarding of policy advisory and analysis work to private consultants should be a matter of concern: "These expenditures are quite large and involve outside actors in policy and managerial decision deliberations who are not only unelected but also un-appointed. They evade scrutiny at the polls but also by civil service commissions and escape the rigours of public service recruitment processes" (Howlett and Migone 2013b, 184). It has been said that it is "extremely rare" to find consultants who give advice that runs counter to market-driven solutions (Bakvis 1997). The private consultants hired by government are usually large firms, typically engaged on a revolving basis.

The growth in the use of external contracts at the federal level, in fact, has stagnated (Howlett and Migone 2013a, 2013b), but this plateauing has less to do with an actual decline in contracting and more to do with the changing nature of those contracts. Although the number of smaller contracts has shrunk, large year-to-year repeat contracts have grown. As well, external contracts tend to be concentrated within several departments, rather than across all of government. Of the forty-six departments and agencies at the federal level at the time of the survey, only eight had spent over $20 million on external contracting (Howlett and Migone 2013a). And only five departments accounted for 75 per cent of federal contracting expenditures (Howlett and Migone 2014). With a few departments relying upon large repeat contracts, 68 per cent of contracting funds were allocated to companies with two or more contracts (Howlett and Migone 2013a). Likewise, less than 5 per cent of contracting agencies accounted for 80 per cent of the total value of federal contracts (Howlett and Migone 2014). In short, a small number of departments engage in contracting activities with a very small number of contractors. This provides some evidence that contracting for services is a permanent and embedded feature, and reflects an "oligopoly" relationship with a handful of external consulting agencies that acquire considerable insider knowledge and expertise and become virtually indispensable (Howlett and Migone 2013a).

With the externalization of policy work, concerns have grown over the influence of external consultants on policy outcomes. Consultants support policy development through a variety of activities, from preparing briefings, exploring policy options, and other process-based work (Howlett and Migone 2013b). Rather than providing partisan advice, however, politicization of consulting has more to do with work in focus groups and public consultations, where consultants are tasked with determining the public's view of government initiatives. With a certain volume of policy work now developed outside of the public service, this obviously leads to a certain questioning of the substance of what informs public policy decisions (Howlett and Migone 2013b).

"Capturing" the Administrative State: The Case of Ontario's Common Sense Revolution

The case of Ontario in the period from 1995 to 1999 provides a rich case study in the construction of neoliberal public administration, including the themes of centralization and politicization of the public service. Ontario is not the only province to have experienced a government with a transformative public sector project and policy agenda. Indeed, Alberta, Manitoba, Saskatchewan, and British Columbia had all seen governments with clear New Right agendas elected in the late 1970s, through the 1980s, and, in the case of Alberta, in 1992. Ontario is unique, however, in several ways, including its sheer size vis-à-vis other provinces – containing 40 per cent of the nation's population and having the second-largest government after the federal. Moreover the sharp ideological expression of Premier Mike Harris's Common Sense Revolution was unique to Ontario. The Progressive Conservatives

(PCs) had governed Ontario, uninterrupted, from 1943 to 1985 as cautious pragmatic centrists. With defeat in 1985, the party reconstructed itself to emerge as rather different: populist, New Right, and prepared to play divisive wedge issues, including poverty and race.

In the mid-1960s, at the height of the Keynesian golden age, Eisenstadt questioned the neutrality of the public service bureaucracy: "the bureaucracy is servant or master, an independent body or a tool, and if a tool, whose interests it can be made to serve" (Eisenstadt 1965, 179). Control over the administrative state was central to the project of constructing a neoliberal state, and consequently the vexing problem for neoliberal state builders was how to address the doctrine of neutrality. Constructing NLPA required an active management to lead cultural and ideological change throughout the public service (Wilson and Doing 1996, 35). From a comparative perspective, public management scholars such as Gregory (1991) and Goldfinch (1998) noted the shift to technocratic and market-oriented managerialism in Australia and New Zealand in the 1980s and the central role of senior state managers in leading the transition to a neoliberal economic policy orientation and an attendant radical restructuring of the public sector. A certain degree of politicization – as opposed to partisanship – or comfort with the neoliberal project was required (Aberbach and Rockman 1988, 609).

Months before the 8 June 1995 election that brought the Common Sense Revolution PCs to power in Ontario, the party had assembled a transition team that included former senior public servants to lay the groundwork for taking control of the provincial government apparatus. The transition team reported to soon-to-be-premier Mike Harris on how to deal with the public service. Their recommendations were based on two criteria: competence, and comfort with the policy direction of the Common Sense Revolution (Cameron and White 2000, 86). Signalling the need to align the public service quickly with the new government's policy agenda, the public affairs organization, Public Policy Forum, was asked to organize a strategy session for November 1995. The event brought together fifty private sector leaders and twenty deputy ministers to discuss how to proceed with restructuring the Ontario public sector. At this meeting, Rita Burak, the newly appointed cabinet secretary (the chief public servant) stated the public service challenge was to "mesh better its role with the government orientation, and to meet the pressing fiscal challenge by cutting faster and deeper than any public service in Canada and possibly in the world" (Public Policy Forum 1995, 1). The discussion focused on the need for greater exchange between the private sector and the public service; a restructuring plan that "cuts deep, cuts fast, cuts once"; a plan to recruit and train future public service leaders with skills in strategic thinking, business-mindedness, familiarity with change management, and entrepreneurialism; and the overhauling of the Ontario public service recruitment and compensation system to better reflect that of the private sector (Public Policy Forum 1995, 1). Towards this goal, the Common Sense Revolutionaries adopted a strategy of alignment that would impose a clear division of labour between the political leadership as policy makers and the public service as policy implementers.

The theme of centralization of control emerged rather strongly as the Common Sense Revolution rolled out. The success with which the PCs were able to align the provincial state to their political project was very much a result of their transition planning and strategy to take power at the centre of the state. This differentiated their approach from that of the New Democratic Party (NDP), according to Cameron and White, who cite a central agency official as saying of the incoming government: "The NDP assumed office, but they never took power. These guys are taking power even before they have assumed office" (Cameron and White 2000, 105). For this agenda to succeed, it "would have to be driven from the top. In turn, the system should see senior ministry staff primarily responding to direction from the top rather than sending ideas and proposals up the line for approval" (87). The policy agenda under the PCs had been nearly entirely framed by political priorities established in their election manifesto. Consequently the role of the public service policy units was narrowed to developing the most efficacious means to implement policy decisions. And the depth of "responsive competence" effectively served to "disable" the public service from exploring and presenting proposals that lay outside the sphere of the platform. In other words, the capacity to be innovative became limited. Ironically, if NLPA was to be capable of sustaining the neoliberal project, these capacities would be essential.

As with any political project, the senior public service has a strategic role to play in supporting that project. An alignment of the public service with political priorities is required through a centralization of political and bureaucratic power. State managers and officials are critical agents in transforming the Keynesian welfare state into a neoliberal state by restructuring the what and how of state functions (Jessop 2002a, 123). Given the degree to which the Ontario public service was responsible for implementing the Common Sense Revolution, it is necessary to ask the uncomfortable question, as a leading observer of the Ontario government did: "Are not senior bureaucrats who are facilitating the implementation of the radical Harris agenda going beyond the professional duty of the public service to do the bidding of the duly elected government and, in effect, adopting a clearly ideological (albeit non-partisan) posture? Can public servants, in other words, be truly neutral players in what amounts to a massive dismantling of the state?" (White 1997, 149).

Of course, one must be cautious in drawing too straight a line from one location and period – for example, from Ontario's 1990s Common Sense Revolution – to more recent and uneven developments that do not correspond to the aggressive, class-war-from-above characterizations of rollback neoliberalism, but are a variant of neoliberalism concerned with rolling back public expenditures and privatization. Paradoxes and contradictions abound, particularly in Canada, given its regional characteristics, the reality of the Quebec subnational state where 80 per cent of the population speaks French as the primary language, and vastly different regional economies that give rise to different capitalist elites and forces of resistance. Such is the colonial and post-colonial history of the Canadian state.

The twenty-first century has seen departures from the rollback variant of neoliberalism that was predominant through the 1980s and 1990s. Examples abound (see Evans and Smith 2015b): in Newfoundland and Labrador, the Progessive Conservative government of Danny Williams, known for exceptionally tense relations with the public sector unions, used windfall oil revenues to fund pay equity and to improve pensions and pay for public sector workers. In 2009 Nova Scotia found itself with an NDP government, but one that chose to be rather conservative. In conservative New Brunswick, the attempt to sell off the state-owned hydro corporation was met with such resistance that the government retreated. In Quebec a new Liberal government, the party of the Quiet Revolution, moved rapidly to dismantle various policy and program arrangements that marked out Quebec as perhaps the most social democratic province in Canada. In the territory of Nunavut, a state corporation led the most significant economic development projects. And in tiny Prince Edward Island, given the relatively large size of the public sector, no government drove forward with an explicit project to downsize the state.

In other words, in Canada, the neoliberal era moved forward, but by remarkably differing means and speeds. Continuing with the case of Ontario under the Liberals, there are continuities, and important discontinuities, in the history of neoliberalization.

Inclusive Neoliberalism? The McGuinty-Wynne Governments

Neoliberalism is the central political concept to the foregoing analysis. However, it has been noted elsewhere that there are two "dangers" in this. The first danger is "the potential to flatten all policy under the label of neoliberalism, thereby missing the variety of policies in contention"; the second is "to put undue causal influence on neoliberalism as opposed to the influence of more general characteristics of capitalism, or of the long-run institutionalization of capitalism" (Graefe and Hudson 2018, 312, 313). To state it another way, just as there were variations of the post-war Keynesian welfare state, there are variations on the forms neoliberalism may take. The hard rollback neoliberalism of the Common Sense Revolution in Ontario, as elsewhere, engendered social conflict and a legitimation crisis. Various social forces mobilized to defend themselves, as we saw, for example, in Ontario's one-day local general strikes ("Days of Action") between late 1995 and 1998, and in the Quebec "Maple Spring" of 2012. In what follows, I briefly review the cases of Ontario under the Third Way Liberals' post–Common Sense Revolution, and the NDP in Alberta during the premiership of Rachel Notley. Both might be viewed as departures from the hard rollback form of neoliberalism of other governments, but they also demonstrate a fidelity to building a sustainable neoliberal state.

The 2003 election in Ontario of the Liberals under Dalton McGuinty and the arrival of Kathleen Wynne in the premier's office in 2013 is one case in point. In the 2003 election, the Liberals differentiated themselves from the PCs and their Common Sense Revolution by profiling the need to reinvest in public services – specifically, health and education. The revenue side, however, was ignored, and instead the Liberal platform committed to "keeping taxes down" (Ontario Liberal Party 2003, 5). To seal their commitment to fiscal conservatism, the Liberals affirmed that "[w]e will not add to the provincial debt. We will pay down the debt as conditions allow, with all surpluses going directly to debt repayment" (5). At the same time, the Liberals promised to return to progressive competitiveness economic policies that had characterized the Peterson and Rae governments. In this, they would focus on investments in support of skills and knowledge acquisition, rather than simply pursue austerity (7). In this sense the Liberals saw a clear role for the provincial state in building an "innovative economy." A review of expenditure in the five main social policy ministries – health, education, post-secondary, social services, and children's services – indicates that, in the first term of the McGuinty premiership (2003–07), budgets increased by between 6.5 and 8 per cent. In the second term (2007–11), budget increases tendeds toward 7 per cent or less (Evans and Fanelli 2018a, 144), reflecting the Third Way progressive competitiveness policy frame adopted by the McGuinty government.

Kathleen Wynne succeeded McGuinty as premier in early 2013. In the leadership campaign, she stated her goal to be the social justice premier. Among her very first acts as premier was to repeal legislation that had intervened in collective bargaining between various teachers' unions and their employers. Settling a politically problematic conflict with the large and politically engaged teachers' unions was necessary for the Liberals' electoral survival. In the 2013 budget, however – the first under Wynne's leadership – a much anticipated overhaul of social assistance turned into mere tinkering. Indeed the budget was characterized by an enduring commitment to fiscal restraint, with a view to achieving budget balance by fiscal year 2017/18 (Evans and Smith 2015a, 183–4).

From 2017 to the end of their term in office, the Wynne Liberals did make a substantive shift in labour policy, as well as proposing some major expansions in the provision of health and social services. In 2017 it was announced that students from families earning less than $50,000 annually would receive grants covering the full cost of university/ college tuition, while about half of students from families earning less than $83,000 would also be covered. The 2017 budget announced 100,000 new child care spaces over five years; a basic income pilot project with 4,000 participants in three cities – Hamilton, Lindsay, and Thunder Bay; and new public drug coverage for people ages twenty-four and under and greater coverage for seniors. In addition, total health care spending was increased by 3.3 per cent, compared with an average of 2.4 per cent annual increases over the 2011–16 period. Education spending increased above 3 per cent, with $1.2 billion set aside for school maintenance/repairs (Block and Hennessy 2017).

The Fair Workplaces, Better Jobs Act (Bill 148 – Amendments to the Employment Standards Act), introduced to the Ontario Legislature on 1 June 2017, brought this shift directly to the labour-capital relationship. This was the most significant upgrading of labour law since the NDP government's overhaul of the Labour Relations Act in 1991, and among the most far-reaching reform of the Employment Standards Act since 1969. Notable changes included the following:

- the minimum hourly wage was increased from $11.40 to $14.00, with another bump to $15 on 1 January 2019;
- parental leave was increased to eighteen months (twelve months of employment insurance parental leave payments over eighteen months);
- all employees would be provided two paid days of leave and eight unpaid days for illness/emergency;
- workers with at least five years' seniority would be entitled to a minimum of three weeks' vacation;

- equal compensation, including benefit coverage, would be provided part-time employees performing substantially the same work as full-time equivalents;
- the onus would be placed on the employer to prove a person was a contractor, not an employee;
- unions would be allowed to obtain a list of employees from the employer; and
- a switch would be made to card-based union certification in building services, home care, community services, and temporary help industries (Stam 2018).

The 2018 budget, the last before the next election, expanded several social policy innovations introduced in 2017:

- the Ontario Drug and Dental program would now become universal, although limited to those without other coverage, and would reimburse eligible expenses up to 80 per cent of the cost;
- free day care would be introduced for pre-school children ages 2 and a half and older;
- education spending would increase 4.1 per cent between 2018 and 2021;
- health care spending would increase 4.3 per cent by 2021;
- hospital spending would increase 4.6 per cent (in comparison, hospital budget growth over the 2013–17 period was only 1.1 percent);
- $2.3 billion would be allocated over three years for income security; and
- the rates of the Ontario Disability Supports Program and Ontario Works would be raised by 3 per cent annually for three years (the rates had lost more than half of their real value since the Harris government's time in office) (Hennessy, Tranjan, and Block 2018).

The final two years of Liberal government in Ontario did mark a shift away from austerity, and with proposals to expand the provision of public services and improve employment protections for workers – particularly those at the lower end of the labour market. This was not a program that sought to reverse the worst of Ontario's experience with neoliberalization, but rather to mitigate its worst effects by protecting low-wage workers generally and by providing new social programs partially to improve certain important services, such as child care, dental care and access to prescription drugs.

Conclusion

The construction of neoliberal public administration has served to narrow the range of debate within and about the role of the state in serious ways. The resilience of neoliberal public policy and management ideas is in part a function of the structure of the state and its policy advisory system. The depth of centralization of power, together with significant politicization, serves to exclude alternative perspectives from entering the policy process. The process is highly exclusionary, and this in turn reflects the uneven distribution of power and resources in society more generally. For all the efforts of the evidence-based policy movement to inject a greater degree of rationality and science into policy making, the reality is that evidence can be curated to rationalize the political objectives of any given government or set of political economic interests. This is particularly so with social and economic policy, where the evidence is nearly always contested and contestable.

It must be noted that no single inevitable formula dictates the rolling out of neoliberal policy reforms and administrative restructuring. Public services and policies that support social reproduction, while progressive, are not necessarily anti-neoliberal, but they do give expression to the disruption in sustainability and legitimacy of capitalism brought on by a previous variant of neoliberalism and the need to mitigate its worst effects.

7 Political Economy and the Canadian Working Class: Conflict, Crisis, and Change

CHARLES W. SMITH

Introduction

Writing in 1977, Canadian journalist Walter Stewart pondered the militancy of Canada's organized working class, questioning why Canadian workers were so much more willing to use the strike weapon than were their counterparts in western Europe and Australia (Stewart 1977, 44–6). Notwithstanding Stewart's concern that Canada's record of strikes was destabilizing the economy throughout the 1970s, his anxieties were premature. In the years since 1977, the militancy of Canada's organized working class has fallen precipitously. As of 2018, Canada's strike numbers have decreased to their lowest levels since the end of the Second World War (Smith and Savage 2018).

The reasons behind this decline in worker militancy are multifaceted and complex. Critical political economists have correctly pointed to structural explanations, examining the broad social transition from an economy based primarily on labour-intensive exports in manufacturing and natural resource extraction in a period of Keynesian state-led growth towards a neoliberal service-based economy driven by lean states, deregulated markets, precarious work relationships, and automation in the workplace (Albo 2010; Harvey 2005a; McBride 2017; Moody 2017); for similar themes in this book, see the chapters by Evans, McBride, Peters, Smardon, and Fridell). Such arguments suggest that the highly mobile nature of capital in the neoliberal period has placed downward employment pressure on workers, leading to a vast increase in the precarious workforce, labouring for one or more employers for static wages, and destabilizing families and communities in the process (Kalleberg 2009; Lewchuk et al. 2016; Lewchuk, Procyk, and Shields 2017; PEPSO 2013). For workers who remain in single-employment unionized firms, their unions have been prone to direct legislative attack by capitalist states (especially in the public sector), restricting their ability to organize, bargain, and strike collectively (Panitch and Swartz 2003; Savage and Smith 2017; Tucker 2014). Taken together, these multiple pressures suggest that workers' collective freedoms in the early years of the twenty-first century are under direct assault from employers, governments, and broader macroeconomic forces. Moreover, the very tool that workers once used to resist such pressures – the collective withdrawal of labour – is no longer being used to challenge power imbalances in society. As David Camfield has argued, the decline in workers' collective action has been profound because it has "undermined (but certainly not eliminated) workers' resistance to employers and governments" and "eroded unity and solidarity among working-class people" (Camfield 2011, 3–4; see also Swartz and Warskett 2012).

To varying degrees, the multifaceted crisis facing Canadian workers suggests that working-class movements are struggling to maintain their existence within the current political economy. How did Canadian workers and their organizations arrive at this crisis, and what are the implications for the organized working classes? This chapter seeks to answer these questions by focusing on how the organized working classes have changed over time and how these classes have sought to resist the coercive power of both employers and capitalist states in the current era. Somewhat contradictorily, the most prominent strategy emerging out of the class conflict between workers and employers (and government) over the past 150 years has been workers' reliance on the legal instruments of the state to offset employers' power in the workplace. Since the 1940s, Canadian federal and provincial labour laws have promoted very specific abilities of workers to organize, collectively bargain, and strike. Yet in relying on the capitalist state to offset the power of employers, workers and their organizations are placed in a contradictory position, as the law surrounding labour seeks to promote certain collective freedoms while simultaneously constraining those freedoms in very specific boundaries (Palmer 2003; Tucker 1991). Working through this contradiction is at the heart of this chapter. I argue that overreliance on the law to offset employers' power – both as a tool to preserve past gains and to advance workers' collective freedoms in the current era – is weakening the ability of workers and their unions to respond to new and aggressive forms of anti-unionism by employers and governments. As I demonstrate, since the 1940s, the law has helped to grow the labour movement – especially as unionization was made available to public sector workers – and, somewhat paradoxically, also led to a crisis of the country's organized working classes, which have been radically transformed in the neoliberal period. I conclude the chapter by examining some of the new forms of working-class activism that are rebuilding the labour movement, and I argue that these movements have the potential to reach beyond the letter of the law and achieve new and progressive forms of worker solidarity in the current era.

The Working Class and the State in Canada: A Short Introduction, 1870–1945

Why do workers continue to organize into unions? The answer to that question is both straightforward and complex. The straightforward answer is that workers have more power in the workplace if they act collectively rather than individually. This power struggle occurs because of how work is organized under capitalism. Workplaces are not democratic spaces. In capitalist workplaces, workers have little capacity to challenge the authoritarian control of employers to manage the remuneration, conditions, and speed of work. Employers purchase the labour capacity of individual workers based on prevailing (and constantly changing) market conditions. How the capacity of labour power is transformed into productive labour is shaped by the power of capitalist managers and owners to control labour time, and thus labour productivity (Albo 1990, 472; Jackson and Thomas 2017). By combining into labour unions, individual workers are better able to challenge and resist those decisions, and thus collectively "defend and promote their common economic and political interests" over those of employers and their political allies (Ross et al. 2015, 6).

Yet, if forming a union leads to greater worker autonomy and power in the workplace and in society, why are only some workers organized into unions while a large majority have no union protection? Asking this second question compels us to think about the complex ways labour is organized and governed in capitalist societies. Capitalist societies inevitably are divided by struggles over how the surplus derived from human labour power is appropriated and distributed. Such struggles are shaped by social divisions of class, which themselves are divided by other socially determined characteristics, such as gender, race, ability, language, religion, nationality, and so forth. At the root of these struggles are fundamental questions about how class power is reflected within society. In capitalist societies, employers have the legal ability to appropriate the surplus derived from human labour power and to return only a fragment of that surplus back to workers in the form of wages or benefits. Outside of legally mandated minimum wages, employers are under few obligations to return larger shares of the surplus of labour power back to workers unless demanded by competitive market conditions or through open class conflict. Subject to state regulations, employers can also govern the pace of work and extend the length of the working day to further squeeze the surpluses derived from human labour power.

Identifying that employers' power to control the wages, labour time, and conditions of work is cemented and legally sustained by the capitalist state implies that the social powers of the ownership class are not limited to the workplace. Recognizing the capitalist nature of the state does not suggest that employers control what the state does or does not do at any given moment in time. Rather, it suggests that the state is a complex field of class struggle that often reflects the balance of class power in different historical moments (Panitch 1977b). Laws that regulate the labour process should be conceptualized and filtered through this lens. Ultimately the state is not a neutral arbitrator of class disputes but, as Poulantzas (1973) acknowledges, a capitalist one, and thus embedded within class struggles at both the subnational and national levels. The level of embeddedness, however, varies depending on the type of state (liberal-democratic, social-democratic, authoritarian, fascist, and so on) and the manner by which it reflects different fragments of class power (i.e. the interests of financial versus manufacturing capital). That is to say, although the state reflects a relative autonomy from direct class control and coercion, it is not neutral as to how classes interact. The structure of class struggle will navigate "the institutionalized power of the capitalist state," and will be presented *"its own unity in its* relations to socio-economic relations (the economic class struggle) in so far as it represents the unity of the people/nation, composed of agents set up, as subjects, as individual/political persons, i.e., in so far as it represents the political unity of an economic isolation which is its own effect" (Poulantzas 1973, 276, emphasis in original). In other words, the state manifests segments of class relations as they struggle for power and control within a legally constructed marketplace in a nationally defined geopolitical state.

Canadian history reflects the class tensions between workers struggling for greater autonomy and remuneration, on the one hand, and employers' determination to resist those demands by relying on both legal and non-legal means, often enforced by the state. In the nineteenth century, the emergence of a class of "free" wage labourers alongside capitalist expansion altered the social dynamics of private employment, albeit unevenly in terms of gender, race, language, religion, and region. Recognizing that women were largely excluded from employment, the private wage relationship emerged as a form of "bilateral labour market contract" between individual workers, who sold their labour power for a wage, and individual employers, who purchased that labour power (Fudge and Tucker 2000, 251–2). The contractual relationship was regulated by the state through laws that "treated employees as 'juridical equals'," leaving the conditions of employment to individual negotiations between the participants (McCallum 1995, 574). As so-called equals, the law recognized that individual workers entered into contracts of employment freely and without legal constraint. Harry Glasbeek has argued that the free contractual relationship was respected by the courts, and thus "enforced as they stood," because to question the content of the individual contract "might have suggested that the contracting parties were seen as not capable of deciding for themselves what was good for them; that is, they would be seen not to be sovereign individuals" (Glasbeek 1985, 283).

The state's ideological proclivity towards the individual – whether an actual living person or the legally personified individual business or corporation – in the governance of nineteenth- and early twentieth-century labour relations embedded a structural acrimony towards workers' collective freedoms. As artisan and small-scale manufacturing capital gave way to larger pools of industrial capitalist organizations, workers were brought together in larger assembly workplaces. Although there is evidence that the state and the law tolerated workers' combinations and that strikes did occur within primarily skilled trades (Palmer 1987a, 1992), these unions were legitimate only so long as they did not conspire to breach the individual employment contract (Tucker 1991). Thus, although historians have recognized that laws restricting workers' combinations were uneven and did not stop workers from organizing unions between 1830 and 1870 (Craven 1984; cf. Tucker 1991), the real (or perceived) illegality of these workers' organizations to bargain or strike collectively handed employers "a powerful repressive tool" to undermine struggles over wages and a shorter working day (Chartrand 1984, 270). As these struggles solidified to form a powerful workers' movement for a nine-hour working day, more militant and coordinated job actions took place throughout southern Ontario's industrial centres (Battye 1979). As a partial response, in the spring of 1872 Parliament formally lifted the criminal sanctions against workers' acting collectively and combining into unions. Two parallel pieces of legislation, the Trade Union Act and the Criminal Law Amendment Act, have long been identified as marking "the beginning of full legality for 'combinations of workingmen' (unions, collective bargaining and strike action)," although the two Acts have also been recognized as containing a paradoxical "negative undertone"(D'Aoust and Delorme 1981, 895).

Under the Trade Union Act, workers were no longer subject to criminal conspiracy charges in restraint of trade, as had been true under the common law. More concretely, the simple act of combining to alter wages, hours of work, or for greater health and safety protection was tolerated, although not promoted. Yet, reflecting the balance of class power in this period, the Act imposed no corresponding legal duties on employers to recognize or bargain with a union. The only way workers' organizations could be recognized in these manners was through raw class conflict. Inconsistently, for unions actually to use their collective power under the Act, they had to register with the federal government, which few did. Under the Criminal Law Amendment Act, the federal government outlined a host of collective activities typically associated with union behaviour during strike actions – such as hiding tools or criminal harassment (such as "watching and besetting") – that were officially criminalized (Palmer 1992, 111–12; Tucker 1991, 41–2). Amendments to the Trade Union Act between 1872 and 1877 recognized the ability of individual workers to combine, but set extreme limits on what those combinations could accomplish, and did little to address workers' concerns for greater collective freedom to challenge unilateral employers' power.

If workers' collective freedoms were precarious after 1877, labour struggles after the turn of the century suggest that governments were more concerned with containing and limiting overt working-class conflict than with legally recognizing workers' ability to act collectively. Piecemeal legislation, such as the 1907 Industrial Disputes Investigation Act, sought to restrain and limit class conflict and to preserve the prerogative of property by accommodating "legitimate" or "respectable" unions willing to accept federal conciliation with legal limits on the ability to strike (Russell 1990). Yet outside the realm of labour respectability, more radical elements of the growing industrial labour movement were often met with violent resistance by the state. Such violent actions were on display in 1919, when a workers' revolt culminated in a dramatic confrontation in Winnipeg that challenged the legitimacy of the fragmented labour relations system and the state itself following the economic downturn after the First World War (Kramer and Mitchell 2010). In addition to the heavy hand of the state crushing the workers' revolt in Winnipeg through violence, employers continued to use the criminal law and judicial injunctions to constrain, weaken, or eliminate the ability of workers across the country to strike effectively throughout this period (Fudge and Tucker 2001, 52–61).

It was not until the 1940s, and the unprecedented militancy of the working class – often outside and in opposition to the leadership of established industrial and craft unions (Bjorge 2017) – under the wartime conditions of full employment that the federal government finally moved to recognize a legally protected freedom of association for workers (Fudge and Tucker 2001; MacDowell 1978; McInnis 2002; Panitch and Swartz 2003). Adopting important elements of the US Wagner model of labour relations law, the government passed Privy Council 1003 (PC 1003), later codified in the 1948 Industrial Relations Dispute Investigation Act.[1] The Act reflected a key compromise between industrial capital and large segments of the industrial and craft-based working class in Canada. At the root of these new labour laws were forms of compulsory bargaining and union recognition (demanded by organized labour) balanced against compulsory grievance arbitration and compulsory conciliation (demanded by capital and the state) to solve workplace disputes and delay strike action, while also guaranteeing defined periods of uninterrupted production (i.e., no legally recognized strikes during the life of a collective agreement) (Fudge and Tucker 2000, 275). To govern this compromise, the federal (and later provincial) states created complex legal instruments to protect the basic abilities of unions to organize, bargain collectively, and strike in individual job sites under very specific conditions (Woods 1955).

The final pillar of Canada's modern system of labour relations law arose out of Supreme Court Justice Ivan Rand's 1946 arbitration decision ending a heated strike between Ford Motor Company and the United Auto Workers (UAW) in Windsor, Ontario. The strike was primarily over the issue of "union security," which was reflected in the union's demand for the automatic dues "check-off" to be administered by the employer (Moulton 1974). In his decision, Justice Rand began by pondering the societal dilemma of post-war labour relations, questioning whether the future would be regulated by "law and convention" or "economic war" (*Ford v. UAW*, para. 9).[2] In his view, the legal compromise embedded in PC 1003 – which restricted labour's collective ability to strike while employers were obligated to recognize unions – must prevail. Justice Rand's basic philosophical premise was that labour regulation in a liberal democratic society was obligated to balance private

---

1 Woods (1955) described PC 1003 as the construction of Canadian labour's "Magna Carta."
2 *Ford Motor Co. of Canada v. International Union United Automobile, Aircraft and Agricultural Implement Workers of America (U.A.W.-C.I.O.) (Union Security Grievance)*, [1946] O.L.A.A. No. 1.

enterprise and the principle of "social justice in the area of industrial mass production" (para. 3). Such a delicate balancing act began with the liberal conviction that, although private property is a social good, it could no longer be interpreted as "absolutist," treating labour as a mere commodity (para. 10). Labour's new collective legal rights, however, were dependent upon the acceptance of added legal obligations. For Justice Rand, only responsible unions that preserved and respected the new industrial legal framework were worthy of state protection, while an "irresponsible labour organization has no claim to be clothed with authority over persons or interests" (para. 13).

Under the now acclaimed "Rand formula," unions were required to abstain from any strike (general or partial) during the life of a collective agreement, union officials were required to "repudiate any strike or other concerted cessation of work by any group or number of employees," and if leaders refused to do so, they would be "liable to the penalty of a suspension of the check-off" (para. 32). In staking out this compromise, Justice Rand sought to eliminate the problem of "free riders" by ruling that all workers benefited from collective bargaining, and suggested that every member share the cost of maintaining the local union; these members, however, were not required to join the union. This clever legal twist allowed him to balance individual and collective rights with a modified form of union security that included the obligatory check-off.

Lest he be misinterpreted as being overtly pro-union or even an activist in the union cause, Justice Rand assured his audience that the basic hierarchy in the capitalist workplace was not on trial in this dispute. Rather, in his view, private "capital must in the long run be looked upon as occupying a dominant position" because "it is in some respects at greater risk than labour; but as industry becomes established, these risks change inversely" (para. 6). In analysing these dangers, Justice Rand acknowledged that the clout of organized labour had grown in the past century. To protect and preserve the balance of power between both parties, he concluded, labour had to be accepted as a legitimate partner in the managing of industry. In his discussion, responsible unions would be required to reject "communistic ends,"[3] but also must respect the new labour law rules, especially those restricting strike

---

3 Justice Rand later softened his position on communist unions. In *Smith & Rhuland Ltd. v. Nova Scotia*, [1953] 2 S.C.R. 95, he rejected the notion that a labour relations board could refuse to certify a communist-dominated union.

activities (para. 16). Supporters of the new model of labour law believed that it heralded a new era of "industrial democracy" in which the class tensions of the past were replaced with balanced, state-mediated legal institutions to benefit both business and labour in a new era of Keynesian, state-directed capitalism (Tomlins 1985, 19).

In both federal and provincial Canadian states, the so-called compromise between capital and labour was sustained by the construction of new and complex system of industrial relations with real statutory authority. Over time, this new legal system would create a whole stratum of middle-class managers addressing 'human resources' in unionized firms (and later as union-avoidance strategies in non-union firms), and grew whole fields of new labour and management lawyers, a tripartite (staffed by labour, capital, and the state) administrative structure to adjudicate union-employer disputes, and growing union bureaucracies to navigate this new legal reality. In the early years, class struggles over the institutionalization of the post-war labour relations framework tended to concentrate on which legal actors would take responsibility for managing the system and how far legal protections would go in protecting workers using these new legal rights, especially when workers exercised their right to strike (Fudge and Tucker 2009–10; McInnis 2002).

When examining the crystallization of these new labour rights, it is clear that for workers who had suffered through the years when government legitimized and encouraged open union repression, blacklisting, company unionism, and outright employer authoritarianism in the workplace, the significance of the new legal freedoms outlined in the Wagner/PC 1003/Rand compromise cannot be underestimated. For the first time, the capitalist state in Canada was pressured by significant components of the working class to address the long-held demands of workers to organize freely into their own unions, to have employers recognize and bargain with those unions, and to strike when collective bargaining broke down. In other words, while the capitalist labour market persisted, the law would now constrain employers' absolute rights of property to dictate unilaterally the conditions of employment when workers legally organized.

Yet these new collective legal rights came with very specific economic, political, and social trade-offs. The compromise was constructed around very specific forms of workers and employers. At its roots, as Anne Forrest (1995) has shown, the post-war labour regime was constructed to accommodate male, breadwinning workers, labouring in vertically integrated, large industrial and natural-resource-extraction jobs. In turn, these firms would be unionized by large industrial and craft unions, themselves largely organized and run by male workers. And when women workers did find success in organizing in female-dominated sectors – including retail, office work, textiles, fur, food, and later the public sector – the struggles in those firms were often shaped and dominated by male employers and male trade unionists (Sangster 2004). The post-war compromise also changed the ideological shape of Canada's organized working class. Following the Cold War chill on the Canadian left and taking care to act legally "responsibly," many industrial and craft unions avoided, or at least downplayed, radical anticapitalist politics in order to maintain the legitimacy associated with their newfound legal rights. Throughout the 1940s, 1950s, and into the 1960s, such responsibility included a very active campaign to raid communist-led unions and to purge communist labour leaders and long-time activists from the broader house of labour (Abella 1973; Palmer 1992, 290–8).

The new post-war compromise also placed very specific legal boundaries around workers' most powerful collective weapon: the strike. No longer were workers or unions legally free to strike for purposes outside the collective bargaining process (Fudge and Tucker 2001; Palmer 1992). Rather, the state's post-war labour laws became the literal archetype of what Ralph Miliband described as the "routinisation of conflict" (1969, 74–5). From this point forward, strikes would be defined by their "legality" or "illegality." Legal strikes were those that occurred after the conclusion of a collective agreement and when collective bargaining negotiations broke down. By contrast, illegal strikes were those not sanctioned by employers, governments, and sometimes union leadership. These strikes, while less frequent, generally occurred during the terms of collective agreements and were waged for a host of economic, political, and social reasons. Yet the institutionalization of Wagner/PC 1003/Rand institutions was meant to tame working-class struggle in order, as Industrial Relations scholars John Pierce and Karen Bentham have argued, "to regulate strikes with an eye to protecting the public interest and maintaining public peace and order" (2003, 339). Whereas past disciplinary action, dangerous workplace conditions, or simple worker alienation might have led to spontaneous strike action, under the new labour laws strikes during the life of a collective agreement were legally forbidden. In other words, Canadian workers had to act "responsibly" by refusing to strike during collective bargaining negotiations or for political purposes. In some cases, strike action was delayed even further, as mandatory conciliation and cooling off periods were required before picket lines were established (Fudge and Tucker 2009–10, 348–9). These constraints were further amplified by continuing common law restrictions that saw actions such as secondary boycotts or secondary picketing activity as violating the "nominate" or "economic" torts (C.W. Smith 2014, 93–4). Taken together, the legal rules of the post-war compromise placed significant legal restrictions on workers' associational freedoms and reshaped the terrain of class struggle "both ideologically and legally, in terms the state recognizes: the rights of property and managerial prerogative on the one hand, and on the other, the right of association and the right to strike" (Panitch and Swartz 2003, 9).

Working-Class Conflict and Crisis, 1946–96

The spectre of industrial legality and the uneasy tension surrounding the state's promotion of certain forms of collective action by workers while maintaining uninterrupted flows of private sector production is at the root of the post-war relationships between workers, employers, and the state. There is clear evidence that, throughout the 1950s and early 1960s, class conflict looked very different than it did prior to the Second World War. The most influential unions were mostly in the private sector, industrial, internationally led, male dominated, and large. These unions ended the war representing close to 28 per cent of the non-agricultural workforce, growing to 37 per cent in the 1970s before levelling off at 33 per cent throughout the 1980s (Figure 7.1). In the years immediately following the war until well into the 1960s, unions were concentrated in manufacturing, construction, natural resource extraction, and within small segments of the municipal sectors (health, utilities, and public works).

In the immediate post-war period, strikes, while not without serious conflict, were much less common than in the turbulent war years. As Figure 7.2 shows, the early years of the post-war compromise were successful in containing – at least on the surface – radical outbursts of working-class anger. Between 1946 and 1964 strikes rarely threatened the political, economic, or institutional structures associated with the post-war economic order. The post-war economic boom, alongside higher wages for largely male workers, seemed to provide the economic foundations for relatively peaceful labour relations, outside of a few sectors that continued to resist the new laws surrounding unionization (see Morton 1998, 213–15). Class struggle in these early years was defined by typical bread-and-butter union issues such as wage increases, pensions, or other forms of workplace benefits. Most often, these strikes were waged by male union members after the breakdown of collective bargaining. Strikes were almost always done with the consent of a growing union bureaucracy, and rarely lasted longer than a

Figure 7.1. Union Membership as a Percentage of Non-agricultural Paid Workers, Canada, 1946–96

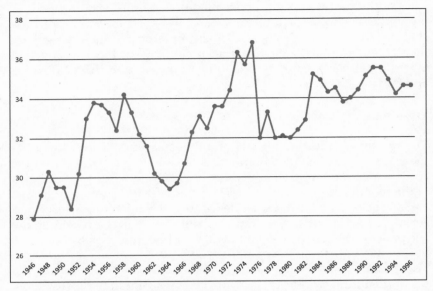

Sources: Historical Statistics of Canada, Series E175–177, "Union membership in Canada, in total, as a percentage of non-agricultural paid workers, and union members with international affiliation, 1911 to 1975"; Statistics Canada, table 2790026, "Number of unionized workers, employees and union density, by sex and industry based on the Standard Industrial Classification, 1980 (SIC), annually (Persons unless specified)."

few weeks. In the short term, at least, the old recognition and political strikes became a thing of the past.

From the middle of the 1960s and through the 1970s, however, workers' relationships with employers, governments, union officials, and the industrial relations system writ large came to define a new form of class struggle. Between 1966 and 1980, workers increasingly engaged in all forms of strike activity, a much larger proportion of them wildcat, or "illegal," strikes. As labour historians have well documented, the shape and characteristics of these strikes reflected a growing demand by rank-and-file workers – often younger and socially divorced from the old political and economic debates that preceded the post-war compromise – to confront employer and government power on the ground. When union officials attempted to clamp down on such militant outbursts by the rank and file, they met with little success. As Peter McInnis (2012) argues in his history of the strike wave of the period, this militancy on

Figure 7.2. Total Strikes, Legal and Illegal, Canada, 1946–2017

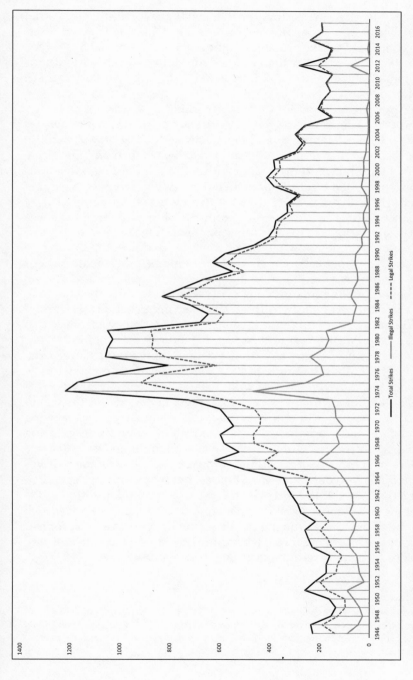

Sources: Statistics Canada, Table 14100352, "Work stoppages in Canada, by jurisdiction and industry based on the North American Industry Classification System (NAICS); Canada, Employment and Social Development Canada, Labour Program occasional (number unless otherwise noted), occasional (Number); *Employment and Social Development Canada, Work Stoppage Directory, 1946–2018.*

158 Charles W. Smith

the part of workers increasingly challenged the rationale that industrial peace should be the defining characteristics of Canada's labour laws. More concretely, workers, and later a new generation of labour leaders, began to use the strike weapon to stand up against workplace and societal "injustice and fairness" (McInnis 2012, 160; see also Palmer 2009, 211–41).

The growing militancy of Canada's working class was not limited to the private sector. Perhaps the most dramatic change to the general post-war labour relations model came between 1965 and 1967. In those years, the federal government responded to the waves of militant strike activity by postal workers by passing the Public Service Staff Relations Act, extending the legal ability of all federal public servants to bargain collectively and strike. Over the next twenty years, provinces (led by militant outbursts in Quebec and British Columbia) conceded these same legal freedoms to their public sector workforces.[4] The transformation expanded the growing ranks of organized labour, leading to changes in the political orientation of the workers' movement. Perhaps most prominent was the push for greater autonomy for Canadian members of international unions, with activists leading the charge to have their unions break away from American organizations. The growing militancy of both private and public sector workers was reflected in increasing strike numbers in both sectors (Figure 7.3).

Further changes were also transforming the country's organized working class. By the middle of the 1960s, women were making new openings for themselves in the workforce and by extension slowly transforming the unions that represented workers in various sectors (Sangster 2010). Women workers were also taking the lead in organizing traditionally underrepresented sectors, launching aggressive organizing campaigns in sectors as diverse as local banking branches and large retailers such as Eaton's department stores. In some cases, these drives were led not by older established unions, but by feminist independent unions (J. Smith 2014). Moreover, the expansion of unionization in the public sector led thousands of newly unionized women workers to kick open the doors to the growing public sector labour movement, forever changing the face of organized labour and how it responded to arbitrary decisions by employers and governments (Ross 2013).

---

4 The one exception to this trend was Saskatchewan. In 1944 the Co-operative Commonwealth Federation government of Tommy Douglas included public servants in its Trade Union Act, granting these workers the ability to organize, bargain collectively, and strike.

Figure 7.3. Strikes in the Public and Private Sectors, Canada, 1946–96

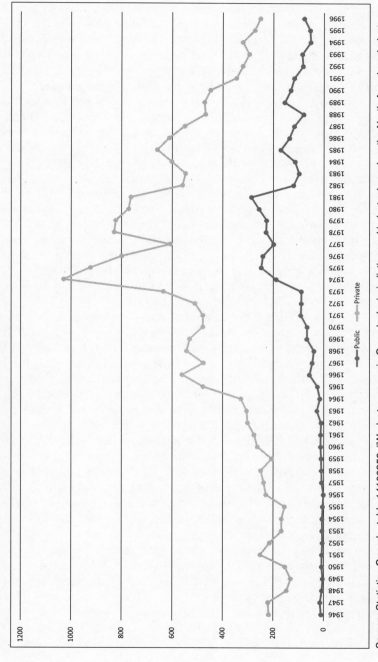

Source: Statistics Canada, table 14100352, "Work stoppages in Canada, by jurisdiction and industry based on the North American Industry Classification System (NAICS)." Employment and Social Development Canada – Labour Program occasional (number unless otherwise noted), occasional (Number).

The height of post-war working-class activism took shape between the tumultuous years of 1966 and 1982, culminating in a one-day national general strike in 1976. Organized by the Canadian Labour Congress (CLC), the one-day strike was called to challenge the Trudeau Liberal government's "6&5" austerity program – its attempt to fight the economic crisis of inflation by attacking the collective bargaining rights of workers (Aivalis 2018, 109–38). However, the policy instrument the Trudeau government used to address the crisis, notwithstanding rhetoric about capping prices, was clearly to attack the free collective bargaining system promoted by its own labour laws. The CLC's collective response was to call 800,000 workers onto the picket line over the course of a single-day walkout. That strike action, in contrast to traditional strikes in the 1950s and early 1960s, was political in nature, and designed to challenge the boundaries of industrial legality beyond workplace issues towards greater societal changes. Similar political strikes occurred in Quebec and British Columbia throughout the decade, as workers led provincial strikes to oppose government crackdowns on collective bargaining rights and the early salvo by right-of centre governments to impose austerity-driven policies – most notably in the Solidarity actions in British Columbia in 1983 (Palmer 1987b).

Yet outside these impressive acts of collective resistance to government and employer power, by the late 1970s and early 1980s cracks had begun to emerge in the now uneasy détente among capital, labour, and the Canadian state. The economic crisis of the 1970s witnessed federal (and later provincial) erosion of free collective bargaining as the state increasingly used its power to end legal strikes through back-to-work legislation (Panitch and Swartz 2003). If there was a symbolic end to the class compromise institutionalized after the war, it was in the 1979 incarceration of Canadian Union of Postal Workers president Jean-Claude Parrot for his refusal to end a strike after the federal government imposed draconian back-to-work legislation. In fact, Parrot's incarceration demonstrated the extent to which the federal government and the legal system itself failed to respect the collective right of workers to strike freely, especially when it conflicted with the political and economic objectives of Canada's ruling classes and the traditional political parties of capital. The blunt instrument of criminalization used so prominently on Parrot has since given way to the disciplining of unions through punitive financial measures if workers defy imposed back-to-work orders by governments.

The increased use of back-to-work legislation and attempts by federal and provincial governments to curtail the capacity of workers to advance their interests through strikes were defining features of

Canada's process of neoliberalization in the 1980s. In fact, the theory of "permanent exceptionalism" advanced by Panitch and Swartz (2003) examines the seemingly contradictory manner by which federal and provincial governments have eroded the ability of workers to strike while only moderately reworking the legal foundations of Canadian Wagnerism. Panitch and Swartz's well-established theory argues that exceptionalism is defined by a coercive regime of industrial legality in which government-led policies allow and even promote the post-war framework of free collective bargaining and the legal ability to strike, while at the same time openly repressing the practice of these freedoms, especially through curtailing workers' ability to strike. For Panitch and Swartz (2003), permanent exceptionalism marks a new, and particularly coercive, form of class politics because it claims to respect the post-war institutions of Wagnerism/PC 1003/Rand, while simultaneously constraining or outright repressing those freedoms on a permanent ad hoc basis. Although Panitch and Swartz point to the public sector as ground zero for exceptionalism's expansion, by the 1990s such treatments extended to private sector strike action as well (Smith and Stevens 2018).

Given this reality, an important component of the shifting realities for Canadian workers has been attempts to weaken workers' collective ability to resist the power of employers to dictate the conditions of work, in both the public and private sectors. In the 1980s, such pressure came from both governments and the courts, as unions' attempts constitutionally to protect important elements of the Wagner/PC 1003/Rand model under Canada's Charter of Rights and Freedoms were met with stunning disdain by the country's top court (Panitch and Swartz 2003; Savage and Smith 2017).

Governments have further eroded long-standing Wagner/PC 1003/Rand institutions, often to the benefit of employers. This restructuring has included eradicating card-check certification in favour of mandatory elections, raising election thresholds to unionize successfully, eliminating the ability of supervisory employees to be included in collective bargaining units, and cutting back and weakening occupational health and safety regulations and workplace inspections. All of these elements of "gradualism" – in which the institution of collective bargaining is weakened through gradual reforms, rather than through abrupt, radical changes – weaken the ability of workers to form new unions and thus undermine the levelling potentials of collective bargaining (Bartkiw 2008; Bentham 2002; Slinn 2004). These top-down restrictions on the rights of labour have severely weakened the movement, especially limiting its influence in the private sector.

Figure 7.4. Union Membership, Canada, 1997–2018

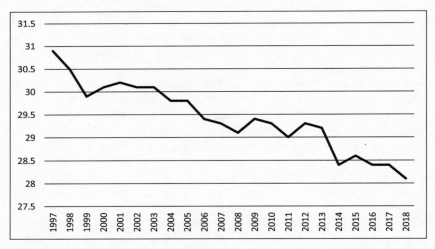

Source: Statistics Canada, table 14100132, "Union status by industry, annually, total employees, all industries, both sexes."

Workers and Unions in a Period of Crisis and Change, 1997–2018

The open attacks on Canada's working-class organizations have led to a serious crisis in the labour movement. Since 1997 the percentage of workers organized in a labour union has declined to the same levels as after the Second World War, at 28 per cent in 2018. Although that decline represents an erosion of over eight percentage points from its post-war high in the 1970s, the absolute density number actually shields the precipitate decline of unionization in the private sector, which fell to 14.3 percent in 2018 (Figures 7.4 and 7.5).

Notwithstanding the decline of unions within the overall workforce, the struggles of earlier generations of feminist union activists, transitions within the economy, and the move of unionization from the private to the public sector have changed the union movement's membership. In 2018 organized workers were far more likely to be female and to have a relatively high level of education. In 2004, for the first time, women workers represented a higher percentage of the unionized labour force than men, and their share has accelerated since then (Figure 7.6). There has also been an absolute decline in the number of workers in traditionally male-dominated private sector industries such as

Figure 7.5. Public and Private Sector Union Membership, Canada, 1997–2018

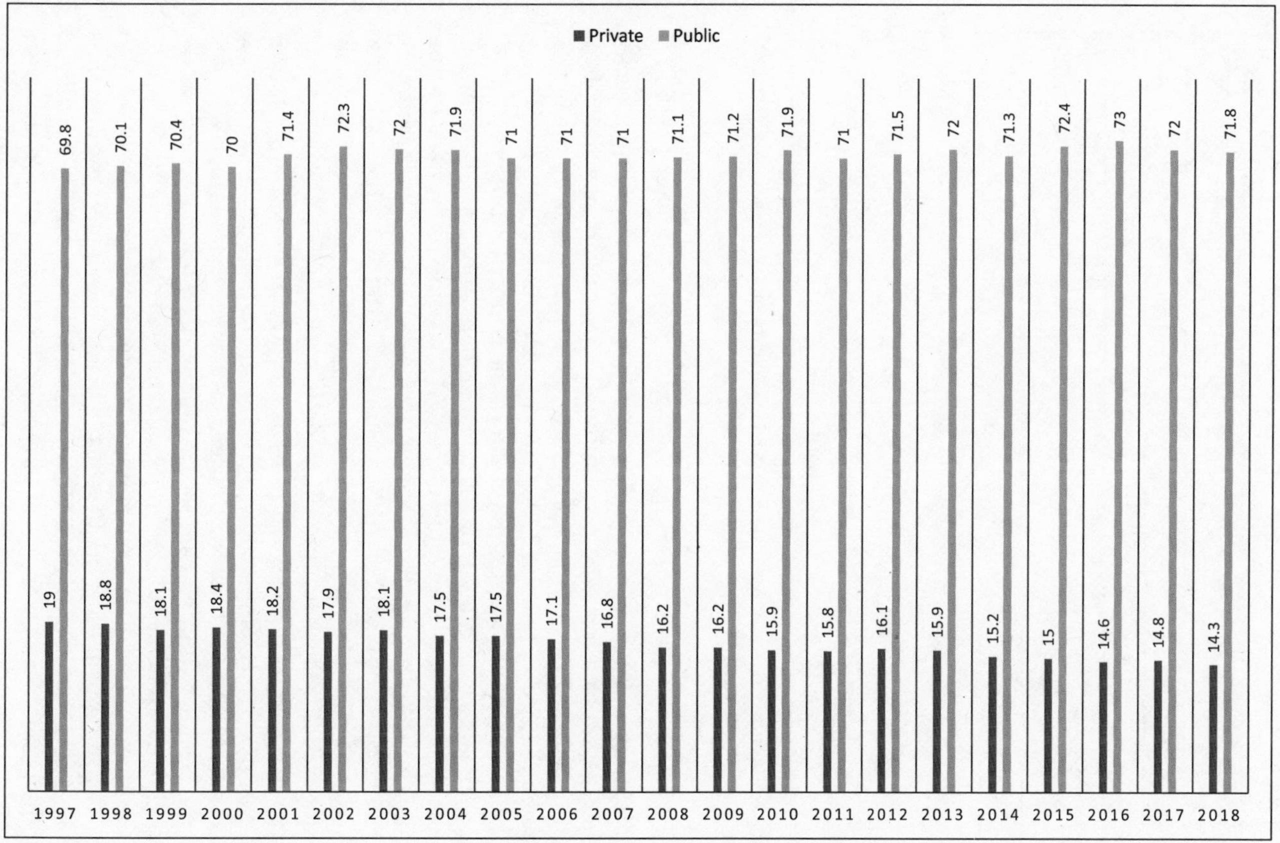

■ Private ■ Public

Year	Private	Public
2018	14.3	71.8
2017	14.8	72
2016	14.6	73
2015	15	72.4
2014	15.2	71.3
2013	15.9	72
2012	16.1	71.5
2011	15.8	71
2010	15.9	71.9
2009	16.2	71.2
2008	16.2	71.1
2007	16.8	71
2006	17.1	71
2005	17.5	71
2004	17.5	71.9
2003	18.1	72
2002	17.9	72.3
2001	18.2	71.4
2000	18.4	70
1999	18.1	70.4
1998	18.8	70.1
1997	19	69.8

Source: Statistics Canada, table 14100132, "Union status by industry, annually, total employees, all industries, both sexes."

Figure 7.6. Male and Female Unionization, Canada, 1997–2018

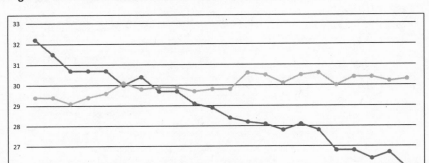

Source: Statistics Canada, table 14100132, "Union status by industry, annually, unionization rate, total industries, all sectors, males and females."

autos, steel, mining, and forestry. The absolute growth of public sector unionization as a total share of all unionized workers has also meant that unions represent a greater percentage of workers who are highly trained (Figure 7.7). In 2015 the Canadian Union of Public Employees (CUPE) was by far the largest union in the country, representing over 635,000 workers, a growth of 100,000 members since 2004. By contrast, the largest private sector union, the CAW, grew by only 40,000 members. The CAW's growth, however, is masked by a large decline in membership until 2012, which rebounded after a merger with the 100,000-member-strong Communications, Energy and Paper Workers Union, creating a new union, Unifor (Canada 2015). The merger of these two unions represented a trend within private sector unionization, as numerous long-standing private unions in various sectors have merged with larger bodies in order to survive. Put another way, the merger trend within private sector unions does not reflect a healthy, growing movement, but rather organizations in crisis.

Changes in the educational status of existing union members are also an interesting phenomenon. On the one hand, they reflect the demands of the labour market for more highly skilled workers, largely subsidized by the public through access to universities and colleges. On the other hand, the educational changes illustrate the high representation of workers from the public sector and from certain sectors in the private sphere.

Figure 7.7. Unionization by Education, Canada, 1997–2018

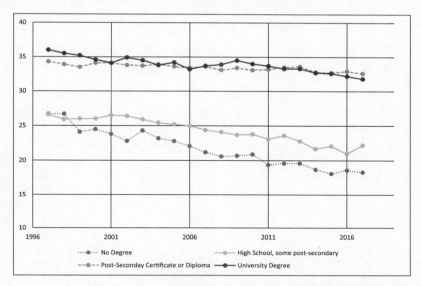

Source: Statistics Canada, table 14100130, "Union status by education level, annually."

Workers with lower levels of education appear to face numerous structural barriers to accessing basic labour union freedoms – an issue that the union movement, especially in the private sector, has yet to address.

The changing rates of unionization in the private sector present numerous social and political challenges for unions. Whereas the movement began in the large private industries in railways, manufacturing, mines, forests, and utilities, today workers in unions are far more likely to be employed by government. This implies that the vast majority of workers in the private sector have no access to the protections provided by unions. Although the extension of union freedoms to women workers is long overdue, this trend is at least partially explained by the growing concentration of unions in the public sector. As employment for thousands of new workers entering the labour market continues to move towards low-end and precarious private sector services industries such as retail, food service, sales, consulting, technology, research, shipping, and online, there is greater pressure on unions and their allies to represent the women and men in these relatively low wage jobs. If that cannot occur, there will be continuing pressure on private sector unions as employers use competitive pressures to squeeze them out of these sectors.

The falling rate of unionization in the private sector also suggests that workers' grievances will have far less weight and be far less

Figure 7.8. Public and Private Sector Strikes, Canada, 1997–2018

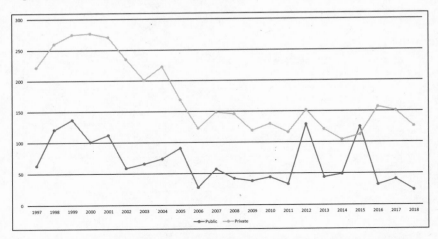

Source: Statistics Canada, table 14100352, "Work stoppages in Canada, by jurisdiction and industry based on the North American Industry Classification System (NAICS)." Employment and Social Development Canada – Labour Program occasional (number unless otherwise noted), occasional (Number).

likely to be addressed by employers (or governments) because there will be few consequences if these demands are not met. Moreover, if workers have no credible threat to strike, employers will have little incentive to bargain effectively or to concede to union demands. There is considerable evidence that, over the past several years, there have been fewer collective agreements settled per year, contracts are taking longer to negotiate (with collective bargaining sometimes going for years after a contract expires), and when settlements are reached the duration of those contracts now averages 40 months, up from 19.6 months in 1984 (Employment and Social Development Canada 2015, 1–2). These trends are amplified by the declining militancy of the organized working class in all sectors. For instance, by 2012, for the first time in Canadian history, more workers in the public sector were engaged in strike action than were their colleagues in the private sector (Figure 7.8).

Given the predisposition of governments to intervene routinely in all forms of strikes by public sector workers, the inability of workers to engage in collective strike action weakens the hands of all workers to regain a greater share of surplus labour power from employers.

The falling rate of union militancy is reflected in the declining number of workers now participating in any form of strike action. As Figure 7.9

Figure 7.3. Number of workers involved in illegal and legal strikes, Canada, 1946–2018

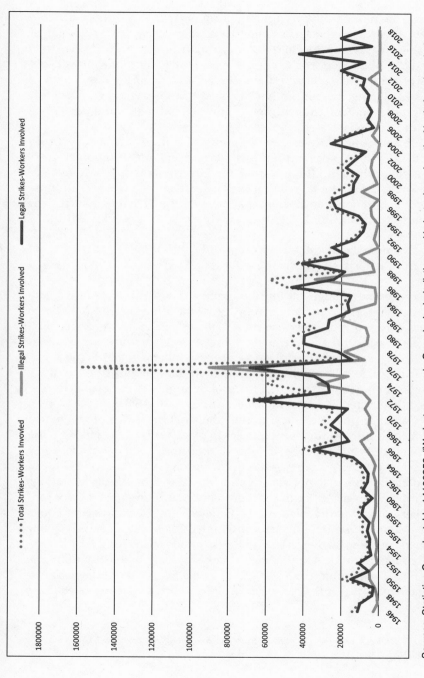

····· Total Strikes-Workers Invovled   —— Illegal Strikes-Workers Involved   —— Legal Strikes-Workers Involved

Sources: Statistics Canada, table 14100352, "Work stoppages in Canada, by jurisdiction and industry based on the North American Industry Classification System (NAICS); Canada, Employment and Social Development Canada, – Labour Program occasional (number unless otherwise noted), occasional (Number); *Employment and Social Development Canada, Work Stoppage Directory, 1946–2018.*

shows, the number involved in any form of militancy against employers (or governments) has dropped to levels unseen since the 1950s. If, as Donald Swartz and Rosemary Warskett (2012) have argued, the strike is the moment when workers collectively realize the core value of solidarity and collective action, then the decline in workers' militancy is also weakening their incentive to conceptualize their own economic and political power, thus further limiting the influence of unions in all Western capitalist states.

This weakening of workers' solidarity, and thus of collective workers' freedoms, also has implications for workers in non-unionized sectors, where there is little incentive for governments to improve basic employment standards, making it more difficult for workers in those sectors and in non-traditional workplaces to be paid a living wage or to be protected from employer abuse (Fudge and Vosko 2001a, 2001b).

Conclusions: Backwards, Forwards, and the Tides of Crisis and Change

The crises and changes facing the organized working class are surely monumental. Governments across the political spectrum continue to attack core workers' freedoms, especially when those freedoms challenge the neoliberal priorities of the ruling classes. Such an event occurred in 2018, when the self-described progressive Liberal government of Justin Trudeau legislated legally striking postal workers back to work because their action threatened the profit margins of businesses during the Christmas retail season (Pedwell 2018; Smith and Savage 2018). Given that Canadian governments continue to restrict the ability of workers to strike while also putting legal hurdles in place to make organizing more onerous, unions' fight-back strategies have been largely defensive. A key component of those strategies has been to protect the Wagner/PC 1003/Rand institutions that, notwithstanding the restrictions these institutions place on workers' collective action, continue to reinforce unionized workers' ability to organize and bargain collectively. In order to protect that system, several unions have attempted to elevate Canada's labour laws to coverage by the Charter of Rights and Freedoms.

This legal strategy saw some success in 2007, when the Supreme Court of Canada ruled, in *Health Services and Support-Facilities Subsector Bargaining Assn. v. British Columbia*,[5] that freedom of association included

---

5 *Health Services and Support – Facilities Subsector Bargaining Assn. v. British Columbia*, [2007] 2 S.C.R. 391.

a constitutional right for workers to bargain collectively, which also included a corresponding duty on the part of employers to bargain in good faith (para. 97). Responding to the unilateral actions of the British Columbia Liberal government of Gordon Campbell, the Supreme Court ruled that the Charter protected "the capacity of members of labour unions to engage, in association, in collective bargaining on fundamental workplace issues" (para. 19). Although the Court framed its ruling as only narrowly applying to a "process of collective action to achieve workplace goals" and not constitutional protection for "the fruits of the bargaining process," the decision nevertheless expanded significantly the ability of unions to challenge governments intent on weakening the bargaining rights of public sector unions (paras. 19, 29). The Court later expanded on the protection of collective bargaining when it acknowledged, in *British Columbia Teachers' Federation v. British Columbia*,[6] that constitutionally entrenched good-faith collective bargaining restricted governments from unilaterally deciding which issues could and could not be bargained.

Unions were given added constitutional support in 2015. In a 5–2 decision, the Supreme Court determined in *SFL v. Saskatchewan*[7] that the Charter included the ability to strike. In making that decision, the Court determined that the freedom to strike is a central component of a "meaningful collective bargaining process in our system of labour relations," supported by Canadian labour history, by court jurisprudence, and by international commitments (para. 3). As the Court had determined in *BC Health Services* that "meaningful collective bargaining" was a constitutionally protected freedom, it recognized that engaging in that process was impossible without a credible threat by workers to withdraw their labour. For the Court, the freedom to "collectively withdraw services for the purpose of negotiating the terms and conditions of employment – in other words, to strike – is an essential component of the process through which workers pursue collective workplace goals (*SFL v. Saskatchewan*, para. 46). The Court determined that, in the process of engaging in a strike, workers "come together to participate directly in the process of determining their wages, working conditions and the rules that will govern their working lives" (para. 54) Under such circumstances, workers are able to act collectively to resist "imposed terms and conditions" of employment and thus further their

---

6 *British Columbia Teachers' Federation v. British Columbia*, [2016] 2 S.C.R. 407.
7 *Saskatchewan Federation of Labour v. Saskatchewan*, [2015] 1 S.C.R. 245.

human dignity by levelling the power imbalance between themselves and employers (paras. 54, 55). It was particularly important, the Court reasoned, to recall that simply engaging in strike action does "not guarantee that a labour dispute will be resolved in any particular manner, or that it will be resolved at all" (para. 57) Rather, the onus is on both workers and employers to solve the dispute peacefully through "good faith negotiations."

Many unionized workers, especially in the public sector, have certainly interpreted this defensive constitutional strategy as furthering their collective rights (C.W. Smith 2019). Yet, as important as those Supreme Court decisions have been for the union movement, they have done little for workers not currently organized into a union (Savage and Smith 2017). Moreover, the constitutionalization of these union freedoms must be understood alongside the already existing legal limitations of the Wagner/PC 1003/Rand labour relations regime. Put another way, constitutional labour rights do little to organize workers as a class. Rather, the courts simply defend the existing system – a system that, as we have seen, is protecting fewer and fewer workers in the Canadian economy.

Recognizing these limitations, where can Canadian workers turn? The seemingly simple yet complex answer is that workers be addressed as a class. What motivates workers to unionize and to strike in the first place? Historically, unionization only really takes off once government removes the legal restrictions on organizing. And yet those restrictions, as we have seen, will not be removed without sustained pressure from the working class itself. It almost goes without saying that workers can be motivated to address the crisis of union density and falling rates of militancy only when they see themselves clearly reflected in the movement itself. In this regard, the increasing prominence of working-class women in the union movement will only strengthen the ability of existing unions to reach out to marginalized women in the labour market. Similar trends in diversifying the labour movement to reflect women and men of colour and reaching out to Indigenous workers reflect clear priorities in both the private and public sectors. Recent successful campaigns in the United States by teachers and workers of colour in campaigns for wage fairness and the improvement of public services show the importance of militancy when campaigns are organized and run by precarious and marginalized workers themselves (on this question, see McAlevey 2016). In many ways, the history of working-class militancy outlined in this chapter suggests that workers need to be wary of the law as an instrument to rebuild workers' power. When workers follow the rules, as they largely have since the 1980s, capital and the state shift the terrain, making it structurally impossible to advance significant working-class goals. Although the law can, as Bryan Palmer (2003) has articulated, be an instrument to blunt the edges of ruling-class power, it will always reflect the material hierarchy at the roots of capitalist society. In that hierarchy, workers are always at a disadvantage.

Notwithstanding those concerns, the positive changes that have occurred within the labour movement in terms of both diversity and skills attainment suggest that a movement that recognizes and builds on how class is framed and shaped in the current era needs to be organized and run by workers themselves. One such worker-driven campaign that has had a great deal of success in both Canada and the United States is the Fight for 15 (FF15). In Ontario, for example, workers were able to win significant concessions in 2017 in terms of improved working conditions, an increase in the minimum wage, and improved employment standards. Driven by workers themselves, the FF15 has proven an effective organizing campaign because it recognized from its early stages that the struggle was not about wages alone, but also about empowering and building working-class capacity. As Dave Bush and Doug Nesbitt (2017) have pointed out, the campaign found success in attracting a diverse cross-section of the working class because it was built and run by "local groups" who were able

> to shape the $15 and Fairness campaign to their needs built internal organizing capacity and buy-in at the same time. The organization's structure encouraged self-activity, new ideas, and new directions as long as activists were willing to do the work. Most of the routine mobilization work involved petitioning, leafleting, holding creative events, postering, organizing town halls, and lobbying politicians. Protests, strikes, and strike support were less common, but they played a crucial role in focusing local and province-wide capacities, building momentum and energy, and providing an ebb and flow to activity that helped prevent burnout.

Whether the workers were conscious of the history or not, the FF15 campaign certainly borrowed from many of the workers' struggles that emerged before the institutionalization of labour relations during the Second World War. Yet it was also new, because it sought to reach out to precarious workers, many of whom were workers of colour, women, young, and other marginalized groups. Moreover, as Bush and Nesbitt (2017) argue, the growth in the movement allowed the activists to frame "the movement's demands in language that spoke to their lived realities as workers." In building in this way, the FF15 was successful at winning concessions from the state, and thus creating a sense of solidarity within a common movement that benefited both the orga-nized and unorganized alike.

To be sure, there is no one recipe for rebuilding the organized work-ers' movement in Canada. The issues identified in this chapter suggest that the organized working classes' reliance on the capitalist state to defend their collective interests comes with very specific trade-offs with respect to workers' collective ability to strike. As the material foundations that promoted the post-war labour relations model began to fade in the 1970s, the union movement itself was thrown into crisis as density and militancy rates fell. The falling rate of unionization and, by extension, the declining militancy of Canada's organized working class suggest that little will be gained by simply defending existing Wagner/PC 1003/Rand institutions. Rather, the future of the move-ment will depend on how workers themselves can be supported to rebuild the solidarity necessary to think as a class. Some of that has begun to occur, but its long-term success or failure will almost certainly depend on how workers in existing unions reach out to non-unionized workers to provide the resources to rebuild and extend workers' strug-gles. Part of that success will also be remembering the militant struggles of the past, while working through and expanding on what a new mili-tancy will look like in the future.

8   Corporations and Corporate Power

JAMIE BROWNLEE

Introduction

In Canada, and to varying degrees in nations throughout the world, the economy, state, and political system are now heavily influenced by corporations. Corporate power has reached unprecedented levels, influencing decisions about who governs and how, the production process, how resources are distributed, the quality and quantity of jobs, and the content of media and communication systems. Some view this development positively, arguing that corporations are an efficient means of creating wealth and employment opportunities and providing useful goods and services. Others, however, are more critical. In his book, *The Corporation*, Joel Bakan (2004, 2, 60) argues that the modern corporation is a "pathological institution, a dangerous possessor of the great power it wields over people and societies ... As a psychopathic creature, the corporation can neither recognize nor act upon moral reasons to refrain from harming others." The rise of corporate power is also associated with growing economic inequality, outsourced and sweatshop labour, complicity in human rights abuses, and environmental destruction. Moreover, as the power of corporations grows, so too does their capacity to overwhelm the democratic process and preside over aspects of life once firmly embedded in the public sphere.

In Canada the vast majority of incorporated businesses are small: in 2015 there were nearly 1.2 million Canadian businesses that employed at least one person, more than half employed between one and four people, 98 per cent had fewer than one hundred employees, and those with over five hundred employees were just 0.25 per cent of the total number (Canada 2016). Although small- and medium-sized firms are important in shaping the lives of Canadian workers and communities, it is a small fraction of large Canadian corporations – or, more accurately, a small fraction within that fraction – that dominates Canada's political economy. As a result, they have been at the forefront of debates about social change and social conflict in Canadian political economy scholarship.

This chapter explores the modern corporation in Canada, focusing on three key empirical issues in the Canadian political economy literature: (1) the economic, social, and political dimensions of corporate power; (2) the relationship between corporations and economic inequality; and (3) the changing nature of corporate regulation in the context of neoliberalism and globalization.

Corporate Power in Canada

Institutionally speaking, corporations are powerful entities. Much of their power is "structural" in that it is rooted in the ability to determine privately the provision of investment and resources, thereby affecting economic growth, consumption, and levels of employment. Structural power is also based in capitalist economic relations and the organization of the corporation itself. To describe this process, William Carroll (2016) distinguishes among operational, strategic, and allocative power. Operational power is the power of corporate management, working through a chain of command, where the power to make decisions decreases as one moves from upper management to workers. Within this pyramidal structure, workers who produce the goods and services have little control over corporate planning or the labour process. Strategic power is the power to determine business strategy and long-term corporate goals, often through the ownership of large blocs of shares. Much like operational power, strategic power is rooted in the "non-democratic character of corporate capital," where workers, communities, and consumers are typically excluded from corporate decision making (one vote per corporate share, as opposed to "one person-one vote") (cf. MacArthur, in this volume). The majority of shareholders are also effectively excluded because share ownership is highly concentrated. Lastly, allocative power belongs to agents and organizations – most notably large financial firms – that control credit and the financial assets to fund new investments.

According to Carroll (2016), corporate boards of directors show traces of all three kinds of power, and strategic and allocative power involve complex alignments of senior managers and major shareholders that cut across individual firms though interlocking ownership and governance structures. Taken together, these relations constitute a structure of "finance capital" – an integrated alliance of banking and industrial corporations under the control of a relatively small group of powerful investors. Finance capital has been integral to the modern capitalist system, "pulling the largest corporations together into configurations of strategic control, capital allocation, and operational command" (Carroll 2016, 14).

Concentrated Ownership and Control

The concentration of corporate ownership is fundamentally a concentration of corporate power. Today, relatively few large enterprises control a dominant proportion of all economic activity. Some corporations even rival nation-states in their size and financial influence. In 2013, thirty-seven of the largest one hundred economies in the world were corporations, with Wal-Mart ranked as the twenty-eighth biggest economy (Ellwood 2015). In fiscal year 2015/16, the world's ten largest transnational corporations (TNCs) had revenues greater than the combined government revenues of 180 countries (Oxfam 2017). In Canada the top sixty Canadian-based corporations listed on the Toronto Stock Exchange (TSX) received 35 per cent of all corporate profits in 1961, rising to 60 per cent by 2010 (Brennan 2012). It is worth noting that this ratio increased even though the number of corporations grew from 153,000 in 1965 to over 1.3 million in 2009. Other economic indicators yield similar conclusions. In the early 1960s, the largest sixty firms on the TSX held 27 per cent of total corporate assets; by 2010, they held 46 per cent (Brennan 2015). In 1988, the year the Canada-US Free Trade Agreement was signed, the top sixty firms accounted for 21 per cent of the equity market value on the TSX. This figure had soared to 65 per cent twenty years later, meaning that the other four thousand or so firms on the TSX accounted for just one-third of the exchange's total equity market value. As Brennan (2012, 20) points out, "when we speak about Canadian business or the corporate sector, we are effectively referring to these 60 firms."

Most large corporations do not accumulate their wealth simply by "slugging it out" in a competitive economic arena. Most grow and expand their operations by combining with other companies through mergers and acquisitions (M&As). At the global level, cross-border M&As now account for approximately 80 per cent of foreign direct investment (FDI) every year, and little of this investment ends up in new productive activity. In Canada, between 1914 and 1988, businesses spent an average of 23 cents on M&As for every dollar spent on expanding industrial capacity (e.g., building new structures, hiring more workers). In the twenty-five years that followed, an average of 93 cents was spent on M&As for every dollar devoted to productive capacity (Brennan 2015).[1]

It is also important to situate levels of corporate concentration alongside the concept of control. In Canada, widely held firms with no identifiable controlling interest are the exception; most major corporations are under the control of a single shareholder or small group of connected shareholders (Burke 2002; Carroll 2004; Morck et al. 2005). For example, one study of 1,120 Canadian-controlled corporations found that only 17.8 per cent did not have a clearly identifiable controlling interest (Gadhoum 2006). It is also common for an individual, a family, or a corporation to acquire enough equity (or voting shares) in a set of companies so as to control them without a major ownership stake. Intercorporate ownership – where many of the top shareholders in large companies are other corporations – and "pyramiding" strategies can tie vast numbers of firms together under a single controlling interest.[2] At the global level, one study estimates that a "super entity" of 147 highly integrated global firms controls 40 per cent of the total wealth in a global network of over 43,000 TNCs (Vitali, Glattfelder, and Battiston 2011).

Compared with other countries, control pyramids are common in Canada, and a considerable portion of Canada's private sector still rests with family-controlled conglomerates (Gadhoum 2006; Morck 2010; Morck et al. 2005). Examples include the Thomson family (Thomson Reuters, Woodbridge), with a net worth of over $41.1 billion; the Rogers family (Rogers Communications), worth $11.6 billion; and the Saputo family (Saputo, Transforce), worth $10.4 billion (*Canadian Business* 2017). Power Corporation, owned by the Desmarais family, had a market capitalization of $12.65 billion in 2017; through pyramiding structures of intercorporate ownership, however, the family actually controlled assets worth $435 billion (Carroll and Sapinski 2018). The key point is that, by tracing links of common ownership and control among dominant corporations and investors, it is possible to reduce the entire economy to a much smaller group of corporate complexes – clusters of companies that are independently registered but effectively controlled by one source.

---

1 According to David Macdonald (2017), Canada's M&A boom has been worth between $100 billion and $200 billion each year since 2011.

2 Morck, Strangeland, and Yeung (2000) assert that a control pyramid ten layers high (with 51 per cent ownership at each level) magnifies a billion dollars of wealth into control of over $840 billion worth of corporate assets.

The Social Organization of Corporate Power

Corporate power does not reside solely in elite control over big industry and high finance. It also has political and cultural dimensions. As Carroll (2016) notes, while some of the work of "manufacturing consent" can be left to the media and intellectuals, business leaders still play an active role in setting the political agenda and recruiting support for a worldview in which the interests of corporations and capitalists are "universalized" as the general interests of society. To accomplish this goal, the business community must have some degree of unity and cohesiveness, with a shared perspective on its long-term goals and how to achieve them.

The growth of corporate power in Canada increased in conjunction with the well-recognized "corporate offensive" that accelerated in the mid-1970s throughout the developed capitalist world. The offensive marked the beginnings of what is now called globalization. Fed up with falling profits, government regulation, and stagnating economic growth, corporate leaders mobilized their collective resources to increase their control over the global economic system and assert themselves more forcefully in the political process (Brownlee 2005; Roman and Arregui 2013). In the Canadian context, the goals of business leaders were consistent with the general objectives of the corporate campaign.

The program of economic and political restructuring that coincided with the corporate offensive later became known as neoliberalism. Neoliberalism brings together a range of elite policy imperatives such as trade and investment liberalization ("free trade"), privatization of publicly owned enterprises, deregulation, the weakening of social programs, emphasis on deficit and/or debt reduction, and business-friendly tax reform (Harvey 2005a; McBride and Shields 1997). Crucially, it involves "rethinking" the role of the state by replacing its functioning with market mechanisms. The transition to neoliberalism was facilitated by economic liberalization and greater corporate mobility, which increased the structural power of corporations and their leverage over the state. However, it was also driven by the social organization of corporate power. Research on the social organization of business power in Canada (e.g., Brownlee 2005; Brym 1985; Carroll 1986, 2004; Clement 1975; Park and Park 1962; Porter 1965) and elsewhere (e.g., Domhoff 1998; Miliband 1969; Mills 1956) focuses on the interlocks and relationships among corporations and corporate elites, as well as the ties between corporations and outside organizations such as policy-planning groups, industry associations, political parties, and think tanks. Much of this literature speaks to the question: to what extent does the business community constitute a "unified" group that can achieve cohesion around public policy issues and promote a common agenda?

A number of "unifying mechanisms" help corporate leaders to foster cohesiveness. As discussed above, heightened corporate concentration has created a situation where there are fewer conflicting interests in the domestic market. Similarly the spread of intercorporate ownership has meant that the investments of top owners and managers have become dispersed among a larger number of companies, providing a structural foundation for the rise of common interests – for example, major Canadian banks collectively own significant pieces of one another through this mechanism. Interlocking directorates represent another core unifying mechanism for corporate leaders. Interlocking directors are individuals who simultaneously sit on two or more corporate boards of directors, whereas interlocking directorates are stable networks of interlocking directors among particular groups of companies. Interlocking directorates draw individual directors into socially integrated networks, just as they draw major firms into a broader network of intercorporate relationships. In this way, they can serve as a means of corporate planning and political and ideological coordination. Studies of interlocking directorates have a long tradition in Canada. The most recent examines Canada's fossil fuel industry (Carroll 2017). It identifies a tightly knit network of carbon-capital firms and their top-level managers (centred in Calgary), which is also heavily interlocked with major financial institutions.[3]

While concentrated ownership, intercorporate ownership, and interlocking directorates create the conditions for corporate cohesion, other mechanisms produce a policy consensus and translate it into action. This largely occurs within the context of a "policy formation network."

The Policy Formation Network

Since the 1980s, Canadian corporations have established a formidable organizational network to influence public policy. In part, this has been accomplished through policy planning organizations. The most influential of these groups are "intersectoral" in that they provide a forum for the development of policies affecting most large companies, regardless of sector or region (e.g., the Business Council of Canada, Canadian Manufacturers & Exporters, the Canadian Chamber of Commerce).

---

3 The fossil fuel sector is also highly concentrated, with the top fifteen revenue earners claiming nearly two-thirds of total revenue. As Carroll (2017, 254) notes, "[t]he architecture of corporate power in and around the carbon-capital sector is integrated, to the point of appearing as an entrenched oligarchy."

Broadly focused intersectoral policy organizations are among the key coordinating points in the capitalist power structure, and are one of most successful means by which corporate Canada has formed and exercised its collective will. By far the most powerful of these groups is the Business Council of Canada (formerly the Canadian Council of Chief Executives). The Council was created in 1976 as part of the corporate offensive to unite Canada's business community and to counter organized labour and the threat posed by state intervention (Davies 1977). Its committees and task forces have covered a wide range of domestic and international policy issues, culminating in many victories in areas such as energy policy, tax reform, deficit reduction, and free trade (Brownlee 2005; Dobbin 1998).

Corporate-oriented think tanks are tightly linked to policy organizations, and a few of the largest – e.g., the Fraser Institute, the C.D. Howe Institute, and the Conference Board of Canada – support the work of the Council to generate consensus. Think tanks have also helped to consolidate neoliberalism through their high volume of research output, well-publicized seminars and conferences, and access to the media.[4] They are also directly tied to Canada's business community through overlapping board memberships (Carroll and Shaw 2001; Fox and Ornstein 1986) and funding. In 2014, twelve of Canada's top fifteen think tanks accepted corporate funding and more than half had officials from large publicly traded corporations on their boards (Thomas 2015).[5]

Although the potential for unity and cooperation does not abolish competition between firms or business sectors, the elite social relations that fortify Canada's business community are different from those of isolated firms struggling in a highly competitive economy. The well-connected "inner circle" leaders at the centre of these networks are in a unique position to promote compromise between competing sectors of capital and to advance the general interests of the corporate sector as a whole (Useem 1984).[6]

---

4 One study found that just four corporate-oriented institutes – the Conference Board of Canada, the Fraser Institute, the C.D. Howe Institute, and the now-defunct Economic Council of Canada – generated 60 per cent of all media citations between 1980 and 1999 (Abelson 2002).

5 Private foundations are also integrated in the network and are an important source of funding for think tanks. The Donner Canadian Foundation, for example, gave $120,000 to the Macdonald-Laurier Institute and over $100,000 to the Fraser Institute in 2017, the latter earmarked for research on the environment and Canada's climate change goals.

6 In Canada, these networks operate nationally but also at the provincial level, as shown in Simon Enoch's (2012) work on corporate power and inner-circle business activism in Saskatchewan.

Political Funding and Corporate Lobbying: A Case Study
of Canada's Fossil Fuel Industry

Corporations also exercise power by other, more direct means. Political
spending allows corporations to play a role in the political decision-
making process. Even if companies rarely – or never – tie specific
demands to the money, their financial support gives them direct access
to political actors. In 2010 the controversial "Citizens United" ruling by
the US Supreme Court removed restrictions on political funding by corporations and other special interest groups, unleashing a flood of corporate money into American politics. Predictably, some of the largest
donors have been businesses and individuals with the deepest pockets,
including the fossil fuel industry and two of its billionaire moguls,
Charles and David Koch. The Koch brothers have tapped their vast
wealth ($46 billion each in 2016) to funnel hundreds of millions of dol-
lars into competitive political races and lobbying activities (Mayer
2016). In Canada, controls on political spending tend to be stricter. At
the federal level, corporations and unions are barred from making
direct political contributions. The provinces vary, however, in the extent
to which they allow or restrict contributions.[7] In 2013, forty-six of the
TSX60 corporations made political contributions to major political parties in one or more provinces (Thomas 2015).

Oil, gas, and coal companies are among Canada's largest political
donors. In British Columbia, researchers with the Corporate Mapping
Project examined fossil fuel industry donations to the Liberal Party and
the New Democratic Party (NDP) between 2008 and 2015 (Graham,
Daub, and Carroll 2017). They found that forty-eight fossil fuel companies and eight industry groups donated nearly $5.2 million to the two
parties, with the vast majority (92 per cent) going to the BC Liberals.
The top ten industry donors – the majority headquartered in Calgary, in
neighbouring Alberta – accounted for 78 per cent of donations, while
just two of these (Teck Resources and Calgary-based Encana) contributed nearly half. As in British Columbia, political parties in Saskatchewan are heavily financed by corporations in Alberta. Between 2008 and
2011, the Saskatchewan Party received over $6 million in corporate con-
tributions, and 42 per cent of its top contributors were Alberta-based
firms (Enoch 2012). These "foreign" donations make sense given the

---

7 At the time of this writing, Alberta, British Columbia, Quebec, Manitoba, and Nova
   Scotia did not allow corporate donations (these restrictions were very recently
   imposed in Alberta and British Columbia), while Ontario and New Brunswick limited
   the size of contributions.

interest in Saskatchewan energy reserves by Alberta's energy sector and its desire to see tar sands oil reach British Columbia waters.

Despite greater controls on political spending inside Alberta, fossil fuel companies have long held a considerable grip on the province's electoral system, especially through the Progressive Conservative (PC) Party. Between 2004 and 2016, the top three donors to Alberta political parties were Encana, Cenovus, and Suncor, three of the largest oil companies in Canada. Sixty percent of their donations went to the PC Party (Schwartz 2018). The influence of the fossil fuel industry has been even more pronounced in party leadership campaigns. For example, Jim Prentice's leadership bid in 2014 raised $1.8 million from over 560 contributors, including between $10,000 and $30,000 each from senior executives at Cenovus, Suncor, and Talisman Energy (Taft 2017).

Clearly, corporate money is no guarantee of electoral success. Although most NDP candidates were significantly outspent in the 2015 Alberta provincial election, the party won a decisive victory. The government immediately moved to limit big money in Alberta politics by banning corporate and union donations to political parties and imposing stricter limits on individual donations (the NDP-Green party coalition in British Columbia has introduced similar legislation). While the impact of these changes remains to be seen, one response has been a sharp rise in third-party spending in the form of "super-PACs" (political action committees) of the kind that now dominate the US electoral system. For example, the Alberta Advantage Fund, a PAC linked to United Conservative Party leader and Alberta premier, Jason Kenney, raised over $635,000 in a three-month period in 2017, more than any of the province's political parties (*CBC News* 2017).

Political donations help to secure access to key decision makers as part of the broader process of corporate lobbying. Since the 1970s, lobbying expenditures by corporations have increased sharply, and are now significantly larger than the value of contributions.[8] Corporations lobby to develop relationships with government officials and regulators, to respond to (or propose) policy initiatives, and to keep policy makers informed of their concerns. Lobbying registries reveal that 956 lobbyists were registered to TSX60 corporations in 2014 (an average of 16 per firm) and that 80 per cent of them had active lobbyists in at least one Canadian jurisdiction (more than half in multiple jurisdictions). Of

---

8 It is estimated that, during the 2000s, the money spent on corporate lobbying and the number of lobbyists employed by corporations doubled in many Canadian jurisdictions (Peters 2012).

the more than 1,800 communications recorded in the federal lobbyist registry in just *one month* in 2014, "301 were in-house lobbyists from corporations, 380 were from industry associations or organizations representing companies, and 352 were consultants hired by corporations" (Thomas 2015, 8).

Fossil fuel lobbying warrants special attention because of its potential impact on environmental and climate policy (see Carter, in this volume). A report by the British organization InfluenceMap (2016) warns that total spending on "obstructive climate policy lobbying" by just two corporations (ExxonMobil and Shell) and the American Petroleum Institute amounts to $114 million a year. Although not as powerful as the US lobby, Canada's fossil fuel industry has a formidable lobbying network that targets energy policy and regulation at all levels of government. It includes the largest fossil fuel and pipeline companies – of the 956 TSX60 lobbyists noted above, 60 per cent are associated with oil and gas companies – as well as industry associations such as the Canadian Association of Petroleum Producers (CAPP), the Canadian Energy Pipeline Association, and the now-defunct Energy Policy Institute of Canada. According to the Polaris Institute, between July 2008 and November 2012, twenty-seven energy companies and eight industry associations held over 2,700 meetings with Canadian public officials; CAPP was the most active, accounting for 536 (Cayley-Daoust and Girard 2012). These lobbying efforts played a key role in the federal Conservative government's 2012 overhaul of Canadian environmental regulations. In British Columbia the ten most active fossil fuel lobbyists – including seven of the province's top ten political donors – reported over 19,500 lobbying contacts with public office holders between April 2010 and October 2016, an average of 14 per business day (Graham, Daub, and Carroll 2017).[9]

The fossil fuel industry's power and influence extend beyond its funding and lobbying efforts. It also funnels money to policy organizations and think tanks. It shapes public attitudes and perceptions through purported citizen-driven campaigns (e.g., CAPP's "Energy Citizens" network) and high-priced advertising and public relations campaigns (e.g., Enbridge's "Life Takes Energy"). It funds "energy and environmental literacy" programs in elementary schools to bring

---

9 Canada's fossil fuel lobby has also been highly active abroad, in alliance with Canadian governments. These efforts have included a series of public relations campaigns aimed at cleaning up the negative image of tar sands oil, and aggressively countering moves by American lawmakers and the European Union to impose restrictions on "dirty oil" imports and their use (see Engler 2014).

industry perspectives to children (e.g., CAPP's "Energy in Action") (Eaton and Day 2020). And it has helped to amass a "carbon-centred scientific-industrial complex" – a densely connected network of universities, research institutes, and extractive firms through which the industry can shape academic and other research priorities (Carroll, Graham, and Yunker 2018).

Corporations and Inequality

Another significant change in Canada's political economy is that levels of wealth inequality have reached unprecedented levels (see Peters, and Fanelli and Hudson, in this volume). In 2012 the eighty-six wealthiest Canadian residents, representing 0.0002 per cent of the population, held the same amount of wealth as the poorest 11.4 million (Macdonald 2014). Statistics on income inequality reveal much the same. From the mid-1970s to the late 2000s, the richest 1 per cent saw its share of income double; the richest 0.1 per cent saw its share triple; and the richest 0.01 per cent saw its share more than quintuple (Yalnizyan 2010; see also Saez and Veall 2005).[10]

The gains made by the proverbial "1 per cent" are driving economic inequality in Canada. But how are corporations and corporate power connected to this trend? One contributing factor is growing corporate concentration. In 1950 the average profit of a top-sixty firm was 234 times larger than the average profit for all firms in Canada; by 2007 that ratio had grown to 14,278, a sixty-fold increase (Brennan 2012). Large corporations occupy a dominant position in the marketplace, as reflected, for example, by their ability to influence prices. They also have greater cash flows and higher profits, which means more money for stock options, dividend payouts, executive salaries, and other forms of compensation. Many of Canada's top income earners are equity owners and/or senior executives in these companies, which helps to explain the tight correlation between the differential performance of the top sixty firms and the rising income share of the richest 0.1 per cent over time. According to Brennan (2012, 29), these firms effectively operate "in a separate political economy." Unlike most other businesses in Canada, they are "price-shapers and price-makers. They have a visible hand in shaping not only the industrial process, but the distribution of income, and therefore the growth or reduction of income inequality as well."

---

10 Using data from Statistics Canada, the Broadbent Institute (2012) claims that, if inflation is taken into account, there was *no increase* in the incomes of the bottom 60 per cent of Canadian families over roughly the same period.

Increases in executive compensation have received a lot of media and policy attention. For years, researchers at the Canadian Centre for Policy Alternatives have documented the growing income gap between Canadian workers and corporate executives (see Macdonald 2018; Mackenzie 2017). They show, for example, that the average pay of Canada's one hundred highest-paid CEOs in 1998 was 103 times that of the average Canadian worker; by 2016 it was 209 times larger. Looking at this gap as a factor of time, by 10:57 a.m. on 2 January, the average CEO will have taken home what the average worker will make all year.

At the global level, increased incomes from capital gains, which mainly benefit the wealthy, are an important contributor to growing inequality (Piketty 2014). In Canada, however, it is interesting to note that wages, not capital gains, appear to be the primary source of surging incomes at the top (Veall 2012; Yalnizyan 2010). In 1946, shortly after the Second World War, Canada's richest individuals relied heavily on unearned income, such as rents from real estate holdings and returns on stock investments. Wages accounted for less than half their incomes. By 2007 wages provided over two-thirds of all income for the richest 1 per cent of Canadians, and almost three-quarters for the richest 0.1 per cent. According to economist Armine Yalnizyan (2010, 15), "the rich today are just as reliant on wages as their primary source of income as the average Canadian. But they are more likely to be handsomely rewarded for the hours they put in." This claim is consistent with research by the Organisation for Economic Co-operation and Development (OECD 2011), showing that a key driver of income inequality has been the growing gap in wages and salaries.

Increasing inequality is also part of a broader shift in the balance of power between capital and labour. At the global level, the share of national income going to workers has trended downward in recent decades, despite consistent growth in the value of what workers produce (Guerriero 2012; Russell and Dufour 2016). According to the International Labour Organization (2017), between 1995 and 2014, workers' wages failed to keep pace with increased productivity and economic growth in 91 out of 133 countries surveyed. In part, this reflects the "super-charged shareholder returns" of recent years, where corporations are paying out an ever-greater share of their profits to their owners (Lawson 2018, 48). But it is also a result of declining trade union density rates, which has occurred alongside outsourcing, the growth in contract labour, and greater worker insecurity (International Monetary Fund 2017) (see also Smith, in this volume). Just as the growth of unions helped to reduce inequality in Canada's post-war period, their decline since the late 1970s has contributed to wage stagnation and the widening income gap (Brennan 2014).

The Impact of Corporate Taxation

Since the 1990s, two key changes in Canadian taxation have enhanced economic inequality. First, the tax bill has been shifted from higher-income to middle- and lower-income families through personal income tax cuts (at the high end) and a reliance on regressive tax measures. Second, the tax bill has been shifted from corporations to families though corporate income tax reductions and a proliferation of business subsidies and tax credits. Tax rates on the wealthiest Canadians have fallen precipitously over the past thirty years, and myriad tax breaks and loopholes have further reduced their tax obligations (Murphy, Veall, and Wolfson 2015; Stanford 2011; Swift 2013). According to Dennis Howlett (2017), executive director of Canadians for Tax Fairness, each year the richest 10 per cent of families receive close to $58 billion in tax breaks. Moreover, Canada's top income earners (especially the top 1 per cent) disproportionately use Canadian-controlled private corporations (CCPCs) to accrue tax benefits (Wolfson et al. 2016).[11]

In the context of globalization, most national governments have reduced corporate taxes in order to attract and retain corporate investment. This process has pitted nations against one another to create favourable business tax environments, and has had a significant impact on developing nations. In Sierra Leone, for example, the government spends nearly as much on tax incentives (largely to attract mining companies) as it does on its development priorities. In 2012, tax expenditures amounted to more than eight times the country's health budget and seven times its education budget (Curtis 2014). Likewise, corporate tax rates have declined in developed nations. In 1990, the average statutory corporate tax rate among the G20 nations – the standard or general rate of corporate tax set by the government – was 40 per cent; by 2015, it was 28.7 per cent (Devereux et al. 2016).

Canada has some of the lowest corporate tax rates in the industrialized world (KPMG 2016; OECD 2018b). In part, this is a product of federal corporate tax cuts that successively reduced the statutory rate

---

11 The advantages gained by earning and retaining income in CCPCs are not included in most studies of income inequality in Canada. If CCPC income is included, the share of income earned by the top 0.1 per cent rises by almost half and the share of the top 0.01 per cent nearly doubles (Wolfson et al. 2016).

from 36 per cent in 1988 to 15 per cent in 2012. Since the late 1990s, the provinces have also cut their statutory rates from an average of 14 per cent to 11 per cent. The *effective* corporate tax rate, however, is what corporations actually pay after exemptions, deductions, deferments, and so on. A study by the US Congressional Budget Office (United States 2017a) found that Canadian corporations pay, on average, an effective rate of just 8.5 per cent, which is far lower than the combined federal and provincial statutory rate of 26 per cent. In fact, some corporations are so adept at tax-reduction strategies that they pay little or no tax at all (Hood 2014). In the early 1950s, individuals and corporations contributed roughly the same amount of income tax to the federal government; in fiscal year 2015/16, Canadians paid $145 billion while corporations paid $41 billion (Oved, Heaps, and Yow 2017). As tax returns from corporate wealth continue to fall, middle- and lower-income Canadians have assumed a greater share of the tax bill, and less money has been made available for public programs and services.

Offshore Tax Avoidance and Evasion

In 2016, 11.5 million files on taxpayer activities were leaked from the database of the Panamanian law firm Mossack Fonseca. The "Panama Papers" exposed how corporations and the wealthy use tax havens and offshore entities to hide their taxable incomes. Later that year, another leak from the Bahamas implicated "thousands" of Canadian companies in questionable tax activities, including the Canadian Imperial Bank of Commerce, Royal Bank of Canada, and Scotiabank, which were found to have administered nearly two thousand Bahamian corporations since 1990 (Cockfield 2017). A third leak in 2017, known as the "Paradise Papers," included additional details on over three thousand individual Canadians and Canadian companies that stash their money offshore. Around the world, the number of high-profile companies accused of dodging their taxes – including Google, Apple, Microsoft, General Electric, Amazon, Ikea, eBay and Starbucks – grows larger every year.

Tax havens provide numerous tax advantages to non-resident TNCs, including tax loopholes, low or zero tax rates, and financial secrecy. For example, a Canadian corporation can shift its profits to a subsidiary in a low-tax jurisdiction that has no genuine connection to the company's economic activities. The company can then repatriate its profits without being taxed, and convert them into dividends, salaries, and bonuses. According to Peter Gillespie (2013, 59), tax havens host "more than two million 'international business corporations,' usually little more than shell companies with a postal address ... One modest building in the Cayman Islands is home to more than 18,000 of these entities." The scale of profit shifting is immense. In 2016, both the British Virgin Islands and the Cayman Islands had greater FDI inflows than Canada, Japan, or France (World Bank 2016). Much of this problem can be explained by the lack of coherence between residence-based taxation and current definitions of corporate residency (Loomer 2015).

At the global level, economist Gabriel Zucman (2015) estimates that corporations and the wealthy are hiding $7.6 trillion from tax authorities.[12] According to Oxfam (2017, 2018), developing nations, which rely heavily on corporate income tax, are losing $170 billion a year in tax revenues. Africa alone loses $14 billion, enough to pay for "healthcare that could save the lives of four million children and to employ enough teachers to get every African child into school" (Oxfam 2017, 5). Looking at Canada, a report by Canadians for Tax Fairness found that Canadian FDI in known tax havens grew from $2.1 billion in 1994 to $284 billion in 2016 (Gibson 2017). Canadian companies employ just one person for every billion dollars invested in Bermuda and six people for every billion invested in the Cayman Islands. Overall, Canadian governments are losing between $10 and $15 billion a year from the use of tax havens by corporations.

Regulating Corporations

Over the course of the past forty years, economic liberalization and greater corporate mobility have increased the structural power of corporations. Governments are now more reticent to impose policies or regulations that could discourage business investment or increase the chances of capital flight. The growing size, power, and mobility of TNCs make them especially difficult to control in the context of a neoliberal ideology that views business regulation in suspicious or even hostile terms. Corporations have a powerful incentive – one might say a fiduciary duty – to fight against regulations that could adversely impact their profits. In tandem, most governments around the world have embraced a *deregulation* agenda. In early 2017, for example, US president Donald Trump signed an executive order that included the implementation of a "two-for-one" rule mandating that, for every regulation introduced by a government agency, that agency must eliminate two existing regulations. Trump's stated goal was to eliminate

---

12 Other estimates suggest higher figures; for an overview, see Cockfield (2017).

business regulations by 75 per cent. The Trump order is not unlike Prime Minister Stephen Harper's "one-for-one" rule, which was the centrepiece of the Conservative government's 2012 Cabinet Directive on Regulatory Management. The directive set a progressively lowered ceiling on the number of federal regulations, and made short-term costs to business the primary test for determining whether a regulatory proposal was accepted. The directive built on regulatory reforms by previous Liberal governments that emphasized "risk management" over "precautionary" approaches to regulatory decision making (Lee and Campbell 2006).

The Harper government's policy changes in the area of environmental regulation are particularly noteworthy. After more than three decades of consistent growth in federal environmental regulations, the government overhauled environmental assessment and energy permit processes with the passage of the 2012 Jobs, Growth and Long-term Prosperity Act and the Jobs and Growth Act (MacNeil 2014). Together, these pieces of legislation led to the cancellation of nearly three thousand environmental assessments; stripped federal protections from more than 99 per cent of Canadian lakes and rivers (previously, close to 100 per cent of Canada's water bodies had been protected under federal jurisdiction); and exempted energy and pipeline development from the requirement to assess (and minimize) the impacts of projects on waterways and the habitats of species at risk. Most of the changes took direct aim at regulations that could inhibit resource extraction and transport.

In recent years, some Canadian regulatory agencies have been subject to "regulatory capture," whereby an industry is routinely able to shape and direct the agency's actions, priorities, and decision making. The result is that regulations are designed to benefit the industry's private interests at the expense of the public's. Bruce Campbell (2015) argues that regulatory capture was a contributing factor in the Lac-Mégantic rail disaster in Quebec, and others have pointed to similar trends involving energy regulators in British Columbia (e.g., the BC Oil and Gas Commission), Alberta, and elsewhere (Parfitt 2019). Charges of regulatory capture have also been made against the National Energy Board (NEB), the former federal agency responsible for regulating the country's oil, gas, and electric utility industries. Although the NEB's mandate was to act independently of industry, researchers have pointed to a "revolving door" relationship between the NEB's executive leadership, energy corporations, and their private sector managers. These close connections facilitated an institutional bias where the interests of regulated companies were often prioritized over those of the public (Brownlee 2018).

Deregulation is driven by the claim that corporate regulation stifles innovation, productivity, and investment, thereby reducing a nation's economic "competitiveness." Although this might be true in some cases, it is challenging to measure the costs and benefits of regulation. Although regulation typically is viewed as imposing additional costs on business, its purpose is often to internalize an "externality" – a cost imposed on a third party in a market transaction. From this perspective, regulation does not impose additional costs, but prevents corporations from externalizing their costs onto workers, consumers, and the environment. Some regulations also save corporations potential future liability or clean-up costs. On the other side of the ledger, quantifying the benefits of regulation – such as the value of better health and safety or clean air and water – is often not possible. The US Office of Management and Budget, which performs an annual cost-benefit analysis of federal regulations to try to quantify their effects, estimates in its 2017 report that the aggregate annual benefits of major regulations amounted to between $287 billion and $911 billion, and the costs at between $78 billion and $115 billion (United States 2017b). Another report, by the Economic Policy Institute, argues that the monetized value of health benefits resulting from the Obama administration's air toxin regulations amount to between $55 billion and $146 billion each year, greatly exceeding the $11.3 billion annual cost of the program (Bivens 2011). Although no in-depth analysis has been undertaken in the Canadian context, these studies challenge the widely held assumption that corporate regulation has a negative impact on the economy and society.

Regulatory Cooperation and Free Trade Agreements

Despite the move towards deregulation, governments can and often do introduce regulations to protect the public interest, such as preventing environmental destruction, protecting consumers from hazardous products, and defending workers against unsafe conditions. Their ability to do so, however, has become more difficult in the context of economic liberalization and free trade. International trade agreements go well beyond "trade" issues and emphasize economic competitiveness. The North American Free Trade Agreement (NAFTA), for example, limited regulations in the name of freedom of investment (see McBride, and Fridell, in this volume). The secretive nature of trade negotiations often means that parliaments and the public do not have the opportunity to scrutinize the regulatory implications of trade agreements before they are signed.

Following the passage of NAFTA in 1993, Canadian governments embraced a process known as "regulatory cooperation" (aligning rules, standards, and regulations) with the United States.[13] Although some degree of regulatory cooperation is to be expected between the two countries, given their level of economic integration, this change has promoted the development of more corporate-friendly regulatory policies, as it assumes that different health, environmental, or consumer protection standards create unreasonable "barriers" to trade. In practice, regulatory cooperation usually means downward harmonization to the cheapest and weakest regulatory option. Key areas of regulatory cooperation to date include chemicals and pesticides, consumer products, food inspection methods, vehicle emissions standards, and the transportation by rail of flammable liquids. According to trade researchers, "the acceptance in Canada of a US norm (supported by the rail industry) allowing a single operator to handle rail shipments of hazardous goods played a role in the 2013 Lac-Mégantic explosion that killed 47 people" (Sinclair, Trew, and Mertins-Kirkwood 2017, 22).

More recently, Canada and the European Union included a stand-alone regulatory cooperation chapter in the Canada-European Union Comprehensive Economic and Trade Agreement (CETA), the first of its kind for a bilateral trade agreement. Canada has also agreed to a similar chapter in the stalled Trans-Pacific Partnership (TPP). These inclusions are aimed at harmonizing regulations and testing the legitimacy of new ones on the basis of how they will affect trade and investment. Similarly, the Trade in Services Agreement (TISA) proposes to harmonize and restrict the regulation of a broad range of privately delivered services. The so-called NAFTA 2.0 negotiations also included expansive rules around regulatory cooperation that could, among other things, significantly delay, weaken, or halt new climate-related policies (Ackerman et al. 2018).

Moreover, free trade and other investment treaties often include investor-state dispute settlement (ISDS) mechanisms. The stated goal of ISDS is to protect foreign investors from arbitrary or harmful government actions. In practice, ISDS provisions go beyond this mandate by empowering foreign investors to sue governments for compensation against measures that might deprive them of future profits. TNCs have used ISDS provisions to challenge a wide range of government policies

---

13 Examples include the 2002 Canada-US Smart Border Declaration, the 2004 "smart regulation" review, the 2007 Cabinet Directive on Streamlining Regulation, and the establishment of a Canada-US Regulatory Cooperation Council in 2011.

and regulations, including measures related to environmental protection (e.g., biodiversity, pollution control, hazardous waste disposal), public health and safety (e.g., drinking water, food safety, pharmaceuticals, anti-tobacco measures), and financial and energy regulation. Their use has expanded from just a few cases a year in the 1990s to over sixty new claims each year.

As of 2017, Canada has been sued more often under ISDS than any other developed country except Spain. With one exception, all of the lawsuits against Canada have come under NAFTA's Chapter 11, and nearly half of all NAFTA-related claims have been made by foreign investors against Canada (Sinclair 2018a). Examples include the Lone Pine Resources challenge to fracking restrictions in Quebec, the S.D. Myers challenge to a federal ban on PCB waste exports, the Bilcon claim against an environmental assessment process in Nova Scotia, and the well-known Ethyl suit against a federal gasoline additive ban (Oliver 2005). At the time of this writing, Canada has paid out more than $314 million related to ISDS claims ($219 million to investors, $95 million in legal costs).[14] Although ISDS decisions cannot force a government to change a law or eliminate a regulation, many contested regulatory proposals have been abandoned or weakened as a result of the process. Governments are, in effect, paying in order to regulate.

Conclusion

The vast majority of corporations in Canada are small businesses: 98 per cent have fewer than one hundred employees and more than half employ between one and four people. Few Canadians take issue with the "mom and pop" shops on Main Street. Many, however, are deeply concerned about the power and policy dominance of Canada's largest firms. Canadians do not trust corporations to regulate themselves, and a large proportion places the onus of rising income inequality on corporations and government policies that favour big business (Broadbent Institute 2017; Lee 2010).[15] Statistics Canada reports that just 30 per cent

---

14 Although Canada has been a frequent target of such claims, Canadian corporations have also sued foreign governments at least sixty times over the past twenty years. Canadian mining companies account for nearly 60 per cent of cases since 2009. Investigations by the *National Observer* found that Canadian corporations have successfully sued governments for roughly $2 billion in damages over the past ten years, mostly in the developing world (Renders 2018).

15 In one poll, 84 per cent of Canadians agreed that corporations "will usually put profit before safety" (Lee 2010).

of Canadians have a "great deal" or "some" confidence in major corporations (Cotter 2015).

Over time, these corporations have grown in size and in reach. They are supported by internal governance structures and external partnerships that increasingly allow them to exert control over the economy and the policy-making process. Social activists and advocacy groups have called attention to growing corporate power and its threat to democracy, with environmental and labour organizations underscoring the need for tougher corporate regulation. In turn, some corporate managers appear to be embracing concepts such as sustainability and corporate social responsibility, but it remains to be seen whether their policies and practices will change substantively to protect the broader public interest. It is for this reason that citizens must continue to acknowledge and challenge growing corporate power, as the welfare and livelihood of millions of Canadians are tied, in a very real way, to the activities, performance, and decision making of Canada's top firms and the people who run them.

9 Co-operatives

JULIE L. MACARTHUR[1]

Introduction

Co-operatives have a long and storied history in Canada, but one that is infrequently featured in either political economy or economic texts (Kalmi 2007; McCollum 2010). This gap is significant, however, because co-operatives represent a unique and potentially transformative form of economic activity that has its roots in collectivist social movements of the eighteenth and nineteenth centuries (MacPherson 2009). One reason for this relative neglect is that the field of Canadian political economy until quite recently has concentrated on issues of nation building, state-society relations writ large, and the role of national versus transnational capital (see the Introduction by Whiteside, in this volume). Prior to the 1990s, scholarship on local and urban economies and interdisciplinary work on firm-level (micro) institutional innovations by political economists were less prevalent, located more often in schools of business or policy, or in disciplines such as geography, rather than political science (Gibson-Graham 2007). However, resurgent interest in alternative economic systems and also how localized institutional innovations may "scale up" to shape national political and economic systems has prompted a re-engagement with the study of co-operatives.

Another reason for the resurgence in academic interest is that co-operatives are currently increasing in number, scope, and impact in Canada as people search for less damaging arrangements for their productive and consumptive activities. The search for eco-social

1 The author would like to thank Celestyna Galicki for her excellent research assistance for this chapter.

alternatives has a well-trodden intellectual history in Canada and abroad, but a number of large-scale destabilizing processes over the past fifty years, including intensifying globalization, the global financial crisis of 2008, and acute awareness of widespread environmental degradation, have reignited this search. The past twenty years in Canada has witnessed increased interest in food co-operatives, car sharing, health, and renewable energy co-operatives, to name but a few recent examples. These new organizations are but one part of a broader "social economy" sector (see also Joy and Shields, in this volume) – a broad umbrella term for a range of voluntary, non-profit, and social enterprise organizations that take seriously social (and sometimes environmental) values as well as economic ones as part of their constitution (McMurtry 2010b; Quarter 1992; Richards 2012).

This chapter explores the nature and significance of co-operatives operating in Canada's political economy. In the following pages, I examine their varied forms and functions together with debates about whether and how co-operatives respond to significant issues around globalization, economic democracy, representation, crisis, and resilience. You will find, as you read the following sections, that co-operatives are no one thing – they are diverse, contested, and adaptable organizations. This makes strong conclusions about their contribution to Canada's political economy difficult to establish; co-operatives can be both radical or conservative, local or international, inclusive or exclusive of marginalized actors. What one can establish, however, are the general contours of the co-operative sector in Canada, key practices, trends, and debates, to which I turn below.

What Is a Co-Operative?

Most Canadians are members of co-operatives, such as Mountain Equipment Co-op and Desjardins, whether they know it or not. As with many aspects of our social and economic reality, Canadians often take for granted the histories, norms, and institutions that underpin our daily lives. According to the International Co-operative Alliance (2020), "[a] co-operative is an autonomous association of persons united voluntarily to meet their common economic, social, and cultural needs and aspirations through a jointly-owned and democratically-controlled enterprise." At their core, co-operatives can be distinguished from shareholder-owned firms in the private sector by the unique principle of "one member, one vote" (cf. Brownlee, in this volume). This means that a co-operative membership allows the member to vote on a business activity – for the board of directors, for example – on an equal basis

Table 9.1. Comparison of Co-operatives and Private Businesses

	Co-operative	Private, Investor-Owned Business
Profit	Surplus refunded to members in proportion to patronage.	Surplus allocated in proportion to investment.
	Surplus earnings or profits belong to members, distributed at annual meeting, yearly as recommended by board.	Surplus earnings or profits belong to the corporation, distributed by board of directors.
Control	A co-operative is a system that guarantees Canadian control of a Canadian enterprise.	Constant vigilance is needed to prevent the takeover of Canadian business and industry by foreign interests.
	Ownership is in the hands of members in the community who use the service.	Ownership is in the hands of investors.
	Control is democratic, with each member having one vote.	Control is unequal: by majority of shares.
	Shares are held in the names of members only and are not traded for speculation.	Shares may be freely traded and fluctuate in value.
	Proxy control is rare.	Proxy control is commonplace.
Organization	An organization of users.	An organization of investors.
	Essentially a union of persons.	Essentially a union of capital.

Source: Gossen (1976), cited in MacArthur (2016, 52).

with other members, rather than by the size of one's economic investment. This prevents a few wealth(ier) owners from controlling the organization, and spreads decision making across the membership.

Co-operatives can operate either on a non-profit basis or a for-profit basis. Profits earned in a co-operative are often called a "surplus," rather than profit, which is then reinvested in the co-operative or distributed to the membership. The fact that co-operatives engage in business activities and often make profits or a surplus distinguishes them from many other actors in the social economy, such as non-profit and voluntary associations (see Joy and Shields, in this volume), although in reality the distinctions are not particularly clear-cut. At the same time, their member orientation differentiates them from more traditional private sector companies, as it is based on the interests of stakeholders in the business, rather than solely on financial interests (Restakis 2010). Despite these distinguishing characteristics, co-operatives vary in their practice of democratic engagement, as well as in their treatment of profit, capital, and commitment to co-op principles (Diamantopoulos 2012; Vieta, Quarter, and Moskovskaya 2016).

Co-operatives are also far more significant economically than many might think, even by traditional measures – employment, sales volume, share of gross domestic product (GDP). Following the 2012 United Nations "Year of the Co-operative," the UN conducted a global census of co-operatives (Dave Grace and Associates 2014). It found that, across 145 countries,

- 2.6 million co-operatives have over 1 billion memberships and clients;
- 12.6 million employees work in 770,000 co-operative offices and outlets;
- US$20 trillion in co-operative assets generate US$3 trillion in annual revenue;
- at the national level, the co-operative economy accounts for 20 per cent of New Zealand's GDP, 18 per cent of GDP in both France and the Netherlands, and 14 per cent in Finland; and
- one in every six people on average in the world is a member or a client of a co-operative.

In the next section, I explore the varied types of co-operatives and their emergence in response to socio-economic crises in more detail.

Crisis: Co-operative Emergence and Differentiation

Co-operatives arose in response to the enclosures of the commons, as well as the effects of industrialization. They were founded on the principles that cooperation and reciprocity, rather than competitive markets, form the natural institutional base of economies. This echoes Karl Polanyi's ([1944] 2001) insight that self-regulating markets are a "dangerous fiction" eroding society. Polanyi articulates the social embedding of markets in society, and the crucial role that social forces and beliefs play in production and consumption. Early co-operators recognized this as well. One important goal for them was to democratize the economy to help counter the power of owners of businesses over their employees and customers. Elite control of access to finance, land, commodities, and basic necessities drew anger and frustration from the working classes. Sometimes the "company store" was the only source of foodstuffs and clothing, charging extremely high prices for basic goods and eroding workers' pay. Worker- or consumer-owned firms, it was argued, could provide products and services at more reasonable prices related to costs, rather than costs plus profits for financial elites, thus providing much needed services and forestalling mass social unrest. John Stuart Mill, in his 1848 *Principles of Political Economy* (IV.7.21), argued that "[t]he form of association, however, which if mankind continue to improve, must be expected in the end to predominate, is not that which can exist between a capitalist as chief, and workpeople without a voice in the management, but the association of the labourers themselves on terms of equality, collectively owning the capital with which they carry on their operations, and working under managers elected and removable by themselves."

Contemporary co-operatives in Canada are part of an international movement for economic democracy begun formally in eighteenth-century Europe – although institutionalized practices of cooperation and reciprocity that underpin co-operatives are far older, and most certainly did not originate in Europe. For Mill, Robert Owen, and the Rochdale pioneers of the 1800s, exploitative relationships between workers and owners could not, and should not, continue. The solution proposed was to "democratize" ownership of firms through the development of a widespread co-operative movement. The Fenwick Weaver's Society in the 1700s was the first recorded consumer co-operative. Together with Robert Owen's villages of cooperation and the Rochdale pioneers in England in the 1830s and 1840s and Germany's co-operative credit banks, these are some of the best-known starting points for the modern movement (MacPherson 2009), providing avenues for a transfer of business control from moneyed elites to a broader swathe of the population.

In Canada, early co-operatives attempted to address the diverse needs of resource extractive forestry and farming communities, as well as francophone communities shut out of access to credit. The geographic scale of Canada and uneven industrial development across the provinces meant that insights and innovations drawn from the UK experience had to be adapted to local circumstances (MacPherson 2009). Early co-operatives focused on farming (dairy and wheat), forestry, and providing retail stores in underserviced communities far from urban centres. In the 1930s and 1940s, Canadian co-operatives also stepped in to provide electricity and then, in the 1960s, natural gas services to rural communities – locations private sector providers could not justify serving due to low returns (MacArthur 2016). Similarly, co-operative housing associations developed through the 1960s and 1970s to fill affordable housing needs not met through private housing markets. Canada's geography, openness to international markets for machinery, and uneven development provided rich and fertile ground for co-operative development, albeit in distinct shapes in the Atlantic region, the Prairie provinces, and industrial centres, as I explore later in the chapter.

The co-operative principles drawn up by the Rochdale pioneers in 1844 were adopted in 1937 by the International Co-operative Alliance, the umbrella organization for co-operatives internationally. This international network was then one of the first non-governmental organizations assigned consultative status at the United Nations in 1946, together with the World Federation of Trade Unions, the International League for Human Rights, and the International Chamber of Commerce. The current international co-operative principles underpinning the international movement are:

1. voluntary and open membership;
2. democratic member control;
3. member economic participation;
4. autonomy and independence;
5. education, training, and information;
6. cooperation among co-operatives; and
7. concern for community.

These principles illustrate the multiple bottom-line approach of co-operatives, which includes a motto of "people before profit" and the integration of social concern and need as central to the organizational form. The principles are periodically revised, most recently in 1995 when the last principle was added to focus on the broader community (rather than just members) and sustainability. Other changes included adding gender as a discrimination to avoid, removing strict limits on dividends to capital investments, and reintroducing the principle of independence present in earlier manifestations but absent in the 1966 principles. While not legally binding, the principles provide an overarching framework for assessing co-operative differences.

One of the puzzles for contemporary political economists when studying the co-operative sector is understanding how these unique institutions either challenge or complement the activities of the other sectors in a mixed economy. This is particularly important in times of economic, social, and environmental crises as we search for solutions to our most pressing challenges (see Carter, in this volume). The Venn diagram in Figure 9.1 illustrates how and why we might conceive of distinct practices in co-operatives and the social economy. The area we call the "social economy" is the segment of productive and consumptive

Figure 9.1. Public, Private, and Social Economy Sectors

Source: Author's adaptation from Quarter and Mook (2010, 11).

activity that is undertaken by civil society. Traditionally much of this activity, based on mutual support, volunteering, and social care, went unrecognized in economic accounting of GDP. However, as neoliberal political economic shifts restructured the balance of state and private sector engagement in the economy through the 1970s and beyond, a larger role began to emerge for this "third" social economy sector (see Joy and Shields, in this volume), including stepping in to provide services from which the state had retreated. Figure 9.1 also illustrates that non-profit elements of the social economy overlap more with public sector organizations than with those oriented more towards trading activities and traditional economic aims, which are closer to actors in the private sector. Co-operatives are organizationally fluid, and can play a role on either side of this third-sector spectrum.

For institutional political scientists such as Nobel Prize winner Elinor Ostrom (1990), the co-operative form provides an important innovation that connects diverse resource users to decision-making control, thus helping to address incentive and rule-making issues that cause environmental degradation. The member-owner connection provides a crucial link to enhancing the quality of information about challenges, effective implementation of solutions, and appropriate rule design. Ostrom's work challenged the idea that the solution to environmental degradation was either privatization or state ownership and top-down regulation. She reframed the issue as one of a need for "polycentric

Figure 9.2. Multiscale Sectors of the Economy

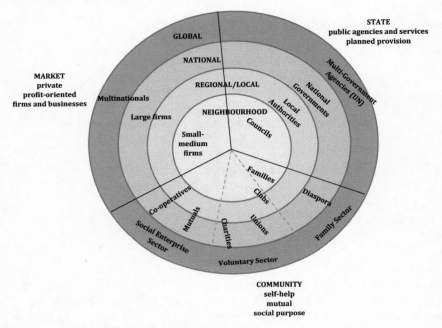

Source: Author's adaptation from Pearce (2003).

governance" at multiple scales, but, importantly, with resource users playing a key role in rule design and enforcement.

One can also construct a multiscaled and more detailed model of where co-operatives fit in the economy (Pearce 2003). Figure 9.2 shows this distinction between the public, private, and social sectors. Within the latter wedge, family, voluntary, and social enterprise wedges operate at local, regional, and global scales. Co-operatives fit most comfortably within this "social enterprise" wedge, as they often operate within the trading economy, providing goods and services for fees, based on members' needs. The scalar element of the diagram, as Ostrom and others have also pointed out, is a crucial addition, because co-operatives and the third sector *may* be locally based, but they may also be internationally active, networked, and often work in complex systems together with public and private actors. The diagram also shows the general driving ethos of each system, as that of "self-help" mutual and social purpose, or public service and planned provision

Table 9.2. Types of Co-operatives

Members	Description	Canadian examples
Consumers	Members are customers (of both goods and services) of the business	Mountain Equipment Co-op (BC), Federated Co-operatives (Saskatchewan)
Producers	Members use the co-operative to sell or market goods; also sell business inputs to members	Agropur (Quebec), Gay Lea (Ontario)
Workers	Members are employees of the business	Girardville Forestry Co-operative (Quebec), Sustainability Solutions Worker Co-op (BC)
Savers/borrowers	Members are customers of the financial institution	Desjardins (Quebec), VanCity (BC), The Co-operators (Ontario)
Multiple stakeholders	Newer form; different members all form the co-operative: workers, service users, and locals, e.g., health care and tourism co-ops	La Corvée (Quebec), Co-op de solidarité en soins et services de St-Camille (Quebec)
Sharing platform users	Emerged as part of peer-to-peer digital economy. Co-operatives provide a digital platform for service exchange (transport, housing, goods sharing, etc.)	Modo Car-sharing (BC)

Source: Author's adaptation from Co-operatives and Mutuals Canada (2020); MacArthur (2016); MacPherson (2009).

(the public sector; cf. Evans, in this volume), or the profit and private gain orientation of the private sector. I return to issues of globalization and scale illustrated in the diagram later in the chapter.

What the two diagrams do not show is the significant variation that exists in the nature of the membership, and thus the structure, of co-operatives (see Table 9.2). As "member-driven" organizations, the type of co-operative can say much about the the type of issues it is trying to address in the economy, as well as the likely interests, needs, and development of the organization. A workers' co-operative, for example, derives organizational control from the labour force of the business (worker-owners). The voting members of consumer co-operatives are the purchasers of the goods and services of the co-op, whereas producer co-operatives are organized around the interests and needs of manufacturers, farmers, or service providers. Credit unions are a type of financial consumer co-operative where the members are the borrowers and savers. More recently we have also seen the rise of multistakeholder co-operatives. In these organizations, workers, service users, and sometimes other local interested parties in a community come together as members of the new entity. Finally, platform co-operatives are a very recent innovation in response to opportunities and challenges presented by the digital economy. These co-ops provide electronic platforms for the exchange of goods and services. In the private sector, platforms such as Air BnB and Uber earn profits from the activities of participants. Platform co-operatives, in contrast, provide a mechanism for the value to be retained by providers and service users, rather than by investors, as part of a new form of digital co-operativism (Bauwens and Kostakis 2016).

Legally, setting up a new co-operative requires identifying the membership link in the organization and the mechanism for members' governance. Generally, members pay a share, sometimes just a few dollars but other times much more than that, to join and participate in the activities of the co-op. Setting up a co-operative in Canada comes with particular benefits and costs. In the benefits column, the co-op might pay different tax rates than a shareholder-owned company if it is structured as a non-profit, or even if it produces a surplus if much of that is returned to members through patronage allocations (Brouard, McMurtry, and Vieta 2015; Quarter 1992). Some jurisdictions, like Quebec, have a well-developed system to encourage and support co-operative development with advice and some grant schemes (Neamtan 2010). On the negative side, the lack of knowledge about co-operatives, the laws that govern them, and the principles underpinning them means that many banks, lawyers, and business advisors are ill equipped to help develop and finance new co-operatives. Lack of awareness of the sector can be costly, frustrating, and time consuming.

Changing Times: Co-operative Growth and Distribution in Canada

Studying co-operatives in Canada is more challenging than studying traditional private sector organizations because state agencies do not collect reliable information on the co-operative sector,[2] although

2 Data on non-financial co-operatives come from an annual survey now conducted by Innovation, Science and Economic Development Canada, so they do not represent the whole sector. Data on financial co-operatives, however, come from Statistics Canada, and is not based on the same voluntary survey. For a discussion on data issues, see Duguid and Karaphilis (2019).

Table 9.3. Growth of Canadian Non-financial Co-operatives, 2010 and 2018

	2010	2018	Percentage increase
Total number of co-ops	5,094	5,846	15
Assets ($ billions)	26.5	42.5	55
Business volume ($ billions)	33.8	49.1	45
Total number of employees	86,452	103,470	20

Sources: Canada (2018, 2019c).

efforts by actors such as Co-operatives and Mutuals Canada and Innovation, Science and Development Canada have done much to close this gap in recent years. We now know that, in 2018, there were more than eight thousand active financial and non-financial co-operatives in Canada, with more than $502 billion in assets – $460 billion by financial co-operatives, $42 billion by non-financial co-operatives – and 31.8 million members (Canada 2019c; Duguid and Karaphillis 2019). Real estate rental, wholesale and retail trade, and health care and social assistance made up more than half of the 5,800 non-financial co-operatives' activities in 2018. Nearly half of these (49 per cent) operated solely with volunteer labour; the vast majority, however, had between 1 and 99 employees, and classified as a small and medium enterprise. Industry Canada reported in 2019 that there were 1.17 million small and medium enterprises in the country (including co-operatives) (Canada 2019b). So, although the financial and non-financial co-operatives sector is larger than many might think and has grown in number, financial assets, activities, and employees, it is still a relatively small part of the larger Canadian economy (see Table 9.3). More than two-thirds of Canadian co-operatives operate as non-profits. Despite this, co-operatives reported paying out $637 million in dividends and patronage returns to their members and service users (Canada 2019a).

Financial co-operatives such as Desjardins and VanCity credit unions are particularly strong in Canada, with more than one in three Canadians holding membership in one. In 2016, according to a Canadian Credit Union Community Impact Report (CCUA 2017), 571 financial co-ops had more than 10 million members, 58,000 employees, and $379 billion in assets (Table 9.4). By comparison, Manulife, one of Canada's largest companies, had assets in 2016 of $705 billion and 34,500 employees.

Table 9.4. Financial Co-operatives (Credit Unions,
Caisses Populaires), Canada, 2016

Number of financial co-ops	571
Members	10,206,049
Assets	$379,424,000,000
Total number of employees	58,000

Source: CCUA (2017).

There are also significant differences in how concentrated co-operatives are in particular provinces. Nearly half of all financial co-op assets and members are in Quebec, while British Columbia has the second-largest concentration by members and assets, with 19.0 per cent and 19.6 per cent of the Canadian total, respectively. This is notable, given that Ontario is the province with the highest population, but perhaps not surprising, since most of the country's private banks are headquartered in Ontario, long the seat of finance capital in Canada. Since credit unions evolved to serve underserved populations and financial needs, it makes some sense that they are comparatively weaker in Ontario, but that province still accounts for the third-largest concentration of members and assets in Canada, at 15.8 per cent and 14.3 per cent, respectively. When provincial populations are taken into account, Saskatchewan and Manitoba also have relatively high financial co-operative membership numbers (CCUA 2017, 13).

Non-financial cooperatives by number are also concentrated most heavily in Quebec (44 per cent), with Ontario (19 per cent) and Saskatchewan (8 per cent) coming second and third, respectively. Membership numbers, however, are highest in British Columbia, with 1.9 million, and Ontario, with 1.4 million. Given the population difference between the two provinces, this is particularly significant, and is likely due to the headquarters in British Columbia of large co-operatives such as Mountain Equipment Co-op. As shown in Table 9.5, Quebec is dominant in terms of its shares of the number of co-ops, employment, and overall sales. This is likely due to the province's strong and enduring regulatory and policy support for the co-operative sector. Adjusted for population, Saskatchewan also represents a strong co-operative presence in the country.

The vast majority of Canadian co-operatives are consumer co-ops like Mountain Equipment Co-op, but there are also many multistakeholder, producers', workers', and financial co-operatives, as Figure 9.3 shows (Canada 2019c).

Canadian co-operatives are also spread across a wide range of economic sectors, from food to finance and health care to housing (Figure 9.4).

Table 9.5. Non-financial Co-operatives, by Province, 2018

Province	Share of number of co-ops (%)	Share of Assets
British Columbia	7.6	4.7
Alberta	8.5	10.8
Saskatchewan	8.0	27.2
Manitoba	4.6	4.4
Ontario	18.9	12.5
Quebec	44.4	38.4
New Brunswick	2.0	0.3
Nova Scotia	3.6	0.4
Prince Edward Island	1.2	0.5
Newfoundland and Labrador	0.6	0.2
Territories	0.7	0.6

Source: Canada (2019a).

Figure 9.3. Co-operatives by Type, Canada, 2018

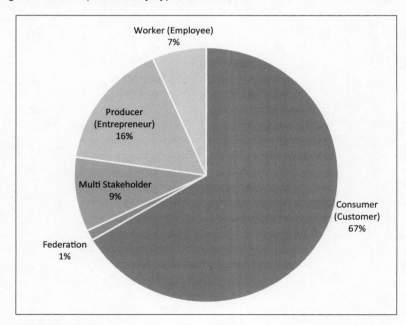

Source: Canada (2019d).

Figure 9.4. Co-operatives in Canada by Activity

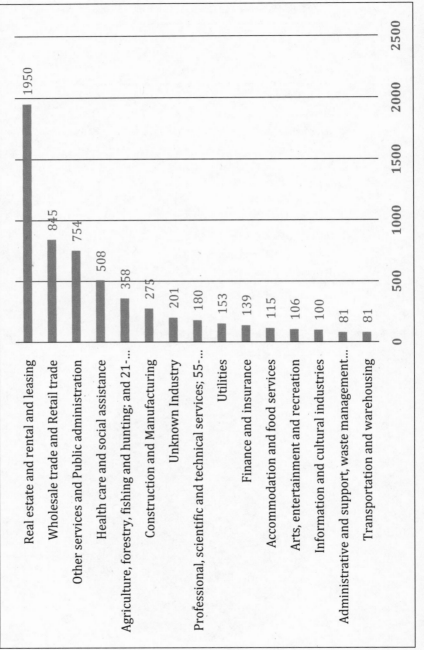

Source: Statistics on Canadian Non-Financial Co-operatives, Open Canada, https://open.canada.ca/data/en/dataset/f241c519-a250-456b-9b1d-a1d48330820

More than half of all non-financial co-operatives are involved in retail trade, with other large concentrations in construction and manufacturing, as well as agriculture, forestry, and mining. Figure 9.4 illustrates the sheer variety of industries and activities undertaken by these member-owned organizations.

Of course, regional and provincial differences within these industry numbers exist due to historical patterns of industrial development (see Smardon, and McBride, in this volume), as well as legacies of specific policies brought in by governments, such as co-operative rural electrification in Alberta in the post-war period. Agriculture, forestry, and fishing co-operatives are most prominent in Quebec, while co-operative utilities for gas and electricity are concentrated largely in Alberta. Construction and manufacturing co-operatives exist almost exclusively in Ontario and Quebec, while those in wholesale and retail trade (such as the Co-op stores across western Canada) are concentrated in Saskatchewan, Alberta, Manitoba, and British Columbia. One stand-out bar in Figure 9.4 is the high number of co-operatives in real estate. Ninety-seven percent of these are non-profit housing co-operatives, concentrated in Quebec, Ontario, and British Columbia. As housing affordability continues to challenge citizens, particularly in cities such as Vancouver and Toronto, these co-operatives provide an important space for housing based on maintenance and cost, rather than on profitability.

Regulating Co-operatives

The regulatory system for co-operatives differs significantly by province, which accounts for many of the differences in distribution and type seen above. This is because most Canadian co-operatives are regulated at the provincial level by legislation outlining rules around reporting, incorporation, and the user-member link. Those that trade across provincial boundaries (such as some credit unions) fall under federal law. Financial co-operatives are regulated separately by the federal Department of Finance. These regulations have evolved over time as new co-operative activities have developed. For example, when renewable electricity co-operatives in Ontario wanted to sell their solar- and wind-generated electricity to the province, they had to contend with a rule that co-operatives need to sell to their members. The emergence of digital and peer-to-peer platform co-operativism likely will also require regulatory attention should these types of co-ops become significant economic actors.

At the federal level, responsibility for co-operatives traditionally sat within the Department of Agriculture and Agri-Food, owing to the historical roots of the sector. In 2012, however, this responsibility was moved to Industry Canada to "better represent the current diversity of businesses that are innovating with the co-operative model, and was a step toward equal access to business support programs" (Richards 2012). In 2017, the federal government passed Motion M-100, establishing a framework to recognize and promote the co-operative model in Canada (Canada 2017).

In addition to formal rule making, a network of associations also provides guidance and resources for co-operatives in Canada. Provinces and territories each have associations to connect, educate, and advocate for the interests of co-operative businesses. At the federal level, Co-operatives and Mutuals Canada is the Ottawa based advocacy and research group for both anglophone and francophone co-ops. One key role these organizations play is helping render the sector visible through supporting research on the co-operative difference and the role that these organizations have played in addressing contemporary challenges. The next section outlines one way in which Canadian co-operatives have demonstrated some unique advantages during the post-2008 era, as governments to differing degrees have adopted austerity measures and retreated from various forms of social service provision.

Crisis, Change, and Co-operative Resilience

Just as early co-operatives were the result of resistance to unfair economic relations, today's co-operatives are also playing a key role in addressing financial and other crises. During the COVID-19 pandemic, co-operatives were among the first firms to respond with differentiated hours for vulnerable citizens, shifting production to health care products, and coordinating rental and mortgage relief (Vieta and Duguid 2020). Following the global financial crisis, the number of co-operatives surged in some countries as citizens sought alternative mechanisms for meeting their needs. For example, in Germany, in 2008 (the height of the recession), twice as many co-operatives were started than in the year before (Birchall and Ketilson 2009). In addition to increased interest, research suggests that co-operatives might have greater resilience during crises than other forms of enterprise. For example, although employment in in Italy as a whole stagnated from 2007 to 2011, with declines in industry and agriculture, employment in the co-operative sector grew by 8 per cent (1.9 per cent per year) (Smith and Rothbaum 2013). Burdín and Dean (2012) found that cooperatives have a 24–38 per cent lower hazard of exit than conventional firms when controlling for other firm characteristics. A study of several thousand French firms

Table 9.6. Co-operative and Business Survival Rates, Quebec

	Average survival rate (%)		
	After 3 years	After 5 years	After 10 years
Co-operatives	75	62	44
Quebec companies	48	35	20
Co-operative survival advantage	1.56 times greater	1.77 times greater	2.2 times greater

Source: Author's adaptation from Clément and Bouchard (2008, 22).

found that co-operatives use their capital and labour more effectively than do traditional firms (Fakhfakh, Perotin, and Gago 2013). Moving to Canada, Clément and Bouchard (2008) have found similar resilience effects, with ten-year survival rates among co-operatives in Quebec more than twice those of conventional businesses (see Table 9.6).

Co-operative banks and credit unions were also more resilient through the financial crisis than were commercial banks (Birchall 2013), which is particularly important given the extent of Canadian banking sector fragility identified by Seccareccia and Pringle (in this volume). (Ferri and Kerola (2014), who analyse changes in banks' credit ratings during the crisis, show that co-operative banks were downgraded to a lesser degree than were shareholder banks. They attribute this to the lower incentives among co-operatives to make risky decisions and to the loyalty of co-operatives' customers.

The reasons for the resilience of co-operatives are complex, but some important factors are that members' control leads to

- reluctance to exit market activities (Burdín and Dean 2012);
- increased willingness to accept survival measures to stave off closures or job losses (Carini and Carpita 2014);
- easier mobilization of co-operative community links to keep businesses running in tough times, including help from other co-operatives (Roelants et al. 2012); and
- increased likelihood of innovating and adapting, particularly on the part of workers' co-operatives, as worker-members can benefit directly (Smith and Rothbaum 2013). For example, workers' co-operatives tend to reduce the number of employees less than for-profit enterprises during an economic crisis (Carini and Carpita 2014). Moreover, in workers' co-operatives, the members can influence business strategies, and democratic decision making can help legitimate changes required for the firm's survival.

Despite the historical emergence of co-operatives in response to crises and evidence suggesting there might be advantages to the co-operative form, challenges also abound. Crises, financial or otherwise, can also lead to co-operative degeneration, where principles such as one-member-one-vote or inclusivity might be abandoned (Narvaiza et al. 2017). Such co-operatives also might begin to restrict membership and to rely on contracting out to provide member surpluses. Co-operative goals also might be replaced by capitalist goals such as profit seeking, or control could become concentrated in the hands of a dominant elite of executives, with little board control. Still, in principle, and sometimes in practice, co-operatives represent a deeply rooted alternative economic form. In the next section, I turn to how radical the co-operative institutional form is in these challenging times.

Conflict: Radical, Reformist, or Conservative Co-operatives

The international co-operative principles and the social movement history of co-operatives suggest there are some unique characteristics of the sector in Canada's political economy. However, the sector has also long been accompanied by critical reflections on how effective this organizational form is. Nova Scotia co-operative pioneer Alexander Fraser Laidlaw (1908–80) put the challenge as follows:

> No co-operative exists in a vacuum but must operate in a given economic and social environment. It must strive, of course, to modify and improve that environment, but it cannot do so unless it recognizes the overriding problems, first of the immediate community, then of the larger region, and finally of the nation and indeed of humanity itself. In the long view the question will be asked: what have these co-operatives and the co-operative movement as a whole done to help people wrestle with the difficulties of life? What is the relevance of co-operatives to the nation's basic problems? (Laidlaw 1980)

Complement or Challenge?

For some, the co-operative form's reliance on market mechanisms to meet social needs blunts the radical potential of the sector to address structural inequality. Many co-operatives do little to challenge key elements of the capitalist system that radical political economy perspectives would seek to change: private property rights, consumer choice, and a current focus on the responsibilization of citizens to solve their own challenges through "self-help" (Argüelles, Anguelovski, and

Dinnie 2017). Some advocates of localized alternative economies through co-operativism are deeply sceptical of the role of the state and its ability to solve crucial challenges such as climate change and poverty. This might lead them to dismiss or deligitimize political movements aimed at "recapturing" the state and instead to focus on socio-economic, rather than politico-institutional, change (Carter 1996).

Co-operative advocates would respond by pointing to the value of a networked sector focused on providing for social needs that is not dependent on any particular party's being in power or government for support. The ethos of "self-help" through mutual cooperation is a virtue, and the emphasis on capitalist market mechanisms has more to do with the current context of co-operativism in the West than with any particular feature of the organizational form. Co-operative and social economy systems in this view can help to build *counterveiling power* that can be mobilized to solve pressing challenges (Wright 2010). That said, some scholars, such as Vieta, Quarter, and Moskovskaya (2016), have also argued that particular co-operative forms are less likely to valorize marketization. They advocate for the increased development of co-operatives that do not rely on individual share capital (financial investments) from members, in order to enhance the inclusivity of the organizations and minimize the role of capital within them. Huertas-Noble et al. (2016) have suggested that co-operatives should be unionized, so that even if they were not run by worker-members, a strong labour voice would be included in the organization and, again, co-operatives could benefit a wider group of actors.

Other criticisms of the co-operative model come from the perspective that they might not be the most efficient or effective way to solve particular challenges. Molk (2014), for example, has argued that they might have higher financing and decision-making costs than more conventional firms. Rather than developing an alternative economy independent from the state, this suggests that, for co-operatives to flourish, state support is essential. Indeed, as we have seen, in Canada the province with the most robust co-operative development system, Quebec, also has the largest number of co-operatives (Diamantopoulos 2012).

Inclusivity: An Ongoing Challenge

Co-operatives have a dual nature as both an enterprise and a social movement, and are not immune to many of the challenges of society more broadly: some are well resourced, skilled, and mobilized communities; others less so. Indeed, some analysts have pointed out that conflicts between co-operative members can pose a significant challenge, particularly conflicts between more entrepreneurially minded and more socially minded members (lliopoulos and Valentinov 2017). The "shared values" and community spirit that are prized in co-operatives can also mask the degree to which values are shared because of the homogeneous backgrounds of members – often white and middle class. One can certainly question the degree to which co-operatives actually embody the values of the sector, particularly those around issues of democratic participation and inclusivity. Sobering (2016) and Miller (2012) have pointed out, for example that women are better off in collectivist organizations such as co-operatives than in traditional firms, but even in the former they are still significantly underrepresented in decision making. The International Co-operative Alliance established a Gender Equality Committee as long ago as 1965 to investigate and address some of these issues, but much work remains (Fraune 2015).

Thus, even though the international co-operative principles begin with open and voluntary membership, co-operatives are by no means devoid of parochial and exclusionary practices of marginalized actors. The challenge has been to use the democratic form and the principles as mechanisms for broadening co-operatives' economic power over time. McMurtry (2010b) indicates that democratic workplace control can help empower workers to challenge inequities. Worker-run organizations also might be more likely to give historically marginalized groups access to skills and knowledge (Meyers and Vallas 2016), and to pressure decision makers on issues such as work/life balance and gender equality (Matthew and Bransburg 2017). The Canadian Credit Union Association recently reported that more than 45 per cent of its volunteer directors were women, "well above the international goal of having more than 30% women on boards" (CCUA 2017, 5). Significant issues remain with respect to the gendered nature of volunteer versus paid positions, but on issues of inclusiveness and diversity, the co-operative sector is making progress and engaging with these debates.

In Canada, the inclusion of Indigenous Peoples in the co-operative sector (or their exclusion from it) is also a key issue. Sengupta (2015) argues that early co-operatives helped to establish settler control over land and resources, In more recent years, MacPherson and other scholars have highlighted how the co-operative form has been taken up by and benefited many Indigenous communities (White 2018). Sengupta (2015) defines Indigenous co-operatives as those located in and owned by Indigenous people, or with primarily Indigenous members but managed by others (see also Starblanket and Coburn, in this volume). Today, examples of Indigenous co-operatives include Great Bear Co-op and Neechi Foods, Northern Saskatchewan fisheries co-operatives,

Buffalo Narrows Sawmill Co-operative, Arctic Co-operatives Limited, SEED Winnipeg, and the Northern Saskatchewan Trappers Association (Sengupta 2015; Thompson et al. 2014; Wuttunee 2010).

Economic Democracy and Co-operative Scale

Globalization and market competition are putting pressure on co-operatives to grow and internationalize to remain competitive. Although many people might assume that co-operatives are small and local, some are truly multinational (e.g., Mondragon). This "scaling up" of co-operatives is accompanied by both challenges and benefits. Increasing the size of the organization introduces a higher degree of complexity, and can erode participatory elements in favour of managerialism and efficiency gains (Ferri and Kerola 2014). The development of networked and federated co-operatives is one way through which organizations can keep a degree of collective decision making in each unit, while still collaborating strategically at a broader scale.

Bretos and Marcuello (2017) highlight a number of tensions and opportunities for the internationalization of co-operatives. They face legislative barriers, geographic and cultural barriers, investment-related barriers (in raising funds, for example), and competitive barriers with existing firms. Internationalization, however, also presents opportunities to develop size and resources to compete and in some areas to supplant the activities of more profit-oriented firms. Internationalization can also lead to organizational learning and facilitate the development of the co-operative sector in other countries.

Conclusion

Co-operatives are a complex set of organizations with a long history in Canada. Understanding them requires awareness of their institutional variety and complexity. It also requires a political economy analysis situating them within the specific historical, geographic, and political contexts that shape their activities. For some, co-operatives are the backbone of a growing alternative economy that puts "people before profit." For others, they are a slight modification of business as usual, providing economic benefits for members, but not a radical challenge to other forms of business. In reality, co-operatives play multiple roles and resist simplistic characterizations. Co-operative members come from across the political spectrum, and the sector holds billions of dollars in assets. Most Canadians are members of financial or non-financial co-operatives, and are increasingly turning to shared and collaborative models. Rural areas have long been familiar with agricultural and retail co-operatives, with extensive farm, natural gas, and electricity networks developed in the inter-war and post-war periods. Today we see a renaissance in new co-operative forms and activities in urban areas for food production and distribution, transport, tools, and digital platforms, and evidence that these organizational forms might be more economically resilient in times of crisis. In a Canadian post-pandemic recovery plan, co-operatives can play an important role in building resilience and democracy, particularly if they are supported to scale up. Co-operatives in Canada are, as they ever have been, evolving, contested, and complex institutions of economic democracy. They contain both the roots and traditions of mutualism, as well as the seeds of a new, more just, and inclusive modern political economy.

10 The Political Economy of the Non-profit Sector

MEGHAN JOY AND JOHN SHIELDS

Introduction: Why Look at the Non-profit Sector through a Political Economy Lens?

Employing a political economy lens to examine the non-profit sector offers valuable insights into both historical and contemporary capitalist society. Such a lens helps to uncover the changing structures of power relations, and reveals that non-profit organizations (NPOs) have always been on the front lines of growing inequality and social exclusion, often providing vital services to disadvantaged communities. The state also "partners" with NPOs to deliver public programs that in some cases were previously offered directly by government and are consequently agents of the state (see Evans, in this volume). In this way, the line between the state and the NPO sector is blurred (see Evans, and Graefe, in this volume). NPOs, however, are also semi-autonomous entities and important agents and resources for progressive change in society (Deverteuil 2016; Moreno, Shields, and Drolet 2018). Hence, the NPO sector embodies many of the tensions and contradictions at work within capitalist society, and is strategically positioned to shed new light on these dynamics.

All too commonly, the NPO sector has been defined in the negative for what it is not – namely, not part of the for-profit or government sectors (cf. MacArthur, in this volume). The NPO sector does in fact rest between the market and the state (OECD 2003, 10), but it is also distinguished by various positive qualities or features – most notably, as mission-driven organizations (Emmett and Emmett 2015, 5) very often guided by social justice orientations. NPOs are private organizations that operate within the public realm and are consequently best understood as being part of civil society. In fact, they have been described as the organizational face of civil society (Fumkin 2009). As civil society organizations, NPOs are a "reservoir of caring, cultural life and intellectual innovation," (Edwards 2004, 14), engaging people in acts of citizenship building. Community-based NPOs "are as much about participation as provision; as much about citizenship as service" (Nowland-Foreman 1996, 4).

Service and advocacy are two key functions that NPOs fulfil in society. These organizations provide a host of supports to members and the general public, and in particular to vulnerable populations with limited access to services provided by the family, private, and state sectors. The service work they engage in tends to be "embedded within a deeper ethic of caring and giving, which enhances the quality of services offered" (Shields, Baines, and Cunningham 2017, 33). Many NPOs also engage in advocacy, promoting the interests, causes, and social justice goals of their missions. In this way, independent NPOs are a vital "voice" for the communities they serve and represent, promoting democratic engagement.

The NPO sector is large, diverse, and growing. The statistical measuring and tracking of the sector, however, has been sporadic and highly uneven. This is due to the challenges of accurately surveying the many small organizations that compose the sector, often run solely by volunteers. Another recent challenge has been austerity-induced cuts at Statistics Canada, which has limited the agency's ability to conduct formal national surveys of the sector. These surveys are consequently now quite dated. Recognizing the limitation of the numbers, figures show that, in 2004, there were 170,000 formally organized NPOs, of which 85,000 were registered charities (Imagine Canada n.d.). It is estimated that some 360 charities are added to the total each year and that the NPO sector is outpacing the growth of both the state and market sectors (Emmett and Emmett 2015, 15). This is perhaps indicative that the sector is not just filling gaps in state provision, but is also taking over core policy domains, such as affordable housing, immigration settlement services, and home care support for the elderly. In effect, the sector's public role is growing – paradoxically to address growing social diversity and to manage public sector costs.

The NPO sector in 2017 contributed material value worth 8.5 per cent of Canada's gross domestic product (GDP) and made up 2.4 million jobs (Statistics Canada 2019). Additionally, based on the most recently available data (from 2013), the sector engaged some 18 million volunteers. These statistics make Canada's NPO sector the second largest in the world just behind that of the Netherlands (Imagine Canada n.d.). Some non-profit charities are large and form part of the para-public sector (hospitals, universities, and colleges), and account for much of the sector's contribution to the GDP. The largest core non-profit bodies contribute an estimated 2.4 per cent of Canada's GDP, more than three times the share of the auto industry (Imagine Canada n.d.). Most core NPOs, however, are small, with revenues below $100,000 (P.R. Elson 2009). In addition, there is a huge number – many times that of formally organized NPOs – of "below-the-radar" entities run totally by volunteers, with extremely limited budgets, and not captured by standard statistical surveys. Such bodies are quintessentially local, and likely constitute the bulk of unreported voluntary activity. This part of the sector is also expanding (McCabe and Phillimore 2018). Hence, the contemporary NPO sector is a substantive component of Canada's political economy.

Despite these trends, there has been very little critical analysis of NPOs either in particular fields or as a sector as a whole through a political economy frame. Much of the literature that does exist focuses on mainstream public administration/management, which examines the sector as an alternative public service delivery agent. There is also an extensive body of American-based literature rooted in a liberal paradigm. This perspective is centred in the early nineteenth-century observations of the French social observer Alexis de Tocqueville, in his book *Democracy in America*. He argued that America's democratic impulse, in contrast to traditionally bound Europe, rested on its genius for nurturing civil society organizations (Ott 2001, 2–4). Such American exceptionalism was seen as a major factor behind the limited size of the state in that country, as voluntary organizations took up the role of addressing many of the social and human needs in American society.

Until quite recently, however, the NPO sector was largely invisible, and hence ignored. Only in the past twenty years or so has it come to be understood and defined, by both itself and others, as an actual sector (Laforest 2011b). Even so, NPOs often are cast as a "third sector" that is somehow lesser than the public and private sectors. At the same time, considerable hope and expectations are placed on the sector to address state fiscal crisis and austerity, the decline of social capital and civic engagement, and diverse and local service needs, as well as to solve social problems through innovative service programs (Evans and Shields 2018).

These changes within the sector illustrate a clear need for an explicit political economy framework with which to understand the sector and how it connects to broader political, economic, and socio-cultural processes. We argue that, through a political economy examination of the non-profit sector, political projects associated with the contradictions of capitalist society can be better understood (see Table 10.1). For instance,

Table 10.1. A Political Economy Examination of the Non-profit Sector

Political Projects	Classic Liberal Individualism	Social Liberalism	Neoliberalism	Communitarian Neoliberalism	Austerity Neoliberalism
Political economy	Pre-welfare state era Laissez-faire capitalism Lack of social policy Expanding social problems	Welfare state era Regulated capitalism Large-scale social policy	Economic deregulation New public management Marketization and privatization of social services	Third way era Continued neoliberalism Service partnerships	Limited communitarianism (big society) Service cuts
Role of NPO sector	Charity in cities Philanthropy Limited state support (filtered through local government) leads to professionalization	NPOs part of "social contract" as junior partners State and NPO sector grow in tandem Services to fill gaps in large-scale social policy programs Advocacy supported	Alternative service delivery contracts with state (competitive, strict accountabilities) Funding cuts Precarity Reduced advocacy and service the most vulnerable	Partnerships coexist with alternative service delivery and competitive contract funding Targeted place-based service delivery Social investment in human capital to local fix social problems No return to support advocacy	Privatization and marketization through new policy tools (social enterprise, social impact bonds) Crackdown on advocacy Emphasis on social problem "solving" that delivers value for money

although the NPO sector has not been seen as central to neoliberal restructuring, the trend towards greater NPO involvement in society has dramatically shifted the mixed social economy to enhance NPOs' role in social service provision, with significant consequences for both the sector and for social policy more broadly (see Graefe, in this volume). Because the NPO sector is so large, we focus more specifically on the social and human service NPOs, since their reorientation is particularly revealing regarding the shifting nature of capitalism, and since they constitute a central component of the core NPO sector.

Changes: Towards a Professionalized Non-profit Sector

At the height of the Industrial Revolution in the nineteenth-century pre-welfare state era, the role of "charities" greatly expanded in countries such as Canada, Britain, and the United States. During this period of classic liberalism (see Table 10.1, under Classic Liberal Individualism), social policy was viewed primarily as a private concern and poverty a consequence of individual moral failure, not the result of the structural dynamics of capitalist political economy and ideological forces rooted in private property, hierarchy, traditional family structures, and class, race, and gendered relations. The so-called deserving poor – orphans, widows, the disabled – were considered worthy of relief (basic subsistence support), but it was to be provided primarily through the private channels of charity, not by the state (Blake and Keshen 2006). In this early period, NPOs, including those in Canada, embodied this voluntary charity model, which was as much a moral regulator of the underclass as a provider of material supports for those in need (Marutto 2005). The moral economies of benevolence were largely rooted in the oppression of the underclass (Chapman and Withers 2019).

In the United States, this was also the period in which wealthy robber barons such as Andrew Carnegie and John D. Rockefeller began to establish philanthropic foundations, applying business principles to charitable giving and provision directed largely at self-improvement and modest non-threatening "social reform" (Raventós and Wark 2018, 155–7). The idea of the wealthy giving back to society was also greatly motivated by fear of communism and revolution from below (Ott 2001, 52). Significantly, the channelling of social policy change through philanthropic private market avenues has once again become a major theme in the post-2008 crisis period, including in Canada, as we discuss later in the chapter.

With the growth of social problems, widening disparity, and increasing social pressures from below, generated by the march of unregulated capitalism, the state sector moved slowly to engage in social reform. In the Canadian case at the time, "federal or provincial interest in the voluntary sector was filtered through local governments" (Marutto 2005, 159). These forces created a shift in the NPO sector towards secularism and more professional-scientific-bureaucratic service provision regulated by the state. Managerialism and efficiency became increasingly important. With some increased state support, charities played an expanding role as a band-aid solution to ever-growing social needs brought on by urbanization and industrialization. Although charities could hand out uneven relief, they were incapable of addressing the increasing inequality and poverty of the Gilded Age.

The case of Quebec was different in that the role of the Catholic Church remained dominant in social provision and moral regulation up until the Quiet Revolution of the 1960s. The Quiet Revolution marked a profound secularization of society in Quebec and the building of a modern progressive welfare state and a rapid decline in the role and influence of religious institutions. Since this time Quebec has had a much more statist orientation than English Canada and also a more vibrant social movement orientation to its politics. Civil society organizations, social movements, labour and co-operatives have been active in building a social economy approach to the 'third sector' in the province distinguishing it from elsewhere in Canada (Bouchard 2013; Shragge and Fontan 2000; Vaillancourt et al. 2002).

Outside Quebec, the political and social fallout from the Great Depression of the 1930s finally broke the hegemony of the old system of small government and minimal commitment to social provision, giving rise in Canada and elsewhere to a social liberalism model of activist government and the Keynesian welfare state. This was a form of regulated capitalism that embraced inclusionary social supports and broad reforms that tamed the worst features of unregulated capitalism. The tremendous expansion in state social spending was validated by the new Keynesian logic of state engagement in demand management (Burke, Mooers, and Shields 2000).

The state's size and role in society expanded considerably, and the general assumption of social scientists was that the NPO sector shrank in this great transformation, displaced by the state. The reality was far more complex. The NPOs' role in social provision and their relationship with the state changed as "charities" moved from being primary providers of relief to being a junior partner with the state in meeting an array of social, health, and educational needs provided by a socially liberal welfare state. This state-NPO relationship featured long-term financing, state funding of both organizations and programming, and minor support for non-profit advocacy (Evans, Richmond, and Shields 2005). It is important to note that the Canadian welfare state was less robust than were social democratic welfare states in Europe. In fact, a core feature of most of the liberal Anglo-American welfare states was the use of NPO service providers to help limit the growth of the size and scope of liberal welfare regimes. There is some discrepancy in Canada, however, as the Quebec welfare state became more robust in the context of the Quiet Revolution in seeking to replace much of the charity once provided by the Catholic Church. Yet this also marked a period of secular NPO development in Quebec, addressing service gaps in the provincial welfare state, but also engaging in robust social justice advocacy (Laforest 2011a).

NPOs throughout Canada actively pushed elements of the state to expand welfare state programs to address other forms of inequality – on the basis of gender, sexuality, race, and age, for instance – and to work with citizens facing these issues to improve programs. As junior partners, NPOs advocated to expand the scope of the welfare state and to fill gaps in social provision to populations the state found more difficult to reach through direct service provision. In this context, the Canadian welfare state continued to expand incrementally up until the mid-1970s. The movement towards NPO secularization and professionalization intensified with these shifts (Salamon 1995). The political economy of state and non-profit sector relations was consequently set within the parameters of the Keynesian policy paradigm (see Table 10.1, under Social Liberalism).

Crises: A Marketized Sector

The economic crisis of the 1970s marked the end of the hegemony of the Keynesian paradigm of social liberalism and the birth of a revamped version of classical liberalism – neoliberalism – in public policy. Neoliberal agents fought against an expansion to the welfare state, believing it would result in heavy taxation, the erosion of property rights, and individuals' dependence on the state. Hence, there was a shift away from more social reform–oriented notions of the operations of the state and society towards neoliberal economics, ideology, and welfare state deconstruction. The social contract that built the welfare state ended and a period of intensified social struggle ensued as neoliberalism gained hegemony. With this, the logic of neoliberal political economy was set in motion.

Neoliberalism promotes a more limited role for the state in the provision of services to the public and a greatly enhanced role for markets and individual "freedom" as consumers, entrepreneurs, and as a form of human capital. Market exchanges and contractual relations are viewed as the basis for all forms of human action, as they are believed to maximize individual freedom and initiative and produce optimal economic benefits. Marketization and privatization are seen as the route to achieving these neoliberal goals. Marketization demands that market criteria be used in the provision of public goods and services, which tend to focus on human capital investment to enhance the competitive position of the state. Privatization calls upon the state to withdraw from the production of goods and services. Government may still be involved in funding "public" services in more austere ways, but the provider should be located increasingly outside the state – in particular, with NPOs (Evans and Shields 2010, 308–9). This process is highly disruptive, resulting in challenging and painful adjustments and crises throughout society, including in the NPO sector.

The NPO sector has had a central place in the political economy of neoliberalism's remaking of state, markets, and society, including in Canada. Neoliberalism seeks to use the NPO sector as an agent in the process of hollowing out the welfare state and marketizing and diminishing the public social sphere (Joy and Shields 2017, 313). The shrinking of public social policy leaves NPO actors with the job of addressing the expanding social needs of society, especially for the most vulnerable, but with access to resources greatly reduced. The shift away from state responsibility towards greater reliance on NPOs to address social needs has been termed the "voluntary/non-profit turn" (Milligan and Conradson 2011, 1). The neoliberal goal is to remake the relationship between government and the people, holding them more responsible for their own individual well-being. In this way, the social risks within society come to be shifted from the state and downloaded onto individuals, families, local communities, and the NPO sector (see Table 10.1, under Neoliberalism).

Neoliberalism makes strong appeals to voluntarism, philanthropy, and other forms of individualized social engagement. It is important, as the state retreats from its social responsibilities, that civil society fill the gaps. At the same time, neoliberalism seeks to narrow the scope and nature of civil society involvement. Voluntarism, as organic grassroots community-centred initiatives, is not being promoted. In fact, popular forms of organization that challenge neoliberal restructuring and austerity are strongly resisted. For example, anti-neoliberal political advocacy has been directly attacked, as have other forms of collective organizing and resistance, such as trade unions. The neoliberal state is pushing voluntarism in a top-down fashion to help manage the absence of government social supports. In this regard, the state is attempting to subsume community action for government purposes (Milbourne 2013, 19). In fact, the neoliberal state in its own way has become dependent on the cheap labour of the NPO sector as well as on the unpaid work in the home and within broader civil society (Joy and Shields 2017, 315). The shift away from the state to informal and less formalized care provided at home or in the community by NPO actors heightens gender inequality, as such care is provided primarily by unpaid or poorly compensated women. Service entitlements also come to be greatly weakened as the right to less formal non-state-provided care is diminished (Powell 2007, 4–5).

At the centre of the relationship between the neoliberal state and social and human service NPOs is the contract-financing regime that was developed to facilitate alternative service delivery of government programs. Under this system, programs are funded through rigid short-term contracts that must be bid on competitively among NPOs and even for-profit organizations. There are strict limitations on how funded dollars are to be spent, greatly limiting costing flexibility. Moreover, funding is inadequate to cover the full costs of delivering the programs, with the expectation that NPO volunteers and donations will fill the gap – estimated to be between 7 per cent and 15 per cent of actual costs (Eakin 2002, 8). This approach has been described as "hollow core funding," whereby the NPO sector in fact subsidizes government-contracted programming. In short, social financing under the neoliberal political economy relies on the NPO sector.

Part of the neoliberal social financing regime is its parallel accountability system, which we have seen in Canada and elsewhere. This involves tightly controlled obligations regarding how funding is directed and spent. Administrative accountability is rigorously monitored, with detailed reporting requirements. The goal is to ensure that government spending enhances efficiency (value for money), but it is through these reporting techniques that the neoliberal state is able to control NPOs from a distance. Hence, neoliberal accountability mechanisms are designed to work in a hierarchical way, with NPOs reporting upward to state funders. It is important to note, however, that NPOs actually have multiple accountabilities. Clearly, upward responsibility to funders is important, but equally so is accountability to the broader public, as is downward accountability to clients and communities served. Moreover, there are horizontal accountabilities to NPO boards, members, volunteers, paid staff, donors, and partners. Under neoliberal governance, however, accountability to government funders trumps all other forms of accountability. NPOs use considerable resources and effort to address the demands made by narrow administrative forms of accountability to the funder, reducing their capacity for broader, more grassroots, and public forms of accountability (Evans and Shields 2010, 312–13).

A key part of the transition from the Keynesian welfare state to the neoliberal state is a change in the model governing public administration, essential for building a different kind of state with a different set of operating values. This shift is particularly important for the NPO sector, given its key role as an alternative service delivery agent for the neoliberal state. New Public Management (NPM) has been the vehicle for neoliberal public administration transformation (see Evans, in this volume). There are two basic elements to NPM: managerialism and modes of control. Managerialism relates to such features as "(1) continuous increases in efficiency; (2) the use of ever more sophisticated technologies; (3) a labour force discipline to productivity; (4) clear implementation of the professional management role; and (5) managers being given the right to manage" (Evans and Shields 2010, 310). In short, the emphasis is placed on a stringent market-oriented approach to running narrowly efficient government as a firm, based on business principles.

The element of modes of control is concerned with the ways in which forms of public administration controls are exercised, particularly more indirect forms of control. NPM is able to manage NPO service providers from a distance through the use of short-term competitive contracts and strong accountability measures by imposing rigorous performance measurement controls, including audit and inspection. This is a case of "centralized decentralization" (Shields and Evans 1998): service delivery is decentralized to NPO providers, but effective control of the management of programs remains with the government funder. It is important to note that 80 per cent or more of the funding of social and human service NPOs is derived from the state, tying these organizations to the NPM approach to manage their affairs (Baines et al. 2014, 76). NPM has been the prime means by which neoliberal ideology and business values and ethics are transmitted to the non-profit sector (Shields and Evans 1998), in effect constituting a "cultural take-over [of the non-profit sector] by stealth" (Taylor 2002, 98–9). The logic of neoliberal political economy becomes hegemonic in this way in the NPO sector.

The NPO sector has been labelled simultaneously the resilient sector (Salamon 2015) and the precarious sector (Shields, Baines, and Cunningham 2017). Resilient because NPOs have been remarkably good at adjusting to adversity and difficult conditions to fulfil their missions.

Their capacity to "do more with less" is renowned, an ability that neo-liberal governments have taken full advantage of in their restructuring of the social sphere.

Yet the NPO sector is in many ways also precarious – the service-providing component of it ever more so. In fact, the NPO sector is a textbook case of the various ways in which precarity is manifested on the ground. Precarity may best be understood as a lack of security and predictability. Precarity is most readily associated with employment conditions related to the growth of temporary, short-term, and other forms of insecure work, which is also generally connected with low pay and few if any employment benefits. Precarious work is counterposed to the so-called standard employment relationship that became the work norm during the welfare state era of capitalism (long-term, full-time, secure forms of paid work) (Lewchuk, Procyk, and Shields 2017, 5–7). Today, precarious work is overtaking standard employment as the new norm.

The NPO sector is a prime example of this development: a core feature of the large majority of paid work in the NPO sector is its precarity. The downloading of care and services onto NPOs under neoliberalism is about finding cheaper, more compliant, and generally more precarious sources of labour to reduce costs to government and to weaken longer-term commitments to state social supports. The NPO labour force is overwhelmingly comprised of female labour, whose pay and benefit compensation are significantly below public and private sector norms (Shields, Baines, and Cunningham 2017, 38). A significant portion of the work of the sector is carried out by the non-paid work of volunteers and sector workers performing hours of extra non-paid labour to meet obligations to "do more with less." The fact that the vast majority of workers in the sector are women, often driven by a commitment to care, means that their work is often purchased at a discount; they are also tightly tied to their jobs since their work is often felt as being a "labour of love" (Baines et al. 2014, 86). An employment discount comes with such caring work, however, that reduces economic compensation and employment security for such workers. Moreover, there is a parallel between the precariousness of NPO clients and the NPO service sector's own workers, as its workforce is generally heavily drawn from the communities it serves (Baines et al. 2014).

Particularly significant is that the funding of the service-providing NPO sector is structured by short-term competitive contracts mostly from government and often subject to cuts. The unpredictability of funding makes even so-called full-time jobs precarious, since if contracts do not come through these jobs will be lost. The funding contract structures precarity into the very DNA of NPO work, making most of the jobs in the sector, in effect, "permanently temporary" (Shields 2014).

Consequently, precarity fosters "conditions of vulnerability, instability, marginality and temporariness" (Baines et al. 2014, 75). Precarity is promoted by neoliberal public policy through restructuring and downloading. Within the NPO sector, it can be clearly observed how precarity operates at multiple self-reinforcing levels: in the workforce (as discussed), in the operation and structure of the organization as a whole, and in the communities and clients served. Neoliberal cuts and restructuring of social welfare programs and supports for NPO clients create multiple vulnerabilities, such as greater needs in marginalized communities, even as NPOs are less able to respond because of restraints on their own government financing and cuts to programming. Underfunding of the sector not only creates precarious employment in NPOs; it also fosters precariousness in the organizations themselves (Shields, Baines, and Cunningham 2017). This greatly weakens their organizational capacities, including the ability to respond quickly to new needs, to engage in longer-term planning, and even to keep together the organizational infrastructure necessary to fulfil their mission. Neoliberal policies, consequently, are producing multiple, self-reinforcing layers of precarity. The political economy of neoliberalism produces conditions of precarity throughout society, but the NPO sector offers a particularly valuable vantage point from which to observe and analyse this growing phenomenon.

Aside from service, as mission-driven organizations, NPOs have "advocacy" as a prime role. It has been long recognized that the sector's engagement in society to fulfil missions and advance social justice causes has been seminal in advancing and enhancing the liberal democratic experience in society. At the height of the welfare state in Canada in the later 1960s to the mid-1970s, governments recognized the importance of NPO advocacy, even funding them in support of this role. The idea of advocacy is often conceptualized as "community voice," as NPO service providers are strategically placed to speak to the needs of clients based in vulnerable communities. Advocacy is sometimes very direct – a case of "big advocacy" – in terms of taking public stances on policy issues and even challenging government. Most often, however, are cases of "small advocacy," involving the everyday interactions and consultations between NPO staff and funders and other government officials. Both forms of advocacy are important for the policy process (Evans and Shields 2014).

Under neoliberal forms of governance, however, NPOs are cast one dimensionally as simply a cheap and compliant source of service provision. The kind of "partnership" model produced for alternative service delivery under NPM is a business model that contributes to a "depoliticization" of the sector. In fact, neoliberalism views advocacy work as "special interest" activity that government funds should not have any part in supporting, especially if they are directed against a government's own policies. Neoliberalism has always been suspicious and less than welcoming of the legitimacy of such a role. For NPOs to become engaged more fully in the policy process will require a degree of acceptance by the state of the legitimacy of a meaningful NPO voice in that process. The hostility to NPO advocacy was especially prominent in Canada during the latter part of the Conservative government of Stephen Harper, which challenged the charitable status of many NPOs that were advocating around various Conservative policy positions such as on energy and global warming (Beeby 2014). In such an environment, the problem of "advocacy chill" within the NPO community grew especially acute, serving to mute the voice of many government-funded NPOs.

The promotion of competition for funding for short-term service contracts among NPOs under NPM also encourages a shift in NPO-government engagement approaches. With government funders, the focus tends to move from broader, mission-based issues to efforts to secure scarce service contracts necessary for the organization's survival. There is thus a strong motivation by NPO agencies to avoid criticizing government and "not bite the hand that feeds them." NPO providers are increasingly compelled to chase after all kinds of government contracts, and mission drift easily sets in. In the process, the deeper democratic impulse related to NPO advocacy is diminished to a narrow business-oriented "pragmatic lobbying" for government contracts, with a "market-driven advocacy" taking hold (Feldman, Strier, and Korch 2016, 6–7). Moreover, NPOs become more disassociated and hence far less effective voices for the communities they serve.

Still, many NPOs, particularly those groups not dependent on government contracts, continue to use advocacy to promote an alternative social justice voice in opposition to the threat of neoliberalism. Other service-providing NPOs dependent on government financing, as in the case of immigrant settlement agencies, channel their advocacy voice through sector-wide organizations such as the Ontario Council of Agencies Serving Immigrants, which are freer to speak forcefully for the interests of their members and clients. In *The Great Transformation* ([1944] 2001), the political economist Karl Polanyi wrote about the double movement that took place as an emerging capitalism in the eighteenth century tore up the fabric of society by undoing long-established social protections to impose a new free market capitalist order. But the forces of capitalist revolution promoted a powerful countermovement in defence of social protection. The same forces of double movement can be observed today in Canada's NPO sector. Neoliberal governments have attempted to contain such social resistance by intervening in the restructuring of the very political economy of the NPO sector itself.

The agenda to marketize and use the NPO sector to hollow out the welfare state and weaken social policy under the neoliberal political economy has created a crisis for the sector. Under the pressures of neoliberal restructuring, the sector struggles to adjust, reinvent itself, innovate, and stay socially relevant in an increasingly hostile and austere environment.

Conflicts: An Innovative Sector

The NPO sector is situated centrally in more recent reconfigurations of the neoliberal project that incorporate the interrelated concepts of communitarianism, localism, social capital, and social innovation. Decades of neoliberal policy, marked by economic deregulation and austerity in social welfare, have expanded and deepened problems such as poverty and inequality, as well as housing and employment precarity, that are increasingly visible (Fanelli and Shields 2016; Procyk, Lewchuk, and Shields 2017; Toronto Foundation 2017). To maintain the dominance of capitalism and to deflect criticism, the neoliberal project has morphed to co-opt communitarian thinking (DeFilippis, Fisher, and Shragge 2010; Fyfe 2005) (Table 10.1, under Communitarian Neoliberalism). Social problems in local places, such as concentrated neighbourhood poverty and gang activity, are framed as illustrative that we have lost our way because modern society lacks community or social capital – understood as the networks of bonds and relations of trust that produce individual and collective benefits (Sullivan 2009). Communitarianism blames both the individualism central to (neo)liberalism and the statist centralized managerialism of the welfare state for declining community (Etzioni 1993; Giddens 1998; Putnam 2000). The latter, however, becomes the dominant villain in neoliberal communitarianism as the previous decades of austerity neoliberalism are downplayed and the project blames statism for drowning out the vibrancy of community self-help and volunteerism. This understanding of the problem conveniently distracts from class-based problems endemic to capitalism intersected with other structures of oppression such as racism and patriarchy.

As the institutionalized arm of community, NPOs are understood as central to the renewal of social capital in local places, and are increasingly lauded for their ability to solve social problems (Kelly and Caputo 2011; Kendall 2008). This extends a pre-existing trend to policy decentralization to the local and to an emphasis on policy development that involves network governance, or partnerships of public, private, and NPO actors addressing localized social problems (Bradford 2002, 2005, 2007a). In the United Kingdom, for example, Tony Blair's New Labour government signed "compacts" between the national government and community-based agencies as part of a third-way alternative that explicitly valued the role of local government and NPOs to deliver services and to enhance democracy and civil society (Fyfe 2005; Morison 2000). In Canada, the Liberals under Jean Chrétien devoted $95 million over a five-year period towards a Voluntary Sector Initiative that encouraged federal and NPO actors to work together to strengthen their relationship by developing "best practices" (Laforest 2011a). The Liberals also introduced the New Deal, an attempt at a more explicit urban policy (Bradford 2007a). These policy innovations recognized the unique role of the NPO sector in working with municipalities to address social problems, and the federal government became interested in place-based policies that targeted local priorities and focused on community development organized through municipal and NPO sector actors (Bradford 2007a). A local example of such a strategy included the Strong Neighbourhoods Strategy in Toronto, which targeted support in neighbourhoods of concentrated poverty and involved a partnership between the city and the United Way Toronto (Joy and Vogel 2015).

These localized strategies have all been critiqued, with the common theme that they fail to address how the problems they seek to solve and the actors they seek to empower are affected by neoliberal policy and can make fundamental changes to these policies (see Fanelli and Hudson, in this volume). On the topic of third-way compacts in the United Kingdom, Morison (2000) and Fyfe (2005) find that the increasing service-oriented professionalization of NPOs has resulted in more passive citizenship. Morison (2000) argues that NPO actors that wanted to move to a more economistic, managerial, and depoliticized model by providing services once the responsibility of government benefited from the compact program. Furthermore, Barnett (2011) notes that simultaneous cuts to social welfare reduced the likelihood that barriers to participation by marginalized groups would decline. Phillips (2009) argues that Canada's version of the third way failed to formulate a non-instrumental vision for NPOs in this country. Although the Voluntary Sector Initiative created a new political constituency, governance changes benefited large, national service-providing agencies, rather than local, community-based, and representational organizations. As well, structural changes, such as limits to advocacy and meager project-based and competitive financing, discussed earlier, were limited (Laforest 2011b). Toronto's Strong Neighbourhoods Strategy has been criticized for being weakly institutionalized and supported by other levels of government (Horak 2013), and for distracting from the systemic roots of neighbourhood poverty (Cowen and Parlette 2011).

These strategies were also short lived, with the election of more conservative governments, such as that of David Cameron in the United Kingdom, Stephen Harper in Canada, Rob Ford in Toronto, and Doug Ford in Ontario, as well as the 2008 global financial crisis, which resulted in renewed austerity-oriented neoliberal projects (Table 10.1, under Austerity Neoliberalism). Communitarianism was taken to another level in the post-recession era of austerity neoliberalism in Britain under Cameron's Big Society project (Szreter and Ishkanian 2012). Cameron claimed that the third-way state overpowered society, and the Big Society aimed to rectify this through policy that encouraged volunteerism, philanthropy, local social entrepreneurialism, and community empowerment (North 2011). Again, however, the Big Society was used to legitimate further austerity cuts aimed at local government and the NPO sector, which was seen as too dependent on central state financing (North 2011). At the same time, NPOs were expected to fill gaps, and in some cases to take over, core areas of service provision in realms such as elder care, housing, and accessible transportation even as they were to engage community and promote social capital (Joy, Marier, and Séguin 2018). These expectations, coupled with continued underfunding and competitive contracts, led to new forms of professionalization in the sector, such as mergers and the turn to professional boards (Blumberg 2009). To continue to support their communities, non-profits increasingly have had to rely on philanthropic donations and own-source revenue through increased user fees, the adoption of business principles, and the creation of social enterprise endeavours (*Economist* 2017; Kelly and Caputo 2011). Although the latter might offer interesting opportunities for the creation of co-operative economies (see MacArthur, in this volume), very small business endeavours to keep social service agencies afloat in a neoliberal political economy seem to be the more common practice, though this merits deeper analysis in the Canadian case (DeFilippis, Fisher, and Shragge 2010; Guo and Bielefeld 2014).

In the post-recession context, neoliberalism has once again mutated to address the critique that social service delivery fails to tackle root problems of so-called complex policy issues. This has resulted in increased pressure on the NPO sector by government and philanthropic funders to show evidence that their service delivery approaches "work" or offer social value for money by fixing social problems (Joy and Shields 2018). NPOs are thus a crucial component of a marketized social innovation agenda, where they are expected to discover solutions to social problems due to their localism and proximity to communities. This requires professionalized organizations to establish research departments and social innovation labs that bring together networks of stakeholders from the community to come up with a solution to a social problem. This is a process of policy development where projects are designed in lab settings, funded after making a pitch to a government, philanthropic, or private investor, and are then piloted and tested – in theory, then scaled up should a solution prove to work. This social innovation agenda is powering the development of an impact investment market in social services (Joy, Shields, and Cheng 2019).

An increasingly popular tool facilitating market creation is the Social Impact Bond (SIB), whereby private investors provide upfront cash for a service delivery approach and receive a return on their investment from government should the approach achieve predefined results (Joy and Shields 2018). This has created a new market for social service provision, making the NPO sector and its social service role a new focus for capital accumulation. As such, there is a risk that these projects skim off the least vulnerable clients (Joy and Shields 2013, 2017). Furthermore, although the trend to social innovation might offer interesting opportunities to engage in research that seeks a more systemic understanding of localized problems, these social policy problems are complex, and there is a tendency to look for simple causes that are purely behavioural in nature. This becomes more about nudging the behaviours of vulnerable people so that they become less costly, and thus represents a sophisticated form of victim blaming repackaged as innovation (Joy and Shields 2018). What is innovative here is that vulnerability becomes a new form of profit making (Joy and Shields 2016). The general acceptance of the benevolence of the market by government, NPOs, and citizens alike presents a striking illustration of the strength of the neoliberal project.

Despite these challenges, the increased emphasis on tackling the roots of complex social problems and involving NPOs and citizens in problem solving in local social innovation labs might create new openings for these actors to push for a conversation and plan to address the more systemic roots of social problems. The state, especially at the local scale, increasingly depends on NPOs to deliver crucial social services, so this might present an opportunity for new forms of urban citizenship that push for more universal social policy to meet diverse needs through meaningful partnerships with NPOs. Hence, the recent central positioning of the NPO sector in public sector restructuring could serve at once to legitimate an extension of neoliberal governance and to push for an expansion of the welfare state that meets both universal and diverse needs. The political economy of neoliberalism is forging a remake of the idea of such concepts as citizenship, community, social responsibility, social cohesion, and more. As such, this is a period of conflict, tension, and paradox for the sector. Continued critical analysis of the sector is required to make sense of recent trends and to search them for more expansive opportunities.

Conclusion

The non-profit organization sector is central to social welfare, economic development, and political participation. As such, it is a crucial subject for political economy analysis, and through it we can learn much about the neoliberal political project as well as more expansive alternative political projects.

The NPO sector, located between the state and market, is positioned to facilitate neoliberalism's push to marketize public provision on its way to achieving a thoroughly market-dominated society. Neoliberalism promotes the idea that freedom and the good society is produced by maximizing individual choice and responsibility, while limiting the role and scope of the state in social provision. Ideas of collective and public social responsibility and the state's social duties to citizens vanish in the "market society," replaced by understandings of an atomized social order governed by the ethic of "possessive individualism" (Macpherson 1962), with little room for collective values related to social citizenship. In this situation, the NPO sector is expected to fill the social gap left by a rapidly shrinking neoliberal state. At the same time, the sector is expected to embrace "innovative" market-oriented and entrepreneurial approaches to reinvent itself to embrace the neoliberal reality through the New Public Management contract culture. NPOs are thus expected to act like a big state, like a lean market, and even like a caring family member, reflecting the difficulty in conceptually orienting the non-profit sector within the capitalist system. The NPO sector, however, is simply too small, too poorly financed, and not structured organizationally to close the social gaps left by a hollowed-out welfare state. The NPO sector cannot replace the state's social role. It is no accident that, as the NPO sector has expanded and the state has retreated, social inequality and deprivation continue to grow, placing enormous pressure on NPOs to "do more with less."

We saw the potential for a more expansive alternative for the NPO sector during the welfare state era, when NPOs provided services tailored to the needs of different population groups while addressing the roots of inequity through their social justice missions. There was consequently an effort to achieve inclusion, where comprehensive supports were provided by different elements of the state and NPOs partnered with the state to ensure that different voices and needs were included. To be sure, this was a case of "limited inclusion" that marked the class and social compromises which constituted the high point of the liberal welfare state in Canada. In this period, inclusionary policies were seen as necessary to produce social harmony for a more regulated capitalism to thrive (Burke, Mooers, and Shields 2000). The capitalist crisis of the 1970s marked an end to this approach, and neoliberalism subsequently pursued aggressive exclusionary policies, what Piven and Cloward (1982) called "new class war conservatism." The neoliberalization of the sector is challenging NPOs to push for an alternative political economy, yet research must continue to examine the potential for this project to take root and perhaps to exploit new openings for the sector, given its greater role in policy design and the state's dependence on its work.

SECTION 3

Applications of Canadian Political Economy

11 Inequality

JOHN PETERS

Introduction

Political scientists, economists, and sociologists have long debated economic inequality. But over the past thirty years, with the widening gap in wages and incomes, as well as the global financial crisis, a new body of research has emerged on inequality, re-evaluating its causes, trends, and consequences (Alvaredo et al. 2018; Salverda et al. 2014). This chapter reviews some of this recent international research as well as contemporary critical political economy literature in Canada, highlighting what is happening to inequality and why. The chapter also notes the many areas where further research on inequality in Canada is required.

One factor driving a renewed interest in the political economy of inequality has been the financial crisis of 2008–09 (Epstein 2015; van der Zwan 2014). The scale of the crisis and its causes led many researchers to examine how financial actors, corporations, and the very wealthy influenced the policy process. Occupy Wall Street, and the global protests that followed in its aftermath, highlighted how widespread public antipathy had become towards income inequality. This activism brought the problems of inequality into the public eye, and led to a great deal of new research on how rising inequality is not simply due to impersonal market forces, but rather a result of politics and policies that too often favour the few at the expense of the vast majority of working people (Hacker and Pierson 2010a; Stiglitz 2013).

In critical political economy, new research has focused on how the largest and most powerful corporations and an ever-expanding array of financial actors have been able to shape public policies within and across countries to their enormous economic and political benefit (see Brownlee, in this volume). But it has also led to an ever-wider set of investigations of how capitalism has come to dominate democracy and, in turn, the need for citizens and unions to press for more egalitarian laws and policies that ensure high wages, public services, and redistributive tax and transfer systems (Brady 2009; Crouch 2019; Gautie and Schmitt 2010).

In examining inequality in this chapter, I first present recent data showing its rise and extent in Canada and other advanced industrial economies. I then turn to review recent work in critical political economy on neoliberalism and how governments have introduced policy reforms to promote economic globalization as well as redirect income into the hands of a wealthy few. In these sections, I examine a number of policy areas in the contemporary international and Canadian literatures that explain the widening gap between rich and poor in both the private and public sectors of the economy. But I also briefly detail how firms and the financial industry have adapted to neoliberalism by taking greater profits and capital incomes at the expense of good jobs and wages for the majority of the workforce. I conclude by noting three research challenges: first, the need for a better understanding of the impacts of financialization and globalization on inequality in Canada; second, the need for further research on the political drivers of inequality in Canada; and, third, the need for further theoretical and empirical work on how to build a stronger democratic public that can effectively challenge neoliberalism and rising income inequality.

Changes: Inequality in Canada

Economic growth and globalization were supposed to bring an increase in incomes and standards of living for all workers, but it is clear that, in many countries, including Canada, the gains have been heavily concentrated at the top. Indeed, income growth among the rich in Canada has been so profound that, over the past forty years – as long as data on inequality have been collected – Canada has never seen higher levels of top income inequality than right now (Osberg 2008; Veall 2012; Yalnizyan 2010). This development follows international trends in rising income inequality among the richest developed countries since the 1980s (OECD 2011, 2015). As the data show, However, in terms of top income shares, Canada is at an extreme among advanced industrial countries, with only the United States regularly witnessing higher levels of top income inequality (Alvaredo et al. 2018; OECD 2015).

Figure 11.1 portrays the scale of the disparity. It combines data calculated for working households – the most comprehensive measure for comparing household incomes – with family incomes of top income earners pre-tax. Typically, Canada is considered a relatively generous and equitable country, and in 2015 average income before taxes and transfers was $62,350. This figure, however, hides massive differences in the distribution

Figure 11.1. Pre-tax Incomes of the Top 1 per cent and Bottom 50 per cent, Canada, 1990–2015

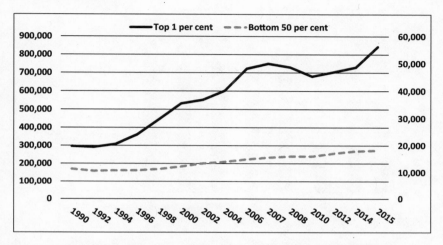

Source: Author's figures based on a custom data request for "Market and After-Tax Incomes of Economic Families under Age 65," Survey of Labour and Income Dynamics; and "Market and After-Tax Incomes of Economic Families," T1 Family File Tax data, Statistics Canada.

of incomes. For example, for the approximately 6.7 million individuals who make up the bottom 50 per cent in Canada, their family earnings averaged just $18,100, or one-third of the average Canadian family income. In stark contrast, those at the top – and especially the very top – witnessed exponential gains between 1990 and 2015. Those whose family incomes put them among the richest 1 per cent of income earners increased their earnings by 185 per cent, while the incomes of the richest 0.01 per cent – the richest 1,500 families in Canada – grew by 256 per cent, to $10.5 million annually. To put this in perspective, the richest 1 per cent in 1990 had incomes twenty-six times those of the average household in the bottom 50 per cent; in 2015, the richest had incomes forty-six times greater.

But the story of rising inequality in Canada does not just stop with the rich and how they have pulled away from everyone else. That is only part of it. Rising inequality in Canada has also been a story of the continuing expansion of bad jobs and the systematic proliferation of low-wage, non-standard employment.

One way of considering how little income many in the labour market receive is by calculating the number in low-paying jobs. The definition of low pay differs considerably across countries, but the Organisation

Figure 11.2. Incidence of Low-Wage Work, Selected OECD Countries, 2015

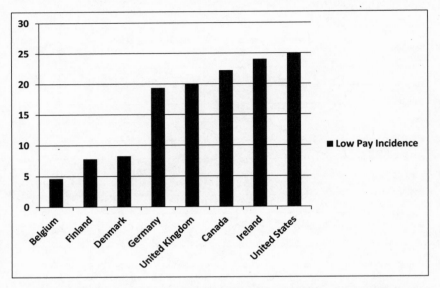

Note: Percentage of workers earning less than two-thirds of median hourly earnings of
all full-time workers.
Source: Organisation for Economic Co-operation and Development, *OECD.Stat*, Labour,
"Incidence of Low Pay," online at https://stats.oecd.org/index.aspx?queryid=64193.

for Economic Co-operation and Development (OECD) has developed a
widely used one that defines low pay as earnings that are less than two-
thirds of the median hourly or annual earnings for all full-time workers. By this definition, Canada currently has the third-highest level of
low-wage work among OECD countries, with 22 per cent of full-time
workers in low-wage employment in 2015, behind only the United
States and Ireland (Figure 11.2).

But if looked at more broadly in terms of all employees – including
part-time and non-standard employment contracts, but not temporary
foreign workers – the data show that the situation is even worse. In
2015, more than 38 per cent of Canadian workers were in jobs that paid
less than half of what a full-time worker received. For these 6.5 million
Canadians, the majority in non-standard employment, average annual
earnings were less than $15,000. Again, although full international
comparative data are limited – notably, the United States does not cal-
culate low-wage work for those in non-standard employment – the

International Labour Organization reports that, in 2011, only Panama and Honduras had overall levels of low-wage employment in their workforces of more than 35 per cent (International Labour Organization 2011, fig. 21). Thus, explaining inequality in Canada is also about coming to grips with what has happened to the labour market and to income distribution more broadly, and what accounts for the spectacular rise in the incomes of the wealthy few, as well as for the exceptionally high share of low-wage and precarious work in the Canadian labour market.

Crises and Response: The Politics of Neoliberalism

Rising income inequality and the growth of low-wage work and nonstandard employment have been recognized by the research community, but the debate continues on the primary *causes* of these changes. The standard explanation in conventional scholarly literatures attributes the widening gap between the rich and the majority of workers to "market forces," and above all to globalization and new technologies that have made many workers less "competitive" in the labour market (Green and Sand 2015a). Some economists, for example, claim rising inequality is due to "skill-biased technological change" – a shift towards greater emphasis on specialized skills, knowledge, and education – that has fuelled the growing divide between the highly educated and the rest of the workforce.

As critical political economy literature has argued, however, the standard explanation of technological change favouring the most educated does not seem to account for much of what has happened (Atkinson 2015; Hacker and Pierson 2010a). Sweden and Denmark, for example, both among the most open and globalized economies in the world, have not seen similar increases in income concentration. Nor do arguments about the level of education take us very far. Certainly, Canada has a slightly lower rate of post-secondary education or vocational school completion, and the gap between the wages of high-skilled and low-skilled workers has increased in Canada compared with the OECD average (Boudarbat, Lemieux, and Riddell 2010). But overall, Canada has one of the highest rates of workers with some post-secondary or vocational schooling, and during the 2000s, levels of post-secondary and vocational education rose (Green and Sand 2015b). These trends challenge arguments about technology rewarding the better educated.

What of the role of government and politics? Could public officials and the policies they enact – or fail to enact – have created this jobs-with-inequality economy? Certainly, over the past decade, more political scientists have begun to suggest as much, pointing out that politicians are doing much less to redress the imbalances of income and resources than they have in previous decades (Banting and Myles 2014; Emmenger et al. 2012). Indeed, this research suggests that politics and public policy are contributing significantly to rising inequality and the polarization of labour markets. Some of the changes to income and wealth distribution have been due to the changing politics of the welfare state, including economic-oriented reforms and retrenchment of programs such as health care or pensions, government-sponsored or -mandated maternity leave and child care programs, and unemployment and activation programs. Graefe and Evans, in this volume, detail changes to social policy and the public sector; Fanelli and Hudson, also in this volume, examine related urban dynamics; and Banting and Myles (2014) also note the effects of faltering tax, transfer, and social program expenditures on rising inequality.

But as a growing literature in critical political economy illustrates, what has been most common in the global economy in recent years is the exponential growth of transnational firms and finance and the ongoing transfer of income and wealth to the wealthiest few (Atkinson 2015; Panitch and Gindin 2012; Piketty 2014; Stiglitz 2013). Recent critical studies argue that such developments have not occurred by chance. To the contrary, they are the result of political choices and changes and the reform of political systems to advantage business and top income earners. In the post-war period, it is argued, governments routinely acted to protect citizens from many of the problems that markets and firms caused – whether pollution, monopolies, or unemployment (McBride and Shields 2004). Governments also took on key roles in providing public goods and policies that enhanced the collective well-being of national societies, while enacting financial regulations that limited systemic risk, and used fiscal policies (taxes, public spending, and deficits) to overcome economic downturns and support employment (Crouch 2006; Hacker and Pierson 2016).

Starting in the 1970s and continuing well into the 2000s, however, governments fundamentally recast their policy priorities to emphasize the profitability of business and the growth of finance and credit – most typically at the expense of workers' bargaining power and political clout (Glyn 2006; Harvey 2005a). As a well-developed literature has demonstrated, under stagflation, slowing economic growth, and the distinct economic calculus of finance and global multinational corporations, the priorities of governments were fundamentally transformed, if not largely reversed, to consider the interests of firms, shareholders, and finance above all else (Brenner 2006; Jessop 2016). At the same time, the world's largest corporations and financial actors grew enormously, and used their new resources to leverage ever more favorable tax, trade, and financial policies. Under these pressures, it became commonplace for governments to overhaul their regulatory environment and to seek ways to make their economies more competitive (Crouch 2013; Neilson and Stubbs 2016).

It is here – in examining these often-neglected conflicts between democracy and an ever more powerful capitalist economy – that critical political economists have made their most significant contributions. For in contrast to conventional arguments on inequality, critical literatures have highlighted how public officials redrafted economic and public policies to serve corporate and financial interests, and in turn how this concentrated the rewards of recent growth into the hands of an elite few at the top. The result has been a major redistribution of income away from labour to those who own major corporations, financial institutions, and capital assets.

Governments, for example, have introduced financial and trade liberalization to stimulate global growth, but the major beneficiaries have been transnational corporations (Lapavitsas 2014; Panitch and Gindin 2012). Governments have also enacted widespread tax cuts and created an international tax architecture. But this too has often worked only to the advantage of corporations and the rich, allowing them to shelter profits and assets (Deneault 2015; Palan, Murphy, and Chavagneux 2013; Shaxson 2012; see also Brownlee, in this volume). And officials have widely sought to reform their labour markets to make them more "competitive," "flexible" (Baccaro and Howell 2017; Smith, in this volume), and more closely aligned with the demands of shareholder-driven businesses and financial markets. Such measures, commonly referred to as neoliberalism or market liberalization, are not only widespread, but increasingly seen as "common sense."

In making these arguments, critical scholars acknowledge that different institutions – whether electoral, industrial relations, or social programs – have shaped conflicts among different political and economic interests, and continue to lead to different responses by firms and governments to such economic problems as the global financial crisis of 2008–09 (Jessop 2016; Neilson and Stubbs 2016; Streeck 2014). Critical scholarship, however, has highlighted how successful business and finance have been in generating ever more unequal outcomes, regardless of institutional setting, by pushing for and winning public policies associated with "competitiveness" and "free markets" (Crouch 2011; Hacker and Pierson 2016).

In highlighting these conflicts between capitalism and democracy, critical political economy frameworks have substantially advanced our understanding of the role government policies play in restructuring the operation of markets and income distribution. If, however, in a number of these policy areas Canadian scholarship has kept abreast of the wider international literature, in others much more research remains to be done. Especially required in Canadian scholarship is a deeper consideration of how these causal dynamics might be better integrated to improve our understanding of rising inequality and its solutions.

Conflicts: Capitalism and Equality

The Rise of Finance and the "Super-Rich"

In the recent international literature, one of the most distinctive trends investigated is the growing importance of finance to economic growth and profit making, and in turn the centrality of finance to rising income inequality (Flaherty 2015; Godechot 2016; Lin and Tomaskovic-Devey 2013; Volscho and Kelly 2012). Over recent decades, states have taken on an ever more active role in promoting, regulating, and coping with debt and debt-based assets, and financial industries and credit markets have increasingly moved from the sidelines to occupy a place at centre stage in the wider economy. As a consequence, one of the most defining features of contemporary advanced societies and the international economy has been the rise of finance across all sectors of the economy (Duménil and Lévy 2011; Durand 2017; Epstein 2015).

For example, the finance, insurance, and real estate industries have continuously increased as a proportion of gross domestic product (GDP) across countries, now averaging more than 18 per cent and more than 25 per cent of GDP in countries such as the United States, Germany, and Canada. The expansion of finance and banking has been such that the ratio of total financial assets to GDP doubled across advanced capitalist countries over the course of the 1990s and 2000 to become eight to ten times larger than GDP by 2008 (Lapavitsas 2014). Cross-border financial flows similarly exploded over those years from $1.1 trillion to over $11 trillion a year (Panitch and Gindin 2012), while daily foreign-exchange transactions more than doubled to twenty-five times world GDP by 2013 (Durand 2017). With rising profits in all these financial sectors, it is argued this is strongly suggestive of a wholesale economic shift towards a new financially driven capitalism, with financial asset investments crowding out investment in real assets and finance engaging in successful rent extraction from the non-financial sector (Durand 2017; Godechot 2016).

For income distribution and rising income inequality, the rapid growth of financial industries and markets has meant skyrocketing returns. Indeed, the rise of finance is closely connected to the emergence of a new class of "super-rich" (Flaherty 2015; Volscho and Kelly 2012). With the vast expansion of the financial and real estate sectors, elite workers in these new growth areas have experienced ever-rising incomes simply from the capital ownership of dividends, fees, mortgage interest, and real estate (Foster and Holleman 2010; Roberts and Kwon 2017). Similarly, with the rise of the banking sector and new patterns of economic growth based on financial channels, wealth and income have concentrated at the top and among those who own the majority of capital assets in fluid financial markets. Whether in the United States (Lin and Tomaskovic-Devey 2013; Hacker and Pierson 2010b), France (Godechot 2012), the United Kingdom (Bell and Van Reenan 2013), or other advanced countries (Flaherty 2015), the common distributional outcome of this financial expansion has not been improvements to equality or wages, but rather a surge of income for the top 1 per cent from new financial investments, racing stock markets, and real estate bubbles.

In Canada, evidence is clear about the role of finance in boosting compensation and returns for those in the financial sector (Lemieux and Riddell 2016; Mackenzie 2012, 2017). We also have a recent study examining the role of pension funds, and how their deregulation in the 1990s and 2000s led to the emergence of new institutional investors driving financial expansion (Skerrett et al. 2018). And Tony Porter has provided a number of studies examining the role of Canadian, US, and international policy developments in setting the context for the expansion of finance in Canada (Porter 2004, 2014). However, there has been no similar contemporary study to match Richard Deaton's *The Political Economy of Pensions* (1989), which tracked the emergence of finance in Canada and its role in fostering capitalism. Nor has there been any examination of the massive expansion of securitization in Canada and its role in expanding finance, as well as the vast returns that institutions and lenders receive from interest and fees on transactions (see Seccareccia and Pringle, in this volume). As Robert Guttmann (2016) has demonstrated, the growth of market-based finance has played a crucial role in creating a "finance-led capitalism." The growing importance of hedge funds, institutional investors, insurance companies, and many others have been key in the ability of the financial sector – and of major financial institutions – to draw profits from the rest of the economy. In Canadian political economy, these changes to finance should be taken into account when considering the rise in income inequality and the growth of the super-rich.

Corporate Financialization

Recent research has also shown how major shifts in public policy have favoured global firms, and provided opportunities for finance to become closely entwined with corporations and how they operate and seek to increase their returns. These too have been key in rising inequality. As critical literatures have recently detailed, neoliberalism and the financialization of firms are responsible for the emergence of "winner-take-all" labour markets, where wealthy executives and shareholders take an ever-increasing share of the rewards at the expense of the jobs and incomes of the majority (Cobb 2016; Hein 2015; Lin 2016). Critical to this transformation has been the effects of finance on firms and employment systems. For in contrast to past practices during the post-war period, when firms used to grow through longer term investment and by hiring on workers full time, long-time contracts, now, it is argued, because of financialization, firms grow by investing in financial markets and by expanding their supplier networks while seeking to boost shareholder value for the benefit of an elite few (Durand 2017). For the majority in the workforce, however, these new hyper-financialized models of corporate operation have meant the loss of good jobs and the emergence of low-wage precarious employment (Grady and Simms 2018; Peters 2011). Because corporations now operate with financially driven targets in mind, they have adopted aggressive labour-cost-reduction strategies, either directly by introducing wage cuts or downsizing or indirectly by expanding their use of low-wage labour and low-cost suppliers (Batt and Appelbaum 2014; Kollmeyer and Peters 2019; Weil 2014).

Within critical political economy, it is argued that several changes have driven firms to be more tightly entwined with finance. For one, public officials have freed large pools of capital for investment in the stock market. This includes legislation that allowed pension funds and insurance companies, for the first time, to hold shares of stock and high-risk bonds in their portfolios (Skerrett et al. 2018). It also includes the loosening of restrictions on the international buying and selling of domestic equity and company takeovers (Horn 2012). Such liberalization of capital and product markets was essential for boosting foreign borrowing and investment, and subsequently spurring enterprises to restructure and expand, thereby increasing profits and employment growth. International tax treaties with tax havens were also crucial in allowing firms to grow and make use of debt and "transfer pricing" in order to shift profits and earnings to low-tax countries while uploading costs and losses to higher-tax countries that offer the most subsidies (Palan, Murphy, and Chavagneux 2013; Panitch and Gindin 2012).

These policy reforms have brought major alternations to firm ownership, to how firms operate, how they generate and distribute revenue, pay executives, acquire other companies through debt financing, outsource and expand offshore, and seek to increase rewards to shareholders through the implementation of global operating "best practices" (Batt and Appelbaum 2014; Lazonick 2014; Lin and Tomaskovic-Devey 2013). Each of these developments, it is claimed, is associated with a fundamental reorientation of firms and their supplier networks to focus on a growing number of financial considerations in their operations (Coe and Yeung 2015). And together, each has made a contribution to shifting corporate priorities away from traditional, long-term investment in productive capital and employees towards a variety of strategies that maximize returns to shareholders and wealthy corporate executives (Durand 2017; Forhoohar 2016).

In Canada, Jim Stanford's *Paper Boom* (1999) still stands out as the best study of the integration of finance into the wider economy, as well as its many perverse effects: limited real investments and job creation, high corporate and financial salaries, and ever-greater government response to the demands of finance and business for "national competitiveness." Stanford's follow-up studies (e.g., Stanford 2011) as well as that of Jordan Brennan (2012) show that, as non-financial corporations increased their involvement with a variety of financial strategies and as profits improved, little in the way of real investment or new employment was created.

Despite this work, there has been very little subsequent research on how finance has changed capitalism in Canada, or its impacts on employment relations more generally. Most missing are more in-depth studies of how contemporary multinationals are increasingly likely to be owned by financial investors and to rely on financial assets for their operations. Also required are more investigations of the ever-widening role of private equity, which in the United States has been signalled out as a key contributor of job loss, wage reductions, and massive returns for corporate partners (Batt and Appelbaum 2014). Equally important, evidence suggests that financialization and new finance-driven "shareholder" business models have been critical in fostering a labour cost-saving approach to employment relations – one focused on wage and benefit concessions and the expansion of flexible employment relations through non-standard employment contracts – and seeking much wider deregulation or non-enforcement of employment and income support policies. A priority of future research should be to delve into these issues and to examine how recent Canadian developments compare to those in the United States and elsewhere.

Globalization, Job Loss, and the Growth of Non-standard Employment

A third link between neoliberalism, capitalism, and worsening labour markets that scholars are exploring is in how non-financial corporations have adopted new global growth strategies and turned to regional and global outsourcing and production chains to boost returns to shareholders in the wake of the massive expansion of free trade and international agreements (Coe and Yeung 2015). Milberg and Winkler (2013), for example, have argued that financialisation and globalization are tightly linked through the expansion of global production networks. One way they claim global firms are generating higher profits to shareholders is through the restructuring of their global operations, disaggregating their activities across countries, and then laying off higher-paid workers and using low-cost suppliers for cheaper inputs (Baud and Durand 2012; Durand 2017). Subsequently, firms use the price markup to reward shareholders – another key driver of inequality.

Critically important for this corporate globalization have been trade and investment agreements. New laws and policies have made Canada and many other countries far more hospitable places for foreign capital, increased foreign direct investment, corporate mergers, and new capital ventures (McBride 2005; Mercille and Murphy 2018; see also chapters by McBride, Fridell, and Brownlee, in this volume). So too have of free trade and investment agreements provided firms the resources to move to regions and countries with lower labour costs and fewer regulations. This in turn has given firms the leverage to pressure domestic workers while freezing wages and eliminating unions at home (see Smith, in this volume).

The result is that multinational corporations have rapidly expanded their use of low-wage work through a wide variety of new organizational methods – from outsourcing and subcontracting, to franchising and third-party management, to contractual arrangements that alter who is the employer of record – all to boost profits and lower labour costs (Weil 2014). In general, highly leveraged firms have often sought to lower costs and gain greater efficiencies by using outsourcing and relocating production to territories with low-cost labour (Coe and Yeung 2015). But multinationals and their suppliers have also "fissured" their employment contracts, shedding their direct employment of workers through franchises, contractors, and temporary staffing agencies (Weil 2014). Such outsourcing and fissuring have been key to the expansion of non-standard employment and widening wage inequality (Appelbaum 2017).

Following from these developments has been the vast expansion of "platform capitalism" and the deployment by firms of online technologies to create new forms of precarious jobs (Standing 2011, 2016). These include "taskers," employed through online platforms in the gig economy/concierge economy (e.g., Uber); those doing online micro-tasks or "human intelligence tasks" (e.g., data collecting); and those doing on-call work. This too has contributed to the dismantling of occupations through online outsourcing, franchising, and subcontracting. Overall, a growing literature has demonstrated how these changes to firms, finance, and their production networks have contributed to the massive expansion of non-standard work across advanced industrial economies, contributing to nearly 60 per cent of all employment growth over the course of the 1990s and 2000s.

Canadian political economy has clearly documented the impacts of free trade and financial liberalization on job loss and rising labour market segmentation. Clarkson (2008) and Chase (2009), for example, have examined how, with the passage of the Canada-US Free Trade Agreement (1987) and the North American Free Trade Agreement (1994), firms undertook hundreds of mergers and acquisitions in everything from steel and mining to forestry and chemicals, in order integrate their operations, close and downsize plants, and lower labour costs. Several studies have also addressed how, in the wake of free trade and the end of the Canada-US auto pact, auto manufacturers built their global value chains by transferring new investment to plants in the non-union US South and Mexico (Rutherford and Holmes 2014; Stanford 2010). This has led to the massive loss of high-paying, unionized manufacturing jobs and their replacement with more non-standard, lower-paying jobs.

Canadian scholars have also investigated a number of aspects of growing non-standard employment. Vosko (2000, 2006b), for example, has examined the erosion of standard employment contracts and their gendered and racialized dimensions. A wealth of literature also exists on the racial dimensions of non-standard employment and the role of racism in consolidating low-wage labour markets (Galabuzi 2006; Kwok and Wallis 2008; Rice and Prince 2013). There is also a growing number of studies on Canada's agri-food industries and how they have expanded their low-wage labour force, becoming the largest employer of casual, temporary, and foreign labour in the country (Binford 2013; Preibisch 2010). As this literature has shown, Canada – like other advanced industrial economies – has dramatically expanded its temporary migrant worker programs as a means of developing a low-wage workforce outside of standard employment models (Binford 2013; Fudge and Strauss 2014; Hennebry 2012). This development has helped consolidate precarious employment across the Canadian labour market, with women, racialized minorities, and immigrants having the largest wage penalties in non-standard work. In turn, the growth of non-standard employment has been a major determinant of wage and income inequality in Canada.

However if the socio-economics of low-wage work have been well explored, there has been less investigation in Canada of its economic forces and of how firms are using a variety of contracting arrangements to lower their labour costs and avoid paying social benefits. The spread of outsourcing, the extent of suppliers, and the impact of franchising and temp agencies on employment relations are all areas requiring further study. Equal attention is also needed with respect to how the "fissuring" of employment has affected jobs and incomes, and how firms have sought to use women, racialized minorities, and immigrants as new sources of cheap labour (Moody 2017). Examining these issues will further deepen our understanding of the causes of inequality in Canada.

The Gloves-Off Economy: Deregulation and the Erosion of Minimum Labour Standards

Associated with the massive growth of precarious employment has been the lack of policy response by governments to uphold wages and working conditions (Bernhardt et al. 2008; Vosko 2013; Vosko and Thomas 2014). Employers, it is argued, have simply begun to sidestep and avoid labour and employment laws, and governments have increasingly looked the other way and stopped enforcing basics such as minimum wages, overtime, and health and safety. This has led to a new norm among employers, a "gloves-off" approach whereby they routinely cheat or systematically avoid their legal responsibilities – a fourth key cause of rising income inequality.

Key to employers' growing use of part-time, temporary, and agency labour has been greater government commitment to "deregulation" and the watering down, erosion, and circumvention of labour law and employment policy. Critical scholars have suggested that there has been a long-term convergence of labour law and employment policy across countries towards deregulation. Driving this convergence, they argue, have been global firms' clear economic objectives of boosting profits and satisfying investors and stock markets (Glyn 2006), and governments' seeking to accommodate these demands by making changes to labour law, employment policy, and hiring and firing regulations (Baccaro and Howell 2017).

Thus, rather than address these violations and take more proactive steps to counter such behaviours, officials instead have rolled back union bargaining rights and decentralized collective bargaining to meet firms' demands for lower-cost unionized labour. Governments have also simply failed to enforce the laws and policies on the books, and allowed firms to avoid employment regulations through an ever-greater array of employment contracts organized by suppliers, subcontractors, agencies, and individuals themselves (Marginson 2016; Vosko, Grundy, and Thomas 2016). As well, officials have sought to make labour markets more flexible by creating new or expanded forms of temporary employment outside regular standard employment contracts, as in the case of temporary foreign workers (Oxfam America 2004; Preibisch and Binford 2007). In these ways, officials hope that public policy changes will increase employer power and managerial discretion in workplaces, thus generating lower labour costs.

In Canada, this research has been pioneered by Vosko and a team of researchers (Vosko et al. 2017; Grundy et al. 2017). Their research has accumulated substantial evidence to suggest that neither laws nor employment standards are effectively upholding a basic floor of labour rights for workers, nor are they allowing workers the basic freedoms to exercise their rights. For rather than improve the job security of workers and constrain employers from engaging in practices that undermine basic worker wages, rights, and conditions at work, employment standards legislation has lacked direct enforcement, and provided few mechanisms for wider education or ensuring employer compliance (Thomas 2009). In addition, officials, through numerous special rules and exemptions for agricultural, hospitality, and small employers, have failed to provide adequate protection for all workers – but especially for women, racialized minorities, and immigrants, who are the most vulnerable to aggressive employers that seek to compete on the basis of a low-wage and precarious labour force (Hennebry 2012; Thomas 2009).

This new "gloves-off" approach to labour market regulation helps to explain the erosion of good jobs and the rise of precarious employment in Canada. But a wider focus on the effects of deregulation, the current lack of enforcement, and routine circumvention of labour laws and employment regulations more generally will serve to improve our understanding of diverse provincial trends, as well as wider international developments in earnings inequality and the persistence of low pay (Gautie and Schmitt 2010; Marginson 2016).

Conclusion

Recent studies in critical political economy have done much to enhance our understanding of how governments affect the distribution of market income between capital and labour in immediate and substantial ways. Under neoliberalism, government policy in Canada and elsewhere has reshaped what people earn to the benefit of a few, while reversing a number of other fundamental economic and labour policies at the cost of citizens' well-being and income security. As numerous studies have shown, income inequality in Canada and in other advanced capitalist countries is not only continuing its rapid rise; there are ever-fewer political efforts to counter it, and even fewer political parties willing to raise it in public debate.

However, if much has been learned about the dynamics and outcomes of inequality, a number of basic research challenges remain for Canadian scholars. As the preceding discussion suggests, one area of future research interest is exploring how recent economic policies have promoted the opening and globalization of financial markets and how, in turn, firms have sought to lower labour costs by creating greater flexibility within their workforces. In examining these interconnected questions, scholars will be able to gain a greater understanding of how the sources of rising inequality are to be found in both capital and labour markets, and how these intertwined processes have contributed to persistent and growing inequalities in income and opportunity.

A second challenge is to better understand the basic political drivers of rising inequality. Hacker and Pierson (2010a, 2016) have argued that business and the most affluent have capitalized on their superior financial and organizational resources to tilt the balance of organized interests in their favour and exert disproportionate political pressure for a "winner-take-all" economy. At the same time, broad publics have become more disorganized, and working-class interests that were once well organized by unions and civic associations have atrophied. Scholars elsewhere have begun to examine these issues for their comparative relevance (Hopkin and Lynch 2016), and the recent soaring of inequality in Canada makes this interpretation highly suggestive. But the key drivers – organized business and financial interests, weakening unions, the capture of political parties by business, and the widening marginalization of citizens from the political process – are still only poorly understood. Establishing the evidence for such "winner-take-all" developments in Canada remains for future research.

More broadly, a third priority for research is to consider what options citizens and workers might have to challenge the power of business and finance (see Smith, in this volume). Over the past few years, there have been numerous national and global protests against inequality and austerity, but if these have helped call into question many of the basic policy nostrums of globalization and the need for "competitive-ness" and "austerity," there have been few major political challenges, let alone policy reversals.

Tackling these will require new inclusionary "Blue-Green" alliances between organized labour and environmental activists, as well as new efforts by unions to develop political challenges to promote democracy and more effective governance in the public interest. But the effort to build such alliances will also demand a real understanding of the hur-dles that exist, as well as of the best organizational means for creating a wider democratic politics that offers an effective alternative and builds a more inclusionary and environmentally sustainable society. Race, gender, and immigration remain major fault lines across labour mar-kets. As well, labour movements still lack the extensive alliances with non-traditional labour and grassroots organizations that represent these groups, but that would make a difference to citizens' engagement and mobilization. In tackling these issues, scholars need to continue to develop and refine their arguments about democracy and how to build progressive alternatives. But by addressing these issues directly, researchers will be able to contribute to debates about the best ways to eliminate and ameliorate inequality in capitalist societies.

12 Urban Political Economy, Poverty, and Inequality in Canada

CARLO FANELLI AND CAROL-ANNE HUDSON

Introduction

Within the broad tradition of Canadian political economy, the "urban question" has long been relegated to the margins as issues of national identity and trade dependency on the British and later American empires dominated the period from the 1930s to the 1970s. Although a distinctively Canadian approach to urban political economy did not materialize, the broader "new" political economy revival of the 1970s went a long way towards establishing the significance of the urban as a space for critical engagement in and of itself. In this regard, our aim in this chapter is threefold: first, to provide a brief overview of the "new" critical urban political economy approach through the 1970s; second, to present a snapshot of poverty and inequality in Canada's largest cities; and third, to evaluate the strengths and weaknesses of current poverty-reduction strategies with a focus on Canada's most diverse and unequal city, Toronto.

Urban Political Economy Takes Form

The critical urban political economy tradition is not a monolith but a broad and interdisciplinary approach concerned with the fundamental nature of capitalism as a framework of social organization. In directing attention to the ways in which the "bourgeoisie has subjected the country to the rule of the towns, created enormous cities, greatly increased the urban population and made the country dependent on the towns," Karl Marx and Friedrich Engels showed in *The Communist Manifesto* (1848) how capitalism imposes its own dynamic on urban development. Unlike classical liberal approaches, however, which claimed that the "propensity to truck, barter, and exchange" derived from age-old practices that gave rise to the division of labour and the Industrial Revolution, Marx and Engels argued that capitalist urbanization is inextricably intertwined with the brutal historical process of separating people from the means of providing for themselves.

> The discovery of gold and silver in America, the extirpation, enslavement and entombment in mines of the Aboriginal population, the beginning of the conquest and looting of the East Indies, the turning of Africa into a warren for the commercial hunting of black-skins, signaled the rosy dawn of the era of capitalist production. These idyllic proceedings are the chief moments of primitive accumulation. On their heels treads the commercial war of the European nations, with the globe for a theatre ... capital comes dripping from head to foot, from every pore, with blood and dirt. (Marx [1867] 1977, chap. 31)

For capitalism to become ever more dominant, the economic self-sufficiency of the feudal manor had to be broken down – that is to say, undermined or destroyed. This required bringing market forces to the countryside, which would remove traditional rights and security over the means of subsistence. The enclosure movement turned formerly communal lands into private property. Where people resisted, a series of state-sanctioned measures, including flogging, branding, and execution, ensured compliance (Perelman 2000).

The need to instil market discipline, "civilize" workers, and stamp out indolence justified the harsh measures (Fanelli and Noonan 2017). Lacking any alternative means of survival, once self-subsistent communities were forced out of the countryside and into cities. This violent historical process of dispossession not only created a wage-dependent working class that migrated in droves to cities; it also ensured that the dictates of the capitalist market – its imperatives of cut-throat competition, profit maximization, and labour rationality – regulated not just all economic activity but social relations in general (Wood 2002). In primitive accumulation's wake, extra-economic measures were of course still used, but only exceptionally. The wage relationship became a seemingly voluntary affair as impersonal market forces both ensured and obscured working-class subordination to capital.

This historical analysis and starting point distinguishes the critical urban political economy tradition from liberal variants that naturalize capitalist social relations.[1] As D.C. Thorns (2002, 7) has noted: "The earliest writers on the city sought to explain urban growth and how city life differed from country or rural life. Therefore, a strong tradition of 'contrast' theory creating typologies of urban and rural life emerged with writers such as Toennies (1956), and Durkheim (1960) as part of this tradition. They provided a view of urban life often overlain by nostalgia for the 'world we had lost,' the rural world of the small-scale, personal 'gemeinschaft' rather than the impersonal, large-scale, heterogeneous world of the city." Whereas the poverty, malnutrition, decrepit housing, ill-health, and unsafe employment vividly detailed in *The Condition of the Working Class in England* appeared for liberal political economists as something inherently urban, a phenomenon of aggregation, or the result of individual pathologies, Marx and Engels tied these dramatic urban upheavals to the very nature of capitalist development (Engels [1845] 2010). Office buildings and large factories with sweatshop working and living conditions proliferated as the churches that once dominated the urban core gave way to new central business districts, with extreme wealth and poverty existing together. From its very start, then, the critical urban political economy tradition appeared as radical, since it sought to get to the root of the problem (capitalism), rather than deal only with its symptoms.

From the late 1880s to the 1930s, early contributions to Canadian urban political economy focused largely on institutions of local government and on British and US influence on their formation (Eidelman and Taylor 2010). Over the next four decades, debates about Canada's dependency on Britain and the United States, fears of continental integration, and questions of national identity, particularly in the context of Quebec separatism, and constitutional reform, as exemplified by the Meech Lake and Charlottetown accords, dominated debates in the field of Canadian political economy (see Helleiner, and McBride, in this volume). Through this period, Canadian urban political economy was largely preoccupied with questions of municipal institutional functions

---

1 "Hence, the historical movement which changes the producers into wage-workers, appears, on the one hand, as their emancipation from serfdom and from the fetters of the guilds, and this side alone exists for our bourgeois historians. But, on the other hand, these new freedmen became sellers of themselves only after they had been robbed of all their own means of production, and of all the guarantees of existence afforded by the old feudal arrangements. And the history of this, their expropriation, is written in the annals of mankind in letters of blood and fire" (Marx [1867] 1977, 508).

and public administration (Brittain 1951; Crawford 1954; Rowat 1955). As urban centres grew and suburban communities proliferated in the aftermath of the Second World War, liberal approaches to urban studies were unable to explain convincingly the growth of urban poverty and inequality through the 1950s and 1960s (Hiller 2010a, 2010b).

As Louis Guay and Pierre Hamel (2014) have argued, liberal approaches posited that urban social dislocations were a temporary stage in the incorporation of immigrant groups and migrants from rural areas. High population turnover, lack of material resources, and ethnic heterogeneity led to the breakdown of social control in immigrant-receiving neighborhoods, creating higher rates of crime and unemployment and general social marginalization. Through processes of neighbourhood invasion and succession, liberal urban political economy argued that ethnic groups that moved upwards in economic status also moved from crowded, impoverished, central city neighbourhoods through a series of concentric zones to progressively better-off areas farther from the urban core. Reality, however, increasingly contradicted this idealized typology.

For a good many working in the broader Canadian political economy framework, the urban was not seen as a politically consequential unit of analysis in the same way that cities appeared to be to US and European scholars (Eidelman and Taylor 2010). In the United States, federal power came increasingly to eclipse that of the states, cementing federal-municipal bilateral arrangements. In Canada, however, the reverse occurred. A Constitution designed to produce strong central authority evolved to make Canada one of the most decentralized federations in the Western world as the provinces jockeyed for more autonomy (Evans and Fanelli 2018). This meant that Canadian municipalities remained, on the one hand, subject to provincial rule in the absence of politically autonomous recognition and, on the other, that federal engagement with municipalities remained largely ad hoc or deinstitutionalized (Fanelli 2016).

Through the 1970s, the class compromise of the Keynesian era that had characterized the previous three decades began to unravel rapidly, with many of its most acute affects – poverty, inequality, racialization, and labour market exclusion – felt at the local level. The crisis of Keynesianism was rooted in the growing strength of labour relative to capital, which resulted in decreased profit margins as workers and poor peoples' movements challenged exploitative labour relations, restrictions on the right to organize and bargain collectively, and racial- and gender-based oppressions (Fainstein and Fainstein 1985; Levitt 1970; Panitch 1977a; Piven and Cloward 1977). The collapse of the Bretton Woods system in 1971 ended the convertibility of gold to US dollars, and the subsequent move to flexible exchange rates further encouraged international capital flows. These changes occurred in concert with the rebuilding of the productive capacities of Europe and Japan, oil instability, capital flight to newly emerging industrial regions with cheaper pools of labour and weaker environmental standards, and technological and organizational restructuring in the manufacturing heartlands of North America and Europe. Inflation and unemployment rose simultaneously, confounding Keynes's most erudite expositors, as incipient neoliberal measures expanded (Clement and Williams 1989; Jenson 1990).

Understood this way, neoliberalism is exposed as a class project that seeks to reaffirm capital's control over labour and cede ever more avenues of social life to the dictates of market imperatives. As articulated more fully elsewhere (e.g., Evans, Joy and Shields, McBride, and Whiteside, in this volume), this vision translates into an economic policy focus on inflation control and supply-side incentives; privatization and commercialization of public sector assets and services, including public-private partnerships; liberalization of trade in goods and capital movements; restructuring of labour and business regulations to reduce market "impediments"; and the societal commodification of goods and services (see Brownlee, in this volume). Additional measures have involved efforts to keep real wages below increases in productivity, monetarist shock therapy followed by inflation targeting by the central bank, regressive tax reform, an export-led growth strategy, and the lifting of controls on foreign direct investment (FDI) and trade liberalization (see Fridell, in this volume). In terms of welfare policy, an ethos of personal responsibility and individual culpability supplemented by private charity, philanthropy, and volunteerism is prioritized in place of state-administered social programs (see Graefe, in this volume). All that said, critical urban political economists increasingly came to argue that, in order to understand what is happening at the local level, it was also necessary to consider the larger political structures of regions, provinces, and nations, including international political processes and relationships, and the ways in which local markets are connected to one another in the larger domestic and global economic environments (see McBride, in this volume).

"New" Political Economy and the Urban Question

It was in this context that a "new" political economy approach challenged mainstream assumptions about geography, technology, and self-regulating markets as the main factors driving political and economic changes (see Whiteside, in this volume). Citing the growing proportion of FDI by American firms, increased plant closures, and fears of cultural homogenization, suspicion of US influence became an important political rallying point for many across Canada through the 1970s and 1980s (Canada 1968; Laxer 1973). As High (2003, 169), notes, "[f]ar from being a tool employed exclusively by Canada's economic and political elites, the new nationalism became a powerful rhetorical weapon in the hands of working people to be used against companies that closed plants." Existential questions concerning the status of Quebec and constitutional changes predominated as urban political economy was viewed, at best, through the prism of intergovernmental relations and, at worst, as derivative of federal and provincial dynamics (Eidelman and Taylor 2010).

Slowly but steadily, the "New Left" Canadian political economy, like its counterparts internationally, increasingly turned its attention to questions of urbanization and urban development, urban public policy, regionalism and land-use planning, municipal elections, and intergovernmental relations, as well as local environmental, urban workers', and poor peoples' movements (Piven and Cloward 1977). This in turn coincided with the revival of critical political economy approaches in the United States and Europe. In France, for instance, Henri Lefebvre (1970) argued that the "urban question" was as much a product of the capitalist system as was any manufactured good. He made the case that the built environment is shaped to serve the needs of the capitalist class, and that it changes in response to periodic and inherent crises which reanimate class struggles in a continuous process of uneven development. In other words, capitalists build a physical city appropriate to a specific moment in time only to replace it later in the course of creative destruction. Lefebvre also introduced the concept of the "right to the city," which called for a radical remaking of urban space through collective actions that challenge the power of capital and its state forms (Kipfer 2002; Purcell 2002). Likewise, Manuel Castells (1977) contended that the alienation experienced in the workplace extended beyond the confines of the factory to the very core of urban life, as evidenced though widespread social inequality and injustice. He argued that liberal urban political economy has been stuck in urbanist thinking and imbued with an implicit ruling-class bias. Castells directed attention to the role of collective consumption and social reproduction in backstopping capital accumulation, while pointing to the growing importance of social movements in challenging unequal class relations.

In the United States, these views found expression in David Harvey's (1973) *Social Justice and the City*, which showed how some Baltimore neighbourhoods fared better than other, largely racially segregated communities because of the profit-oriented priorities set by real estate investors, financiers, and government officials, which were linked to the decay of the central city and suburbanization of the population. Relatedly, John Logan and Harvey Molotch (1987) focused attention on urban growth coalitions – development interests, financiers, business elites, and politicians – that pressure governments to create a "good business climate." Members of this "machine," or pro-growth coalitions, share a common assumption that the best interests of the city and its residents are served by pursuing continuous economic growth irrespective of the social costs. The growth machine cuts to the ideological core of city power and politics as elites exert their influence on local governments to advance their own interests over those of others, such as unemployed workers and antipoverty groups.

Others drew attention to how cities serve as important nodal points in the global economy, linking together money, people, production, and commodities, with information and communication technologies and the relative ease of shipping by tanker, train, and cargo jet as key elements of the "global city" (Friedmann and Wolff 1982). Cities such as New York, London, Tokyo (and, more recently, Toronto) function as highly concentrated command posts in the organization of the world economy, standing at the apex of the global urban hierarchy because they are the financial capitals of the nations that dominate the global economy. As Sassen (1991, 2005) has argued, the concentration of finance capital in urban centres has gone hand in hand with the fragmentation and dispersal of manufacturing to non-metropolitan subsidiaries, offshore plants, and low-wage, precarious enclaves the world over. The deindustrialization of cities and entire regions dramatically altered the landscapes of metropolitan areas as many of the jobs earlier immigrants used as a path towards economic security vanished, precipitating a broader fiscal crisis of the state, since revenue needs could not keep up with service level demands (O'Connor 1973; Tabb 1982).

While distinctively urban issues remained largely peripheralized within the broader Canadian political economy tradition, contributions through the 1970s and 1980s increasingly dealt with issues specific to Canada and gained attention in the international literature. James Lorimer (1970) and others, to an extent anticipating Logan and Molotch (1987), drew attention to how private development coalitions came to dominate urban politics, which precipitated a range of local protest movements that rebelled against unchecked growth, new demands for electoral and governing reforms, and wider mechanisms for community engagement (Aubin 1972; Caulfield 1974; Sancton and

Magnusson 1983; Sewell 1972). Still others drew attention to historically undertheorized aspects of urban social life. For instance, feminist and antiracist political economists emphasized how gender differences in the experiences and uses of urban space were mediated by class, race, and sexuality, informed by the legacies of colonialism and patriarchy. They showed how women, Indigenous and racialized communities, and people with disabilities, immigrants, seniors, and youth, are more vulnerable to poverty (Massey 1984; McDowell 1983; Waldinger and Bozorgmehr 1996).

It was in this context that the Canadian subfield of urban political economy emerged from its three-decades-long eclipse by the national unity crisis. By the 1990s concerns about urban politics, economics, and social life more generally increasingly shifted from the margins of Canadian political economy to become a burgeoning field of investigation in its own right. An endogenous Canadian urban political economy, however, remained thin, "made up of orphans and islands – clusters of studies on particular topics, sometimes developed over time, other times abandoned, that are rarely connected to mainstream, national level studies of Canadian politics" (Eidelman and Taylor 2010, 967). Despite the lack of disciplinary coherence, newfound concerns proliferated, including those related to multilevel governance and urban policy (Bradford 2007; Young and Leuprecht 2006); municipal elections and voting behaviour (Cutler and Matthews 2005; MacDermid 2009; Stanwick 2000); urban planning, municipal restructuring, and public administration (Boudreau 2006; Frisken 2008; Kipfer and Keil 2002); new labour and urban social movements, as well as issues related to identity, citizenship, and group rights (Abu-Laban and Garber 2005; Fernando 2006; Stasiulis 1997).

Through the 2000s, Canadian urban political economy approaches increasingly drew attention to how multiple deprivations – lack of quality employment, low income, poor housing, ill-health, inadequate public transit, limited public services – spatially segregated inequalities among urban residents. Combined with urban sprawl, these reductions to public services further individualized responsibility (Bashevkin 2006; Wekerle 2010). Patterns of racialized urban labour market inequality intensified as neoliberalism weakened labour market protections and income security policies (Peters, Smith, in this volume). As a consequence, racialized groups and new immigrants remained trapped in low-income occupations across the labour market, with overall employment earnings below the Canadian average. This has contributed to the broader racialization of poverty, social exclusion, and urban spatial segregation (Wallis and Kwok 2008).

It is in this wider context that urban populations are finding their ability to express their collective agency and influence political decisions largely procedural and symbolic, as working-class institutions built up over generations have been eroded over some four decades of capitalist-class militancy. Many terms have been used to describe the movement away from the local provision of social welfare and services to more market-oriented development and private sector–led economic growth, including the "competitive," "entrepreneurial," and "corporate" city (Fanelli 2016; Keil 2009; Kipfer 2002; Kirkpatrick and Smith 2011; Leitner 1990; Peck 2014; Zukin 2009). Together, these changes can be understood as an uneven process of political economic restructuring in a matrix of multiscalar institutional relationships and labour-capital conflicts; as an urban policy regime promoting local processes of marketization, public sector austerity, and flexibilization of work relations; and as a process of internationalizing the local economy.

To summarize the broad history discussed above, we can identify four general principles at the core of both international and Canadian variants of critical urban political economy approaches. The first proposes that any analysis of urban forms or urban politics must be specific to the social formation concerned. In other words, a city's growth and particular form are not natural processes, but shaped by decisions of people and organizations that control wealth and other key resources.

Second, urban social arrangements reflect conflicts over the distribution of resources and among different elements of the urban population, notably social classes, and gender, racial, and ethnic groups. Social change – to know how urban life is formed and inequalities can be transformed through collective agency – is thus a primary concern of critical urban political economy (Albo and Fanelli 2019; Macionis and Parrillo 2009; Paddison and McCann 2014; Walton 1993; Zukin 1995).

Third, as a state is articulated on various spatial scales, scale becomes an important issue in understanding urban development trajectories (Brenner 2004; Cox 1993; Jessop 2002b). The local state, for instance, plays a significant role in urban life via the allocation of scarce resources, planning and zoning, spending priorities, housing and transit, business locations, and public spaces. Federal and provincial states are also a major influence on urban life through direct transfers, social programs, and infrastructure spending, as well as indirectly though the management of the prime interest rate for credit markets and rules governing investors. Together, these multiscalar governance arrangements provide consistent and reliable enforcement of contractual relations and general fiscal conditions for economic growth via private enterprise; underwrite the private risks of production at the public expense through tax incentives, subsidies, and depreciation allowances; maintain a stable and predictable social order, while preserving conditions amenable to capital accumulation; and use legal and juridical means, including overtly authoritarian measures, to mediate and, when necessary, discipline working-class resistance (Albo and Fanelli 2014; Hackworth 2007; Peck and Whiteside 2016).

And fourth, economic restructuring is a key influence on urban growth patterns. In contradistinction to classical liberal perspectives that posited urban economic activity was guided by self-regulating markets, critical urban political economy emphasizes the role of capital accumulation on cities and the interplay of political and economic forces in shaping the urban form as well as possibilities for change (Le Gales 2016; May and Perry 2005; Milicevic 2001; Oosterlynck 2012).

Cities increasingly are becoming the spatial location where the wealthiest and poorest members of society coexist and interact. Where the world's poor were once located largely in rural areas, today they are concentrated mostly in cities, although in the United States poverty predominates in suburban spaces. In Canada, seven out of ten of the poor live in an urban area, with particularly high concentrations of poverty in Edmonton, Montreal, Toronto, Vancouver, Quebec City, and Winnipeg. Although urban poverty is heightened in the city, it is not just an effect of the city, as larger regional, provincial, and international public policies play major roles in alleviating or accelerating poverty and inequality. In this sense, cities and their wider metropolitan regions have become pivotal sites for both the extension of neoliberal projects and of contestation. In what follows, we provide a snapshot of inequality in some of Canada's most populous cities, before turning to an assessment of Big City policies for reducing poverty.

Trends in Poverty and Income Inequality in Canada's Big Cities

Canada's development over the past 150 years has been characterized by a steady increase in urbanization. In 1867, only 18 per cent of the population resided in cities. Today, 84 per cent of the country's residents live in urban centres (see Figure 12.1). However, almost 19 million people – approximately half of Canada's population – dwell in ten major cities along the country's southern border with the United States: Toronto, Montreal, Vancouver, Calgary, Ottawa, Edmonton, Quebec City, Winnipeg, Hamilton, and Kitchener.

As discussed above, over the last three decades of the twentieth century, economic restructuring, technological change, and political reorganization significantly transformed the geographic and social landscape

Figure 12.1. Urbanization in Canada, 1851–2016

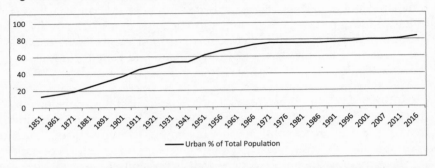

Source: Authors' compilation from diverse sources, including national census products and historical regional employment and income data (numbers rounded up).

of big cities in Canada, as elsewhere. Major urban centres across the country are marked by deeply segregated social spaces and extremes of poverty and wealth (see Peters, in this volume). One of the outstanding features of this change has been the surge in the share of total market incomes of the top 1 per cent.[2] Using historical national data as a basis for comparison, between 1920 and 1940, the top 1 per cent of taxfilers in Canada received between 15 and 20 per cent of all market income. This share declined during the Second World War and continued to drop until 1978, when it stood at just under 8 per cent. The trend then began to reverse itself, moving steadily upwards during the 1980s, then rising sharply over the next two decades. At its peak, the share of market income earned by the top 1 per cent was almost 14 per cent. Although still below levels seen in the late 1920s, this shift represented an increase of 75 per cent over thirty years (see Figure 12.2).

Conversely, as income became more concentrated among the top earners, the lower half of income earners saw their share of total market earnings decrease. Between 1982 and 2014, the proportion of market income earned by the bottom half of earners fell dramatically, by 28 per cent, while the share earned by the top half increased by only 5 per cent. The largest gains were made in the highest earning brackets: the top 1 per cent saw their share rise by 53 per cent, the top 0.1 per cent by 90 per cent, and the top 0.01 per cent by 133 per cent (see Figure 12.3).

---

2 This section draws·exclusively on the data findings in Statistics Canada (2018).

Figure 12.2. Change in the Share of Market Income of the Top 1 per cent, Canada, 1920–2015

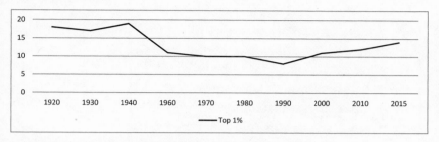

Source: Statistics Canada, CANSIM database, table 204-0001.

Figure 12.3. Differences between Top and Bottom Income Earners, Canada, 1982–2014

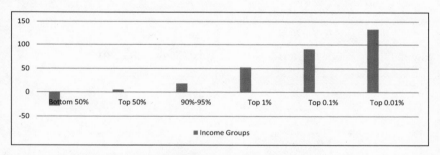

Source: Statistics Canada, CANSIM database, table 204-0001.

The surge in the top 1 per cent's share of market income between 1982 and 2014 occurred in all large Canadian cities, but, as Figure 12.4 shows, the increase was largest in Toronto and Calgary (see also Heisz 2015). In Toronto, the ratio roughly doubled from about 6:1 in 1982 to 12:1 in 2014. In Calgary, it rose from about 6:1 to about 11:1 (Murphy and Veall 2015). Put differently, as cities have increased in size over the past thirty-five years, whether through agglomeration, migration, or changing labour markets, urban inequality and poverty have also increased (Baum-Snow and Pavan 2012).

After peaking in the mid-1990s, poverty rates in Canada's largest cities declined slowly until the Great Recession of 2008. Since then, poverty rates have trended upward once again. In Toronto, however, poverty declined the least of any of the big cities during the pre-recession period,

Figure 12.4. Share of Total Market Income of the Top 1 per cent, Canada's Biggest Cities, 1982 and 2014

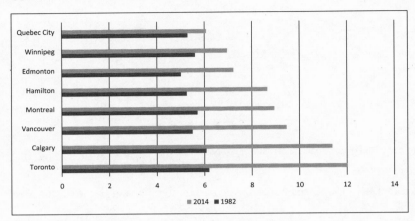

Source: Statistics Canada, CANSIM database, table 204-0002.

Figure 12.5. Poverty in Canada's Ten Largest Cities, 1980–2016

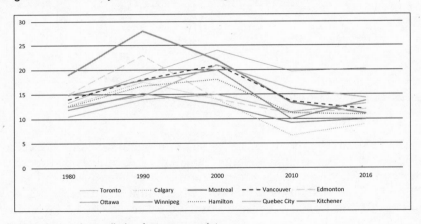

Source: Authors' compilation from census data.

and during most of the years since 2008 has remained the highest, at around 20 per cent. Toronto, in fact, has become the most unequal and polarized city in Canada, with inequality increasing by 68 per cent between 1980 and 2016, and poverty by 51 per cent (see Figure 12.5).

Canada's biggest cities have become more unequal. Although the extent and pace of change have varied from one city to another, the gap between rich and poor is widest in Toronto, followed closely by Calgary and Vancouver. Profound changes on both the economic and social fronts over the past thirty-five years have given rise to diverse political responses and experiments in urban policy making. Recently, many large municipalities have developed plans, policies, and strategies to reduce poverty and income inequality.

Surveying Big City Poverty-Reduction Plans, Policies, and Strategies

In 2010, the City of Ottawa became the first major Canadian city to adopt a poverty-reduction strategy, *Poverty Affects Us All: A Community Approach to Poverty Reduction*. The strategy is currently the most comprehensive and community-driven antipoverty policy of any of Canada's big cities. It seeks to reduce poverty along three major axes: enhancing, improving, and streamlining social services; strengthening marginalized communities and neighbourhoods through social infrastructure development, housing, and workforce development (training, education, apprenticeships); and promoting a communication plan to confront the myths and stigmas related to poverty and low income (Ottawa 2010).

The City of Calgary released its poverty-reduction strategy in 2015, *Enough for All*. Although the strategy is the boldest of any city with a dedicated plan in terms of targets and timelines (cutting poverty by 50 per cent by 2023), its asset-building approach to reducing poverty is the narrowest and most top-down. Programs designed to increase financial literacy and access to (financial) educational services and entrepreneurial opportunities, such as starting a small business and obtaining micro-loans, are centralized in community hubs across poor and low-income neighbourhoods. The strategy seeks to build public awareness and align poverty-reduction activities around financial empowerment (Calgary 2015).

The City of Edmonton released its poverty-reduction strategy, *End Poverty in a Generation: A Road Map to Guide Our Journey*, in 2016, and is the most innovative of the big city strategies in terms of partnerships. This plan takes a mid-range approach to reducing poverty, attempting to combine a top-down, asset-building approach with a bottom-up, community-building implementation model. The strategy is driven by a unique governance model, a secretariat, that draws on keystone partners – such as the United Way Alberta Capital Region, Edmonton Community Foundation, University of Alberta Community University Partnership, and Edmonton Social Planning

Council – to oversee implementation, track progress, and ensure continued and extensive community engagement. The core of the strategy, however, focuses on asset building, underpinned by social investments in early childhood, youth, and adult education and training (Edmonton 2016).

The City of Hamilton released its poverty-reduction strategy in 2017, but the plan lacks clarity around targets and timelines as well as programs and implementation mechanisms, and focuses, almost entirely, on the issue of affordable housing.

Vancouver, Kitchener, Quebec City, Montreal, and Winnipeg have not yet released dedicated poverty-reduction strategies. They do, however, have a range of antipoverty policies in place, and Vancouver is in the early stages of community consultations towards a dedicated strategy (see Table 12.1).

Lastly, the City of Toronto released its poverty-reduction strategy in 2015 (Toronto 2015). We have singled out this strategy for a more detailed examination for two reasons. First, Toronto's antipoverty policy might be of special interest to students of urban political economy because, as noted above, Toronto is the most unequal city in Canada, with the highest and most persistent rate of poverty. Second, by taking a closer look at how the biggest and most diverse city in the country has proposed to address these issues, we will be able to tease out and highlight some of the complex linkages among economic restructuring, spatial reorganization, social crises, and neoliberal urbanization in Canada.

Table 12.1. Plans, Policies, and Strategies to Reduce Poverty, Canada's Ten Largest Cities

City	Rank and Population	Strategy Name, Date, Targets	Priority Areas
Toronto	#1 5,928,040*	*TO Prosperity Poverty Reduction Strategy* (Toronto 2015); twenty-year plan.	Housing stability, service access, transit equity, food access, quality jobs, livable incomes.
Montreal	#2 4,098,927	No dedicated strategy; social development plan, *Montréal de tous les possibles!* (Montreal 2017).	Housing, food, homelessness, immigrant integration, education and training.

City	Rank and Population	Strategy Name, Date, Targets	Priority Areas
Vancouver	#3 2,463,431	No dedicated strategy; *A Healthy City for All*, four-year action plan (Vancouver 2015) to reduce poverty by 75% by 2025.	Food security, homelessness, housing, recreation, transportation.
Calgary	#4 1,392,609	*Enough for All Poverty Reduction Strategy* (Calgary 2015); goal is to reduce poverty by 50% by 2023.	Food security, homelessness, housing, recreation, transportation, payday lending.
Ottawa	#5 1,323,783	*Poverty Affects Us All: A Community Approach to Poverty Reduction* (Ottawa 2010).	Health, education and learning, community participation, public awareness, income and employment, affordable housing.
Edmonton	#6 1,321,426	*End Poverty in a Generation: A Road Map to Guide our Journey* (Edmonton 2016); goal is to lift 100,000 people out of poverty by 2021.	Eliminate racism, livable wages, affordable housing, accessible and affordable transit, affordable and quality child care, access to mental health services.
Quebec City	#7 798,162	No dedicated strategy; city is part of the Quebec Regional Development Plan, 2021.	Inclusive economic development with a focus on Indigenous engagement.
Winnipeg	#8 778,489	No dedicated strategy.	None.
Hamilton	#9 747,545	Housing strategy; $50 million, ten-year plan to reduce poverty (2017).	Housing; strategy sets aside $10 million specifically to address Indigenous poverty and housing.
Kitchener	#10 523,894	No dedicated strategy; community strategy, *Love My Hood* (Kitchener 2017).	18 actions to improve quality of life.

Note: Population figures are for the Census Metropolitan Area, 2016 census.

From Bust to Boom to Bust: Reducing Poverty
in Canada's Most Unequal City

The economic recession that engulfed most of the country in the early 1990s was especially severe in Toronto. For example, the median family income in the city fell 13 per cent compared with 2 per cent in all of Canada. Lone-parent families were particularly hard hit: their already-low median income declined a further 18 per cent. The financial situation also worsened for single people, whose median income fell by 12.5 per cent (United Way of Greater Toronto 2002). While struggling to recover, the city was profoundly affected by a restructuring in governance, a shift in demographics, and intensification of redevelopment in the urban core.

In the mid-1990s, Progressive Conservative premier Mike Harris's neoliberal growth strategy centred on transforming Toronto into a global city, one able to compete with top-tier cities such as New York, London, Paris, and Tokyo (Ibbitson 1997; see also Evans, in this volume). Harris's plan included, among other things, amalgamation of Metro Toronto's lower- and upper-tier municipalities. Prior to restructuring, Metro Toronto consisted of six cities: Toronto, North York, East York, York, Scarborough, and Etobicoke. Each of the lower-tier municipalities had councillors directly elected by the people, and Metro Council was composed of representatives from the lower-tier municipalities. In 1998, the premier amalgamated the six lower-tier cities and the upper-tier Metropolitan Toronto into one government and one administration that would be called the City of Toronto. One hundred and twenty councillors and six mayors were reduced to forty-four councillors and one mayor.

Government restructuring resulted in unexpected social costs. Because medical facilities, social services, and transit were much better in Toronto than in smaller surrounding municipalities, after amalgamation many low-income people, particularly those with special needs, migrated into the city centre. In addition to these pressures, population growth produced unprecedented demographic changes. From 1976 to 2016, the population in the downtown core doubled, from 102,000 to over 200,000. Furthermore, in 2016, 63 per cent of the population identified as a visible minority and more than 50 per cent were immigrants (Toronto Foundation 2017). In a very short span of time, Toronto became the most multi-ethnic and multiracial city in Canada.

Urban redevelopment further transformed the new "City of Toronto." At the end of the 1990s, Toronto's inner city underwent a major building boom that continues to this day. A 2013 TD Bank report found that, between 2009 and 2012, 4.7 million square feet of office space were built. With only 3 per cent of the City of Toronto's land area, the downtown core produces 51 per cent of its GDP, 33 per cent of all jobs, and has 25 per cent of the city's tax base. Over 100,000 people work in high-paid jobs in the banks, brokerage houses, and insurance companies along Bay Street. Government, financial services, and tourism are the core of the city's economy. Low-paid retail, however, is the largest employment sector (cited in Freeman 2017, 108–10).

As a result of these socio-economic changes, a chasm developed between high-paid white-collar jobs and low-paid services sector work that transformed Toronto's neighbourhoods into three cities. City #1 increased in size from 7 per cent of the city to 15 per cent, and included wealthy neighbourhoods in the downtown core, where incomes were 40 per cent greater than the metropolitan average. City #2, the middle-income area of the city, shrank dramatically. The proportion of middle-income neighbourhoods with incomes less than 20 per cent above or below the metropolitan average declined from 66 per cent of the city to 29 per cent, forming a narrow ring around the wealthy downtown core. City #3 comprised the lowest-income neighbourhoods on the edge of the city, including Scarborough, the northern fringe of North York, almost all of Etobicoke, as well as large parts of the former municipalities of York and East York. In a period of thirty-five years, the size of poor neighbourhoods increased from 19 per cent to 53 per cent of the city (Hulchanski 2010).

Globalization in the first half of the first decade of the new millennium produced a booming economy, new jobs, and increased opportunities for improved market incomes. For many, however, especially women, youths, immigrants, lone-parent families, and racialized groups, new prosperity would be short-lived. The global financial collapse of 2008 caused a spike in metropolitan poverty rates and a deepening of urban spatial inequality (see Figure 12.6). Although poverty rates have since decreased slightly, poverty persists, especially among certain population segments and in neighbourhoods on the outer margins of the city (Hulchanski 2015).

Census data show that, in 2016, 20.2 per cent of Toronto's population, or 543,390 people, live on low incomes, according to Statistics Canada's Low-income measure after tax. Although Toronto's low-income rate had declined by a modest 2 per cent since 2010, it was still higher than that for Canada as a whole (14.2 per cent) or Ontario's (14.4 per cent). The census data also show that the low-income rate is higher among visible minority groups in Toronto, and not just because many are recent immigrants – in some populations, such as Black and Latin

Figure 12.6. Neighbourhood Income Change: Toronto's Divided Three Cities, 2005 and 2012

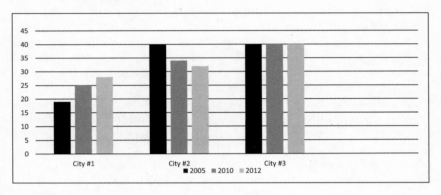

Source: Hulchanski (2015).

American Torontonians, low-income rates are higher among those whose families have been in Canada for three generations or more (Toronto 2017).

Poverty among lone-parent families is on the rise. In 2016, 19.7 per cent of lone-parent families lived in poverty compared with 17.6 per cent in 2008. Of poor, lone-parent families in 2016, 89 per cent were female-led. Notably, in the years since the Great Recession of 2008, the poor have become very poor. By 2016, the poverty gap – the difference between the poverty line and actual household income, expressed as a percentage of the poverty line – had reached 33 per cent (Toronto 2017). According to the Daily Bread Food Bank, food bank usage increased by 9 per cent in one year from 2016 to 2017. The share of Daily Bread member agencies' clients ages sixty-five and older increased by a stark 27 per cent in 2017. In food bank surveys, 14 per cent of clients who were children reported going hungry at least once a week, while 41 per cent of all clients reported not eating for an entire day. The four most-cited living costs paid at the expense of buying food were rent, utilities, phone, and public transit (Daily Bread 2017).

Perhaps the most striking change of all has been the sharp increase in the working poor – defined as someone with earnings of at least $3,000 a year, between the ages of eighteen and sixty-four, not a student, and who lives independently (Stapleton 2019). As Figure 12.7 shows, the rate of working poverty in Toronto increased from 7.2 per cent in 2000 to 10.7 per cent in 2012. Working poverty, moreover, is concentrated

Figure 12.7. Working Poverty Rate, Toronto, 2000, 2006, and 2012

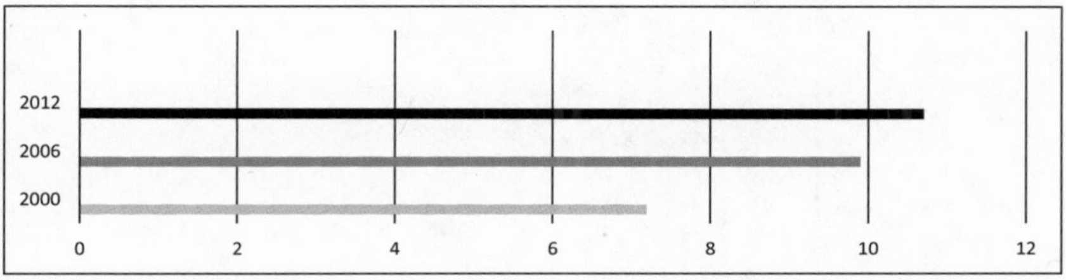

Source: Stapleton (2019).

among younger workers ages eighteen to twenty-nine (23 per cent), singles (34 per cent), and lone parents (29 per cent). A job no longer guarantees freedom from poverty.

In 2015, Toronto City Council unanimously approved *TO Prosperity: Toronto Poverty Reduction Strategy*. Designed as a twenty-year strategy, *TO Prosperity* contains seventeen recommendations divided into six core areas: housing stability, service access, transit equity, food access, quality jobs and livable incomes, and systemic change. *TO Prosperity* was conceived as part of two larger political processes. One was existing City policies and programs aimed at leveraging Toronto's economic power to drive inclusive economic development. The second was the provincial government's ten-year roadmap to structural reform of Ontario's income security system, *Income Security: A Roadmap for Change* (Toronto 2017).

As a starting point, City Council allocated $24.5 million to its first poverty-reduction efforts in the 2015 budget. In the City's first Action Plan (2015–18), City Council approved a set of immediate priorities and spending of $58.3 million from existing funding commitments as well as $11.4 million in new funds. The $58.3 million included new provincial funding for the child care system and a new request for the expansion of the Toronto Urban Health Fund. The $11.4 million in new funds included the City's contribution towards its 20 per cent share of the Child Care Growth Strategy, the low-income transit pass, and student nutrition programs.

The first Action Plan (2015–18) saw the implementation of a broad range of initiatives (see Table 12.2). However, the City's poverty-reduction strategy was designed to leverage interconnected and complementary policies and strategies to focus on inclusive economic development. This included the following policies: Social Procurement, Anchor Institutions, Decent Work & Job Quality, and Community Benefits Framework. Specifically, in 2017, the City adopted a new Social Procurement program

Table 12.2. Toronto Poverty-Reduction Strategy Action Plan, 2015–18

Issue	Housing Stability	Service Access	Transit Equity	Food Access	Quality Jobs and Liveable Wages	Systemic Change
Primary plan(s)	Housing Opportunities Toronto 2010–20 housing plan	Child care	Free and fair transit passes	Food Reach web portal	Partnership to Advance Youth Employment & Youth Employment Partnerships	Created Lived Experience Advisory Group (LEAP)
Targets & objectives	1,000 new affordable rental and 400 new affordable ownership homes	To serve 50% of children ages 0–4 by 2026; reduce parent fees by 25% to 40%	Free transit passes for children 12 and under; reduced fair for low-income adults 18–64	Provide information to community agencies to purchase food at wholesale prices	To connect youths with employers	To provide advice on development of various programs and policies across the City
New policy instrument(s)	Housing allowance	Recreation subsidies	Equity assessment tool; low-income advisory group	Technology-based, multilingual website	Learning and networking events	Enhanced public consultations

with two components: a Supply Change Diversity component aimed at certifying diverse suppliers, and a Workforce Development component to provide training, apprenticeship, and employment opportunities for people experiencing economic disadvantage, including women and Indigenous and racialized people. The City also created the AnchorTO initiative in 2017 to embed social procurement processes across the public sector. To this end, the City partnered with the Atkinson Foundation, eight post-secondary institutions, four provincial agencies, corporations, and divisions, and two non-profit builders (Toronto 2017).

The City has yet to respond fully to the Ontario government's 2018 legislation, the Fair Workplaces, Better Jobs Act, which increases the minimum wage and strengthens the Employment Standards Act of 2000 and the Labour Relations Act of 1995 to reduce precarious employment. The City also has in place a Fair Wage Policy that expects subcontractors to pay a fair wage. The policy is reviewed every three years, but has no enforcement mechanism.

In 2015, prior to these antipoverty initiatives, the City created a Community Benefits Framework that allows it to ask developers to provide community benefits when requesting a zoning by-law amendment for increased height and/or density. These benefits include affordable housing, recreation centres, child care centres, park improvements, public art, heritage preservation, streetscapes, and space for non-profits. Lastly, the City's *Poverty Reduction Strategy* proposes to align with Ontario's 2017 income assistance review – *Income Security: A Roadmap for Change* – in three key areas: financial benefit adequacy and simplification, the need to provide robust housing supports (and move essential health and housing benefits outside the social assistance system), and the importance of promoting a culture of respect, dignity, and collaboration between clients and staff (Toronto 2017).

Assessing Big City Strategies to Reduce Poverty

The recent proliferation of poverty-reduction strategies, plans, and policies in big cities across Canada suggests that the redistributive function of the welfare state has either become weaker or remained more or less the same as in the 1980s. In other words, the Canadian welfare state has been unresponsive in the face of the deep recession of the early 1990s and the global financial collapse of 2008. In the rare cases where redistribution increased (e.g., child benefits and working tax credits), these have not been enough to check the increase in poverty and market income inequality against the backdrop of urban globalization: the rise of global cities in Canada.

In September 2015, the United Nations' seventeen Sustainable Development Goals (SDGs) were affirmed by leaders of all 193 UN member states, and apply to countries at all income levels. Among these goals are achieving full gender equality, quality education, universal access to health and well-being, decent work, and sustainable cities and communities. The number one SDG, however, is ending poverty in all its forms – a useful objective and commitment against which to assess big city poverty-reduction strategies in Canada. This goal is also helpful to gain a deeper understanding of the potential for urban poverty-reduction strategies to check and then reverse the increase in income inequality, to halt the decline of the middle class, to protect the rights of workers, and to reorient the spatial divide between rich and poor neighbourhoods.

In signing on to the SDGs, the UN members agreed to cut their national poverty rate by half by 2030. In this regard, McArthur and Rasmussen (2017, 1–3) evaluated Canada's cities based on no fewer than seventy-one indicators, and determined that none of the poverty-reduction strategies then in place in Calgary, Toronto, Montreal, Vancouver, and Winnipeg fully aligned with the UN goal or was on track to meet the 2030 target. Municipal strategies tend to have better-defined targets than their provincial counterparts, but they are not ambitious nor do they adequately tackle the issues of social inequality or economic opportunities. Additionally, city strategies appear limited in what they can achieve in terms of community building and neighbourhood-to-neighbourhood equity, access to green spaces and parks, affordable housing, and public transportation for low-income people. On the upside, all major cities have surpassed standards for addressing extreme income poverty (the number of people living below $8,000 per year) and average educational outputs. Nonetheless, market incomes (wages), social inequality, and food insecurity are heading in the wrong direction (McArthur and Rasmussen 2017, 30–1). That is, poverty-reduction strategies that privilege inclusion in economic development with few social development or redistributive mechanisms will not be enough to correct our current course as major Canadian urban centres continue to globalize.

Conclusion

Although it is too soon to provide a more comprehensive evaluation of big city poverty-reduction strategies, even a limited empirical assessment of urban antipoverty strategies as measured against the UN's Sustainable Development Goals can inform political debate. It was, after all, political changes over the past thirty-five years, and especially since the mid-1990s, that weakened the welfare state, stripped labour of its bargaining power, and flattened progressive taxation. It was political decision making that led to the concentration of wealth and market income in a few individuals in the top 1 per cent and big cities that are growing poorer and more unequal. In this regard, the critical urban political economy perspective is a holistic approach to understanding urban social life in a manner that denaturalizes capitalist social relations. In this framework, the starting point is not individuals and their values, beliefs, or attitudes, but the structural reproduction of urban space and society as a whole.

A distinctively Canadian urban political economy approach has been slow to emerge, but the broader New Left revival of the 1970s emphasized that "urban" issues could not be understood outside the wider political and economic context of capitalism. Canadian cities have yet to experience an urban crisis of commensurate social, political, and economic significance to that of their US neighbours, yet they are starting to experience many of the same symptoms, including ethno-racial and income segregation, urban-suburban conflicts, and a revenue crisis begat by decades of tax cutting and constitutional constraint, provincial downloading, and federal ad hockery. In this regard, the "Canadian" urban political economy perspective continues to offer fertile terrain on which to begin thinking critically about the interplay of sociopolitical and economic forces, their effects on everyday life, and the transformative potential of urban spaces in larger domestic and international contexts.

13 The Political Economy of Social Policy in Canada

PETER GRAEFE

Introduction

After forty years of neoliberal politics, social policy is in a moment of change. The majority of Canadian provinces, a number of cities (Fanelli and Hudson, in this volume), and the federal government have adopted or are in the process of adopting antipoverty strategies. The post-2015 Trudeau Liberal government has made steps to re-enter the field of housing policy, and has started to engage with provinces around mental health and long-term care policies. Changes were made to employment insurance that, while minor, represented the largest liberalization of the program since 1971.

What is driving this change? Canadian political economy provides some tools for making sense of this moment – for assessing its compatibility with the underlying neoliberal regime of accumulation. For some, new social policies "roll out" neoliberalism by introducing market-like mechanisms into new social realms. For others, social policies in themselves might not be market extending, but they nevertheless serve to "flank" neoliberalism by ensuring that its dislocations do not undermine economic efficiency.

Political conflict nevertheless remains salient in shaping how these moments of "rollout" and "flanking" are translated in people's lived realities. It helps explain, for instance, why parents in Quebec have rights to affordable and accessible child care that do not exist elsewhere in Canada, but also why fifteen years of electing right-wing parties have reduced the Quebec-Canada difference.

This chapter discusses the complex relationship of social reproduction to capitalist accumulation, and how this manifests itself in proposals that alternatively roll out neoliberalism or attempt to flank its shortcomings. It then presents two short capsules on recent changes in

Canadian poverty and child policy to ground these abstract ideas in concrete policy study. The capsules grapple with how social policy reform responds to crises within neoliberalism and the varying ways they roll out and flank neoliberalism. Here conflict matters: it helps explain how the scope and content of the change varies across time and space, and what openings might present themselves for pushing beyond neoliberalism.

Canadian Social Policy

In the early traditions of Canadian political economy, social policy was largely absent. Indeed, early feminist critiques of the Innisian tradition underlined how its emphasis on waves of staples-led development obscured any attention to social reproduction and, by extension, the contributions of women. For instance, the role of non-market social reproduction in Ontario farm households in sustaining the labour force across the seasonal and boom-bust cycles of staple commodity production was ignored (Cohen 1988). Social policy was also tangential to the leading debates of Canadian political economy in the 1970s about the character of Canadian development and its place in the global political economy. Nevertheless, a political economy of Canadian social policy did develop, drawing on neo-Marxist debates on the subject. Although this work started as being about applying political economy theories to Canada, the strength of the socialist feminist presence in the field has created a somewhat distinctive Canadian approach (Luxton 2006). The manner in which social policy affects social reproduction (and not simply labour commodification) has been more present in Canadian work in the field, as has been the importance of agency in shaping policy, including the agency of a range of actors beyond capital and labour, such as the women's movement or community-based organizations (e.g., McKeen and Porter 2003).

In terms of specifically understanding Canada, the country's status in the international literature as a "welfare state laggard" drove much early analysis. Whereas a number of continental European countries began developing pensions, workplace compensation, and even unemployment insurance schemes in the early twentieth century, in Canada many of these policies developed later. The first major policy was workers' compensation, followed in the 1920s by some meagre, means-tested allowances for widowed or abandoned mothers. A means-tested pension was passed in 1927, but only with subsequent reforms in 1951 and 1966 were the major pieces of our current retirement security system put into place. Universal hospital insurance was launched in 1957 and universal medical insurance in 1966, while the upgrading of the scattered provincial social assistance programs for single mothers, people with disabilities, and the unemployed was greatly pushed forward with the launch of the Canada Assistance Plan (CAP) in 1966. In other words, the major pieces of the traditional welfare state were in place in Canada only in the late 1960s (Guest 1997).

Given this laggard status, much effort has been placed on understanding "what went wrong?" Here, it makes sense to ask "what went right?" – what political contestation produced Canadian social policy, as meagre as it mighty look in international comparison (see Noël, Boismenu, and Jalbert 1993)? Two major schools of thought contend on this issue. One argues that the development of social policies reflected the strength of the labour movement in the workplace and in politics as Canada industrialized and urbanized. Given the decentralization and fragmentation of the Canadian labour movement, and the New Democratic Party's (NDP's) inability to win federal elections, it is not surprising that Canada's welfare state is small and ungenerous. The major moments of policy expansion, particularly the development of the Canada Pension Plan, universal medicare, and the CAP in the mid-1960s, can be related to the threat of the newly formed NDP, its kingmaker potential in the minority governments of the period (Boychuk 2009; Johnston 2013), and perhaps the upsurge of labour radicalism in that decade.

The alternative school believes that the "strength of the left" argument can only really explain "what went wrong," as the NDP and the labour movement were never strong enough to spur the development of social policy reforms. In this account, the development of the welfare state resulted from regional and national competition. In other words, given Canada's relatively decentralized constitutional framework in the 1930s and 1940s, elites around the central government felt the need to create central institutions to strengthen the sense of Canadian citizenship. In the post-1945 Keynesian era, when the national scale became pre-eminent in defining spaces of economic and social management, this nation-building project looked to social policy to created pan-Canadian solidarities. This centralist nationalism, however, offended Quebec's dualist or binational conception of Canada. Post-war Canadian nationalism therefore provoked the rise of a counternationalism in that province in the 1960s. Both the federal and Quebec governments used social policy as a means of harnessing Quebecers to their respective national projects, feeding the 1960s social policy surge noted above as well as improvements in child benefits and reinvestments in health in the late 1990s and early 2000s (Béland and Lecours 2008; Jenson 2013).

The Political Economy of Social Policies:
Two Sides to Every Story

Social policies have a contradictory place in political economy. On the one hand, they organize a large slice of society's daily production. Spending on health care systems, for instance, accounts for over 10 per cent of the gross domestic product in most advanced industrial countries, with further outlays for various forms of income support (pensions, unemployment insurance, social assistance, workers' compensation), education, and social services (child and elder care, primary and secondary education). When these services are provided under a public sector auspice, it means that a significant share of social resources is pulled into the state through taxation and invested for ends other than private profit making.

Although this explains why supporters of capitalist development often portray social spending as a wasteful drag on the economy, it is also true that capitalist production depends on the reproduction of inputs that are not automatically replenished. When these inputs are natural resources, this reproduction engages the ecological relationships raised by Carter (in this volume). It is similar with labour power: people cannot magically appear at work each day, but must be able to feed, clothe, and shelter themselves. Over a longer period, new generations of workers need to be reared. As production becomes more complex, it relies on the production and reproduction of skills, and thus on systems of education and training (Cameron 2006). The organization of an economic system also requires shared cultural understandings to produce the predictability that enables actors to make and enforce contracts and coordinate their activities (Boyer and Hollingsworth 1997). Contemporary economic competitiveness increasingly calls upon "extra-economic" inputs such as trust, social cohesion, and creativity (Jessop 2000). The investment of resources in social policies that ensure this social reproduction underwrites the success of the market economy and thus private accumulation. This relationship can help explain how states may undertake new investments – for instance, in early childhood education – even if they remain steadfast in fighting against the power of labour (see Smith, in this volume).

The "optimal" level of social reproduction cannot be set in the abstract. Employers reliant on low-paid, unskilled labour tend to see social spending as wasteful, as they do not require skilling and can keep wages low if people have to treat any job as a good job. Such employers are less willing to pay taxes, and are keen to push the costs of social reproduction onto individuals. Employers reliant on a stable or highly skilled workforce also favour pushing costs onto individuals, but are quicker to recognize when this produces suboptimal outcomes, such as when new workers need extensive on-the-job training, or when reliable employees have to quit to care for dependents if care policies are lacking.

Social policies are not solely about the economic relations of capitalism. In providing or denying resources to people, they contribute to social stratification: they can upset traditional social hierarchies or reinforce them. Feminist scholars underline that social policies can be designed to support a variety of different "gender orders." For example, such policies can reinforce a "male breadwinner, female homemaker" order by supporting labour force participation and security for men and caregiving roles for women. Alternatively, a "dual breadwinner, dual caregiver" model results from policies that open access to the labour market to all, that reconcile care work with paid work, and that encourage men to increase their household work (Mahon 2002).

Political economists therefore have to make sense of how social reproduction is related to production and accumulation. James O'Connor's (1973) distinction between the accumulation and legitimation functions of the capitalist state was an early attempt to do so. In his view, part of the state's social policy effort reflected capital's need for the reproduction of the inputs necessary for accumulation. Another part of the distinction, by contrast, involved ensuring the continued legitimacy of capitalist relations of production by spending part of the economic surplus to ensure sufficient economic security for working people that they continued to support the system.

Another way of capturing this was Gough's (1979) argument that welfare state policies came from twin sources. First, they reflected structural necessities of ensuring continued accumulation. As capitalist production grew in scale and sophistication, old ways of ensuring reproduction proved insufficient, and so the state had to develop new interventions such as education and unemployment insurance. Second, welfare state policies reflected the agency of working people, organizing either to overturn or to find more security within capitalism. In many countries, the development of social policies came from working people exercising power through unions and social democratic parties. There was tension in this analysis: social policies seemed structurally necessary in modern capitalism, yet these necessary interventions were lived as political victories by subordinate classes against capitalists.

These early explanations, however, are weakened by their functionalism: they read off state policies from a deductive understanding of capitalism's needs, rather than from the push and pull of social movements, interest groups, parties, and bureaucrats involved in their crafting. They treat the "needs" of capital as self-evident, as opposed to something negotiated between capitalists themselves – for instance, between employers of high-skilled and low-skilled workers. The explanations are also "class reductionist," in that they capture how social policy relates to capitalism and class, but do not consider other dimensions of these policies, such as how they affect gender relations or ethno-racial hierarchies. In Canada, they also miss the importance of managing Quebec's nationalist claims, and the institutional effects of dividing social policy powers between the federal and provincial governments (Cameron 2006). The early explanations nevertheless have the virtue of understanding social policies as the result of social conflict against the background of historically specific forms of capitalism.

Two-Sided Neoliberalism

In the 1980s, political economists underlined how the move to neoliberal forms of accumulation changed the logic of the welfare state. While the welfare state might have once decommodified labour by providing some income security independent of one's employment, neoliberalism employed social policy to recommodify labour by pushing people into the labour market (McBride 1992). In order to reduce state expenditure, the neoliberal project also foresaw a reduction in the scope and generosity of social protection, thereby privatizing responsibility. Individuals could insure themselves privately through the market or through calling on the care resources that were assumed to exist in families and communities. In terms of the gender order, while neoliberalism presented as "gender blind" by treating people equally as genderless individuals, pushing care responsibilities onto families in practice placed additional burdens on women, with knock-on effects on their ability to secure their own income and social protection. In other words, neoliberalism pretended equality had arrived, which meant it did little to actively transform actually existing gender inequality, violence, and discrimination.

These forms of recommodification, retrenchment and reprivatization/refamilialization were critiqued from the get-go by critical social policy scholars (e.g., McBride 1992; McKeen and Porter 2003), and by the late 1990s they were visible to state policy makers and mainstream policy scholars. In Europe, this was packaged in a discussion of "new social risks": while the post-war welfare state was involved in "social protection" of the male breadwinner and his dependents when his relationship to paid work was interrupted (e.g., through illness, involuntary unemployment, workplace injury, old age), this no longer worked given dual breadwinner families and flexible labour markets. The male breadwinner model relied on families to carry a heavy care burden, but this was not realistic in a world of dual-earner families. Instead, welfare needed to come through market participation, and social policy's role was to support that participation – for instance, through care policies (to encourage women's labour force participation), life-long learning policies, and strategies to delay retirement (Esping-Andersen 2002, 19–21).

These responses mainly covered one side of the story: how to remake the welfare state into a "social investment state" in order to reconcile social policy with economic imperatives. There was an implicit political economy to this story – namely, that success in the knowledge economy required a well-educated and flexible workforce. However, the responses to this demand were seen as mainly functional and voluntarist: all actors were assumed to share an interest in crafting policies that achieved this knowledge society.

Political economists who studied these changes nevertheless wished to go further in relating production and social reproduction. Beyond considering these changes as the result of social learning about a changing world, and thus focusing analysis at the institutional level of policy debates between actors, political economists sought to relate new social policy initiatives directly to economic forces. Two approaches have had particular influence in the Canadian case, discussed below. However, given the "two-sided" nature of social policy and the importance of ongoing conflict, I argue for making less definitive claims, and instead for assessing how social policy might simultaneously roll out and flank neoliberalism.

The first analytical approach is drawn from Craig and Porter's (2004) work on "inclusive liberalism." Porter and Craig adopt the Polanyian conceptualization of the "double movement" – namely, that increased commodification of the "fictitious commodities" of land, labour, and money (fictitious because they are not produced with the purpose of market exchange) will cause social strains and induce a countermovement to protect society from being ground down by the market (Polanyi [1944] 2001). Neoliberalism represents the push of market mechanisms deeper into the life-world, and has given rise to a counterpolitics of "inclusive liberalism," which embraces market liberalization but nevertheless seeks to protect core public services. The agents pushing protection are less traditional working-class actors than centre-left parties that can mobilize a middle-class electorate of public sector employees and those who value public health care and education. This concept has been adapted to the Canadian case by Rianne Mahon (2008), who strips away the functionalist Polanyian political economy of the double movement, and instead emphasizes social conflict over reconciling the moments of production and social reproduction. In particular, she identifies how neoliberal ideas are now challenged by inclusive liberal ones that accept the market emphasis of neoliberalism, but argue that economic efficiency requires a greater state role in correcting market failures, particularly in human capital formation. This opens space for social policy actors to demand greater investment. In this approach, social policy exists in a series of historical forms, where particular sets of dominant liberal ideas create a unique balancing of production and social reproduction.

The second trajectory involves a historical analysis of neoliberalism as a form of class rule. It considers how the program of market liberalization and commodification has been tweaked in response to economic crises and negotiated in response to the alternatives proposed by competing social forces. In Peck and Tickell's (2007) early telling, we witnessed the transition from a "proto-neoliberalism" in the thinking and planning of Hayekian and Friedmanite economists working in the shadows of the Keynesian welfare state, to a period of "roll-back neoliberalism" where the electoral successes of Margaret Thatcher in Britain and Ronald Reagan in the United States led to governments cutting back the welfare state. There were limits to these cuts, as they undermined the level of social reproduction required for continued growth by excluding people from economic participation, even as they came up against continued electoral support for some core programs such as pensions and health care. This led to a "rollout" stage, where the state reinvented social policies using market and quasi-market mechanisms. This could take the form of creating "quasi-markets" for state services by developing systems of competitive bidding for services that might once have been contracted on a longer-term, sustained basis to nonprofits (see Moreno et al. 2018). It could also mean privatizing public assets – for instance, through contracting out services or through integrating private financing and management in the construction and operation of public infrastructure such as hospitals (Whiteside 2009).

The benefit of this approach, compared to that of "inclusive liberalism," is that it understands neoliberalism within a geographic and historical process. Rather than taking it at its "free market" word, it considers how neoliberalism unfolded through specific projects of state retrenchment and reform. Rather than treating deviations from market-based regulation as evidence of a break with neoliberalism, it relates these to an unfolding process of neoliberalization and the need to experiment with new forms of statecraft to overcome crises and challenges.

One difficulty with this approach is that it almost becomes tautological in its inability to define what might stand outside of neoliberalism. Because the state is expected to be neoliberal, neoliberal aims or consequences are read into every action. In the process, the aspects of policies that reproduce neoliberalism are overemphasized, while aspects that point to non-neoliberal possibilities are ignored (Leitner et al. 2007).

For scholars such as Jane Jenson (2012), this is a fundamental problem: it underplays that both the Keynesian state and the "rollback" neoliberal state shared an understanding of social policy as providing security in the "here and now" when one's relationship to paid work was severed due to predictable risks (such as unemployment, sickness, injury, old age). Where they differed was in their assessments of the extent of state responsibility and of necessary labour discipline. For Jenson, social policy debates changed fundamentally in the 1990s as social policy goals moved from emphasizing social protection to stressing social investment to counter the "new social risks." This shift in the idea sets gets flattened in the analysis of neoliberalization. Inclusive liberalism, by contrast, is better placed to capture this shift, as it can make sense of how these ideas represent a new expression of liberalism, marrying the neoliberal status quo to a defence of limited state interventions to ensure some basic equality of opportunity in confronting new social risks (Mahon 2008).

Another danger of the rollback/rollout approach is that it downplays the "two-sided" nature of social policy. Although crises of social reproduction might spur new forms of statecraft, the interest is largely in how these are themselves patently market oriented and contribute to further commodification. It ignores that policies might be adopted to deal with the tension within neoliberal capitalism between an economic competitiveness reliant upon many extra-economic inputs (skills, knowledge, trust, social cohesion) and the inability of that capitalism to reproduce those inputs (Jessop 2000).

An alternative to both the inclusive liberalism and the rollback/rollout approaches is to relax the urge to label. Just as social policy can be about both production and social reproduction, so too can specific policies relate in complex ways to neoliberalism. In the abstract, we could consider at least three forms of relation. First, policies could serve to *roll out* neoliberalism – for instance, by the privatization of public services through the development of managed competition in service delivery. Second, policies could serve as *flanking mechanisms*, with the policies themselves based on a non-neoliberal logic, but nevertheless serving to shore up a neoliberal development strategy by containing negative externalities, such as poverty, homelessness, or low human capital formation (Jessop 2002a). Third, such policies could contribute to *alternative development projects* outside of or beyond neoliberalism. While political economists have been especially interested in social democratic or ecological alternatives, there are also movements of the political right that disapprove of the abstract individual equality of neoliberalism, and seek a return to a more authoritarian order that rebuilds patriarchal power and a male breadwinner/female caregiver model. The recent rise in authoritarian political movements certainly complicates social policy by bringing conservative voices to the social policy table that had been sidelined by neoliberalism's ascendency. These voices might wish to expand social provision selectively to reward the "deserving" (such as traditional nuclear families or members of the majority ethnicity), but deny protection to the "undeserving" (such as queer families or racialized communities). For left movements that wish to expand social protection, but in a project of increasing equality, this produces some tactical quandaries.

These three possibilities of rollout, flanking, and alternative development projects are defined "in the abstract," because social policies exist in a field of contest between organized social forces that are trying to shape the direction of development. A given social policy might serve as part of a neoliberal strategy, but might take on a decidedly different coloration if the broader development strategy were to change. This is in some way the conclusion Peck and Theodore (2015) reach about conditional cash transfers in Latin America: while originally rolled out as a neoliberal governmentality to encourage poor women to mother in ways that enhanced human capital development, in some countries they have evolved into de facto unconditional social transfers. As such, they have become a flanking mechanism, and provide the foundation for more thoroughgoing redistribution if the transfers were significantly increased. By keeping the question of the relationship of specific policies to a wider neoliberalism contingent, space is retained for politics, as social actors with competing development models seek to change the "policy ecology" not only by changing existing policies, but also by introducing new initiatives that might affect how current policies contribute to the reproduction (or non-reproduction) of social relationships.

Recent Trends in Canadian Social Policy

How might this threefold framework help us understand recent Canadian social policy? Canadian policy makers have followed the international trend in assessing the fit of a "social protection" welfare state with new social risks. In the late 1990s and early 2000s, this discussion tried to define a "new social architecture" to meet "new social risks" (Jenson 2004; Scott 2005). These risks included childhood poverty (and associated effects on brain development and human capital formation), in-work poverty, the impact of child care and elder care deficits on labour market participation, and efficiency losses from the non-optimal inclusion of newcomers in the labour market.

Canadian political economists have criticized the work on new social risks for capturing aspects of change (in labour markets, life courses, and families, for instance) and of crisis (in the mismatch of policies to these risks), but of missing important dimensions of conflict arising from deeper connections of social policy to capitalist production and labour-capital relations. For those in the rollback/rollout tradition, the observed changes are seen as extending neoliberalism. If there is a moment of crisis, it is related to the need to deepen commodification in order to find new opportunities for profit making. For instance, in assessing Ontario's social housing policy, Hackworth (2008) emphasizes how the government developed a set of market-based management strategies that squeezed social purposes out of the sector. In health services, attention has been paid to how work has been restructured to emphasize doing more with less, squeezing out the time for true caring (e.g., O'Neill 2015). Others have underlined the development of profit centres within health care through privatization, whether through the contracting out of ancillary services (food preparation, cleaning) in hospitals, the use of private firms for diagnostic and rehabilitation services, or the involvement of large private consortia in the financing, construction, and management of new hospital facilities (see Whiteside 2015). Engaging the non-profit sector in delivering new solutions to social problems through the offer of "social impact bonds" provides another example (Joy and Shields 2018, and in this volume).

Scholars using concepts of inclusive liberalism have a broader sense of change, recognizing that it might involve interventions that break from neoliberalism – for instance, to compensate for insufficient human capital formation or to reduce care deficits. Crisis is generally considered more on the side of social reproduction than of production: whereas neoliberals stress the need for further commodification and marketization, inclusive liberals see the state as developing new cases for intervention in order to palliate the care crisis or to ensure sufficient human capital formation. This produces a form of "after-neoliberalism" where the main commitments of neoliberalism to market-centred growth and a fiscally constrained state persist, but with new state spending at the margins to underwrite a fuller equality of opportunity (Mahon 2008).

These two accounts, one stressing the rollout of neoliberalism and the other the development of new flanking mechanisms to sustain a neoliberalized political economy, reflect decisions to focus on one side or the other of what remains a two-sided story. In surveying a couple of policy areas, such as poverty policy and child policy, we can see that both dynamics are taking place concurrently, and that ongoing political conflict is important in shaping which dynamics predominate. Moreover, in observing that political conflict, one can recover imaginaries pointing to development projects beyond neoliberalism.

Poverty

One area with a high degree of policy engagement has been poverty policy. In the early neoliberal period, poverty fell off the policy agenda. The assumption guiding policy makers was that increasing labour market participation, particularly of people on social assistance, would solve the problem of poverty (Jenson 2004), and policies and programs were revamped to encourage participation. For instance, federal employment insurance eligibility rules were tightened by increasing the work hours needed to qualify and by disqualifying those who voluntarily quit their jobs, even as benefits were reduced. Likewise, provincial social assistance systems adopted "employability' measures to push recipients into paid work, often taking the form of structuring job search activities around low-paid, non-standard work. Mothers of young children, who previously had been encouraged to stay home, were also compelled to search for work when their children reached toddler age (Mahon 2008; Porter 2015).

This strategy had popular appeal, given its association with widely held ideas about the work ethic, but it lost purchase as poverty rates remained high even as unemployment and welfare caseloads plummeted. As concern about the social and economic costs of poverty grew, policy thinking began to change (Jenson 2012). The mix of policy instruments also changed as the focus shifted from employability to child and in-work poverty. Since the turn of the twenty-first century, nine provinces have elaborated poverty-reduction strategies; the Trudeau government also proposed its own, but let it die on the order paper ahead of the 2019 election. Overall, these poverty strategies serve as limited forms of flanking. The proposed policy solutions try to compensate for the long-run human capital costs of child poverty – for instance, through school or community programming – but aim especially to lift the children of parents with work earnings to the poverty line by subsidizing low-wage employment through child and employment benefits.

The idea that poverty is not a fatality, but could be reduced or eliminated through sustained political commitment, does open spaces to alternative development strategies. To the extent that provinces enact laws requiring the development of action plans and the ongoing measurement of results, poverty is foregrounded in state activity and decision making. To date, however, the poverty strategies have largely avoided questions of increasing social assistance rates or of increasing minimum wages and working conditions. Instead they focus on how relatively small investments could be deployed to undercut some of the most flagrant social costs induced by poverty (e.g., Hudson and Graefe 2011).

The particular mix in a given place or time is nevertheless affected by political conflicts. For instance, Quebec was a first mover with the adoption of a law against poverty in 2003. The framing of Quebec's efforts in poverty stands out both in emphasizing that poverty limits people's rights to participate in society and in asserting the collective responsibility to develop plans to fight poverty. These ideas point to the possibility of pursuing development beyond neoliberalism, by defining poverty elimination, not just private profit (sometimes rendered as economic growth or rising incomes), as the primary goal. The strength of the Quebec initiative and its survival under a strongly neoliberal government elected immediately after its adoption reflect the sustained campaign of women's and community sector activists for the law and their ability to find relays within the then-governing Parti Québécois (PQ). Starting from the mobilization of the Women's March against poverty and violence in 1995, the campaign took root in communities across the province, and gave rise to high-profile events such as the organization of a Street Parliament across from the National Assembly (for a fuller account, see Dufour 2011).

In the intervening fifteen years, the law against poverty, with its requirements for five-year action plans and annual reports, has provided a structure around which antipoverty actors have organized. This organizing has nevertheless often been defensive, devoted to ensuring that right-leaning governments develop the next five-year plan or respect their engagements not to further impoverish social assistance recipients (Noël 2013). Recently, social assistance reforms have signalled a partial return to rolling out new mechanisms for instilling labour market discipline. This change in the mix reflects the difficulty of sustaining the mobilization of antipoverty actors against the state and the fact that an ideologically right-wing Liberal Party has held power for thirteen of the past fifteen years.

In Ontario, the 2008 Poverty Reduction Strategy emphasized the economic inefficiency of poverty rather than rights. The biggest expense involved adopting the Ontario Child Benefit, which it hoped would bring the province close to its announced goal of reducing child poverty by 25 per cent in five years. The government also repackaged a number of planned initiatives as part of the strategy, including Crown Wards, and investments in programming for at-risk youth. The strategy studiously steered clear of social assistance or the labour market, making no commitments to improve the adequacy of social assistance rates and only limited commitments to consider improved minimum wages or employment standards. The Ontario strategy's weaker rights frame than that of Quebec and its growing invisibility – quietly renewed in 2013; absent from public discussion by 2018 – reflect the lack of strong social movement promoters. The Liberal government adopted the idea of poverty reduction in the 2007 election to head off a successful NDP campaign on the minimum wage. Within the antipoverty advocacy community, the organizations seeking to expand the social rights of those in poverty through robust investments in housing and income assistance were largely sidelined by organizations closer to the Liberals that advocated for making investments at the margins to give a richer sense of equality of opportunity. In other words, the "inclusive liberals" beat out the "social democrats," and poverty policy would act more as a flanking mechanism than as an opening to an alternative development project (Hudson and Graefe 2011).

In sum, contemporary social policies around poverty seem designed to "flank" neoliberalism by addressing certain problems that poverty poses for production and social reproduction. At the margins, these new directions in poverty policy can give rise to glimmers of alternative development projects, particularly when people living in poverty mobilize to demand an expanded a set of rights to inclusion, including rights to housing, care, and public transportation. These new directions are nevertheless still contested by conservative political actors who wish to roll out new programs to push people into the low end of the labour market and dampen wages and working conditions. The Harper Conservatives' 2012 changes to employment insurance, which pushed recipients to accept lower-paying jobs sooner, rather than waiting for more appropriate work, provide an example (Porter 2015).

Child Policy

Policies around employment insurance and social assistance bear the stamp of the post-war welfare state, and so it was not unexpected to find the stronger presence of a "rollback neoliberalism" dynamic that then spurred rollout and flanking responses. But what of "newer" policy concerns? Given the "everybody works" orientation of neoliberalism, the question of who will care for the young and the elderly becomes a pressing one. In a pure neoliberal mindset, the answer would be that the market will sort it out. Either families will choose to provide their own care and forego parental income, or they will purchase care in the market. Given the importance of labour force attachment, Canadian governments have provided some subsidization of care to low-income families since the late 1960s.

By the late 1990s, shortcomings were identified with this policy package, reflecting slow-moving crises of social reproduction. For the bulk of the population that neither earned high incomes nor qualified for low-income subsidies, the cost of child care either encouraged reduced labour force participation (with life-long earning implications) as parents stayed home or the use of substandard care arrangements as parents traded off cost and quality (Jenson, Mahon, and Phillips 2003). Meanwhile, given the scientific evidence of the impact of early childhood poverty on brain development and on future social costs – for instance, in child services, mental health, and incarceration – Canada's high rates of child poverty could be seen as imposing significant economic costs, as opposed to presumably less important "social" costs. The changes needed to meet this crisis included child benefits to reduce the severity of child poverty and child care to provide early learning opportunities and facilitate full labour force participation (Jenson 2004). The shape of these interventions, and their relations to the broader neoliberal project, nevertheless remained to be worked out through political conflict. Given that significant levers for child policy are located in the provinces, the forms of this conflict varied across the country. This is particularly the case given the attempts of the Harper Conservative federal government to stymie the development of publicly subsidized non-parental child care in favour of traditional family forms and a smaller social state (see Findlay 2015). Kate Bezanson (2017) qualifies the Harper Conservatives' initiatives as "Mad Men" social policies, trying to bring back a 1960s gender order by creating incentives through the income tax and child benefit systems for mothers to withdraw from the labour force to provide caring labour. The provinces nevertheless did not follow suit, but experimented with new social investment ideas, albeit rarely putting much money behind them (White 2017). The account below focuses on Ontario and Quebec as provincial examples, as they account for roughly two-thirds of Canada's population.

On the child benefits front, policy makers championed the idea of an income-tested benefit that declined as income rose, and indeed that replaced or came close to replacing the child portion of social assistance benefits – so that social assistance recipients who moved into the labour market would not be left worse off, since they would not lose benefits for their children. At the federal level, this involved decisions in the 1980s and early 1990s to "roll back" the family allowances inherited from the early Keynesian era and to "roll out" a National Child Benefit regime with a clear labour market participation bias. A similar emphasis on commodifying labour was evident in Quebec's child benefits, which the province had been experimenting with alongside workfare-inspired social assistance reform since the early 1980s.

As these benefits matured, they nevertheless provided a significant guaranteed transfer to low-income families, with smaller benefits reaching well up the income distribution (Jenson 2004). They are an important part of the story of moving children in families where the parent or parents are in low-wage employment close to or above the poverty line. As such, they can be seen as a successful form of "flanking" in diminishing the social dislocations of neoliberalism and countering problems of social reproduction at the generational time scale (e.g., reducing child poverty improves long-term human capital formation). In redistributing income to low-income families without strings attached, these benefits also pointed to the possibility of alternative development projects. Proponents of developing some form of "citizenship income," providing a basic minimum without the stigmatizing oversight of current social assistance, often see child benefits as a building block upon which other benefits – say, for disability or unemployment – might be layered (see Battle, Mendelson, and Torjman 2006).

The variety of possibilities opens the question of conflict: what mix of possibilities might come to the fore? By the mid-2010s, levels of child benefits delivered to Quebec families were two to three times those available to Ontario families. Although the pro-commodification policy design was similar in both provinces, the capacity to "flank" by addressing child poverty was clearly greater in Quebec. What accounts for this difference? According to Jenson (2002), the reasons for Quebec's particularity are political: unlike in other provinces, a "family movement" formed in Quebec in the 1970s and 1980s that demanded supports for families, providing an additional impetus for demanding higher child benefits. When combined with a strong women's movement that also supported benefits to alleviate mothers' poverty and a left-right consensus that such benefits encouraged the employability of parents, these transfers expanded. The left-right consensus provided political cover for a nationalist PQ government seeking to reinforce a sense of Quebec's distinctiveness in the difficult budgetary environment of the late 1990s (see also Arsenault 2018). In Ontario, by contrast, the Progressive Conservative provincial government in power when the National Child Benefit was introduced was unwilling to invest in a matching provincial benefit. Only with the election of a Liberal government in 2003 did Ontario begin moving to layer a provincial benefit onto the federal one.

A similar, if more tortuous, story can be told for child care. It is too easy to tell the story in stark terms: after 1998, Quebec developed a universal, low-cost, high-quality public child care system, while Ontario continued in the "Canadian" track of very low public spending on early childhood education with minimal emphasis on raising educational quality, and leaving the provision of spaces to the private sector. In this simplified version, Quebec's policy responses can be seen as a form of "flanking," in addressing crises of care through developing a system that makes a large space for non-profit, community-managed provision. Although some conservative promoters of the project point to its effects on commodifying labour, thus explaining the rapid rise in women's labour force participation rates, the program could also be seen as opening the door to alternative social projects. For instance, child care workers were able to unionize, and through their mobilization were successful in increasing wages for a highly feminized workforce. The idea of having services organized at the community level and run through not-for-profits also opened the door to considering new modes of organizing public services that might enhance local democracy and participation (Lévesque 2014; cf. Joy and Shields, in this volume).

The source of divergence can be placed on factors similar to those for child benefits: a stronger women's movement and the nationalist strategies of the PQ in Quebec versus the weakness of the movement and partisan actors in conflict with the neoliberal status quo in Ontario (Jenson 2002; Noël 2013). In time, the effect of partisan political considerations on policy outcomes has come more clearly to the fore. For Quebec, the long-term presence of right-wing parties has given rise to the stealthy "rollout" of child care privatization. The non-profit sector bias of the PQ's original model has been supplanted by the growth of state subsidies for spaces offered in privately owned centres, as well as a watering down of the system's community-centred governance (Lévesque 2014). For Ontario, a decade and a half of a Liberal government attentive to the crisis of social reproduction led to a gradual closing of the gap with Quebec (Graefe and Orasch 2013), first through extending public schooling downward to four-year-olds and then through greater investment in spaces and subsidies. The election of a Progressive Conservative government in June 2018 halted these new investments, although so far there is little evidence of its adopting Harper's project of incentivizing traditional family forms.

Conclusion

In this chapter I have argued that the political economy of social policy is complicated due to the complex ways that production and social reproduction are intertwined. At one and the same time, a policy can have dimensions where it is rolling out market relationships, engaging in social reproduction outside the market, and opening possibilities of a transition to forms of economic and social development that break with capitalist dynamics. Analysts often tend to foreground a particular dimension – to note how social policies at a given time are rolling out neoliberalism or reflecting an "inclusive liberalism" that breaks with neoliberalism. My approach, however, has been to hold off on such determinations, and instead to canvass the variety of relationships and consider their relative importance in particular times, places, and policy areas. This also allows one to move from more functionalist understandings of social policy under capitalism to consider politics and political conflict. The manner in which these relations are worked out through concrete social conflicts helps explain why different societies might move broadly in a similar direction – such as from the Keynesian welfare state to neoliberalism – yet adopt different policies.

In a context where public austerity leads to crises in social reproduction and hence to changed idea sets about social policy challenges, much of the conflict around social policy involves the fate of neoliberalism. Although the push to reconfigure social policy to deepen market relations – either through privatizing existing public services or through using policy designs to increase competition (say, among non-profit service providers) – and commodification has not disappeared, the costs of such a strategy in terms of foregone social reproduction produce openings for counterstrategies. These can be considered as "flanking mechanisms" to the extent that they mop up the dislocations of neoliberalism without attempting to change the broader political economy. However, the presence of such mechanisms does provide some institutional bases for imagining alternative development projects, as they might be turned to other purposes in a context where the balance of social forces has shifted.

This crisis of social reproduction is being worked out in Canada as it is elsewhere: through political conflict. The conflict takes particular forms in different provinces as social and political forces mobilize and bring their power to bear. As the examples of child care policy and poverty policy indicate, changes have occurred in the past decade. However, the extent to which they balance production and social reproduction, or the current functional needs of capital and the visions of alternative models of development, is very much at play, with clear consequences of how well (or poorly) people live. Although neoliberalism has long been critiqued from the left, it is now besieged by an authoritarian conservatism to its right. As such, renewed attention needs to be paid to how egalitarian alternative development projects can successfully reach constituencies that might otherwise be susceptible to the promises of protection and order offered by the new right.

14 Canadian Trade and Trade Agreements: Free or Fair?

GAVIN FRIDELL

Introduction

"Free trade" is an extremely popular term in Canada. It is so popular, in fact, that it is hard to imagine any debate or discussion on trade that does not inevitably end up being about "free trade." Since the 1970s, moreover, the growing popularity of the idea of free trade has been combined with massive growth in global trade and investment. Free trade is often depicted as the driving force behind this growth. Free trade theory posits that the even elimination of barriers to international trade (tariffs and other forms of protectionism) leads to the greatest economic gains for all trading nations, and by extension promotes peace, liberal political values, and general prosperity (Krugman, Obstfeld, and Melitz 2018). The world we live in today, we are often told, is increasingly a free trade world – despite occasional bumps along the road to prosperity by misguided protectionists.

While the idea of free trade might be popular, whether *we actually live* in a free trade world and whether this is something positive and desirable are both highly contested assumptions. Beginning with the first, researchers have evoked numerous examples that call into question whether we live in a free trade world. Two examples are particularly revealing. First, as I discuss later in the chapter, although the world has witnessed an explosion of "free trade agreements" since the 1980s, most of these agreements contain extensive components that go beyond free trade, and in some cases even run contra to it. Second, despite common assumptions linking free trade to *successful trade*, many of the world's most rapidly growing economies – including those of the United States, the United Kingdom, Germany, Japan, and, more recently, South Korea, China, and several other Asian countries – historically have developed behind protective walls of import controls, tariffs, quotas, and preferences designed to protect domestic industry and enhance export industry (Chang 2008; Fridell 2013). Increases in global trade flows are not necessarily about *free* trade, but rather about *expanded* trade under a variety of policies.

This leads us to the second assumption, whether free trade is something positive and desirable. In many ways, one's approach to this question hinges on the previous assumption. Free trade supporters – in particular, trade economists and corporate business councils – argue that global prosperity has been driven by free trade and that liberalizing trade is always "in Canada's long-run economic interests" (Globerman and Sands 2017, i). Opponents, often led by civil society groups and unions, argue that the goal of trade policy should be "fair trade." They reflect on a different history, challenging the view that free trade agreements are about genuine free trade, and point to growing corporate power and rising inequality in the era of globalization. As an alternative, they propose trade relationships in which trade is regulated or managed to make sure workers' rights, environmental sustainability, social justice, transparency, and democracy are promoted (Patterson 2016; Unifor 2014).

In this chapter, I examine the great free trade/fair trade debate in Canada, placing specific emphasis on North American economic integration and Canada's trade relationship with the United States. Despite decades of talk about diversification, Canada remains overwhelmingly dependent on its trade relationship with the United States. I explore the political economy of change, crisis, and conflict in trade, looking specifically at whether Canadian trade policy is truly about free trade, the conflicts that have emerged out of actually-existing-trade, and the alternative visions advanced by Canadian groups for fair trade. But first, I offer a brief discussion of free trade theory, and situate it within the context of Canadian political economy (discussed further in Helleiner, in this volume; see also McBride, Smardon, and Whiteside, in this volume).

Free Trade and Its Discontents

Outside of its popular use, which often has many meanings attached to it, at its core free trade is an economic theory rooted in the work of classical economists – in particular, Adam Smith and David Ricardo – that posits that the even elimination of trade barriers leads to the greatest "gains from trade" for all trading nations, by allowing them to pursue their "comparative advantage." Although not all nations may be able to compete in the global economy in "absolute" terms, free trade allows each to specialize in what it does the most efficiently. This means that, if Country A is most efficient at producing both cars and apples, but is particularly efficient at cars, it will specialize in car production, allowing another country (Country B) to pursue apples. Country A would then trade cars to Country B for apples, to their mutual benefit. The idea of comparative advantage has been passionately defended by trade economists (Bhagwati 2008; Krugman, Obstfeld, and Melitz 2018), as well as widely critiqued for being based on highly speculative assumptions – two-country trade, homogenous technology, balanced trade, full employment, perfect information – that ignore the real history of world trade, which is grounded in unequal power, violence, and geopolitics (Chang 2008; Fridell 2013).

These global debates have been played out in Canada, where the dispute on free trade has pivoted on a classical defence of comparative advantage versus critiques by "left nationalists" who depict Canada as a semi-peripheral neocolony, subservient to the United States and dependent on it for investment and markets for Canadian staples or raw materials exports (see Clarkson 2002; Levitt 1970; Watkins 1963). Left nationalists have called for state regulations to limit foreign private investment, promote public investment and ownership, protect Canadian sovereignty from the external constraints imposed by US capital and monetary policy, and develop strategic protections and supports to stimulate domestic manufacturing, entrepreneurship, technology, quality jobs, and innovation to avoid becoming a resource-dependent, branch-plant economy of the United States. Their ideas were particularly influential from the 1970s to the early 2000s, when political opposition to free trade was at high tide. In 1988, Liberal Party leader John Turner, fearing the impact free trade could have on jobs, the industrial sector, and national sovereignty, fought against the signing of the Canada-US Free Trade Agreement (CUFTA), losing a tight election to the pro–free trade incumbent, Progressive Conservative Brian Mulroney.

Flash ahead to today, and left nationalism continues to have an important influence on Canadian debates around free trade, especially among the social movements and unions I discuss in the final section of this chapter. In parliamentary politics, however, left nationalism's influence has waned, with today's Liberal Party an unwavering promoter of free trade and free trade agreements. In 2017, US president Donald Trump triggered renegotiations over the North American Free Trade Agreement (NAFTA), claiming the agreement was imbalanced and threatened US sovereignty. Canada's Liberal prime minister, Justin Trudeau, emerged as a staunch advocate of free trade, defending NAFTA's core components – including, as discussed below, its controversial investor protections – while proposing a "progressive" trade agenda to further support labour rights, the environment, gender equality, and Indigenous rights. In doing this, Trudeau was echoing a long tradition of liberal reformism, underpinned by the belief that, while trade liberalization brings economic growth and prosperity, there is a role for regulation to protect workers' and human rights and to promote a more equitable sharing of benefits than the market, on its own, would produce (Zini 2016).

Clearly, a lot has changed within the Liberal Party and its thinking on free trade. This change has also sparked debate within Canadian political economy around the nature of the Canadian state as it relates to global trade and investment. While left nationalist accounts effectively point to the uneven power of Canada and its much larger neighbour, critics assert they have downplayed the power and assertiveness of Canadian capital and the Canadian state, which has actively pursued its own strategic objectives through international trade agreements (Froese 2010; Krikorian 2012). This might help explain Trudeau's enthusiasm for free trade, as it represents the goals of a successful, wealthy, and assertive advanced capitalist economy. The Canadian state, as Paul Kellogg (2015) has argued, has aggressively sought out, and received, investment and trade opportunities for Canadian companies in the United States and internationally.

These debates, in many ways, extend well beyond trade, but they also frame several significant questions that are central to understanding the political economy of trade in Canada. To what extent is Canadian trade policy driven by a dedication to free trade? Is this a desirable goal, as opposed to alternative visions of fair trade? To promoters, the goal of free trade is to increase Canada's total wealth. In economics, the dominant approach for assessing the success of this policy is to measure the economic growth of the nation *as a whole* in relation to other nations. In political economy, however, relationships between nations are only one way of assessing trade. Trade and trade agreements also have uneven impacts *within nations*, shaped by relations of power around class, race, gender, and nationality. From this political economy view, trade policy is not developed in a neutral, apolitical, or strictly technical space. Instead, it is highly political, and emerges out of struggles to define trade policy and its goals between dominant and subordinate sectors of society (Roman and Velasco Arregui 2015).

Changes

Over the past forty years, Canadian trade has changed in important ways. Perhaps the most significant change has been in import patterns. Although US imports to Canada have grown substantially in total value, and still represent more than those from the rest of the world combined, their relative share has declined. Following the rise of a number southern economies, countries such as China, Mexico, South Korea, Vietnam, India, Thailand, and Malaysia have increased their shares of Canada's imports. In 1980, China was Canada's twenty-fourth largest import partner, Mexico was sixteenth, and South Korea was fifteenth; by 2016, China had risen to second place, Mexico to third, and South Korea to seventh (see Figure 14.1).

Exports tell a different story. From 1980 to 2016, the share of Canadian merchandise exports going to the United States increased from around 63 per cent to 76 per cent. Markets in China, Mexico, and South Korea also increased in importance relative to other countries, but Canadian export dependence on the US market intensified (see Figure 14.2). Canada is also an important market for the United States, and remains its largest export market. Given the immense size of the US economy, however, the reliance is not nearly to the same degree: in 2016, around 18 per cent of US exports went to Canada, followed by Mexico at 16 per cent, and China at 8 per cent (see Figure 14.3).

The most significant changes to trade, however, cannot be measured solely in economic terms, but also by trade policy. Since the 1980s, Canada has signed numerous multilateral, regional, and bilateral trade agreements. This has been part of a global movement towards neoliberal reforms (discussed by Evans, and McBride, in this volume) involving deregulation, privatization of state assets and state enterprises, market liberalization, and declining commitments to public spending on social programs such as health care and education (Clarkson 2002; Roman and Velasco Arregui 2015). Top among these agreements is NAFTA – renegotiated as the United States-Mexico-Canada Agreement (USMCA) – which has had the most substantive impact on the Canadian economy, and is a revealing case for understanding Canadian trade policy.

Figure 14.1. Canada's Top Import Partners, 1980 and 2016

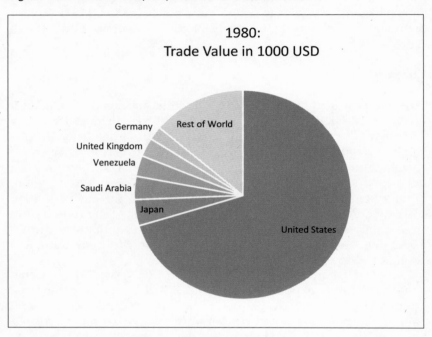

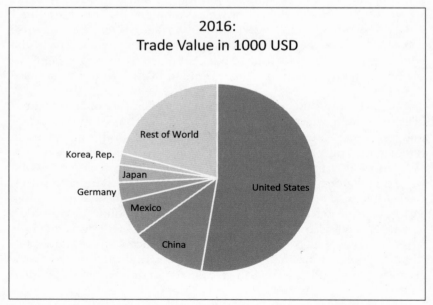

Source: World Integrated Trade Solution (WITS), United Nations Commodity Trade Statistics Database (UN-COMTRADE), online at https://wits.worldbank.org, accessed 30 January 2018.

Figure 14.2. Canada's Top Export Markets, 1980 and 2016

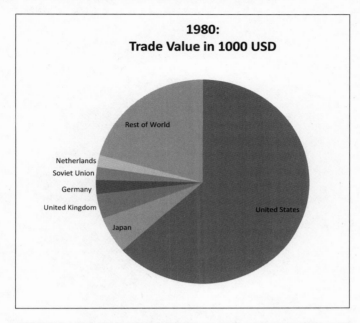

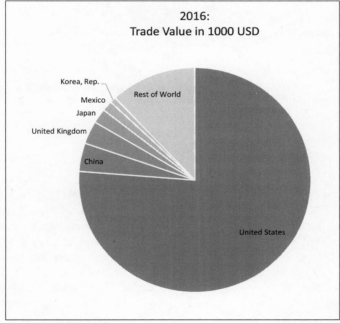

Source: World Integrated Trade Solution (WITS), United Nations Commodity Trade Statistics Database (UN-COMTRADE), online at https://wits.worldbank.org, accessed 30 January 2018.

Figure 14.3. The United States' Top Export Markets, 2016

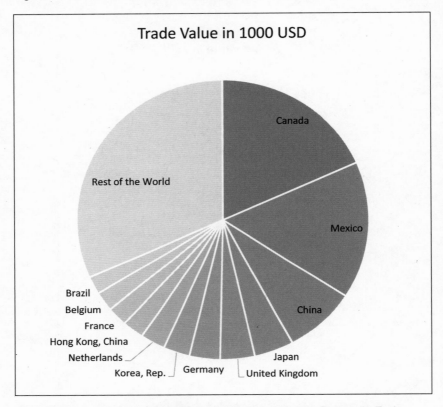

Source: World Integrated Trade Solution (WITS), United Nations Commodity Trade Statistics Database (UN-COMTRADE), online at https://wits.worldbank.org, accessed 30 January 2018.

NAFTA Dreams

On 1 January 1989 Canada and the United States established the bilateral CUFTA, followed five years later, on 1 January 1994, by NAFTA, which extended the agreement to include Mexico. Both agreements were hotly contested, with opponents arguing they would lead to job losses and a "race to the bottom" for working conditions. Proponents, for their part, argued the agreements would improve competitiveness and market access, leading to more and better jobs. Canadian and Mexican business elites were particularly interested in ensuring access to the US market, whereas the US elite were concerned to lock in access to raw materials from Canada and Mexico (Clarkson 2002; Hufbauer, Cimino, and Moran 2014; Roman and Velasco Arregui 2015; Villarreal and Fergusson 2014).

Aside from the immediate interests at play during its emergence, it is important to explore NAFTA's deeper significance for the political economy of Canada and the continent. To begin with, to what extent was NAFTA truly about "free trade"? Many trade economists and pro-liberalization commentators have taken this as a given, grounded in the fact that NAFTA eliminated or reduced tariffs (custom taxes on imports or exports) between member countries on most products, with some restrictions remaining on such things as dairy, poultry, eggs, sugar, meat, and food products (Dadush and Leycegui 2016; Walmsley and Minor 2017).

Although NAFTA did reduce tariffs significantly, the agreement also did many other things that challenge the view that it was truly about free trade. Passionate free trade promoter Jagdish Bhagwati (2008), for example, has criticized bilateral and plurilateral trade agreements such as NAFTA for not being about free trade, but rather about "preferential" trade. Whereas NAFTA reduced tariffs among Canada, Mexico, and the United States, this does not apply to other countries. As a result, the three partners gained *preferential* access to each other's markets, while those outside the trade bloc experienced, in effect, increased trade barriers, given that they did not have the same access as NAFTA members. This situation was reinforced by other NAFTA rules – in particular, its rules of origin, which stated that goods must have 50–60 per cent of their value originate from within North America to circulate free of tariffs. This rule limited access to the North American market for non-NAFTA members, and served, essentially, as a "regional content requirement" (Leblond and Fabian 2017, 3).

NAFTA rules not only subverted the idea of genuine free trade; they also contained numerous components that went well beyond trade. For example, many rules liberalized foreign investment and manufacturing within North America, while regulating or imposing new restrictions on intellectual property rights, public ownership, agriculture, investment, energy policy, food, and consumer safety (Karpilow et al. 2014, 1); Weisbrot et al. 2017). Defenders viewed these rules as a "golden straightjacket" (Friedman 2000) that promoted economic reforms, but critics argued that they in fact represented a "supraconstitutional" (Clarkson 2002) or "new constitutionalist" (Gill 2003) framework that placed the rights of transnational corporations above those of citizens, limiting elected officials' ability to regulate for the public good.

Perhaps the most well-known example of NAFTA's new constitutionalist underpinnings was its Chapter 11, which dealt with foreign investment rights and investor-state dispute settlement mechanisms. Whereas investment treaties had been around since the 1960s, NAFTA was considered pioneering because it included investment rights within a trade agreement in a manner considered "to represent best practices at the time" (Leblond and Fabian 2017, 11; Finbow 2016). Chapter 11 allowed foreign investors from NAFTA countries to challenge government policy directly by unilaterally triggering international arbitration if they believed they had lost potential profits over a violation of investor rights. NAFTA tribunals were ad hoc, transcended the authority of domestic courts, and entailed only limited public input and transparency. Through Chapter 11, member states ceded a portion of their sovereignty, "not just to international entities, but to private ones," governed not by public authority but by commercial arbitration (McBride 2006, 755).

Given its broad definition of investor rights, corporations evoked Chapter 11 to challenge numerous government policies. As of 1 January 2018, out of eighty-five Chapter 11 claims, forty-one had targeted Canada (48 per cent), twenty-three Mexico (27 per cent), and twenty-one the United States (25 per cent). The Canadian government had won nine disputes and lost eight (with the remainder still pending), costing $219 million in damages and around $95 million more in legal fees (Sinclair 2018a). A sample of some of the most notorious NAFTA cases include the following:

- In 1997, US-based Ethyl Corporation challenged the Canadian government over its ban on methylcyclopentadienyl manganese tricarbonyl (MMT), a gasoline additive and suspected neurotoxin. The government settled, paid Ethyl $19.5 million in damages, issued a formal apology, and overturned the ban (Leblond and Fabian 2017, 8; Sinclair 2018a, 5).
- In 2008, US-based Bilcon challenged the Canadian government for rejecting a proposed quarry and marine terminal in Nova Scotia after a joint federal-provincial environmental assessment. In 2015, the tribunal ruled against Canada, awarding Bilcon $7 million in damages (Sinclair 2018a, 21).
- In 2015, Exxon Mobil and Murphy Oil challenged a requirement of the government of Newfoundland and Labrador that companies involved in offshore oil production conduct research and development within the province, to promote local benefits. The Canadian government lost, and paid $20 million to ExxonMobil and $5 million to Murphy Oil (Sinclair 2018a, 29).

Examples of cases that have not yet been resolved include (as mentioned by Carter, in this volume) a $250 millon suit against Canada by Lone

Pine Resources, a US-based oil and gas company, challenging Quebec's partial moratorium on hydraulic fracturing (or fracking), instituted out of concerns over toxins used in the fracking process, drinking water contamination, and possible links to earthquakes (Karpilow et al. 2014, 8).

Although corporations do not always win investor-state disputes, critics point out that, either way, Chapter 11 created a "chilling effect" that could "deter governments from acting in the public interest or distort policy choices towards options that are more amendable to foreign commercial interests" (Sinclair 2018a, 8). The impact of Chapter 11 lies in sharp contrast to the main labour and environmental components of NAFTA, which were side agreements that contained major hurdles to trigger any sort of formal dispute settlement. The most significant of these hurdles was that disputes had to be initiated by governments (as opposed to triggered unilaterally by private companies, as was the case with investor disputes) (Clarkson 2002; Knox 2004).[1] As a result, no formal dispute was ever launched under NAFTA concerning labour or the environment.

NAFTA's Shortcomings: Failure or Design?

How did these disparities come about? To some, they were unintended distortions of the original goals of NAFTA. Leblond and Fabian (2017), for example, argue that Chapter 11 was designed to encourage investment – in particular, by Canadian and US investors in Mexico. In practice, however, Chapter 11 provisions were "used to challenge governments' regulatory measures, which was not the negotiators' original intention, although this is part of a wider trend globally" (ibid, 8). In contrast, others have argued that the imbalances in NAFTA and other trade agreements were no accident, but "reflect a fundamental choice to empower some rights holders, including foreign investors, above others" (Finbow 2016, 70).

In their book, *Continental Crucible: Big Business, Workers and Unions in the Transformation of North America*, Richard Roman and Edur Velasco Arregui (2015) maintain that the political economy of NAFTA must be understood not as stemming from the goal of free trade, but rather from continental market integration in a manner that entrenches corporate

---

1 The two side agreements were the North American Agreement on Labour Cooperation (https://www.canada.ca/en/employment-social-development/services/labour-relations/international/agreements/naalc.html) and the North American Agreement on Environmental Cooperation (http://www.cec.org/about-us/NAAEC), both accessed 20 March 2018.

power and neoliberal reforms (see also McBride, in this volume). There is widespread recognition among scholars and researchers that NAFTA was primarily about regional value-chain integration, where various component (or intermediate) parts produced in one country are imported into another for partial or final assembly. In North America, this is prominent in automobiles, wearing apparel and leather, machinery, livestock and fishing, textiles, and electronic equipment (Baldwin and Lopez-Gonzalez 2015, 1696); Walmsley and Minor 2017, 24).

Roman and Velasco Arregui (2015) argue that North American market integration was not a mere technical arrangement, but a highly political one driven by transnational corporate interests. They chart the emergence and growth of powerful business lobbies in all three countries, and how they have developed their own shared agenda and used their economic power to impose it on politicians and society as a whole, spending "vast sums of money in carrying out a multi-faceted offensive in their class interests" (Roman and Velasco Arregui 2015, 2). Faced with growing worker militancy, economic nationalist policies, declining profits, and escalating global competition in the 1970s, North American corporations sought to weaken labour, open public services to privatization, and strengthen investor rights. The fact that investor rights under NAFTA were powerful while other rights were weak or ignored was not an oversight, they argue, but the goal of the business groups who envisioned, developed, and promoted NAFTA in the first place (Roman and Velasco Arregui 2015).

An Explosion of Free Trade Agreements

Since the signing of CUFTA and NAFTA, Canada has continued to expand its commitment to a range of trade and investment agreements. In 1995, Canada joined in the creation of the World Trade Organization (WTO). Composed of 164 members today, the WTO is tasked with promoting and enforcing market liberalization among its member states, and is the most important international trade organization. Canada has also agreed to fourteen free trade agreements and thirty-seven foreign investment promotion and protection agreements, with many more under negotiation.[2] In 2016, in part to promote trade diversification away from the United States, Canada signed the Canada-European Union Comprehensive Economic

---

2 See Canada, "Trade and Investment Agreements," online at https://www.international. gc.ca/trade-commerce/trade-agreements-accords-commerciaux/agr-acc/index. aspx?lang=eng, accessed 14 March 2018.

and Trade Agreement (CETA), and agreed to the Comprehensive and Progressive Agreement for Trans-Pacific Partnership (CPTPP) – composed of Australia, Brunei, Canada, Chile, Japan, Malaysia, Mexico, New Zealand, Peru, Singapore, and Vietnam – which still requires full ratification by all member states.

Despite the diversity of these agreements, they all contain components similar to those of NAFTA, and have been resisted and critiqued for similar reasons. The Canadian labour movement has protested the ways in which these agreements empower unelected bodies to intrude on government policies, often with destructive outcomes. For example, starting in the 1960s, the Canadian auto industry expanded and thrived, in part due to the Canada-US Automotive Products Agreement (commonly called the "Auto Pact"). This allowed tariff-free trade in vehicles and parts between Canada and the United States as long as a certain number of vehicles and value-added parts were produced in Canada. In 2001, a WTO dispute panel ruled that the Auto Pact violated WTO rules and had to be eliminated – resulting in the loss of thousands of Canadian jobs (Unifor 2014, 8). Overall, under liberalization from 1993 to 2013, manufacturing jobs in the auto sector declined by 10 per cent in Canada and 30 per cent in the United States, while it increased by over 350 per cent in Mexico (Hufbauer, Cimino, and Moran 2014, 15–16).

Unions have also opposed burgeoning free trade agreements for continuing to favour strong corporate investment rights while having unenforceable labour protections. In response, both CETA and the CPTPP were negotiated with various reforms. CETA, for example, replaces ad hoc investment tribunals with permanent panels, allows for greater public participation and transparency in tribunals, and adopts language protecting government's ability to regulate in the public interest (Leblond and Fabian 2017). Both CETA and the CPTPP also integrate labour provisions into their core texts, and provide a mechanism that, in theory, could trigger binding dispute settlement. Member states, however, remain in charge of advancing disputes – meaning, as with NAFTA, they are very unlikely to happen (Knox 2004). The agreements also come with various exceptions in side letters; Vietnam, for instance, has a temporary exemption from meeting requirements for freedom of association and collective bargaining in the CPTPP.[3]

---

3 See the CPTPP text online at http://international.gc.ca/trade-commerce/trade-agreements-accords-commerciaux/agr-acc/cptpp-ptpgp/text-texte/index.aspx?lang=eng, accessed 19 March 2018.

Indigenous groups and their allies have also raised opposition to free trade agreements around their role in the on-going process of colonial dispossession, marginalization, exploitation, and state-orchestrated attacks on Indigenous rights, customs, and culture. Trade agreements generally have excluded "Indigenous peoples from the drafting, negotiation and approval processes of agreements and from the settlement of disputes" (Schwartz 2017, 13). Concerned that trade agreements could impede Indigenous land claims, the Hupacasath First Nation legally challenged the signing of the 2014 Canada-China Foreign Investment Promotion and Protection Agreement, which the Canadian government hoped would expand trade and investment with China's rapidly growing economy. The courts rejected the challenge, however, ruling that there was no clear evidence linking investment protections and adverse effects on Indigenous rights. International law expert Risa Schwartz (2017) suggests that, as a result, future land claims could be held up or challenged by investment tribunals. As an example, in 2017, China Minerals Mining Corp. sought to block the transfer of land, on which it had purchased subsurface rights, as part of a land claim agreement with the Kaska Dene Council by challenging it in the British Columbia Supreme Court. The case was not heard, for unrelated reasons, but China Minerals made clear its position that investors should be "protected or properly compensated" for any land claims transfers (quoted in Schwartz 2017, 9). This raises the prospect of future investor-state disputes around Indigenous land claims, and has led to calls for stronger language in agreements to protect Indigenous rights.

Crises

Despite the dominance of free trade in Canadian political discourse and debate, that focus has always been contested, and Canadian social movements have played active roles in campaigns opposing free trade and neoliberal reforms at home and internationally. A proposed thirty-four-country Free Trade Agreement of the Americas (FTAA), for example, was shelved due to political disagreements among nations and political resistance from protestors throughout the Americas. Canadian groups played a key role here, symbolized by a massive demonstration during the 2001 Summit of the Americas in Quebec City (Unifor 2014).

Today, free trade is on the ropes once again. This time, however, the most powerful political opposition comes from far-right nationalists. In the United States in the 1990s, political figures such as Pat Buchanan and Ross Perot led right-nationalist movements that stoked racist and xenophobic fears about immigrants and the loss of US jobs to Mexico

(Zini 2016, 118–41). Today, right nationalists have been reinvigorated with the presidential election of Donald Trump in 2016, the "Brexit" vote in the United Kingdom the same year, and the rise of far-right political parties throughout Europe. President Trump has combined attacks on Blacks, Mexicans, Muslims, and migrant communities – unjustly accused of violence, stealing jobs, or dragging down wages – with massive corporate tax breaks and calls for the United States to renegotiate existing trade agreements that he has deemed unfair. During his first year in office, Trump withdrew from negotiations for the CPTPP, threatened to pull out of the WTO, and triggered a renegotiation of NAFTA.

Most significant for Canada were the NAFTA renegotiations in 2017 and 2018, which involved intense political struggles, and ended with the new USMCA. Scared of losing preferential access to the US market, Canada and Mexico made several concessions to US demands, including raising the regional content requirement on tariff-free North American cars (passenger vehicles increased from 62.5 per cent to 75 per cent regional content), a sunset clause to revisit the agreement every sixteen years, reduced cross-border duties and taxes on US retail goods imported into Canada and Mexico, and greater access for US farmers to the regulated Canadian dairy market – with potentially harmful consequences for Canadian dairy farmers in the context of oversupply. The new agreement also contains several important modifications of the old NAFTA – for example, labour and the environment are now chapters within the core text.[4] Unions are particularly hopeful that the new labour rules, including a "rapid-response" enforcement mechanism with the power to investigate labour violations and impose penalties, will make the labour chapter genuinely effective for the first time. Also of major significance, investor-state dispute mechanisms were removed from the agreement regarding the United States and Canada, and continued, with new restrictions, between the United States and Mexico. Canada at first resisted this move, preferring modified investment chapters such as those in CETA despite intense and effective opposition to such mechanisms by the Council of Canadians and other groups, as I discuss below (McGregor 2018). The United States, however, demanded their removal, viewing them as a threat to its national sovereignty. At the time of writing, the USMCA had not yet gone into force,

---

4 See the draft text of the USMCA online at https://ustr.gov/trade-agreements/free-trade-agreements/united-states-mexico-canada-agreement/agreement-between.

and the full impact of its changes, in North America and globally, remained to be seen.

Winners and Losers of North American Economic Integration

Trump's attack on NAFTA and his insistence that the United States was on the losing end of the agreement sparked renewed debate on the impact of North American economic integration. The issue is by no means clear, as it is extremely difficult to sort out the effects of NAFTA from those of countless other economic and political variables, from changing global economic conditions to changing technology to the influence of dozens of other trade agreements (Sinclair, Trew, and Mertins-Kirkwood 2017; Villarreal and Fergusson 2014). Numerous debates exist, but one can discern two general observations.

First, NAFTA's overall impact on the three countries involved, in standard economic terms, appears to have been less than originally anticipated (Brennan 2015; Globerman and Sands 2017; Hufbauer, Cimino, and Moran 2014; Sinclair, Trew, and Mertins-Kirkwood 2017; Villarreal and Fergusson 2014). Although NAFTA contributed to regional economic integration, the NAFTA bloc, faced with growing competition from Asian economies, experienced a significant drop in its share of world trade, from 17 per cent in 1994 to 13 per cent in 2014 (Dadush and Leycegui 2016, 4). Free traders argued that NAFTA would close the gap between the higher labour productivity in the United States and that of Canada and Mexico, but both continued to lag behind, with Mexico experiencing particularly poor results. From 1994 to 2014, the labour share of income declined in all three NAFTA countries and income inequality increased (Brennan 2015; Sinclair, Trew, and Mertins-Kirkwood 2017). Canadian corporations successfully globalized their operations – foreign operations of Canadian businesses accounted for 23 per cent of total corporate income in 1998, but 47 per cent by 2010 – while the Canadian economy in general, Jordan Brennan (2015, 5–6) observes, was "marked by lackluster growth, underinvestment and weak employment results."

Second, there is little evidence that the United States experienced a disproportionately negative impact from NAFTA than its partners. In fact, contra Trump's proclamations, Mexico and Mexicans seem to have experienced the worst results. Many had assumed Mexico would be the biggest beneficiary of NAFTA, as it would draw investment from the

United States and Canada due to its relatively low wage workforce. Instead, much of Mexico's assumed competitive advantage was undercut by China, which combined cheaper labour with an active state-led industrial policy, high spending on research and development, and a government-controlled banking system (Weisbrot et al. 2017). As a result, Mexico experienced slow economic and income growth, and its national poverty rate actually *increased* under NAFTA, from 52.4 per cent in 1994 to 55.1 per cent in 2014 (Weisbrot et al. 2017, 2; Remes 2014; Villarreal and Fergusson 2014).

Particularly hard hit in Mexico have been small family farms, which, as a result of reduced tariffs, have had to compete with subsidized and high-technology agriculture in the United States, especially in the corn industry. From 1991 to 2007, Mexico experienced a massive net loss in total agricultural employment of around 1.9 million jobs, which fed domestic and international migration (Weisbrot et al. 2017). In 2013, there were over 11.5 million Mexican-born residents in the United States, many of them poorly paid and confronted by institutionalized racism (including lack of citizenship rights), making them a vulnerable and exploitable workforce (Weisbrot et al. 2017, 15; Roman and Velasco Arregui 2015). Canada has also received thousands of Mexican workers, many on temporary worker programs such as the Seasonal Agricultural Worker Program. Although these jobs offer income and employment, they are frequently onerous, with long hours and dangerous working conditions. Temporary workers are bound to a single employer, prohibited from forming unions, and often scared to complain about labour and safety violations for fear they will be sent home (Preibisch and Otero 2014; UFCW Canada 2011). These Mexican workers are among those who have experienced the worst of North American economic integration, denied good-paying, safe, stable, and decent livelihoods at home and abroad.

Conflict: Free Trade or Fair Trade?

Free trade's popularity as an idea is not necessarily matched by its ability to prescribe policies that spur growth, employment, and general well-being, or to explain the most significant political and economic drivers behind trade patterns and policy. This has led to opposition to free trade from a range of groups – environmental organizations, unions, Indigenous groups, church groups, global justice activists – that have often coalesced around demands for "fair trade." One of the

longest-standing proponents of fair trade in Canada is the left-leaning
Council of Canadians, a non-profit environmental activist group that
has campaigned against free trade agreements since the 1980s. Today,
the Council of Canadians has sixty volunteer chapters across the country, looking at issues around trade, water, health care, green energy, and
democracy.[5] Although originally focused on Canadian sovereignty and
progressive nationalism, over the years the Council has shifted its
efforts towards global justice, democracy, and confronting corporate
power (Kellogg 2015, 212–13). This shift, in part, reflects dialogue and
solidarity with groups that seek to decolonize Canada, such as Indigenous groups working to protect the land and water, as well as global
partners in Mexico, the United States, Europe, the Americas, and
beyond that have been protesting NAFTA, the FTAA, CETA, CPTPP,
and other trade agreements (Karpilow et al. 2014). Against the far right,
which has opposed trade agreements in combination with xenophobic
and bigoted beliefs, the Council has put forward an alternative vision
to free trade rooted in "the progressive concept of 'fair trade' and the
aspiration to build economies and trading relationships that are based
on social and ecological justice, on the primacy of democratic rights
over the profits of transnational corporations, and on the free movement of people rather than capital" (Patterson 2016).

Another long-standing advocate for fair trade has been Unifor, Canada's largest private sector union. While believing international trade
can be beneficial, Unifor has actively lobbied against the current free
trade agreements for promoting corporate rights and weakening
democracy, calling for alternative agreements that eliminate investment protections and promote fairness, transparency, inclusiveness,
mutual benefits, the protection of public services, industrial and social
development, cultural sovereignty, workers' and Indigenous rights,
sustainability, and national self-determination (Unifor 2014). During
the NAFTA renegotiations, Unifor advised the Canadian government
while applying pressure outside the negotiations on all three governments. Unifor has strengthened its bonds with independent Mexican
unions, and invited ten union representatives to Ottawa in March 2018
to explain the challenges faced by Mexican workers. The union has also
adopted a position paper outlining its fair trade vision, and from 2017
to 2018 carried out a series of community town halls across the country

to discuss what a "Peoples Trade Agenda" could look like. The goal, according to Angelo DiCaro, Unifor national representative and trade policy analyst, was to pressure government to recognize that "we can't just sign trade deals for the sake of signing trade deals. If we want to build a more cooperative, development-focused approach to globalization and global trade then we're going to have to spell that out as pre-conditions to free trade accords."[6]

Fair Trade Certification

While Unifor and the Council of Canadians have demanded changes to government policy and sought to confront rising corporate power, others have envisioned fair trade in less explicitly political terms. Fair trade certification has sought to work with corporations, co-operatives, social enterprises, and small businesses to better integrate poorer and marginalized small farmers and workers from the global South into global markets. Formed in 1997, Fairtrade Canada today certifies over two hundred companies that buy from licensed producer groups under the terms of a guaranteed floor price; additional social premiums to build such things as infrastructure, schools, roads, and hospitals; no exploitation of child labour; and environmental sustainability. Fair trade certification has grown substantially, and the global fair trade network now works with over 1.66 million farmers and workers.[7]

Despite its growth, however, important limitations to fair trade remain. In general, fair trade farmers cannot find a market for all of their certified products – coffee farmers, for example, on average can find a fair trade buyer for only around 35 per cent of their beans (*Coffee & Cocoa International* 2014) – and impact assessments have suggested that fair trade has modest or mixed results. One such assessment in Uganda and Ethiopia determined that workers on small, fair trade farms were being paid less and received fewer benefits than those on large-scale, non-certified farms (Cramer et al. 2014). Fair trade groups have responded to these limits by expanding both their standards – for example, Fairtrade International and other groups are working towards "global living wage" standards – and their advocacy, calling on governments to integrate labour standards into trade agreements, combat

---

6 Author's interview with Angelo DiCaro, National Representative, Research Department, Unifor, online from Ottawa, 25 March 2018.

7 For more information, see Fairtrade Canada, online at http://fairtrade.ca/en-CA/ What-is-Fairtrade/Facts-and-Figures, accessed 15 March 2018.

global inequality and gender discrimination, clamp down on tax evasion and avoidance, and respect Indigenous rights (Canadian Fair Trade Network 2017).[8]

Founding fair trade organizations continue to evolve, seeking to further differentiate themselves from a narrow corporate social responsibility model and assert their social justice roots. JustUs! coffee, for example, a co-operative in Nova Scotia, has long been a leader of fair trade in Canada. JustUs! pays farmers a much higher price than the fair trade minimum, and most of its coffee is certified by the Small Producers' Symbol from Latin America, which involves higher standards developed by small producers, workers, and artisans themselves (Coscione 2014). JustUs! also works in solidarity with its global South partners: when an attack of coffee leaf rust destroyed much of Nicaragua's crop from 2012 to 2016, JustUs! offered its Nicaraguan partners 30 cents more per pound to help cover the losses, and worked with two co-operatives to support replanting and diversification. To JustUs! general manager Joey Pittoello, trade is not just about economics, but also about relations between people, community, and the environment and the belief "that human transformation should be our goal in our societies, not gross domestic product."[9]

State-to-State Disputes

Conflict over trade – what is free and what is fair – occurs not only within countries but also between them. Trade agreements are designed to reduce these conflicts by diminishing the power of individual states to impose trade barriers for protectionist reasons and by removing conflicts out of the realm of power politics, where the strongest can dictate terms over the weak, and into juridical dispute resolution bodies (Froese 2010). In practice, however, things are far more complex. First, power politics continues to play a central role regardless of what might be written on paper. A common example of this is Canadian softwood lumber exports, which, since the 1980s, have been subject to rounds of countervailing and antidumping duties from the United States. Despite dispute resolutions favouring Canada under both NAFTA and the

---

8 See also Global Living Wage Coalition, online at https://www.isealalliance.org/about-iseal/our-work/global-living-wage-coalition, accessed 15 March 2018.
9 Author's interview with Joey Pittoello, General Manager, JustUs! Coffee, Grand-Pré, NS, 29 March 2018.

WTO, Canada has been compelled to sign a series of bilateral agreements limiting its lumber exports to the United States through export taxes and quotas (Leblond and Fabian 2017, 21).

Second, rather than tempering trade conflicts, dispute mechanisms have often been just another tool states have used to "gain a strategic advantage" over competitors (Froese 2010, 77). Nowhere is this more evident than in the aerospace industry, which, as political scientist Marc Froese (2010, 82) observes, has been driven, not by free trade, but by "explicitly mercantilist objectives," with competing states providing huge subsidies and other supports to national firms. Bombardier, headquartered in Quebec, is a global leader in the aerospace industry. In 1996, Canada triggered a WTO dispute tribunal against Brazil, accusing it of offering unfair subsidies through its export credit program to the Brazilian company, Embraer, also a world leader in the aerospace industry. Brazil countersued, triggering its own dispute against Canada for unfair subsidies to Bombardier. Both tribunals ruled that the subsidies were non-WTO compliant, and authorized both countries to retaliate against the other – Canada could retaliate up to C$344 million and Brazil could retaliate up to US$248 million. This led to bilateral negotiations, and the issue was essentially shelved (Froese 2010, 77). Subsidies, often hidden in complex ways, and other forms of government support remain the norm in the industry. In 2018, for example, the United States temporarily imposed a 299.45 per cent tariff on Bombardier C series jets in response to complaints from US aerospace leader, Boeing. Although the tariff was eventually removed, tensions and disputes over the politics of subsidies continue (Zhang 2018).

The Future of Canadian Trade Policy: Progressive Trade?

Few if any commentators anticipated the massive impact of the global COVID-19 pandemic on public health and the global economy, which was ongoing in 2020 when this chapter was finalized. In Canada, the pandemic claimed the lives of thousands and revealed the vulnerability of its trade-dependent economy, most notably by the lack of medical masks, COVID tests, ventilators, and a range of protective equipment that put everyone, frontline workers most of all, at unnecessary risk. In response, the government took measures to encourage domestic production of these essential products. This reflected growing recognition that trade could not be relied on to provide essential goods in time of global crisis, although it was not clear what impact this would have on Canada's overall trade pattern. For instance, looking to the future, Canada is likely to remain highly dependent on the US market, a situation which could even increase if Canada begins to rely less on other global trading partners.

In terms of trade policy, Prime Minister Trudeau was likely to continue with his "progressive trade" agenda that seeks to combine the traditional aspects of free trade agreements with new or more rigorous language around labour rights, gender equality, the environment, and Indigenous rights. This agenda was mostly rebuffed by the Trump administration during the NAFTA/USMCA negotiations. Trudeau has had more success with other trade agreements, in which Canada has negotiated some new gender components. For instance, Canada and Chile added a new gender appendix to the pre-existing Canada-Chile Free Trade Agreement in 2017, and a gender chapter was included in an amendment to the pre-existing Canada-Israel Free Trade Agreement in 2018.[10] Both offer a range of general commitments to cooperate around promoting gender equality, advancing gender-responsive policies, and fostering financial inclusion, leadership, entrepreneurship, and capacity building for women. Although the recognition of the significance of gendered inequality is a major advance, concerns have also been raised that gender additions such as these could serve as a "Trojan horse" (Bissio 2017). In this guise, they could perpetuate neoliberal free trade agreements without regard for their own gendered impacts: cuts to public spending, higher costs for medicines due to intellectual property rights, the denigration of societally necessary unpaid care work, and the feminization of low-paid, precarious work (Bissio 2017; D. Elson 2009; Roman and Velasco Arregui 2015, 98–109). The Canada-Chile gender appendix, moreover, is explicitly not open to any form of dispute settlement. The Canada-Israel gender chapter, in contrast, does contain the possibility of binding arbitration, but the vague and general nature of the commitments and the fact that, as is so often the case, disputes would need to be brought forward by states make them extremely unlikely to occur. As things currently stand, the new gender components reproduce the unevenness of all free trade agreements: strong,

---

10 For the Canada-Chile agreement's gender appendix (Appendix II – Chapter N bis-Trade and Gender), see http://international.gc.ca/trade-commerce/trade-agreements-accords-commerciaux/agr-acc/chile-chili/fta-ale/2017_Amend_Modif-App2-Chap-N.aspx?lang=eng, accessed 5 October 2018. For the Amending Protocol to the Canada-Israel agreement, see http://international.gc.ca/trade-commerce/trade-agreements-accords-commerciaux/agr-acc/israel/fta-ale/index.aspx?lang=eng, accessed 5 October 2018.

enforceable investment rights for transnational corporations; mostly unenforceable commitments for gender equality.

Where do these imbalances originate? Do they stem from oversights or negotiating errors? A political economy approach to trade, such as the one advanced in this chapter, argues that these imbalances are not a result of mistakes or omissions, but rather are a reflection of the interests and goals of the most powerful sectors in Canada and the world. Trade policy changes, but not strictly as a result of economic, scientific, or technical assessments; instead, it is highly influenced by struggles to define and redefine what it should look like and what it should achieve. In the end, trade and trade agreements do not emerge out of a pure, objective selection between "free" and "fair" trade, but out of the battles between their proponents on the highly uneven terrain of trade politics.

15 Money and Finance

MARIO SECCARECCIA AND DAVID PRINGLE

Introduction

On 6 March 2018, the Bank for International Settlements warned that Canada was displaying strong indicators of financial system vulnerabilities tied to debt accumulation, real estate prices, and risks posed by rising interest rates. These vulnerabilities correlate with past financial instability. The warning was the latest in a series of reports drawing Canadians' attention to the possibility that our financial system is vulnerable to instability.

This is the entry point into a broader discussion of a dimension of social relations in Canada, that of lender and borrower. The narrative begins in the mid-1970s, when the mass use of credit by Canadian households becomes well established. It is in this historic period, from 1975 to the present, when structural transformations in three related spheres are observed in the larger Canadian political economy of finance: the chartered banking industry, lender-borrower relations, and the central bank and its conduct of monetary policy.

In this chapter, we reveal how institutional developments, believed to explain both the rise of a bank-dominated financial industry in Canada as well as a strong financial regulatory system, have steered the banking system away from instability. Adjacent to the suppliers of finance are the users of financial services – in particular, credit. During this historic period, there has been an inversion of lending-borrowing roles between private actors. Traditionally, Canadian households had been net savers in the aggregate, thereby building up financial assets within the bank-dominated financial system, while Canadian businesses generally were net borrowers whose debt normally went towards financing their capital expenditures. In the 1990s, as data from the national accounts indicate, this traditional relationship inverted, with households becoming net borrowers and firms becoming net lenders. A key economic device common to both the banking order and credit relations is the institution of interest rates.

The third sphere features monetary policy conducted by the Bank of Canada. The evolution of this macroeconomic policy lever during this historic period, particularly with the Bank's adoption of the inflation-targeting regime in 1991, has revealed monetary policy to be about interest rate policy. The key policy interest rate set by the Bank has enormous influence on the wider menu of credit offerings and their associated prices, including housing mortgages, within the Canadian credit market. Instead of dwelling on the use of interest rate policy as a tool to manage price inflation, this chapter frames the rate of interest as both a policy variable for income distribution and a critical device for the maintenance of credit system stability.

American political scientist Harold Lasswell famously said politics is about who gets what, when, and how. In many ways, this chapter takes a similar approach to the political economy of money and finance: who pays and who earns interest, when and how? Given the intimate links between credit use, macroeconomic demand, and growth, we assert that there exists a *credit crux* – that the credit system is a major driver of the contemporary Canadian macroeconomic system of production and distribution. This is not unique among advanced capitalist economies, but the unique historical path of its evolving financial system, with its concomitant institutions, situates Canada as an exceptional case with respect to the distribution of risks tending to crisis.

Compared to scholarship on other sectors of the Canadian economy – namely, the primary resource (staples) and manufacturing sectors – the existing political economy literature on Canadian finance is relatively thin and indistinct. This might be explained by the choice of emphasis on primary resources as a driver of economic development by the original staple theorists H.A. Innis and W.A. Mackintosh, as well as by the first-generation scholars in the New Canadian Political Economy (NCPE), such as M.H. Watkins. However, even in the original Innisian staples analysis, where emphasis was placed on the nature of commodity production/trade relations and on the importance of overhead costs, the latter needed financing, thereby explaining the deep and enduring links between finance (whether domestic or foreign) and the Canadian state that go back centuries. Thin though it be, the political economy of Canadian finance literature does display the interdisciplinary approach characteristic of the larger NCPE literature, with contributions by political scientists, economists, and historians, as well as by business studies and legal scholars. See Coleman and Porter (2003) for a more contemporary examination of the Canadian political economy of finance.

The political economy method we follow in this chapter differs from that generally employed in the relatively recent research program that also calls itself the "political economy of finance," distinguished by its framing of finance as a public choice problem, where actors are defined by the rational choice model of behaviour and where the method employed borrows heavily from neoclassical economics (see Calomiris and Haber 2014; Perotti 2014; and Helleiner, in this volume). Focusing on a recent interval of Canadian economic history, from 1975 to 2018, we examine three spheres of the Canadian economy in terms of evolving structures and the social processes operating within this structured system. One of these spheres is the national financial order, defined here as a particular configuration of structures that define how private and state actors combine to supply financial services. This exploration focuses on how institutional and technological changes have enabled Canadian chartered banks not only to shift away from conventional banking towards the universal banking model, but also to become the dominant financial services industry group in the system. The second sphere features the social relations of lender and borrower, organized and aggregated into economic groups of households, businesses, governments, and non-residents, the four general sectors of the macroeconomic framework. The third sphere includes the institutions of macroeconomic policy, with specific focus on the monetary policy responsibilities of the Bank of Canada.[1]

We argue that, although the bank-dominated national financial order that took shape during this historical period is characterized by strength and resilience, the adjacent, larger sphere of macro credit relations was transformed in such a way as to elicit concerns about the financial fragility of Canadian households. Examining the economic processes operating within this structured system will help to reveal the character of these concurrent structural transformations.

We enlist two bodies of economic theory from the post-Keynesian schools of thought. The first, the *sectoral balance framework* developed by Godley (see Godley and Lavoie 2007) for the macroeconomic analysis of national economies, is grounded on the underlying principle that

---

1 Readers familiar with Robert Cox's (1981) method of historical structures will note similarities with this method of elucidating the structures underpinning different spheres of social activity at a specific moment in time.

every economic transaction between two (or more) actors is reflected or recorded as symmetric offsetting entries in the actors' accounts. This principle, which provides the basis of national accounting, allows sectoral net lending and borrowing positions to be related to a sector's contribution to economic growth. On this basis, structural analysis and short-term forecasting can be performed.

Closely related to the sectoral balance framework is the *financial instability hypothesis* developed by Minsky (1982). Key aspects of his hypothesis are important for understanding contemporary financialized economies because they are based on a model of a capitalist economy animated through the circulation not only of income, but also of credit between agents and sectors. Minsky's model demonstrates how an economic system is capable of endogenous instability through debt accumulation by private borrowers (in our analysis, private households), where some borrowers, no longer able to service their debt through income revenues, prompt lenders to scale back credit flows. This triggers a collapse in asset values, and the system spirals into crisis. Government intervention, depending on how it is designed and wielded, can either dampen these tendencies or amplify them.

Change: Evolution of the Chartered Banking Sphere, 1975–2018

Canada's banking system stands out among those of other advanced capitalist economies, notably for its relative resilience amid international financial crises not only in 2008, but also in the 1930s during the Great Depression (Bordo, Redish, and Rockoff 2011). Further, the system has avoided domination by the United States, despite American economic strength and the shared history, language, legal system, and culture between the two countries. Indeed, Canada's banking system stands out as among the exceptions to broader continental integration (Clarkson 2008; McBride, in this volume). Much of the distinctiveness of Canada's banking system vis-à-vis that of the United States is explained by the different historical paths the two nations have taken that have shaped the institutions underpinning their respective national financial orders. Canada's banking system is characterized by fewer larger banks, organized nationally as branch banks and overseen almost exclusively by the federal government. Up until the past few decades, the American system had tended towards hundreds of unit banks restrained from operating branches across state lines. This, combined with the fact that bank regulation is an area of shared federal-state jurisdiction, has entailed a fragmented regulatory system (Calomiris and Haber 2014). The strength of Canada's domestic market meant that

Canadian banks were able to rely far less on foreign liabilities than were banks in peer countries before the 2008 financial crisis. Since they were less integrated in the international financial system, Canadian banks were more insulated from external turmoil (International Monetary Fund 2012, 106). Canada's financial service providers are dominated by the chartered banks: at the end of 2017, they held 57 per cent of loans outstanding, 80 per cent of deposits, and about 30 per cent of both total financial assets and liabilities in Canada's overall financial sector, which includes credit unions, insurance companies, pension funds, and independent mutual fund managers.[2] Historically, Canada's banking industry has been a stable profit centre amid the rise and fall of other industrial sectors such as primary resources and manufacturing. The following describes the development of the Canadian banking order over the past four decades. But first, we offer two contrasting views of how banks work.

Two Theories of Banking

The "intermediation" theory of banking is a deeply rooted, yet misleading, view of the role of banking widely held in our society and by most economists. This theory portrays banks as largely passive economic entities engaged in the activity of deposit taking. By attracting a community's flow of saving and receiving them as deposit liabilities, bankers can then make loans to agents in need of finance. Hence, in this intermediary role, saving can be channelled towards financing business investment, household investment (say, in housing), or consumption expenditures, or towards financing government spending if the state refuses to adjust tax revenues to its expenditures. Based on this conception of the banking process, "deposits make loans." Moreover, as compensation for this intermediary service they render to the public and for their risk-taking activity in lending depositors' funds to creditworthy borrowers, banks earn revenue on the interest rate spread – that is, on the difference between the interest they charge borrowers for each dollar of loan and what the banks pay out as interest on their clients' deposit accounts.

A second theory concerning actual banking processes does not view banks as passive financial intermediaries between savers and investors, allocating scarce credit within organized financial systems. Rather, according to this view, banks are, and have always been, primarily

---

2 Statistics Canada, National Balance Sheet Accounts, CANSIM table 378-0121.

creators of deposit money by actively seeking to make loans to borrowers associated with varying degrees of creditworthiness. Through a balance sheet operation, they make loans to the public that generate an equivalent amount of deposits in the banking system, thereby suggesting an actual causal mechanism consistent with the less well-known expression that "loans make deposits" (Lavoie and Seccareccia 2016).

Also, in the modern context, banks earn profits not only on the basis of interest income, constituting about half of bank net revenues in Canada. Banks also earn non-interest revenue for a multitude of services they provide, such as transaction fees for payment of services they offer, insurance fees charged borrowers against the risk of credit default, fees for investment banking services such as underwriting a business's share issuance, and payments for wealth management fees such as administering bank-sponsored mutual funds. These changes in the sources of bank revenues over the past few decades have actually been associated with the growing profitability of the banking sector and, concomitantly, with a significant long-term expansion of the share of gross domestic product (GDP) by the banking and overall financial sector (Seccareccia 2012, 2014).

Transformation of the Canadian Banking Order

The history of the Canadian chartered bank system during this interval is best delineated along two policy tracks, with one track addressing the competitiveness of the Canadian financial system and the other transforming the bank supervision system.

Bank Supervision

Ever since the Porter Commission on Banking and Finance reported in 1964, increasing competition in the financial services industry has been a policy priority. Measures to promote competition were included in the 1980 Bank Act, creating the Schedule A and B bank systems to encourage foreign entrants into the banking industry while protecting widely held, Canadian-owned banks. This resulted in the entry of sixty new banks over the next six years (Estey 1986, 3). However, the combination of high interest rates, recessionary conditions, and falling oil prices led to the collapse in 1985 of both the Alberta-based Canadian Commercial Bank and Northland Bank. A federal inquiry into their failure revealed the need to overhaul the existing system of bank supervision.

This initiated a policy movement that would transform the federal financial regulatory apparatus, beginning with the creation of the Office of the Superintendent of Financial Institutions (OSFI) in 1987. Tasked with the prudential regulation of banks, OSFI would respond actively to early signals of bank distress, exercise enhanced powers to inspect the loan portfolios of supervised banks, and issue cease-and-desist orders. OSFI would join the Bank of Canada, the Canada Deposit Insurance Corporation (CDIC), and the Department of Finance to form the Financial Institutions Supervisory Committee (FISC),[3] a group mandated to maintain an on-going dialogue on issues of regulation and supervision, share information, and jointly develop strategies to address banks and other regulated institutions in distress (Dodge 2011). Together, they form the federal safety net.

OSFI is the agency that provides on-going oversight of the regulated banks. Its coercive powers remain in the background, however, as OSFI has pursued a responsive regulatory[4] relationship with the banks it oversees, emphasizing self-regulation and co-production of rules and guidelines. The banks participate in the development of the regulations to which they then are publicly expected to adhere. Failure to self-regulate is discouraged by the latent threat of coercive intervention by the regulator.

Financial Competition

For most of the twentieth century, the private supply of financial services to Canadians could be described as a five-pillar system, with each pillar being a large industry group operating in its own core business

---

3 The Financial Consumer Agency of Canada (FCAC) became a member of FISC upon its establishment in 2002. The regulatory role of each agency is as follows: prudential supervision (OSFI), lender of last resort (Bank of Canada), deposit insurance (CDIC), and consumer protection (FCAC). Although having fewer regulatory responsibilities in the operational sense, the Department of Finance, headed by the minister of finance, is responsible for developing financial sector policy (such as the Bank Act) as well as for managing wider economic, fiscal, and tax policy. The minister is responsible for these four financial agencies, despite their ability to operate at arm's length of the minister. Further, the Department develops much of the legislation shaping the Canadian mortgage market, including the mortgage securitization market.

4 Among the core tenets of responsive regulation are the principles of maintaining a dialogue with the regulated firm and of demonstrating a willingness to escalate or de-escalate intervention in response to a firm's or industry's performance with respect to regulatory goals (Ayers and Braithwaite 1992, 6). Pringle (2018) argues that the theory of responsive regulation describes the approach of OSFI. Although not widely followed by other national prudential bank regulators, OSFI's principles of responsive regulation have been found to describe the practice of the Australian Prudential Regulatory Authority (Wood et al. 2015).

lines: chartered banks, trust and mortgage loan companies, life insurance companies, securities brokerages, and credit unions.[5] Beginning in 1954, when chartered banks were permitted to issue mortgage loans to households, these pillars would gradually erode through federal policy efforts to enhance competition in the financial sector, often through periodic amendments of legislation such as the Bank Act. The Bank Act contains a sunset clause that provides for a periodic statutory review and update of the Act. Originally every ten years, the review now takes place every five years, providing a timetable for both the government and interest groups to organize strategies to influence any amendments of the Act.

In 1987, a key amendment to the Bank Act allowed chartered banks to engage in securities dealing. Four of the large chartered banks subsequently acquired large domestic securities dealers, giving each an investment bank wing while hollowing out the independent brokerage industry. The impetus behind this move was to respond to the encroachment of securities brokerages on the corporate lending business of the banks, while allowing the brokerages to consolidate and compete with their larger American counterparts. This move was the equivalent of the repeal in the United States of the 1933 Glass-Steagall Act, which had separated commercial banking from investment banking, by the 1999 Gramm-Leach–Bliley Act. One difference between the legislative changes in the two countries, apart from the twelve-year lag, was that the 1987 Bank Act facilitated greater de facto regulatory consolidation as more financial activities were gathered under fewer regulated firms. Similar regulatory consolidation did not follow from the 1999 US Act, and so a fragmented regulatory system remained in place there.

Following this, the 1992 Bank Act sought to level the playing field for the remaining pillars, as both the chartered bank and trust and mortgage loan company sectors had long been encroaching on each other's core activities. This resulted in the large chartered banks acquiring weaker trust companies and offering financial services traditionally offered only by trust companies, such as wealth management services.

---

5 Credit unions are a unique pillar in the system, as they have tended to share the same traditional business lines as chartered banks (business lending) and trust and mortgage loan companies (household saving and lending). Unlike these two pillars, co-operative credit providers tend to be regulated at the provincial level. Historically, they have distinguished themselves by providing financial services in communities underserved by other pillars. See MacArthur, in this volume, for a broader consideration.

By the mid-1990s, institutional changes aimed at enhancing competition within the Canadian system collapsed the original five-pillar system to three, leaving chartered banks, life insurance companies, and the provincially regulated credit unions as the remaining large pillars. Through this, the chartered bank industry moved to its present position of dominance within the wider financial services industry, offering services along the universal bank model (Coleman and Porter 2003; Freedman 1998).

A National Financial Order Coalesces

Yet, despite their expansion, the banks continued to press policy makers for additional flexibility to move into other business lines, such as auto leases, as well to consolidate into larger entities. This pressure was partly motivated by a perceived growing threat of foreign competition. The federal government responded by setting up the 1996 Task Force on the Future of the Canadian Financial Services Sector (Mackay Task Force). Amid the process, in early 1998, two of the so-called Big Six banks, Royal Bank of Canada (RBC) and Bank of Montreal (BMO), announced their intention to merge, to be followed three months later by a similar merger announcement by the Toronto-Dominion Bank (TD) and the Canadian Imperial Bank of Commerce (CIBC). These merger proposals ultimately were rejected by Finance Minister Paul Martin in late 1998 on the grounds of an unacceptable concentration of economic power. Although this might seem at odds with the broader neoliberal policy legacy of the Chrétien years, with its support of the North American Free Trade Agreement in 1993 and fiscal retrenchment beginning with the sharp budget cuts of 1995 (e.g., see Fridell, Graefe, McBride, in this volume), large numbers of the Liberal caucus opposed the bank merger proposal, fearing voter backlash at the next election if financial services declined as a result of the mergers.

When the Mackay Task Force did ultimately report, it featured a wide variety of recommendations organized around four themes: giving flexibility to financial institutions, promoting competition, updating the regulatory framework, and improving consumer protection. Several of its recommendations would be implemented in the 2002 Bank Act, including putting in place a formal process to review merger proposals among large banks, which included the submission of a public interest impact assessment. This braked any rekindled movement towards disrupting the structure of the banking industry.

The 2002 Bank Act, along with OSFI's 1999 Supervisory Framework – which formalized its evolving supervisory approach towards the regulated banks – were the final major policy events in the maturing of the new national financial order of this period, an order characterized by a bank-dominated financial services system with a stable industrial structure and a strengthened regulatory apparatus. This order would endure the 2008 financial crisis and beyond.

Prelude to a Global Financial Crisis

Within this new financial order, several large banks experienced losses between 1999 and the 2008 financial crisis[6] that led bank managers to shift towards more conservative business models – such as reducing their exposure to securitized financial products – and to change their approach to risk management. It is noteworthy that this shift in strategy among Canadian banks contrasted with that pursued by peers in the United States and Europe, who continued to embrace securitized financial products. This self-corrective bank behaviour was broadly aligned with the principle of self-regulation in the new regulatory relationship. Yet these behavioral changes did not alter the banks' longer-term trend of growth and profit.

The self-corrective responsiveness of the large Canadian banks was also evident in the months after international credit markets began to seize up in August 2007. In terms of relative asset write-downs and share price declines, Canadian banks outperformed peers in jurisdictions such as the United States and the United Kingdom. Further, they were able to tap private investors and rebuild bank capital depleted from asset write-downs and overall losses. Except for a few quarters of losses for specific banks, the Big Six remained profitable, and continued to lend to customers in the run-up to the acute stress observed in September and October 2008, when several financial institutions abroad collapsed or needed public rescue.

Although the Canadian banks did benefit from the various programs put in place by the Canadian state to support the continued supply of financial services (including bank lending) in the uncertain wake of fall 2008, notably absent was a bank recapitalization program using public funds – a course of action taken in several other countries. The resiliency of the Canadian bank-centred financial system during the 2008

---

6 Among the large six banks, RBC, TD, and CIBC were all exposed to the fallout of the 2001 Enron accounting scandal, contributing to lower quarterly profits. In the cases of TD and CIBC, Enron exposure combined with other factors, such as losses related to the dot com bubble, led to sharp quarterly losses early in the new millennium.

crisis drew the world's attention to Canada's approach to bank regulation. In some respects, this Canadian resiliency was the product of policy intentions (by both the government and the banks) and good timing. Yet pressures that could undermine the resiliency of this national financial order were never entirely absent. In 2008, on the eve of the crisis, the Competition Policy Review Panel organized by the Harper government recommended the removal of the "de facto prohibition on bank, insurance and cross-pillar merger of large financial institutions subject to regulatory safeguards" (Canada 2008, 52).

Canadian Banks in the Post-crisis Era

Despite a general movement of re-regulation initiated nationally (e.g., the Dodd-Frank Act in the United States) and internationally (e.g., the formation of the Financial Stability Board), the international financial system continued to be rocked by destabilizing events well after the 2008 crisis, undermining confidence in the soundness of national systems and the broader global network. The most immediate event was the European sovereign debt crisis in 2010, when several smaller Eurozone economies, such as Greece and Ireland, tottered on the brink of default. Signs of lingering fragility, combined with slow economic recovery from the recession triggered by the crisis, led central banks to keep their key policy interest rates low for nearly a decade – in some instances at the zero per cent boundary.

Meanwhile, the Big Six banks took advantage of their positions of relative strength, and invested abroad while cultivating their domestic bases. The banks continued to lend, sell, manage, and advise, and have remained among the most profitable corporations in the economy. This is not to say that there have not been emerging pressures, such as the disruptive effects of new computer-mediated financial technologies (such as robo-advisors and blockchain record management) that could undo this particular national financial order. However, the most significant pressure on the national financial order to emerge is the condition of the balance sheet of Canadian households.

Change: Structural Transformation in Sectoral Balances, 1975–2018

Changes in institutional structures and technological forces over the past four decades (such as the rapid spread of information and communication technologies) have not only shaped the Canadian banking order, but have also influenced demand for financial services. Canadian households and businesses are more closely entwined with the bank-dominated financial system than ever. This increased financialization, reflected in the public's greater dependence on financial services, is due to the growing complexities of a payments system in which the banking sector is both the gatekeeper and principal supplier of the means of payment (whether through cash or through credit). This trend of greater financialization is not unique to Canada, but the concentration of the supply of financial services among six large banks does contrast with the more decentralized US system.

Labour Market Outcomes and Income Distribution

At the macroeconomic level, growing bank profits have risen not only through bank market power, but also through the way the distribution of income and wealth has evolved as a result of stagnant real (or inflation-adjusted) wages over the past few decades. This situation has resulted from declining union density rates in Canada since the 1980s because of growing anti-unionism, promoted via legislated changes and direct government actions (see Smith, in this volume). It is also the result of the restructuring of social spending at both the federal and provincial levels, which has sought to move individuals off social programs, thereby weakening labour's bargaining position, especially that of unskilled workers (see Graefe, in this volume).

This broad real-wage stagnation has also been influenced, perhaps even more so, by a trend of growing long-term unemployment that is reinforced by the overall forces of globalization and changing labour market conditions, as well as by the adoption of neoliberal policies, beginning in the latter half of the 1970s, that favour restrictive monetary and fiscal policy. Figure 15.1 highlights in a rather dramatic way what happened to the evolution of real wages and average labour productivity after the 1970s – in this case, in the manufacturing sector. By implication, this general decoupling of real wages and productivity is also reflected in the longer-term decline in the share of labour income in national income and the growing polarization of market wages, especially between those of skilled and unskilled workers.

Household Balance Sheets

The consequence of this shift in income distribution away from labour's share of national income, combined with more easily accessible bank

Figure 15.1. Evolution of Output per Person-Hour and Real Average Hourly Earnings in the Manufacturing Sector, Canada, 1950–2016

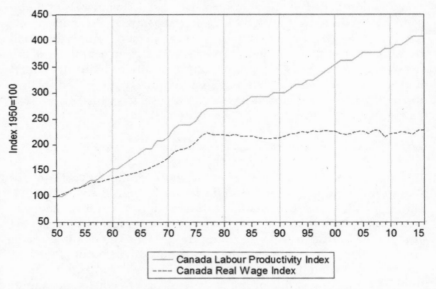

Source: Conference Board of Canada, Total Economy database, May 2017.

credit at increasingly lower interest costs since the early 1990s, has been a tremendous expansion of household indebtedness (see Peters, in this volume). In many ways, it can be said that the Canadian economy has become increasingly dependent on household debt for its continued growth, by replacing the traditional roles of private business investment and, since the financial crisis, even net exports as drivers of growth. As can be seen from Figure 15.2, bank mortgage lending expanded from less than 20 per cent of GDP in 1970 to almost 70 per cent of GDP in 2017, with most of the expansion taking place since the late 1980s. Hence, even as consumer credit expansion slowed down as a share of GDP after the global financial crisis of 2008, mortgage lending has continued its steep rise. This credit expansion has fed what appears to be an unsustainable housing bubble that eventually could burst unless supported by strong growth in household disposable income.

Figure 15.2. Household Credit as a Share of GDP, Canada, 1970–2017

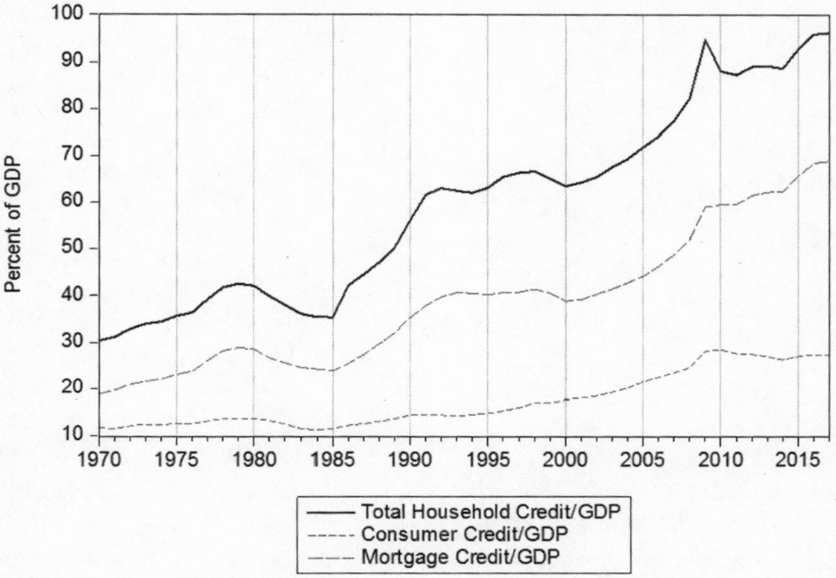

Source: Statistics Canada, CANSIM V36408, V36409, V36410, and V62295576.

Corporate Balance Sheets

This continued expansion of household credit, which has sustained both strong bank net revenues and the profits of the non-financial business sector, has partly compensated the slowdown in private business investment that has been associated with Canada's relatively anemic overall real GDP growth since the 1980s. Despite the overall business sector's sustained profits, the share of business investment has never much recovered from the 1990–92 recession and the 2008 financial crisis, thereby reinforcing a significant downward trend (see Figure 15.3). One can infer that this is hardly a characteristic of a strong dynamic business sector in Canada. Smardon (in this volume) makes a similar argument about the low commitment of Canadian business to privately funded research and development. Furthermore, since the late 1990s, an increasing share of actual business

Figure 15.3. Business Gross Fixed Capital Formation as a Share of GDP, Canada, 1988–2017

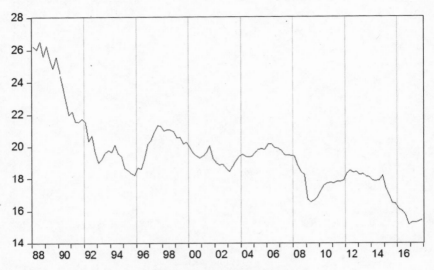

Source: Statistics Canada, CANSIM V62305733 and V62305783.

investment has been in the form of intercompany investment, where Canadian firms acquire existing business assets rather than spending on new ones. Moreover, an increasing proportion of this intercompany investment has been directed abroad, rather than in Canada (Tomas 2006, 7–8).

Except for periods of steep recession or economic slowdown, the return on capital in all industries tends to gravitate around a relatively fixed trend. Indeed, with sustained profitability in the face of declining investment, the net lending position of corporate enterprises in the aggregate has mirrored the decline in the share of investment spending. Moreover, Canadian corporations have deleveraged in a similar step-wise fashion since the early 1990s, with business debt-to-equity ratios displaying a longer-term downward trend. These factors have combined to leave many corporations with the task of managing growing corporate surpluses. As the late federal finance minister Jim Flaherty often complained, many business enterprises seemed more concerned with stashing their net cash revenues or engaging in speculative financial acquisition than in pursuing productive investment (see Whittington 2012).

Confronting the Sectoral Balance

These changes in the evolution of household spending and business investment have led to a very important macroeconomic accounting identity that explains the dramatic reversal of the traditional pattern of indebtedness in Canada. There exists a fundamental macroeconomic relationship, sometimes referred to as the Godley equation, derived from the definition of GDP and based on the principle that what is an expenditure for someone in a market transaction must necessarily be a receipt or income for someone on the other side of the transaction. Hence, if we sum up these agents into sectors (households, business enterprises, governments, and foreigners), and if one of these sectors is spending more than it is receiving – thus running a deficit financed, say, through bank borrowing – some other sector, of necessity, will be receiving more than it is spending, and find itself in a surplus position. For instance, if we assume a closed economy with no outside trade, a government sector running a budget deficit would mean the domestic private sector, whether households or businesses, is in a surplus or net lending position. If we further assume an open economy and that a surplus in the government account is offset by a deficit in the foreign account, an increase in the net expenditures of the household sector necessarily would be reflected in an increase in the net receipts or flow of funds to the business sector.

The estimated net accounting balances of the three domestic macroeconomic sectors can be found in Figure 15.4 for the 1970–2017 period. What is obvious from the net lending/borrowing positions of these three sectors is that there was a dramatic shift in the household position in the mid-1990s, from its peak as a net lender in the early 1980s to becoming a persistent net borrower. Conversely, the other sectors were on the receiving end of increasing household indebtedness, especially the business sector, which converted in the early 1980s from a traditional net borrower to primarily a rentier net lender.[7]

This reversal of the traditional roles of the two major sectors of the private economy reflects the fact that, with sustained business profits from the growing net spending of the household sector since the mid-1990s, there is less incentive for businesses to invest in domestic productive enterprises. All that net cash flow has been funnelled progressively into financial markets, and has brought the Canadian economy into a

---

7 This shift in net lending-borrowing positions among sectors is not unique to Canada. However, there is not a uniform pattern among developed economies, in part due to different fiscal policies and trade positions pursued among them (Wray 2012).

Figure 15.4. Net Lending/Borrowing by Sector, Canada, 1970–2017

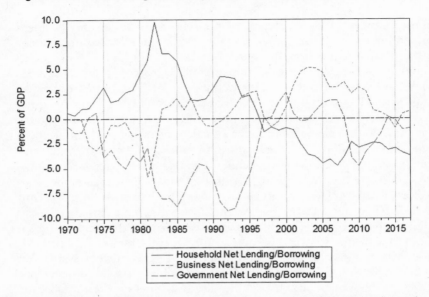

Note: The foreign sector's current account balance was excluded to avoid clogging up the chart. Source: Statistics Canada, CANSIM V62295576, V62306045, V63207123, V63255673.

brave new world of what US economist Hyman Minsky dubbed "money manager capitalism." Canada's non-financial business sector continues to rely on a relatively steady long-term stream of profits, while building up and becoming ever more dependent on the gains that can be made in financial markets through the portfolio management of existing assets. Chapters by Peters and Brownlee in this volume describe the trend of corporate financialization as a key explanatory factor behind the widening income inequality among Canadians.

The Consequence of the Shift in Debt Relations

This evidence suggests that growth in Canada has become more dependent on spurts of consumer spending, financed through bank credit, and much less on investment spending and net exports, the traditional drivers of growth. In the aggregate, this trend in consumer expenditures might appear to be underpinned by cheaper imported goods and a wealth effect induced by a highly speculative housing market, as in the United States just before the 2008 financial crisis. But what is perhaps most disturbing about the nature of this growing household indebtedness is the perversity of the incidence of indebtedness when classified by income groups. A better understanding of the nature of this household indebtedness may be gained by decomposing the saving rate by income quintiles.

Figure 15.5 displays graphically the flow of total household saving as a percentage of total personal disposable income. The data suggest

Figure 15.5. Saving Rates by Income Quintile, Canada, 1999–2017

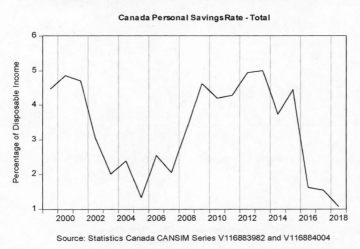

Canada Personal Savings Rate - Total

Source: Statistics Canada CANSIM Series V116883982 and V116884004

Canada Personal Savings Rate - Lowest Quintile

Source: Statistics Canada CANSIM Series V116884005 and V116884027

Figure 15.5. *(Continued)*

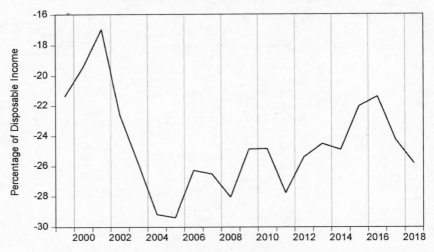

Source: Statistics Canada CANSIM Series V116884028 and V116884050

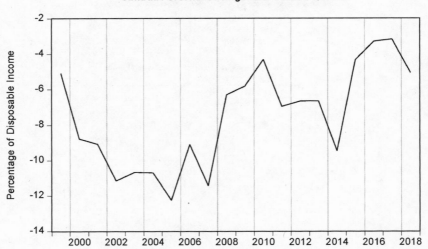

Source: Statistics Canada CANSIM Series V116884051 and V116884073

Figure 15.5. *(Continued)*

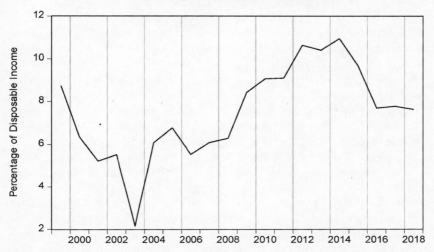

Canada Personal Savings Rate - Fourth Quintile

Source: Statistics Canada CANSIM Series V116884074 and V116884096

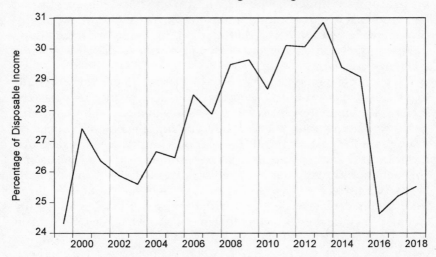

Canada Personal Savings Rate - Highest Quintile

Source: Statistics Canada CANSIM Series V116884097 and V116884119

what we would expect as the normal behaviour of the saving rate before and after the financial crisis. During the run-up to the financial crisis in 2008 and ensuing Great Recession of 2009, we see the overall saving rate reach a trough in 2005 and remaining historically low until 2008. Immediately following the crisis, fearing job uncertainty, households sought to deleverage by raising their saving rate, which peaked in 2013 and then slowly declined.

Breaking down that saving rate by income groups, however, reveals that only the top two quintiles actually had a *positive* saving rate out of disposable income throughout the whole period from 1999 to 2017, with patterns similar to the aggregate saving rate. The middle quintile and the two lower quintiles all display a *negative* saving rate. What is striking is that not even the "middle class" of household income groups was able actually to deleverage during the crisis. Its saving rate was never able to "break even" at the zero threshold, and it peaked at only around −3 per cent of disposable personal income. As for the lowest and second-lowest quintiles, not only were these households unable to deleverage during the recession, many poorer Canadian households were stuck in what one can describe as a vicious cycle of indebtedness: a debt trap. This is especially the case with the lowest quintile, where individuals seem to have built up debt at an alarming rate. Although the negative rates observed in the lower-income quintiles might be influenced by the inclusion of individuals temporarily in these quintiles − such as post-secondary students who were borrowing heavily to pay tuition fees − other individuals and families in the lower and middle quintiles might have been accumulating debt, including mortgage debt, in a pattern similar to that witnessed just prior to the US subprime mortgage crisis.

The evolution of the saving rate and household indebtedness points to the way bank credit fills the gap in our increasing income-polarized society. Although higher-income earners essentially had been increasing their saving rate, thereby building up their wealth position throughout the post–financial crisis period, the evidence suggests that lower-income earners appear to have become stuck in an unsustainable debt vortex, with many within the lower half of the income scale at risk of sinking ever deeper. Given the role of the banking sector in feeding this explosive debt accumulation by households, especially among some of the most vulnerable in our society, this would explain why the Bank for International Settlements has identified Canada's banks as vulnerable to a level of risk perhaps not seen since the financial crisis.

Change: Transformation of Monetary Policy at the Bank of Canada, 1975–2018

The behaviour of the banking sector, which seems to be profiting from and sustaining more and more of the growing indebtedness of Canadian households, is taking place within an environment marked by increasing risk in the housing sector, jeopardizing the viability of Canada's financial system. This evolution would not have been possible during the past few decades without the policy of the Bank of Canada itself, especially since the 1990s, coupled with a restrictive fiscal policy mix that remained in place until the global financial crisis.

The Keynesian era in Canadian macroeconomic policy ended during the Pierre Trudeau years of the 1970s with the departure in 1973 of Louis Rasminsky as governor of the Bank of Canada, which coincided with the emergence of high inflation rates triggered by the first oil price shocks. By 1975, the Bank had officially adopted a monetarist policy stance to combat double-digit inflation by focusing on control of the growth rate of one key measure of the money supply in Canada, a narrow monetary aggregate called M1.[8] The intellectual cover for the Bank's singular focus on fighting inflation, rather than reducing unemployment, was provided by monetarist theory developed by Milton Friedman and later by the New Classical Macroeconomics pioneered by fellow Chicago School economist Robert Lucas. These schools of macroeconomic thought emphasized that both the monetary and fiscal authorities had but one principal objective: to combat inflation. If not perturbed by discretionary activist Keynesian policies, the private economy naturally would tend towards some long-term non-accelerating inflation rate of unemployment.

However, some central banks that had adopted a monetarist policy framework, including the Bank of Canada, found in the early 1980s that they were repeatedly unable to achieve their M1 target (see Lavoie and Seccareccia 2006, 2013). With the collapse of the monetarist framework,[9] Bank of Canada policy entered a period of realignment until it embraced

---

8 M1 includes physical currency outside banks plus all chequable deposits held at chartered banks and other deposit-taking institutions.
9 The Bank had attributed the collapse to a technical problem resulting from financial innovations by the private banking system during an era of high interest rates. This had even prompted Governor Gerald Bouey in 1982, when abandoning the M1 monetary aggregate, to say, "[w]e did not abandon M1, M1 abandoned us." For a discussion, see Freedman (2003, 319).

a policy regime of inflation targeting in February 1991, following the lead of the Reserve Bank of New Zealand, which pioneered the framework. Canada's inflation-targeting regime was founded on the belief that, ultimately, the Bank's capacity to control inflation rested *not* on its control of some broad measure of the money supply, but on its ability *to set* the interest rate prevailing in the interbank market for funds within the clearing and settlement system – that is, the central bank–administered interest rate for borrowing funds overnight. Through the adoption of an explicit interest-rate operating rule to conduct monetary policy, the Bank sets a target overnight rate that is then transmitted to a whole array of interest rates in the economy. In turn, this key policy rate affects interest-sensitive components of aggregate spending and, finally, the rate of inflation. Although this framework initially sought to control inflation within a 1–3 per cent target range, the Bank refined this system after 1995, when it began to target a precise number – its familiar 2 per cent inflation rate – situated at the mid-point of the range. The essence of this policy operation is that, whenever the inflation rate moves outside the target range, the Bank is expected to adjust its nominal key policy rate and, to a lesser extent, the inflation-adjusted (or real) rate in the same direction. A rise in the inflation rate is met with a rise in the interest rate.

The evolution of monetary policy regimes followed by the Bank of Canada can be organized as historical periods or conjunctures. Using the Bank Rate[10] as indicator, we can compare the four monetary policy regimes since the Second World War by the average inflation rate, the average (or mean) Bank Rate for the period, and the degree to which individual observed rates during the period are spread out around the average rate (the variance) – see Table 15.1.

- The Keynesian era (1946–75): This period was dominated by concerns over unemployment that largely outweighed preoccupations with inflation until the first oil price shocks of the 1970s. During this early period, the inflation-adjusted (or real) Bank Rate gravitated around approximately zero, but was characterized by significantly high variance around the mean, signifying strong discretionary policy actions by the Bank of Canada, which was not wedded to

---

10 The Bank Rate is the interest rate at which the central bank lends funds to banks. The time series for the rate goes back to the 1930s. In the current inflation-targeting framework, the Bank Rate serves as the upper limit of the interest rate target range or corridor, set at 0.25 of a percentage point above the target for the overnight rate.

any simple type of policy rule that would be introduced in the succeeding era. The average inflation rate was 3.1 per cent.

- The monetarist era (1975–90): During the monetarist era, as well as the transition period leading up to the introduction of the inflation-targeting regime in 1991, real interest rates peaked alongside high inflation – at 6.9 per cent over the period when including the disinflationary trend of the 1980s – even though the variance somewhat narrowed. Accompanying these high real interest rates was high unemployment, which, in turn, slowed real wage growth. Coupled with other policy measures relating to trade liberalization and fiscal austerity, this monetary policy regime would be associated with a decoupling of real wages and productivity (as shown in Figure 15.1 above).
- The inflation-targeting regime (1991–2008): During the official inflation-targeting period leading up to the 2008 financial crisis, the real Bank Rate fell mildly while variance around the mean contracted significantly in this era of relatively low inflation (2 per cent on average) – the so-called Great Moderation (Bernanke 2004). Under inflation targeting, a fluctuation in the inflation rate was expected to be met by a change (in the same direction) in the nominal interest rate. The empirical outcome of this distinct policy rule was to stabilize the real Bank Rate at a relatively high level, as evidenced in Table 15.1. By consequence, intended or not, the interest income earned by investors was stabilized largely at the expense of wage earners.
- The hybrid or flexible inflation-targeting regime (2009–17): This brings us to the most recent period, the decade after the global financial crisis. As the last column of Table 15.1 highlights, the Bank of Canada slashed the nominal Bank Rate virtually to its lower bound of 0.25 per cent as a response to the crisis in 2008. Because of relatively positive rates of inflation that, with the exception of 2009, had remained within the central bank's target of 2 per cent, this meant that the average real Bank Rate in the post-crisis period was negative. Further, there was little variance around that mean, since with a relatively stable inflation rate (1.7 per cent on average) and a nominal rate essentially parked at a very low level, real rates remained very stable.

The behaviour of Canada's monetary authorities over the hybrid inflation-targeting regime is best described in Figure 15.6 below, which traces the evolution of the nominal overnight rate and the rate of inflation from 1996 to 2017. Although throughout the post-crisis period the Bank of Canada had retained its official policy position that it would stay the course and not abandon inflation targeting, in reality inflation appears no longer to be the Bank's single focus as was the case before

Table 15.1. Mean and Variance of the Inflation-Adjusted/Real Bank Rate during Various Monetary Policy Regimes, Canada, 1946–2017

	Post-war Keynesian Era, 1946–74	Monetarism and Policy Realignment, 1975–90	Official Inflation-Targeting Regime, 1991–2008	Hybrid Inflation-Targeting Regime, 2009–17
Rate	*(per cent)*			
Real Bank Rate, average	0.08	3.76	2.64	−0.50
Real Bank Rate, variance (as square of standard deviation)	14.70	8.57	2.88	0.34
Inflation rate, average	3.1	6.9	2.0	1.7

Source: Statistics Canada, CANSIM tables 176-0048,326-0021, 326-0023.

Figure 15.6. Canada's Inflation Rate and the Bank of Canada's Key Policy Rate, 1996–2017

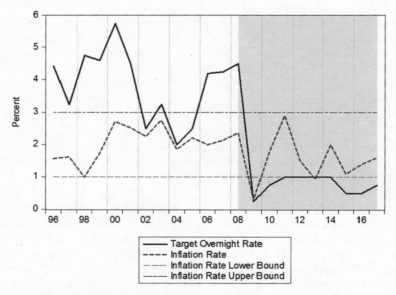

Source: Statistics Canada, tables 1760048 and 326-0021.

the 2008 crisis. Under both governors Mark Carney and Stephen Poloz, the Bank has shown much concern with sustaining the economic recovery through extremely low interest rates (depicted in the shaded area of Figure 15.6). These rates were certainly not warranted if the Bank was only monitoring fluctuations in the inflation rate or observing its measure of the macroeconomic output gap as a predictor of future expected inflation. Although the sharp cut in the overnight rate might well be explained by initial fears of deflation during 2009, the fact that the inflation rate quickly recovered and remained within the 1–3 per cent target range would be sufficient *prima facie* evidence that other policy objectives (such as financial stability) have guided Bank decisions since 2008, when interest rates have remained persistently low. If not, why did the overnight rate not return to the pre-crisis level around which it had been gravitating since the 1990s?

Even if the Bank of Canada remained committed to combatting inflation exclusively, the movement of the overnight rate until 2015 is more consistent with the view that the Bank was pursuing a *de facto* multigoal monetary policy mandate. In other words, it undertook an expansionary monetary policy both to stimulate private sector spending through negative real interest rates, but also to maintain nominal interest rates low enough so as to prevent a collapse of the Canadian housing market. It is here, at the central bank, the heart of the credit crux, where the interest rate authority proceeds with great caution in its policy announcements so as not to upset the fragile balance between Canadian borrowers and lenders.

After emergency Keynesian macroeconomic stimulus in 2008 and 2009, when both monetary and fiscal policy were moving in the same direction to pump prime the Canadian economy, by June 2010 the Harper government had reversed its fiscal stance and sought to return to the fiscal orthodoxy that had existed in the 1990s during the Chrétien and Martin years. While the federal government sought to restrict public spending through its commitment to a "fiscally responsible" balanced budget, expansionary monetary policy was still part of the broader macroeconomic policy mix aimed at stimulating private sector expansion.[11]

---

11 It is noteworthy that this expansive monetary policy direction in Canada, signified by near-zero key policy rates, was followed elsewhere in the international system. Furthermore, the eurozone (which was struggling with a sovereign debt crisis), the United States, the United Kingdom, Switzerland, Sweden, and Japan all enlisted forms of quantitative easing, where central banks buy selected financial assets from private financial institutions in exchange for cash to support banking sector liquidity and lending.

In the era before the financial crisis, the federal government had been able to achieve balanced budgets and surpluses thanks to the high growth of exports to the United States and declining interest rates on public debt throughout the 1990s and early 2000s. Further, these falling interest rates helped fuel growing household indebtedness. This macroeconomic policy strategy did not work very well after 2010, however, not only because of weak exports, but also because Canadian households sought to reduce their debts somewhat despite the low interest rates (an exception being the lower-income groups described above). The result was a homegrown recession in Canada during the first half of 2015.[12]

Since the Trudeau Liberals came to power in fall 2015, we have seen a rebalancing of the macroeconomic policy mix, with greater reliance on a mild fiscal expansion while still maintaining a relatively low interest rate policy as a strategy for growth. Notwithstanding the distributive effects of mild public sector deficits in recent years, the Canadian banking sector as supplier of credit still remains very much the key player in sustaining private sector spending as a driver of economic growth, as well as the risks associated with rising household indebtedness that have characterized much of the growth process of the past three decades.

Conclusion: Change Culminating in Potential Crisis

The conduct of monetary policy by the central bank since the crisis, combined with the sustained upward trend in household indebtedness and the entrenchment of the large chartered banks at the core of the credit supply system, brings this story to the present juncture. The largest issue in post-crisis Canada has been the growing risk of continued aggregate growth in household indebtedness, largely fuelled by mortgage borrowing. This growth has taken place alongside rising aggregate household net worth, driven by rising real estate prices. Although this trend in household indebtedness began much earlier than the 2008 financial crisis, the sharp reduction in the Bank of Canada's key policy interest rate during the crisis and its parking the rate near zero have sustained household demand for credit, much of it supplied by the large banks.

---

12 Whether or not the slowdown in the first two quarters of 2015 was a recession is a controversial point. For example, the C.D. Howe Institute (2016) has argued that it was not – that, "while GDP contracted in both Q1 and Q2 2015, the downturn was restricted to only a few industries, and national employment expanded over this period,"

To dampen the growing risk to macrofinancial stability and to the broader economy, the federal government in 2008 began to introduce more restrictive rules about mortgage loans (e.g., length of amortization period, minimum down payment), mortgage refinancing, and mortgage insurance. More recently, OSFI has required regulated private lenders to stress-test mortgage applicants to assess if they can withstand a possible deterioration of economic conditions, such as a rise in mortgage rates. At the provincial level, the governments of British Columbia and Ontario have introduced surtaxes on non-resident purchases of real estate in urban centres to dampen spiralling house prices.

While the eyes of market watchers are fixed on each data release, from home sales to new mortgage loans, to divine how the Canadian real estate and mortgage system unfolds, they also scrutinize every response by policy makers. One recent policy action is revealing of the politics of the present institutional arrangement. When the federal government held a public consultation in 2016 on proposals to change the mortgage insurance regime so that private lenders would shoulder more of the risk in the event of mortgage default, the initial response by stakeholders (including mortgage lenders) was to resist such a plan. Among their reservations, some stakeholders believed changes to the regime could dampen mortgage lending, which could exacerbate a decline in house prices. Under the status quo, however, the federal government's balance sheet is exposed to the risk of a housing market correction. Thus, Canadian taxpayers would be on the hook if there were ever mass mortgage defaults on the scale observed in the United States in the lead-up to the 2008 crisis.

As this illustrates, Canadian policy makers are performing a precarious balancing act as they seek to guide the financial and larger macroeconomic system through these fragile conditions. This is nowhere more apparent than through the monetary policy actions of the Bank of Canada. Despite signalling to Canadians that it will gradually raise its key policy rate in the near term to its "normal/neutral" level, the Bank has raised it only a few times, by a quarter of a percentage point each time, in the last ten rate announcement dates since September 2017. At the time of writing, it was 1.75 per cent. In a speech in April 2018, Governor Stephen Poloz warned that "this [household] debt still poses risks to the economy and financial stability, and its sheer size means that its risk will be with us for some time. But there is good reason to think we can continue to manage these risks successfully" (Poloz 2018). This cautious restraint in raising its key rate, despite evidence that the annual inflation rate has been above the

Bank's 2 per cent target over the last while, underscores the possible incongruence between the Bank's inflation-targeting mandate and actual practice. It is the latter that addresses a challenging reality that has evolved within a space of ten years, in which Canada has moved from having a resilient banking sector, the envy of the world in 2008, to becoming one of the three nations most vulnerable to a future banking crisis.

Conclusion: Advancing Canadian Political Economy

HEATHER WHITESIDE

The three "C"s of changes, crises, and conflicts are themes found throughout this book, as indeed they pervade Canadian political-economic development more generally. We see *changes* (and continuity) across historical eras, in forms of state power, the nature of trade agreements, technological development, and the activities of corporations, co-operatives, and non-profit organizations. We see (looming) *crises* in banking and finance, ecological sustainability, income distribution and inequality, public and private sector governance, and urban life. We see *conflicts* in relations between labour and capital, capital and the environment, state and society, among gendered and racialized subjects, and within the public sector.

This collection brings these three strands together to form a coherent, if not complex, treatment of long-run and multifaceted political economy phenomena *of* and *in* Canada. Political economy analysis requires both a nuanced and a holistic understanding of interrelated political, economic, social, racial, gendered, environmental, spatial, and temporal developments. The venue for these events – in this case, Canada – matters. In that sense, Canada is the fourth, and indispensible, "C" that combines with the three Cs of political economy to form the unique field of CPE. The objective of this book has been to highlight the multidimensional 3Cs and the Canadian experience, in particular.

Canadian Political Economy, however, goes beyond what is currently available in CPE studies to provide up-to-date interpretations, analyses, and descriptions; accessible writing suitable for academic engagement along with teaching and learning; novel chapter combinations, broader subject treatment; and a better-rounded, interdisciplinary, cadre of CPE theory and debate than is typically presented in the extant literature. Section 1, on approaches to CPE, covered theory and policy from liberal, nationalist, Marxian, ecological, Indigenous, and feminist perspectives; Section 2 addressed various agents in CPE (corporate, public sector, union, co-operative, and non-profit); while Section 3 delved into applications of CPE through trends in inequality and urban poverty, and the evolution of social policy, trade, and banking.

At times, the field and practice of CPE is at the forefront of theoretical and empirical developments; in other instances, CPE takes its cues from broader political economy events and understandings. This might be because Canada is subject to international or regional trends, or because Canadian analyses are sometimes more firmly rooted within disciplines such as geography, history, sociology, political science, and economics. This book has developed existing thought and has driven research in new directions. Helleiner, for example, uncovers a missing piece of history in CPE (conservative nationalist thought in the nineteenth century); Smardon corrects the track record of Canadian economic-technological development; Carter urges an enhanced inclusion of ecological political economy within CPE; Starblanket and Coburn establish Indigenous feminist pathways beyond the colonial present; MacArthur and Joy and Shields contemplate the role and possibility for ignored third sector agents (social economy actors such as co-ops and non-profits) in a political economy dominated by capitalist relations; and Fanelli and Hudson describe how earlier ignorance of the "urban question" in classical CPE has been usefully engaged over the past few decades but lacks a unique CPE variant.

For Evans, a political economy approach expands our understanding of public administration. Graefe asks that political economy analyses move beyond binary interpretations of social policy. Helleiner suggests that the gap between international political economy and CPE in academe should be narrowed. Smardon establishes that studies of neoliberal era CPE could benefit from better understanding the National Policy era (the antecedent to Fordism). Peters cautions that inequality remains underaddressed in the CPE literature. His chapter, and those by Brownlee and Fanelli and Hudson, thus provide important contributions in this vein.

Changes in CPE are evident. Evans examines how transformations in the public sector and public administration approaches have constructed a neoliberal state over the past few decades; Smardon analyses a century of changes across three phases of Canadian technological and economic development; McBride reveals the tensions created by Canada's subordinate but evolving position within international and North American political economies; and Smith charts changes with union strategies, density, and sectoral coverage in Canada.

Conflicts in CPE are multifaceted. Intersectional contradictions and concerns have emerged through increasingly unequal distribution of wealth and income (Peters, Fanelli and Hudson, Brownlee), corporate power (Brownlee), environmental destruction and resource exploitation (Carter), land rights and treaties (Starblanket and Coburn), and ever-expansive trade agreements (Fridell, McBride). Conflicts over the role and interpretation of social policy (Graefe), within labour markets through anti-union policies (Smith), and public sector restructuring more broadly (Evans) have fundamentally challenged the capacity of capitalism – and the ability of liberalized public and private markets – to deliver the good life. Alternatives such as co-operatives (MacArthur) and the non-profit sector (Joy and Shields) are abundant in Canada, but they present debates of their own. Both MacArthur and Joy and Shields query whether these "alternatives" to state and private for-profit employment and service delivery actually offer opportunities for substantial progressive change, and how these third sector or social economy actors have been equally empowered and challenged by the neoliberalization of public and private sectors over the past few decades.

Crises abound. Seccareccia and Pringle identify fragility within a once-resilient Canadian banking sector. Understanding this potential for crisis in domestic banking requires a Canadian approach and delving into long-run CPE-specific dynamics. Easy comparisons with events elsewhere in 2008 will not entirely suffice. Carter reminds us that the "staples" theory at the heart of early CPE has translated into a looming ecological crisis. Whether these crises can be absorbed, or transformed in any way through reforms to the public sector and policy around finance, trade agreements, labour markets and unions, corporate regulations, urban affairs, and income/wealth inequality dynamics, remains to be seen.

Crises are not merely academic; capitalism is riven with tensions and conflicts. Just as the capitalist system is prone to booms and busts (Arrighi 1994; Harvey 1982), so contemporary neoliberal era policies and practices have inbuilt contradictions. Variations within the policy mix (Graefe, in this volume), in tandem with economic turbulence over the past forty years, indicate evolution and tenacity. Neoliberalism is prone to "failing forward" (Peck 2010) following moments of crisis, as opposed to its replacement by a coherent alternate paradigm. With stagflation in the 1970s, recession in the 1980s and 1990s, and a series of stock market bubbles and crashes along the way, the global financial crisis of 2008 provides the most recent, if most painful, illustration of a historically familiar pattern: the deepening of market relations, the discovery of new avenues of profit making, and the contradictory forms of state intervention that intertwine liberal and illiberal moments within a framework of ever-evolving capitalism. Two notable aspects of Canada's political economy, domestically and elsewhere, capture this tension. At home, we see the persistent and pernicious racialization of poverty, inequality, and class (e.g., Bakan and Stasiulis 2012; Choudry and Smith 2016; Wallis, Sunseri, and Galabuzi 2010); abroad, Canadian governments and corporate actors remain involved in imperial campaigns of violence and extractivism in Latin America (e.g., Gordon and Webber 2008).

After 2008, high government debt and vexing deficits earned through fiscal stimulus, corporate bailouts, and economic stagnation urged the reassertion of tight fiscal policy through cutbacks to public sector spending and employment, along with punitive structural reforms to labour markets (for more on Canadian austerity, see Evans and McBride 2017; McBride and Evans 2017). If, for some commentators, the 2008 crisis discredited neoliberal narratives of socially optimizing, self-correcting markets, and the 2009 stimulus and government intervention efforts called for a return of Keynesian economics (e.g., Krugman 2012), the return of austerity in 2010 was a clear signal that neoliberalism might be bruised intellectually but not defeated politically – this being a time of zombie neoliberalism (Peck 2010) and zombie economics (Quiggin 2012). By 2015, the austerity doctrine of spending restraint had been reconfigured in many Canadian jurisdictions, with much enthusiasm for private finance through public-private partnerships (Whiteside 2015, 2016, 2017a, 2018a, 2018b).

What follows from here remains uncertain. Right-wing nationalist-populist parties and governments challenge liberalism around the world, but so too do socialist feminism and left-progressive discontent with fiscal austerity, the assault on public support for social reproduction, and environmental depletion (Fraser 2013). By late 2018, ten years on from the global financial crisis, finance industry insiders and global political-economic leaders were predicting another economic crisis as being all but certain in the near future (Gatehouse 2018).[1] Whether millennialism proves accurate is beside the point. It is clearly a turbulent time in global, national, and local political economy. Changes, crises, and conflicts of material and ideational dimensions are upon us, much as they have been in previous eras. We might better understand where Canadian political economy is going if we know where the thought and practice of political economy in Canada – with its tangled settler-capitalist socio-economic relations – has been. Perhaps it is now, more than ever, in light of the changes, crises, and conflicts both behind and ahead of us, that a rejuvenated field of Canadian political economy is most needed.

---

1 And indeed, as this book goes to press, the 2020 COVID-19 crisis rages.

Bibliography

Abele, F. 1997. "Understanding What Happened Here: The Political Economy of Indigenous Peoples." In *Understanding Canada: Building on the New Canadian Political Economy*, edited by W. Clement, 118–40. Montreal; Kingston, ON: McGill-Queen's University Press.

Abella, I. 1973. *Nationalism, Communism, and Canadian Labour*. Toronto: University of Toronto Press.

Abelson, D.E. 2002. *Do Think Tanks Matter? Assessing the Impact of Public Policy*. Montreal; Kingston, ON: McGill-Queen's University Press.

Aberbach, J., and B. Rockman. 1988. "Mandates or Mandarins? Control and Discretion in the Modern Administrative State." *Public Administration Review* 48 (2): 606–12. https://doi.org/10.2307/975761.

Abramovitz, M. 1994. "Catch-Up and Convergence in the Postwar Growth Boom and After." In *Convergence of Productivity*, edited by W. Baumol, R. Nelson, and E. Wolff, 86–125. New York: Oxford University Press.

Abu-Laban, Y., and J.A. Garber. 2005. "The Construction of the Geography of Immigration as a Policy Problem: The United States and Canada Compared." *Urban Affairs Review* 40 (4): 520–61. https://doi.org/10.1177/1078087404273443.

Acheson, T.W. 1973. "Changing Social Origins of the Canadian Industrial Elite, 1880–1910." *Business History Review* 47 (2): 189–217. https://doi.org/10.2307/3113402.

Ackerman, F., A. Álvarez Béjar, G. Laxer, and B. Beachy. 2018. *NAFTA 2.0: For People or Polluters?* Ottawa: Sierra Club, the Council of Canadians and Greenpeace Mexico.

Acoose-Miswonigeesikokwe, J. 2016. *Iskwewak kah'ki yaw ni wahkomakanak: Neither Indian Princesses nor Easy Squaws*. Toronto: Canadian Scholars' Press.

Adaman, F., and B. öZkaynak. 2002. "The Economics-Environment Relationship: Neoclassical, Institutional, and Marxist Approaches." *Studies in Political Economy* 69 (1): 109–35. https://doi.org/10.1080/19187033.2002.11675182.

Adkin, L.E. 1994. "Environmental Politics, Political Economy, and Social Democracy in Canada." *Studies in Political Economy* 45 (Fall): 130–69. https://doi.org/10.1080/19187033.1994.11675377.

Adkin, L.E. 2003. "Ecology, Political Economy, and Social Transformation." In *Changing Canada: Political Economy as Transformation*, edited by W. Clement and L. Vosko, 393–421. Montreal; Kingston, ON: McGill-Queen's University Press.

Adkin, L.E., ed. 2016. *First World Petro-Politics: The Political Ecology and Governance of Alberta*. Toronto: University of Toronto Press.

Adkin, L.E. 2017. "Crossroads in Alberta: Climate Capitalism or Ecological Democracy?" *Socialist Studies* 12 (1): 2–31. https://doi.org/10.18740/s4bp7h.

Aivalis, C. 2018. *The Constant Liberal: Pierre Trudeau, Organized Labour, and the Canadian Social Democratic Left*. Vancouver: UBC Press.

Albo, G. 1990. "The New 'Realism' and Canadian Workers." In *Canadian Politics: An Introduction to the Discipline*, edited by A.-G. Gagnon and J. Bickerton, 471–504. Toronto: Broadview Press.

Albo, G. 2006. "The Limits of Eco-Localism: Scale, Strategy, Socialism." In *Socialist Register 2007: Coming to Terms with Nature*, edited by L. Panitch, C. Leys, B. Harriss-White, E. Altvater, and G. Albo, 337–63. London: Merlin Press.

Albo, G. 2010. "The 'New Economy' and Capitalism Today." In *Interrogating the New Economy: Restructuring Work in the 21st Century*, edited by N. Pupo and M. Thomas, 3–20. Toronto: University of Toronto Press.

Albo, G., and C. Fanelli. 2014. "Austerity Against Democracy: An Authoritarian Phase of Neoliberalism?" Socialist Intervention Pamphlet Series 13. n.p.: Socialist Project.

Albo, G., and C. Fanelli. 2019. "Fiscal Distress and the Local State: Neoliberal Urbanism in Canada." In *Change and Continuity: Canadian Political Economy in the New Millennium*, edited by M.P. Thomas, L. Vosko, C. Fanelli, and O. Lyubchenko, 269–96. Montreal; Kingston, ON: McGill-Queens University Press.

Allen, B. 1999. *Why Kosovo? Anatomy of a Needless Way*. Ottawa: Canadian Centre for Policy Alternatives.

Alook, A., N. Hill, and I. Hussey. 2017. "Seeking 'Good Jobs' in the Oil Patch." *Monitor*, 1 November, 28–32.

Alook, A., N. Hill, and I. Hussey. 2019. *Indigenous Gendered Experiences of Work in an Oil-Dependent, Rural Alberta Community*. Edmonton: Parkland Institute.

Altamirano-Jiménez, I. 2004. "North American First Peoples: Slipping Up into Market Citizenship?" *Citizenship Studies* 8 (4): 349–65. https://doi.org/10.1080/1362102052000316963.

Altvater, E. 2006. "The Social and Natural Environment of Fossil Capitalism." In *Socialist Register 2007: Coming to Terms with Nature*, edited by L. Panitch, C. Leys, B. Harriss-White, E. Altvater, and G. Albo, 37–59. London: Merlin Press.

Alvaredo, F., L. Chancel, T. Piketty, E. Saez, and G. Zucman. 2018. *World Inequality Report 2018*. Paris: World Wealth and Income Database.

Anderson, K. 2000. *A Recognition of Being: Reconstructing Native Womanhood*. Toronto: Second Story Press.

Appelbaum, E. 2017. "Domestic Outsourcing, Rent-Seeking, and Increasing Inequality." *Review of Radical Political Economics*. Online at https://doi .org/10.1177/0486613417697121.

Argüelles, L., I. Anguelovski, and E. Dinnie. 2017. "Power and Privilege in Alternative Civic Practices: Examining Imaginaries of Change and Embedded Rationalities in Community Economies." *Geoforum*. Online at https://doi.org/10.1016/j.geoforum.2017.08.013.

Armstrong, C., and H.V. Nelles. 1973. "Private Property in Peril." In *Enterprise and National Development, Essays in Canadian Business and Economic History*, edited by G. Porter, and R.D. Cuff, 20–38. Toronto: Hakkert.

Arnot, D.M. 1998. *Statement of Treaty Issues: Treaties as a Bridge to the Future*. Saskatoon: Office of the Treaty Commissioner for Saskatchewan.

Arrighi, G. 1994. *The Long Twentieth Century*. London: Verso.

Arsenault, G. 2018. *L'économie sociale au Québec: une perspective politique*. Quebec City: Presses de l'Université du Québec.

Arvin, M., E. Tuck, and A. Morrill. 2013. "Decolonizing Feminism: Challenging Connections between Settler Colonialism and Heteropatriarchy." *Feminist Formations* 25 (1): 8–34. https://doi.org/10.1353/ff.2013.0006.

Asch, M. 2014. *On Being Here to Stay: Treaties and Aboriginal rights in Canada*. Toronto: University of Toronto Press.

Atkinson, A.B. 2015. *Inequality – What Can Be Done?* Cambridge, MA: Harvard University Press.

Atleo, C. 2008. "From Indigenous Nationhood to Neoliberal Aboriginal Economic Development: Charting the Evolution of Indigenous-Settler Relations in Canada." *Canadian Social Economy Hub*. Occasional paper.

Atleo, C. 2015. "Aboriginal Capitalism: Is Resistance Futile or Fertile?" *Journal of Aboriginal Economic Development* 9 (2): 41–51.

Aubin, H. 1972. *City for Sale*. Toronto: Lorimer.

Aucoin, P. 1988. "Contraction, Managerialism and Decentralization in Canadian Government." *Governance: An International Journal of Policy and Administration* 1 (2): 144–61. https://doi.org/10.1111/j.1468-0491.1988.tb00256.x.

Aucoin, P. 1995a. *The New Public Management: Canada in Comparative Perspective*. Montreal: Institute for Research on Public Policy.

Aucoin, P. 1995b. "Politicians, Public Servants and Public Management: Getting Government Right." In *Governance in a Changing Environment*, edited by G.B. Peters, and D. Savoie, 113–37. Montreal; Kingston, ON: McGill-Queen's University Press.

Aucoin, P. 1996. "Political Science and Democratic Governance." *Canadian Journal of Political Science* 29 (4): 643–60. https://doi.org/10.1017/s0008423900014414.

Aucoin, P. 2010. "The Policy Roles of Central Agencies: Bruce Doern's Original Ideas." In *Policy: From Ideas to Implementation, in Honour of Professor G. Bruce Doern*, edited by L. Pal, M.J. Prince, and G. Toner, 59–76. Montreal; Kingston, ON: McGill-Queen's University Press.

Ayers, I., and J. Braithwaite. 1992. *Responsive Regulation: Transcending the Deregulation Debate*. New York: Oxford University Press.

Ayres, J.M. 1998. *Defying Conventional Wisdom: Political Movements and Popular Contention against North American Free Trade*. Toronto: University of Toronto Press.

Baccaro, L., and C. Howell. 2017. *European Industrial Relations: Trajectories of Neoliberal Transformation*. New York: Cambridge University Press.

Bagehot, W. [1876] 1885. *The Postulates of English Political Economy*. Student ed., preface by A. Marshall. New York: G.P Putnam's Sons.

Bagelman, J., and S.M. Wiebe. 2017. "Intimacies of Global Toxins: Exposure and Resistance in 'Chemical Valley'." *Political Geography* 60 (September): 76–85. https://doi.org/10.1016/j.polgeo.2017.04.007.

Baines, D., J. Campey, I. Cunningham, and J. Shields. 2014. "Not Profiting from Precarity: The Work of Nonprofit Service Delivery and the Creation of Precariousness." *Just Labour: A Canadian Journal of Work and Society* 22 (Autumn): 74–93.

Bakan, A., and D. Stasiulis. 2012. "The Political Economy of Migrant Live-in Caregivers: A Case of Unfree Labour?" In *Legislated Inequality: Temporary Labour Migration in Canada*, edited by P. Lenard and C. Straehle, 202–26. Montreal-Kingston: McGill-Queen's University Press.

Bakan, J. 2004. *The Corporation: The Pathological Pursuit of Profit and Power*. Toronto: Penguin.

Bakvis, H. 1997. "Advising the Executive: Think Tanks, Consultants, Political Staff and Kitchen Cabinets." In *The Hollow Crown: Countervailing Trends in Core Executives*, edited by P. Weller, H. Bakvis, and R.A.W. Rhodes, 84–125. New York: St. Martin's Press.

Baldwin, R., and J. Lopez-Gonzalez. 2015. "Supply-chain Trade: A Portrait of Global Patterns and Several Testable Hypotheses." *World Economy* 38 (11): 1682–721. https://doi.org/10.1111/twec.12189.

Banting, K., and J. Myles. 2014. *Inequality and the Fading of Redistributive Politics*. Vancouver: UBC Press.

Barnett, N. 2011. "Local Government at the Nexus?" *Local Government Studies* 37 (3): 375–90. https://doi.org/10.1080/03003930.2011.571253.

Bartkiw, T.J. 2008. "Manufacturing Descent? Labour Law and Union Organizing in the Province of Ontario." *Canadian Public Policy* 34 (1): 111–31. https://doi.org/10.3138/cpp.34.1.111.

Bashevkin, S. 2006. *Tales of Two Cities: Women and Municipal Restructuring in London and Toronto.* Vancouver: UBC Press.

Batt, R., and E. Appelbaum. 2014. *Private Equity at Work: When Wall Street Manages Main Street.* New York: Russell Sage.

Battye, J. 1979. "The Nine Hour Pioneers: The Genesis of the Canadian Labour Movement." *Labour* 4: 25–56.

Baud, C., and C. Durand. 2012. "Financialization, Globalization, and the Making of Profits by Leading Retailers." *Socio-Economic Review* 10 (2): 241–66. https://doi.org/10.1093/ser/mwr016.

Baum-Snow, N., and R. Pavan. 2012. "Understanding the City Size Wage Gap." *Review of Economic Studies* 79 (1): 88–127.

Bauwens, M., and V. Kostakis. 2016. "Towards a New Reconfiguration among the State, Civil Society and the Market." *Journal of Peer Production* 2 (6): 1–6. http://www.p2plab.gr/en/wp-content/uploads/2016/02/Journal-of-Peer -Production.pdf.

Bear, T.L. 2016. "Power in My Blood: Corporeal Sovereignty through the Praxis of an Indigenous Eroticanalysis." PhD diss., University of Alberta.

Beeby, D. 2014. "Canada Revenue Agency's 'political' targeting of charities under scrutiny." *Globe and Mail*, 3 August. Online at https://www.theglobeandmail.com/news/politics/canada -revenue-agencys-political-targeting-of-charities-under-scrutiny /article19900854/.

Béland, D., and A. Lecours. 2008. *Nationalism and Social Policy: The Politics of Territorial Solidarity.* New York: Oxford University Press.

Belcourt, B.R. 2016. "A Poltergeist Manifesto." *Feral Feminisms* 6: 22–32.

Bell, B.D., and J. Van Reenan. 2013. "Extreme Wage Inequality: Pay at the Very Top." *American Economic Review* 103 (3): 153–7. https://doi.org/10.1257 /aer.103.3.153.

Bennett, M., C. Blackstock, and R. De La Ronde. 2005. *A Literature Review and Annotated Bibliography on Aspects of Aboriginal Child Welfare in Canada.* Ottawa: First Nations Child & Family Caring Society of Canada.

Bentham, K.J. 2002. "Employer Resistance to Union Certification: A Study of Eight Canadian Jurisdictions." *Industrial Relations* 57 (1): 159–87. https:// doi.org/10.7202/006714ar.

Bernanke, B. 2004. "The Great Moderation." Remarks at the meetings of the Eastern Economic Association, Washington, DC. Washington, DC: Federal Reserve Board.

Bernhardt, A., H. Boushey, L. Dresser, and C. Tilly, eds. 2008. *The Gloves off Economy: Problems and Possibilities at the Bottom of America's Labor Market.* Ithaca, NY: Cornell University Press.

Bezanson, K. 2017. "*Mad Men* Social Policy: Families, Social Reproduction and Childcare in a Conservative Canada." In *Caring for Children: Social Movements and Public Policy in Canada*, edited by S. Prentice, R. Langford, and P. Albanese, 19–36. Vancouver: UBC Press.

Bezanson, K., and M. Luxton, eds. 2006. *Social Reproduction: Feminist Political Economy Challenges Neo-Liberalism.* Montreal; Kingston, ON: McGill-Queen's University Press.

Bhagwati, J. 2008. *Termites in the Trading System: How Preferential Agreements Undermine Free Trade.* Oxford: Oxford University Press.

Binford, L. 2013. *Tomorrow We're All Going to the Harvest: Temporary Foreign Worker Programs and Neoliberal Political Aconomy.* Austin: University of Texas Press.

Birchall, J. 2013. "The Potential of Co-Operatives during the Current Recession; Theorizing Comparative Advantage." *Journal of Entrepreneurial and Organizational Diversity* 2 (1): 1–22. https://doi.org/10.5947/jeod.2013.001.

Birchall, J., and L.H. Ketilson. 2009. *Resilience of Co-Operatives in Times of Crisis.* Geneva: International Labour Organization.

Biro, A., and R. Keil. 2000. "Sites/Cities of Resistance: Approaching Ecological Socialism in Canada." *Capitalism, Nature, Socialism* 11 (4): 83–102. https://doi.org/10.1080/10455750009358942.

Bissio, R. 2017. "Is 'Gender' a Trojan Horse to Introduce New Issues at WTO?" *Third World Network*, 10 December.

Bivens, J. 2011. "A Lifesaver, not a Job Killer: EPA's Proposed 'Air Toxics Rule' Is No Threat to Job Growth." Economic Policy Institute Briefing Paper 312. Washington, DC: Economic Policy Institute. June 14.

Bjorge, M. 2017. "The Workers' War: The Character of Class Struggle in World War II." PhD diss., Queen's University.

Black, D., and C. Turenne Sjolander. 1996. "Multilateralism Re-constituted and the Discourse of Canadian Foreign Policy." *Studies in Political Economy* 49 (Spring.): 7–36. https://doi.org/10.1080/19187033.1996.11675341.

Black, T. 2014. "Petro-Chemical Legacies and Tar Sands Frontiers: Chemical Valley Versus Environmental Justice." In *A Line in the Tar Sands: Struggles for Environmental Justice*, edited by T. Black, S. D'Arcy, T. Weis, and J. Kahn Russell, 134–45. Toronto: Between the Lines.

Black, T., S. D'Arcy, T. Weis, and J. Kahn Russell, eds. 2014. *A Line in the Tar Sands: Struggles for Environmental Justice.* Toronto: Between the Lines.

Blake, R.B., and J.A. Keshen, eds. 2006. *Social Fabric or Patchwork Quilt: The Development of Social Policy in Canada*. Peterborough, ON: Broadview Press.

Bliss, M. 1973. "Another Anti-Trust Tradition: Canadian Anti-Combines Policy, 1889–1910." *Business History Review* 47 (2): 177–88. https://doi.org/10.2307/3113401.

Bliss, M. 1974. *A Living Profit: Studies in the Social History of Canadian Business, 1883–1911*. Toronto: McClelland and Stewart.

Block, S., and T. Hennessy. 2017. "Ontario budget is balanced, but province is still in a fiscal straightjacket." *behindthenumbers.ca*, 27 April. Online at http://behindthenumbers.ca/2017/04/27/ontario-budget-balanced -province-still-fiscal-straightjacket/.

Blumberg, M. 2009. "Mergers and Acquisitions in the Canadian Nonprofit and Charitable Sector." *Philanthropist* 21 (1): 40–59.

Bonnett, J. 2013. *Emergence and Empire: Innis, Complexity and the Trajectory of History*. Montreal; Kingston, ON: McGill-Queen's University Press.

Bordo, A., M. Redish, and H. Rockoff. 2011. "Why Didn't Canada Have a Banking Crisis in 2008 (or in 1930, or 1907, or …)?" NBER Working Paper 17312. Cambridge, MA: National Bureau of Economic Research.

Borins, S. 1999. "Trends in Training Public Managers: A Report on a Commonwealth Seminar." *International Public Management Journal* 2 (2): 299–314. https://doi.org/10.1016/s1096-7494(00)89039-x.

Borrows, J. 2017. "Canada's Colonial Constitution." In *The Right Relationship: Reimagining the Implementation of Historical Treaties*, edited by J. Borrows and M. Coyle, 17–38. Toronto: University of Toronto Press.

Bouchard, M.J., ed. 2013. *Innovation and the Social Economy: The Québec Experience*. Toronto: University of Toronto Press.

Boudarbat, B., T. Lemieux, and C. Riddell. 2010. "The Evolution of the Returns to Human Capital in Canada, 1980–2005." IZA Discussion Paper 4809. Bonn: IZA.

Boudreau, J.-A. 2006. "Intergovernmental Relations and Polyscalar Social Mobilization: The Cases of Montreal and Toronto." In *Municipal-Federal-Provincial Relations in Canada*, edited by R. Young and C. Leuprecht, 161–80. Kingston, ON: Institute of Intergovernmental Relations.

Bourque, J.C., and J. Martin. 2013. "How John F. Kennedy helped Diefenbaker lose an election." *Globe and Mail*, 3 April. Online at https://www.theglobeandmail .com/news/politics/how-john-f-kennedy-helped-diefenbaker-lose-an-election /article10844078/.

Bowen, F. 1856. *The Principles of Political Economy*. Boston: Little, Brown, and Company.

Bowles, P., R. Broomhill, T. Gutierrez-Haces, and S. McBride, eds. 2008. *International Trade and Neoliberal Globalism: Towards Re-peripheralisation in Australia, Canada and Mexico*. London: Routledge.

Bowles, P., and H. Veltmeyer, eds. 2014. *The Answer Is Still No: Voices of Pipeline Resistance*. Halifax, NS: Fernwood Publishing.

Boychuk, G. 2009. *National Health Insurance in the United States and Canada: Race, Territory, and the Roots of Difference*. Washington, DC: Georgetown University Press.

Boyer, R., and J.R. Hollingsworth. 1997. "From National Embeddedness to Spatial and Institutional Nestedness." In *Contemporary Capitalism: The Embeddedness of Institutions*, edited by J.R. Hollingsworth and R. Boyer, 433–84. Cambridge: Cambridge University Press.

Bradford, N. 1998. *Commissioning Ideas: Canadian National Policy Innovation in Comparative Perspective*. Toronto: Oxford University Press.

Bradford, N. 2002. *Why Cities Matter: Policy Research Perspectives for Canada*. Ottawa: Canadian Policy Research Networks.

Bradford, N. 2005. *Place-based Public Policy: Towards a New Urban and Community Agenda for Canada*. Ottawa: Canadian Policy Research Networks.

Bradford, N. 2007a. "Placing Social Policy? Reflections on Canada's New Deal for Cities and Communities." *Canadian Journal of Urban Research* 16 (2): 1–26.

Bradford, N. 2007b. *Whither the Federal Urban Agenda? A New Deal in Transition*. Ottawa: Canadian Policy Research Networks.

Brady, D. 2009. *Rich Democracies, Poor People: How Politics Explain Poverty*. New York: Oxford University Press.

Braithwaite, J. 2008. *Regulatory Capitalism*. Cheltenham, UK: Edward Elgar.

Brennan, J. 2012. *A Shrinking Universe: How Concentrated Corporate Power is Shaping Income Inequality in Canada*. Ottawa: Canadian Centre for Policy Alternatives.

Brennan, J. 2014. *The Creation of a Shared Prosperity in Canada: Unions, Corporations and Countervailing Power*. Ottawa: Canadian Centre for Policy Alternatives.

Brennan, J. 2015. *Ascent of Giants: NAFTA, Corporate Power and the Growing Income Gap*. Ottawa: Canadian Centre for Policy Alternatives.

Brenner, N. 2004. *New State Spaces*. New York: Oxford University Press.

Brenner, N., J. Peck, and N. Theodore. 2010. "Variegated Neoliberalization: Geographies, Modalities, Pathways." *Global Networks* 10 (2): 182–222. https://doi.org/10.1111/j.1471-0374.2009.00277.x.

Brenner, R. 2006. *The Economics of Global Turbulence*. New York: Verso.

Bretos, I., and C. Marcuello. 2017. "Revisiting Globalization Challenges and Opportunities in the Development of Cooperatives." *Annals of Public and Cooperative Economics* 88 (1): 47–73. https://doi.org/10.1111/apce.12145.

Bridge, G. 2014. "Resource Geographies II: The Resource-State Nexus." *Progress in Human Geography* 38 (1): 118–30. https://doi.org/10.1177/0309132513493379.

Brittain, H. 1951. *Local Government in Canada*. Toronto: Ryerson.

Broadbent Institute. 2012. *Towards a More Equal Canada: A Report on Canada's Economic and Social Inequality*. Ottawa: Broadbent Institute.

Broadbent Institute. 2017. *Progress Summit 2017: Progress in the Age of Trump*. Ottawa: Broadbent Institute.

Brodie, J. 1990. *The Political Economy of Canadian Regionalism*. Toronto: Harcourt Brace.

Brodie, J., and J. Jenson. 1988. *Crisis, Challenge and Change: Party and Class in Canada Revisited*. Ottawa: Carleton University Press.

Brouard, F., J.J. McMurtry, and M. Vieta. 2015. "Social Enterprise Models in Canada – Ontario." *Canadian Journal of Nonprofit and Social Economy Research* 6 (1): 63–82. https://doi.org/10.22230/cjnser.2015v6n1a195.

Brownlee, J. 2005. *Ruling Canada: Corporate Cohesion and Democracy*. Halifax, NS: Fernwood.

Brownlee, J. 2018. "Pipelines, Regulatory Capture and Canada's National Energy Board." In *Corporatizing Canada: Making Business Out of Public Service*, edited by J. Brownlee, C. Hurl, and K. Walby, 193–208. Toronto: Between the Lines.

Brownsey, K., and M. Howlett. 2001. "Class Structure and Political Alliances in an Industrialized Society." In *The Provincial State in Canada: Politics in the Provinces and Territories*, edited by K. Brownsey and M. Howlett. Toronto: Broadview Press.

Bruff, I. 2014. "The Rise of Authoritarian Neoliberalism." *Rethinking Marxism* 26 (1): 113–29. https://doi.org/10.1080/08935696.2013.843250.

Brym, R.J. 1985. *The Structure of the Canadian Capitalist Class*. Toronto: Garamond Press.

Buchanan, I. 1864. *The Relations of the Industry of Canada with the Mother Country and the United States*. Montreal: John Lovell.

Buckley, K. 1974. *Capital Formation in Canada, 1896–1930*. Toronto: McClelland and Stewart.

Burdín, G., and A. Dean. 2012. "Revisiting the Objectives of Worker-Managed Firms: An Empirical Assessment." *Economic Systems* 36 (1): 158–71. https://doi.org/10.1016/J.ECOSYS.2011.06.003.

Burke, K.S. 2002. "Regulating Corporate Governance through the Market: Comparing the Approaches of the United States, Canada and the United Kingdom." *Journal of Corporation Law* 27: 341–80.

Burke, M., C. Mooers, and J. Shields. 2000. "Critical Perspectives on Canadian Public Policy." In *Restructuring and Resistance: Canadian Public Policy in an Age of Global Capitalism*, edited by M. Burke, C. Mooers, and J. Shields, 11–23. Halifax: Fernwood.

Burn, D.L. 1970. "The Genesis of the American Engineering Competition, 1850–1870." In *Technological Change: The United States and Britain in the 19th Century*, edited by S.B. Saul. London: Methuen.

Bush, D., and D. Nesbitt. 2017. "Workers Win Big in Ontario." *Jacobin,* · 22 November. Online at https://www.jacobinmag.com/2017/11 /ontario-fight-for-15-fairness-campaign-labor-ndp-liberals.

Cadigan, S. 2014. "Want Amidst Plenty: The Oil Boom and the Working Class in Newfoundland and Labrador, 1992–2010." In *Workers in Hard Times: A Long View of Economic Crises,* edited by L. Fink, J.A. McCartin, and J. Sangster, 187–212. Urbana: University of Illinois Press.

Calgary. 2015. *Enough for All: Calgary's Poverty Reduction Strategy.* Calgary: City of Calgary. Online at http://www.calgaryunitedway.org/impact/poverty /enough-for-all.

Calomiris, C., and S.H. Haber. 2014. *Fragile by Design: The Political Origins of Banking Crises and Scarce Credit.* Princeton, NJ: Princeton University Press.

Cameron, B. 2006. "Social Reproduction and Canadian Federalism." In *Social Reproduction: Feminist Political Economy Challenges Neoliberalism.,* edited by K. Bezanson and M. Luxton, 45–74. Montreal; Kingston, ON: McGill-Queen's University Press.

Cameron, D.R., and G. White. 2000. *Cycling into Saigon: The Conservative Transition in Ontario.* Vancouver: UBC Press.

Camfield, D. 2007. "Renewal in Canadian Public Sector Unions: Neoliberalism and Union Praxis." *Relations Industrielle* 62 (2): 282–304. https://doi.org /10.7202/016089ar.

Camfield, D. 2011. *Canadian Labour in Crisis: Reinventing the Workers' Movement.* Halifax: Fernwood.

Campbell, B. 2015. *Lac-Mégantic: Loose Ends and Unanswered Questions.* Ottawa: Canadian Centre for Policy Alternatives.

Canada. 1878. *Debates of the Senate of the Dominion of Canada, 3rd Parliament,* 5th session, vol. 1. Ottawa: C.W. Mitchell.

Canada. 1879. *House of Commons Debates, 4th Parliament, 1st session, vol. 1.* Ottawa: C.W. Mitchell.

Canada. 1968. Task Force on the Structure of Canadian Industry. *Foreign Ownership and the Structure of Canadian Industry.* Ottawa: Government of Canada.

Canada. 1991. Office of the Comptroller General. *Treasury Board Program Evaluation Policy.* Ottawa: Comptroller General.

Canada. 2008. Competition Policy Review Panel *Compete to Win: Final Report.* Ottawa: Industry Canada.

Canada. 2015. Employment and Social Development Canada. *Collective Bargaining Trends in Canada, 1984–2014.* Ottawa: Employment and Social Development Canada. Online at https://www.canada.ca/content/dam /esdc-edsc/migration/documents/eng/resources/info/publications /collective_bargaining/Trends_in_Canada_e.pdf.

Canada. 2016. Innovation, Science and Economic Development Canada. "Key Small Business Statistics." Ottawa. Online at https://www.ic.gc.ca/eic /site/061.nsf/eng/h_03018.html, accessed 11 July 2018.

Canada. 2017. "Motion M-100 Adopted in Unanimity by House of Commons." Ottawa. Online at http://canada.coop/en/news/motion-m-100-adopted -unanimity-house-commons.

Canada. 2018. Industry Canada. "Co-operatives in Canada in 2015." Online at https://www.ic.gc.ca/eic/site/106.nsf/eng/h_00151.html, accessed 10 May 2020.

Canada. 2019a. "Canadian Co-operatives 2018." Online at https://open .canada.ca/data/en/dataset/f241c519-a250-456b-8b1d-a1d483308c20, accessed 10 May 2020.

Canada. 2019b. Industry Canada. "Key Small Business Statistics – January 2019." Online at http://www.ic.gc.ca/eic/site/061.nsf/eng/h_03090.html, accessed 10 May 2020.

Canada. 2019c. Innovation, Science and Economic Development Canada. "Co-operatives in Canada, 2018." Online at https://www150.statcan.gc.ca /n1/en/pub/11-627-m/11-627-m2019087-eng.pdf?st=Ql7PtGME.

Canada. 2019d. Innovation, Science and Economic Development Canada. "Open Data." Online at https://open.canada.ca/data/en/dataset /f241c519-a250-456b-8b1d-a1d483308c20.

Canadian Business. 2017. "Canada's Richest People: The Complete Top 100 Ranking." 9 November.

Canadian Fair Trade Network. 2017. *2020 Strategic Framework*. Vancouver. Online at http://cftn.ca/about-us, accessed 19 March 2018.

Carey, H. 1858. *Principles of Social Sciences*. Vols 1 and 2. Philadelphia: J.B. Lippincott.

Carey, H. 1859. *Principles of Social Sciences*. Vol. 3. Philadelphia: J.B. Lippincott.

Carini, C., and M. Carpita, 2014. "The Impact of the Economic Crisis on Italian Cooperatives in the Industrial Sector." *Journal of Co-Operative Organization and Management* 2 (1): 14–23. https://doi.org/10.1016/j.jcom.2014.03.001.

Carroll, W.K. 1986. *Corporate Power and Canadian Capitalism*. Vancouver: UBC Press.

Carroll, W.K. 1989. "Neoliberalism and the Recomposition of Finance Capital in Canada." *Capital and Class* 38 (1): 81–112. https://doi.org /10.1177/030981688903800106.

Carroll, W.K. 2004. *Corporate Power in a Globalizing World: A Study in Elite Social Organization*. Don Mills, ON: Oxford University Press.

Carroll, W.K. 2016. "The Changing Face(s) of Corporate Power in Canada." In *Social Inequality in Canada*. 6th ed., edited by E. Grabb, J.G. Reitz, and M. Hwang, 12–23. Don Mills, ON: Oxford University Press.

Carroll, W.K. 2017. "Canada's Carbon-Capital Elite: A Tangled Web of Corporate Power." *Canadian Journal of Sociology* 42 (3): 225–60. https://doi.org/10.29173/cjs28258.

Carroll, W.K., N. Graham, and Z. Yunker. 2018. "Carbon Capital and Corporate Influence: Mapping Elite Networks of Corporations, Universities, and Research Institutes." In *Corporatizing Canada: Making Business Out of Public Service*, edited by J. Brownlee, C. Hurl, and K. Walby, 58–73. Toronto: Between the Lines.

Carroll, W.K., and J.P. Sapinski. 2018. *Organizing the 1%: How Corporate Power Works*. Halifax: Fernwood.

Carroll, W.K., and M. Shaw, 2001. "Consolidating a Neoliberal Policy Bloc in Canada, 1976–1996." *Canadian Public Policy* 27 (2): 195–216. https://doi.org/10.2307/3552197.

Carter, A. 2016. "Environmental Policy and Politics: The Case of Oil." In *Canadian Environmental Policy and Politics: The Challenges of Austerity and Ambivalence*, edited by D. VanNijnatten, 292–306. Don Mills, ON: Oxford University Press.

Carter, A. 2018. "Policy Pathways to Carbon Entrenchment: Responses to the Climate Crisis in Canada's Petro-Provinces." *Studies in Political Economy* 99 (2): 1–24. https://doi.org/10.1080/07078552.2018.1492083.

Carter, A. 2020. *Fossilized: Environmental Policy in Canada's Petro-Provinces During the Last Oil Boom*. Vancouver: UBC Press.

Carter, A., G. Fraser, and A. Zalik. 2017. "Environmental Policy Convergence in Canada's Fossil Fuel Provinces? Regulatory Streamlining, Impediments, and Drift." *Canadian Public Policy* 43 (1): 61–76. https://doi.org/10.3138/cpp.2016-041.

Carter, A., and L. Fusco. 2017. "Western Newfoundland's Anti-Fracking Campaign: Exploring the Rise of Unexpected Community Mobilization." *Journal of Rural and Community Development* 12 (1): 98–120.

Carter, A., and A. Zalik. 2016. "Fossil Capitalism and the Rentier State: Towards a Political Ecology of Alberta's Oil Economy." In *First World Petro-Politics: The Political Ecology and Governance of Alberta*, edited by L. Adkin, 51–77. Toronto: University of Toronto Press.

Carter, N. 1996. "Worker Co-Operatives and Green Political Theory." In *Democracy and Green Political Thought*, edited by B. Doherty and M. de Geus, 56–76. New York: Routledge.

Castells, M. 1977. *The Urban Question: A Marxist Approach*. London: Edward Arnold.

Caulfield, J. 1974. *The Tiny Perfect Mayor. David Crombie and Toronto's Reform Aldermen*. Toronto: Lorimer.

Caulfield, N. 2010. *NAFTA and Labor in North America*. Urbana: University of Illinois Press.

Cayley-Daoust, D., and R. Girard. 2012. *Big Oil's Oily Grasp*. Ottawa: Polaris Institute.

CBC News. 2017. "Alberta political parties raise big money, but political action committees raise more." 19 October.

CCH. 1994. *NAFTA Text*. Chicago: CCH Inc.

CCUA. 2017. "Canadian Credit Union Community and Economic Impact Report." Ottawa.

C.D. Howe Institute. 2016. "Evidence mounts that 2015 downturn was no recession." Statement from the C.D. Howe Institute's Business Cycle Council. Toronto.

Chandler, A. 1990. *Scale and Scope: The Dynamics of Industrial Capitalism*. Cambridge, MA: Harvard University Press.

Chang, Ha-Joon. 2008. *Bad Samaritans: The Myth of Free Trade and the Secret History of Capitalism*. New York: Bloomsbury Press.

Chapman, C., and A.J. Withers. 2019. *A Violent History of Benevolence: Interlocking Oppression in the Moral Economies of Social Working*. Toronto: University of Toronto Press.

Chartrand, M. 1984. "The First Canadian Trade Union Legislation: An Historical Perspective." *Ottawa Law Review* 16: 271–2.

Chase, K.A. 2009. *Trading Blocs: States, Firms, and Regions in the World Economy*. Ann Arbor: University of Michigan Press.

Chase, S., R. Fife, and L. Stone. 2018. "China criticizes new North American trade deal." *Globe and Mail*, 5 October.

Choudry, A., and A.A. Smith, eds. 2016. *Unfree Labour? Struggles of Migrant and Immigrant Workers in Canada*. Oakland, CA: PM Press.

Clarkson, S., ed. 1968. *An Independent Foreign Policy for Canada?* Toronto: McClelland and Stewart.

Clarkson, S. 1985. *Canada and the Reagan Challenge*. Toronto: Lorimer.

Clarkson, S. 1993. "Constitutionalizing the Canadian-American Relationship." In *Canada Under Free Trade*, edited by D. Cameron and M. Watkins. Toronto: Lorimer.

Clarkson, S. 2002. *Uncle Sam and Us: Globalization, Neoconservatism and the Canadian State*. Toronto: University of Toronto Press.

Clarkson, S. 2008. *Does North America Exist? Governing the Continent After NAFTA and 9/11*. Toronto: University of Toronto Press.

Clément, M., and C. Bouchard. 2008. "Taux de survie des coopératives au Québec." Quebec City: Government of Quebec. Online at http://numerique.banq.qc.ca/patrimoine/details/52327/1813852.

Clement, W. 1975. *The Canadian Corporate Elite: An Analysis of Economic Power*. Toronto: McClelland and Stewart.

Clement, W. 1997a. "Introduction: Whither the New Canadian Political Economy?" In *Understanding Canada: Building on the New Canadian Political*

Economy, edited by W. Clement, 3–18. Montreal; Kingston, ON: McGill-Queen's University Press.

Clement, W., ed. 1997b. *Understanding Canada: Building on the New Canadian Political Economy*. Montreal; Kingston, ON: McGill-Queen's University Press.

Clement, W., and D. Drache. 1978. *A Practical Guide to Canadian Political Economy*. Toronto: Lorimer.

Clement, W., and L. Vosko, eds. 2003. *Changing Canada: Political Economy as Transformation*. Montreal; Kingston, ON: McGill-Queen's University Press.

Clement, W., and G. Williams, eds. 1989. *The New Canadian Political Economy*. Montreal; Kingston, ON: McGill-Queens University Press.

Clow, M. 1984. "Politics and Uneven Capitalist Development: The Maritime Challenge to the Study of Canadian Political Economy." *Studies in Political Economy* 14 (January): 117–40.

Cobb, J.A. 2016. "How Firms Shape Income Inequality." *Academy of Management Review* 41 (2): 324–48. https://doi.org/10.5465/amr.2013.0451.

Coburn, E. 2016. "Alternatives: New Canadian Political Economy and the Relations of Ruling: A Comment on C. Hurl and B. Christensen." *Studies in Political Economy* 97 (2): 206–15. https://doi.org/10.1080/07078552.2016.1220072.

Coburn, E. 2017. "Défaire et refaire le sexe, le genre, la sexualité: le sujet intersexe, trans et queer." *Socio: La nouvelle revue des sciences sociales* 9: 9–31. https://doi.org/10.4000/socio.2900.

Cockfield, A.J. 2017. "Policy Forum: Examining Canadian Offshore Tax Evasion." *Canadian Tax Journal* 65 (3): 651–80.

Coe, N., and H.W.-C. Yeung. 2015. *Global Production Networks: Theorizing Economic Development in an Inter-Connected World*. New York: Oxford University Press.

Coffee & Cocoa International. 2014. "Certifiers Claim Key Role in Response to Fluctuating Prices." Coffee & Cocoa International, 26–7.

Cohen, M.G. 1988. *Women's Work, Markets, and Economic Development in Nineteenth-Century Ontario*. Toronto: University of Toronto.

Cohen, M.G. 1991. "Exports, Unemployment, and Regional Inequality: Economic Policy and Trade Theory." In *The New Era of Global Competition*, edited by D. Drache and M.S. Gertler, 83–102. Montreal; Kingston, ON: McGill-Queen's University Press.

Coleman, W., and T. Porter. 2003. "'Playin' Along': Canada and Global Finance." In *Changing Canada: Political Economy as Transformation*, edited by W. Clement and L. Vosko, 241–64. Montreal; Kingston, ON: McGill-Queen's University Press.

Colvin, F. 1998. "Building an Automobile Every 40 Seconds." In *The Rise and Fall of Mass Production*, edited by S. Tolliday. Cheltenham, UK: Edward Elgar.

Commercial and Financial Chronicle. 1875. "Political Economy in Europe." *Commercial and Financial Chronicle*, 24 July, 74–5.

Conde, R.C. 1992. "Export-Led Growth in Latin America: 1870–1930." *Journal of Latin American Studies* 24 (S1): 163–79. https://doi.org/10.1017 /s0022216x00023828.

Co-operatives and Mutuals Canada. 2020. "Types of Co-operatives." Online at https://canada.coop/en/co-operatives-and-mutuals/co-op-types, accessed 10 May 2020.

Cordell, A. 1972. *The Multinational Firm, Foreign Direct Investment, and Canadian Science Policy*. Ottawa: Information Canada.

Cordell, A., and J. Gilmour. 1976. *The Role and Function of Government Laboratories and the Transfer of Technology to the Manufacturing Sector*. Ottawa: Information Canada.

Corntassel, J. 2012. "Re-envisioning Resurgence: Indigenous Pathways to Decolonization and Sustainable Self-determination." *Decolonization: Indigeneity, Education & Society* 1 (1): 86–101.

Coscione, M. 2014. *In Defense of Small Producers: The Story of CLAC*. Black Point, NS: Fernwood.

Cotter, A. 2015. "Public Confidence in Canadian Institutions." Cat. no. 89-652-X2015007. Ottawa: Statistics Canada.

Coulthard G. 2014. *Red Skin, White Masks: Rejecting the Colonial Politics of Recognition*. Minneapolis: University of Minnesota Press.

Cowen, D., and V. Parlette. 2011. *Toronto's Inner Suburbs: Investing in Social Infrastructure in Scarborough*. Toronto: Cities Centre, University of Toronto.

Cox, K. 1993. "The Local and the Global in the New Urban Politics: A Critical View." *Environment and Planning D: Society and Space* 11: 433–48. https://doi .org/10.1068/d110433.

Cox, R. 1981. "Social Forces, States and World Orders: Beyond International Relations Theory". *Millennium* 10 (2): 126–55. https://doi.org/10.1177/0305 8298810100020501.

Cox, R. 1996. *Approaches to World Order*. Cambridge: Cambridge University Press.

CPSA (Canadian Political Science Association). 2018. *Indigenous Content Syllabus Materials*. September. Online at https://www.cpsa-acsp.ca /documents/committees/Indigenous%20Content%20Syllabus%20 Materials%20Sept%202018.pdf.

Craft, J. 2015. "Conceptualizing Partisan Advisers as Policy Workers." *Policy Sciences* 48 (2): 135–58. https://doi.org/10.1007/s11077-015-9212-2.

Craft, J., and J. Halligan. 2017. "Assessing 30 Years of Westminster Policy Advisory System Experience." *Policy Sciences* 50 (1): 47–62. https://doi .org/10.1007/s11077-016-9256-y.

Craft, J., and M. Howlett. 2013. "The Dual Dynamics of Policy Advisory Systems: The Impact of Externalization and Politicization on Policy Advice." *Policy and Society* 32 (3): 187–97. https://doi.org/10.1016/j .polsoc.2013.07.001.

Craig, D., and D. Porter. 2004. "The Third Way and the Third World: Poverty Reduction and Social Inclusion in the Rise of 'Inclusive Liberalism.'" *Review of International Political Economy* 11 (2): 387–423. https://doi.org/10.1080/09 692290420001672881.

Cramer, C., D. Johnston, C. Oya, and J. Sender, 2014. *Fairtrade, Employment and Poverty Reduction in Ethiopia and Uganda: Final Report to DFID*. London: University of London, SOAS. http://ftepr.org/wp-content/uploads /FTEPR-Final-Report-19-May-2014-FINAL.pdf.

Craven, P. 1980. *'An Impartial Umpire': Industrial Relations and the Canadian State 1900–1911*. Toronto: University of Toronto Press.

Craven, P. 1984. "Workers' Conspiracies in Toronto, 1854–72." *Labour* 14: 49–70. https://doi.org/10.2307/25140481.

Crawford, K. 1954. *Canadian Municipal Government*. Toronto: University of Toronto Press.

Crouch, C. 2006. *Post-Democracy*. Malden, MA: Polity Press.

Crouch, C. 2011. *The Strange Non-Death of Neo-Liberalism*. Malden, MA: Polity Press.

Crouch, C. 2013. *Making Capitalism Fit for Society*. Malden, MA: Polity Press.

Crouch, C. 2019. *The Globalization Backlash*. Medford, MA: Polity Press.

Curtis, M. 2014. "Losing Out: Sierra Leone's Massive Revenue Losses from Tax Incentives." Online at http://curtisresearch.org/wp-content/uploads /Losing-Out.-Final-report.-April-2014.pdf, accessed 14 June 2018.

Cutler, F., and S. Matthews. 2005. "The Challenge of Municipal Voting: Vancouver 2002." *Canadian Journal of Political Science* 38 (2): 359–82. https:// doi.org/10.1017/s0008423905040151.

Dadush, U., and B. Leycegui. 2016. *TPP, the NAFTA Countries, and the Integration of the Americas*. Washington, DC: Wilson Center, Mexico Institute.

Daily Bread. 2017. "Who Is Hungry: 2017 Profile of Hunger in Toronto." Online at https://homelesshub.ca/resource/whos-hungry-2017-profile-hunger-toronto.

Dalby, S. 2019. "Canadian Geopolitical Culture: Climate Change and Sustainability." *Canadian Geographer* 63 (1): 100–11. https://doi.org/10.1111 /cag.12472.

Dalby, S., and S. Keil. 2003. "Introduction: Political Ecology and Canadian Political Economy." *Studies in Political Economy* 70 (1): 5–9. https://doi.org /10.1080/07078552.2003.11827127.

D'Aoust, C., and F. Delorme. 1981. "The Origin of the Freedom of Association and the Right to Strike in Canada." *Industrial Relations* 36 (4): 894–921. https://doi.org/10.7202/029209ar.

Daschuk, J.W. 2013. *Clearing the Plains: Disease, Politics of Starvation, and the Loss of Aboriginal Life.* Regina: University of Regina Press.

Daub, S., and Z. Yunker. 2017. *BC's Last Climate "Leadership" Plan Was Written in Big Oil's Boardroom (Literally).* Vancouver: Canadian Centre for Policy Alternatives.

Dave Grace and Associates. 2014. *Measuring the Size and Scope of the Co-Operative Economy: Results of the 2014 Global Census on Co-Operatives.* Madison, WI: Dave Grace and Associates. Online at https://www.un.org/esa/socdev/documents/2014/coopsegm/grace.pdf.

David, C.-P., and S. Roussel. 1998. "'Middle Power Blues': Canadian Policy and International Security after the Cold War." *American Review of Canadian Studies* 28 (1-2): 131–56.

Davies, C. 1977. "The Origins of the BCNI." *Board of Trade Journal* (April): 30–1.

Deaton, R. 1989. *The Political Economy of Pensions: Power, Politics, and Social Change in Canada, Great Britain, and the United States.* Vancouver: UBC Press.

DeFilippis, J., R.J. Fisher, and E. Shragge. 2010. *Contesting Community: The Limits and Potential of Local Organizing.* New Brunswick, NJ: Rutgers University Press.

De Finney, S. 2017. "Indigenous Girls' Resilience in Settler States: Honouring Body and Land Sovereignty." *Agenda* 31 (2): 10–21. https://doi.org/10.1080/10130950.2017.1366179.

Dempsey, J. 2016. *Enterprising Nature.* Hoboken, NJ: John Wiley & Sons.

Deneault, A. 2015. *Canada: A New Tax Haven.* Vancouver: Talon Books.

Deschamps. T. 2018. "Shopify founder fears U.S. tech in Canada." *Toronto Star,* 26 September.

Devereux, M., K. Habu, S. Lepoev, and G. Maffini. 2016. "G20 Corporation Tax Ranking." Oxford: Oxford University, Centre for Business Taxation.

Deverteuil, G. 2016. *Resilience in the Post-Welfare City: Voluntary Sector Geographies in London, Los Angeles and Sydney.* Bristol: Policy Press.

Dewitt, D., and J. Kirton. 1983. *Canada as a Principal Power: A Study in Foreign Policy and International Relations.* Toronto: Wiley.

Diamantopoulos, M. 2012. "Breaking Out of Co-Operation's 'Iron Cage': From Movement Degeneration to Building a Developmental Movement." *Annals of Public and Cooperative Economics* 83 (2): 199–214. https://doi.org/10.1111/j.1467-8292.2012.00461.x.

Dimand, R. 1998. "Rae and International Trade." In *The Economics of John Rae,* edited by O.F. Hamouda, C. Lee, and D. Mair. London: Routledge.

Dobbin, M. 1998. *The Myth of the Good Corporate Citizen: Democracy under the Rule of Big Business.* New York: Stoddart.

Dodge, D. 2011. "Public Policy for the Canadian Financial System: From Porter to the Present and Beyond." In *New Directions for Intelligent Government in Canada: Papers in the Honour of Ian Stewart*, edited by A. Sharpe and F. Gorbet, 81–100. Ottawa: Centre for the Study of Living Standards.

Doern, G.B., and B.W. Tomlin. 1991. *Faith and Fear: The Free Trade Story*. Toronto: Stoddart.

Dolha, L. 2009. "First Nations leaders stunned by Harper's G-20 remarks." *First Nations Drum Newspaper*, 25 October.

Domhoff, G.W. 1998. *Who Rules America? Power and Politics in the Year 2000*. Mountain View, CA: Mayfield Publishing.

Dorow, S. 2015. "Gendering Energy Extraction in Fort McMurray." In *Alberta Oil and the Decline of Democracy in Canada*, edited by M. Shrivastava and L. Stefanick, 275–92. Edmonton: AU Press.

Drache, D. 1978. "Rediscovering Canadian Political Economy." In *A Practical Guide to Canadian Political Economy*, edited by W. Clement and D. Daniel. Toronto: Lorimer.

Drache, D. 1991. "Harold Innis and Canadian Capitalist Development." In *Perspectives on Canadian Economic Development*, edited by G. Laxer, 22–49. Toronto: Oxford University Press.

Drache, D., and W. Clement, eds. 1985. *The New Practical Guide to Canadian Political Economy*. Toronto: Lorimer.

Driskill, Q.L. 2004. "Stolen from Our Bodies: First Nations Two-Spirits/Queers and the Journey to a Sovereign Erotic." *Studies in American Indian Literatures* 16 (2): 50–64. https://doi.org/10.1353/ail.2004.0020.

Drummond, I. 1987. *Progress without Planning: The Economic History of Ontario from Confederation to the Second World War*. Toronto: University of Toronto Press.

Dubuc, A. 1966. "The Decline of Confederation and the New Nationalism." In *Nationalism in Canada*, edited by P. Russell, 112–32. Toronto: McGraw-Hill.

Dufour, P. 2011. "Anti-Poverty Policies and the Adoption of Bill 112 in Quebec." *Canadian Review of Social Policy* 65–66: 45–57.

Duguid, F., and G. Karaphillis. 2019. *Economic Impact of the Co-operative Sector in Canada*. Ottawa: Co-operatives and Mutuals Canada. Online at https://canada.coop/sites/canada.coop/files/coop_gdp_report_english_web.pdf, accessed 10 May 2020.

Duménil, G., and D. Lévy. 2011. *The Crisis of Neoliberalism*. Cambridge, MA: Harvard University Press.

Dunleavy, P. 1997. "The Globalization of Public Services Production: Can Government Be 'Best in the World'?" In *Globalization and Marketization of Government Services: Comparing Contemporary Public Sector Developments*, edited by A. Massey. New York: St Martin's Press.

Durand, C. 2017. *Fictitious Capital: How Finance is Appropriating Our Future*. New York: Verso.

Durkheim, E. 1960. *The Division of Labor in Society*. New York: Macmillan.

Eagleton-Pierce, M. 2016. *Neoliberalism: Key concepts*. New York: Routledge.

Eakin, L. 2002. *Supporting Organizational Infrastructure in the Voluntary Sector.* Ottawa: Voluntary Sector Initiative Secretariat.

Eaton, E., and N. Day. 2020. "Petro-Pedagogy: Fossil Fuel Interests and the Obstruction of Climate Justice in Public Education." *Environmental Education Research* 26 (4): 457–73.

Eaton, E., and S. Enoch. 2018. "Oil's Rural Reach: Social Licence in Saskatchewan's Oil-Producing Communities." *Canadian Journal of Communication* 43 (1): 53–74. https://doi.org/10.22230/cjc.2018v43n1a3305.

Eaton, E., and D. Gray-Donald. 2018. "Socializing and Decolonizing Saskatchewan's Oil." *Briarpatch*, 30 April.

Eaton, E., and A. Kinchy. 2016. "Quiet Voices in the Fracking Debate: Ambivalence, Nonmobilization, and Individual Action in Two Extractive Communities (Saskatchewan and Pennsylvania)." *Energy Research & Social Science* 20 (October): 22–30. https://doi.org/10.1016/j.erss.2016.05.005.

Economist. 2017. "Charities Are Becoming More Professional." 30 September. Online at https://www.economist.com/international/2017/09/30/charities-are-becoming-more-professional.

Eden, L., and M.A. Molot. 1993. "Canada's National Policies: Reflections on 125 Years." *Canadian Public Policy* 19 (3): 232–51.

Edmonton. 2016. *End Poverty in a Generation: A Road Map to Guide Our Journey.* Edmonton: City of Edmonton. Online at https://www.endpovertyedmonton.ca/our-strategy.

Edwards, M. 2004. *Civil Society.* Cambridge, UK: Polity.

Eidelman, G., and A. Taylor. 2010. "Canadian Urban Politics: Another 'Black Hole'?" *Journal of Urban Affairs* 32 (3): 305–20. https://doi.org/10.1111/j.1467-9906.2010.00507.x.

Eisenstadt, S. 1965. *Essays on Comparative Institutions.* New York: John Wiley.

Ellwood, W. 2015. *Globalization: Buying and Selling the World.* Oxford: New Internationalist.

Elson, D. 2009. "Gender Equality and Economic Growth in the World Bank World Development Report 2006." *Feminist Economics* 15 (3): 35–59. https://doi.org/10.1080/13545700902964303.

Elson, P.R. 2009. "Independence in a Cold Climate: A Profile of the Nonprofit and Voluntary Sector in Canada." In *The First Principle of Voluntary Action: Essays on the Independence of the Voluntary Sector from Government in Canada, England, Germany, Northern Ireland, Scotland, United States of America and Walesirst Principle of Voluntary Action*, edited by M. Smerdon, 13–34. London: Baring Foundation. Online at https://baringfoundation.org.uk/wp-content/uploads/2014/09/FirstPrincipleofVA.pdf.

Emmenger, P., S. Hausermann, B. Palier, and M. Seeleib-Kaiser, eds. 2012. *The Age of Dualization: The Changing Face of Inequality in De-industrializing Societies.* New York: Oxford University Press.

Emmett, B., and G. Emmett. 2015. "Charities in Canada as an Economic Sector: Discussion Paper." Toronto: Imagine Canada.

Engels, F. [1845] 2010. *The Condition of the Working Class in England*. London: Cambridge University Press.

Engler, Y. 2014. "Canadian Diplomatic Efforts to Sell the Tar Sands." In *A Line in the Tar Sands: Struggles for Environmental Justice*, edited by T. Black, S. D'Arcy, T. Weis, and J. Kahn Russell, 55–63. Toronto: Between the Lines.

Enoch, S. 2012. *Mapping Corporate Power in Saskatchewan*. Regina: Canadian Centre for Policy Alternatives.

Environics Unifor 2017. *Canadian Attitudes toward NAFTA and Progressive Trade Issues*. November.

Epstein, G. 2015. "Financialization: There's Something Happening Here." Working Paper Series. Amherst, MA: University of Massachusetts Amherst, Political Economy Research Institute.

Esping-Andersen, G. 2002. "Towards the Good Society, Once Again?" In *Why We Need A New Welfare State*, edited by G. Esping-Andersen, D. Gallie, A. Hemerijck, and J. Myles, 1–25. Oxford: Oxford University Press.

Estey, W.Z. 1986. *Report of the Inquiry into the Collapse of the CCB and the Northland Bank*. Ottawa: Supply and Services Canada.

Etzioni, A. 1993. *The Spirit of Community: Rights, Responsibilities, and the Communitarian Agenda*. New York: Crown.

Evans, B., and C. Fanelli. 2018. "The Permanent Unequal Union: Canada's Provinces and Territories in an Era of Neoliberalism." In *The Public Sector in an Age of Austerity: Perspectives from Canada's Provinces and Territories*, edited by B. Evans and C. Fanelli, 3–22. Montreal; Kingston, ON: McGill-Queen's University Press.

Evans, B., and S. eds. McBride. 2017. *Austerity: The Lived Experience*. Toronto: University of Toronto Press.

Evans, B., T. Richmond, and J. Shields. 2005. "Structuring Neoliberal Governance: The Non-Profit Sector, Emerging New Modes of Control and the Marketisation of Service Delivery." *Policy and Society* 24 (1): 73–97. https://doi.org/10.1016/s1449-4035(05)70050-3.

Evans, B., and S. Ross. 2018. "Policy Analysis and Advocacy in the Canadian Labour Movement: When the Force of Argument Is Not Enough." In Policy Analysis in Canada. 2nd ed., edited by L. Dobuzinskis and M. Howlett, 331–50. Bristol: Policy Press.

Evans, B., and H. Sapeha. 2015. "Are Non-government Policy Actors Being Heard? Assessing New Public Governance." *Canadian Public Administration* 58 (2): 249–70. https://doi.org/10.1111/capa.12115.

Evans, B., and J. Shields. 2010. "The Third Sector and the Provision of Public Good: Partnerships, Contracting, and the Neo-Liberal State." In *The Handbook of Canadian Public Administration*. 2nd ed., edited by C. Dunn, 305–18. Don Mills, ON: Oxford University Press.

Evans, B., and J. Shields. 2014. "Nonprofit Engagement with Provincial Policy Officials: The Case of Canadian Immigrant Settlement Services and NGO Policy Voice." *Policy and Society* 33 (2): 117–27. https://doi.org/10.1016/j .polsoc.2014.05.002.

Evans, B, and Shields, J. 2018. "The Third Sector, The Neo-liberal State, and Beyond: Reshaping Contracting and Policy Advocacy." In *The Handbook of Canadian Public Administration*. 3rd ed., edited by C. Dunn, 489–500. Don Mills, ON: Oxford University Press.

Evans, B., and Smith, C. 2015a. "The Transformation of Ontario Politics: The Long Ascent of Neoliberalism." In *Transforming Provincial Politics: The Political Economy of Canada's Provinces and Territories in the Era of Neoliberalism*, edited by B. Evans, and C. Smith, 162–92. Toronto: University of Toronto Press.

Evans, B., and C. Smith, eds. 2015b. *Transforming Provincial Politics: The Political Economy of Canada's Provinces and Territories in the Era of Neoliberalism*. Toronto: University of Toronto Press.

Evans, P. 2018. "'Astonishing' clause in new deal suggests Trump wants leverage over Canada-China trade talks: experts." *National Post*, 2 October.

Fakhfakh, F., V. Perotin, and M. Gago, 2013. "Productivity, Capital, and Labor in Labor-Managed and Conventional Firms: An Investigation on French Data." *ILR Review* 65 (4): 847–79. https://doi.org/10.1177/00197939 1206500404.

Fanelli, C. 2016. *Megacity Malaise: Neoliberalism, Public Services and Labour in Toronto*. Halifax, NS: Fernwood.

Fanelli, C., and J. Noonan. 2017. "Capital and Organized Labour." In *Reading Capital Today*, edited by I. Schmidt and C. Fanelli, 138–59. London: Pluto Books.

Fanelli, C., and J. Shields, eds. 2016. *Alternate Routes: Precarious Work and the Struggle for Living Wages*. Edmonton: Athabasca University Press.

Fast, T. 2014. "Stapled to the Front Door: Neoliberal Extractivism in Canada." *Studies in Political Economy* 94 (1): 45–53. https://doi.org/10.1080/19187033 .2014.11674953.

Feldman, G., R. Strier, and M. Koreh, 2016. "Liquid Advocacy: Social Welfare Advocacy in Neoliberal Times." *International Journal of Social Welfare* 26 (3): 254–62.

Ferguson, B. 1993. *Remaking Liberalism: The Intellectual Legacy of Adam Shortt, O.D. Skelton, W.C. Clark, and W.A. Mackintosh, 1890–1925*. Montreal; Kingston, ON: McGill-Queens University Press.

Fernando, S. 2006. *Race and the City: Chinese Canadian and Chinese American Political Mobilization*. Vancouver: UBC Press.

Ferri, G., and E. Kerola. 2014. "Organizational Structure and Exposure to Crisis among European Banks: Evidence from Rating Changes." *Journal*

of Entrepreneurial and Organizational Diversity 33 (1): 35–55. https://doi
.org/10.5947/jeod.2014.003.

Finbow, R.G. 2016. "Restructuring the State through Economic and Trade
Agreements: The Case of Investment Disputes Resolution." *Politics and
Governance* 4 (3): 62–76. https://doi.org/10.17645/pag.v4i3.639.

Findlay, T. 2015. "Child Care and the Harper Agenda: Transforming Canada's
Social Policy Regime." *Canadian Review of Social Policy* 71: 1–20.

Findlay, T. 2018, "Gendering the State: Women and Public Policy in Ontario."
In *Divided Province: Ontario Politics in the Age of Neoliberalism*, edited by
G. Albo and B. Evans, 212–46. Montreal; Kingston, ON: McGill-Queen's
University Press.

Flaherty, E. 2015. "Top Incomes under Finance-Driven Capitalism, 1990–2010:
Power Resources and Regulatory Orders." *Socio-Economic Review* 13 (3):
417–47. https://doi.org/10.1093/ser/mwv011.

Flanagan, G. 2015. *From Gap to Chasm: Alberta's Increasing Income Inequality.*
Edmonton: Parkland Institute.

Flanagan, M. 2007. *America Reformed: Progressives and Progressivisms,
1890s–1920s.* New York: Oxford University Press.

Folbre, N. 1994. *Who Pays for the Kids?* New York: Routledge.

Forhoohar, R. 2016. *Makers and Takers: The Rise and Fall of American Business.*
New York: Crown.

Forrest, A. 1995. "Securing the Male Breadwinner: A Feminist Interpretation
of PC 1003." In *Labour Gains, Labour Pains: 50 Years of PC 1003*, edited by
C. Gonick, P. Phillips, and J. Vorst, 139–62. Halifax, NS: Fernwood.

Foster, J., and B. Barnetson. 2015. "Exporting Oil, Importing Labour, and
Weakening Democracy." In *Alberta Oil and the Decline of Democracy in
Canada*, edited by M. Shrivastava and J. Stefanick, 249–73. Edmonton:
Athabasca University Press.

Foster, J.B., and H. Holleman. 2010. "The Financial Power Elite." *Monthly
Review* 62 (1): 1–19. https://doi.org/10.14452/mr-062-01-2010-05_1.

Fournier, S., and E. Crey. 1997. *Stolen from Our Embrace: The Abduction of First
Nations Children and the Restoration of Aboriginal Communities.* Vancouver:
Douglas & McIntyre.

Fox, J., and M. Ornstein. 1986. "The Canadian State and Corporate Elites in
the Post-War Period." *Canadian Review of Sociology and Anthropology* 23 (4):
481–506. https://doi.org/10.1111/j.1755-618x.1986.tb00819.x.

Fraser, N. 2013. *Fortunes of Feminism.* New York: Verso.

Fraune, C. 2015. "Gender Matters: Women, Renewable Energy, and Citizen
Participation in Germany." *Energy Research and Social Science* 7 (May): 55–65.
https://doi.org/10.1016/j.erss.2015.02.005.

Freedman, C. 1998. "The Canadian Banking System." Bank of Canada
Technical Report 81. Ottawa: Bank of Canada.

Freedman, C. 2003. "Reflections on Three Decades at the Bank of Canada." In *Macroeconomics, Monetary Policy, and Financial Stability: A Festschrift in Honour of Charles Freedman*. Ottawa: Bank of Canada.

Freeman, B. 2017. "Toronto." In *The Rise of Cities*, edited by D. Roussopolous, 93–151. Montreal: Black Rose Books.

Fridell, G. 2013. *Alternative Trade: Legacies for the Future*. Halifax, NS: Fernwood.

Friedel, T., and A. Taylor. 2011. "Digging beneath the Surface of Aboriginal Labour Market Development: Analyzing Policy Discourse in the Context of Northern Alberta's Oil Sands." *Aboriginal Policy Studies* 1 (3): 29–52. https://doi.org/10.5663/aps.v1i3.12559.

Friedman, T. 2000. *The Lexus and the Olive Tree*. New York: Anchor Books.

Friedmann, J., and G. Wolff. 1982. "World City Formation: An Agenda for Research and Action." *International Journal of Urban and Regional Research* 6 (3): 309–44. https://doi.org/10.1111/j.1468-2427.1982.tb00384.x.

Frisken, F. 2008. *The Public Metropolis: The Political Dynamics of Urban Expansion in the Toronto Region, 1924–2003*. Toronto: Canadian Scholars' Press.

Froese, M. 2010. *Canada at the WTO: Trade Litigation and the Future of Public Policy*. Toronto: University of Toronto Press.

Fudge, J., and K. Strauss, eds. 2014. *Temporary Work, Agencies, and Unfree Labour: Insecurity in the New World of Work*. New York: Routledge.

Fudge, J., and E. Tucker. 2000. "Pluralism or Fragmentation?" The Twentieth-Century Employment Law Regime in Canada." *Labour* 46: 251–306. https://doi.org/10.2307/25149101.

Fudge, J., and E. Tucker. 2001. *Labour Before the Law: The Regulation of Workers' Collective Action in Canada, 1900–1948*. Oxford: Oxford University Press.

Fudge, J., and E. Tucker. 2009–10. "The Freedom to Strike in Canada: A Brief Legal History." *Canadian Labour and Employment Law Journal* 15 (2): 333–53.

Fudge, J., and L. Vosko. 2001a. "By Whose Standards? Re-Regulating the Canadian Labour Market." *Economic and Industrial Democracy* 22 (3): 327–56. https://doi.org/10.1177/0143831x01223002.

Fudge, J., and L. Vosko. 2001b. "Gender, Segmentation and the Standard Employment Relationship in Canadian Labour Law and Policy." *Economic and Industrial Democracy* 22 (2): 271–310. https://doi.org/10.1177/0143831x01222005.

Fumkin, P. 2009. *On Being Nonprofit: A Conceptual and Policy Primer*. Cambridge, MA: Harvard University Press.

Fyfe, N. 2005. "Making Space for 'Neocommunitarianism'? The Third Sector, State and Civil Society in the UK," *Antipode* 37 (3): 536–57. https://doi.org/10.1111/j.0066-4812.2005.00510.x.

Gadhoum, Y. 2006. "Power of Ultimate Controlling Owners: A Survey of Canadian Landscape." *Journal of Management and Governance* 10 (2): 179–204. https://doi.org/10.1007/s10997-006-0004-0.

Galabuzi, G.-E. 2006. *Canada's Economic Apartheid: The Social Exclusion of Racialized Groups in the New Country.* Toronto: Canadian Scholars' Press.

Gale, F.P., and R.M. M'Gonigle, eds. 2000. *Nature, Production, Power: Towards an Ecological Political Economy.* Cheltenham, UK: Edward Elgar.

Gamble, A. 1988. *The Free Economy and the Strong State: The Politics of Thatcherism.* Durham, NC: Duke University Press.

Gamble, A. 2001. "Neo-liberalism." *Capital and Class* 25 (3): 127–34. https://doi.org/10.1177/030981680107500111.

Gamble, A. 2006. "Two Faces of Neoliberalism." In *The Neo-Liberal Revolution: Forging the Market State,* edited by R. Robison, 20–35. London: Palgrave Macmillan.

Garvie, K., and K. Shaw. 2016. "Shale Gas Development and Community Response: Perspectives from Treaty 8 Territory, British Columbia." *Local Environment* 21 (8): 1009–28. https://doi.org/10.1080/13549839.2015.1063043.

Gatehouse, J. 2018. "IMF warns of looming financial crisis, says world is woefully unprepared to handle it." *CBC News,* 11 December. Online at https://www.cbc.ca/news/thenational/national-today-newsletter-imf-warns-kevin-hart-grow-light-1.4939070.

Gauthier, B. 2016. "Impact = Content x Influence: Evaluation, Evidence and Policy in Canadian Government Contexts." *Evaluative Voices* 1: 1–14.

Gautie, J., and J. Schmitt, eds. 2010. *Low-Wage Work in the Wealthy World.* New York: Russell Sage Foundation.

Germain, R. 2009. "Of Margins, Traditions, and Engagements: A Brief Disciplinary History of IPE in Canada." In *Routledge Handbook of International Political Economy,* edited by M. Blyth. London: Routledge.

Gibson, D. 2017. "Bay Street and Tax Havens: Curbing Corporate Canada's Addition." Ottawa: *Canadians For Tax Fairness.*

Gibson, D., A. Thompson, D. Thompson, and G. Flanagan. 2016. *A Better Future: Building a Jobs-Rich, Fair, and Sustainable Economy for Newfoundland and Labrador.* n.p.: Common Front NL.

Gibson-Graham, J.K. 2007. "Beyond Global vs Local: Economic Politics Outside the Binary Frame." In *Geographies of Power: Placing Scale,* edited by A. Herod and M.W. Wright. New York: John Wiley & Sons.

Giddens, A. 1998. "The State and Civil Society." In *The Third Way: The Renewal of Social Democracy,* 69–98. Cambridge, UK: Polity Press.

Gill, S. 1995. "Globalisation, Market Civilisation and Disciplinary Neoliberalism." *Millennium* 24 (3): 399–423. https://doi.org/10.1177/03058298950240030801.

Gill, S. 2003. "National In/Security on a Universal Scale." In *Power, Production and Social Reproduction,* edited by I. Bakker and S. Gill, 208–23. New York: Palgrave Macmillan.

Gillespie, P. 2013. "The Trouble with Tax Havens: Whose Shelter? Whose Storm?" In *The Great Revenue Robbery*, edited by R. Swift, 54–65. Toronto: Between the Lines.

Glasbeek, H.J. 1985. "Law; Real and Ideological Constraints on the Working Class." In *Law in a Cynical Society: Opinion and Law in the 1980s*, edited by D. Gibson, and J.K. Baldwin, 282–301. Calgary: Carswell.

Globerman, S., and C. Sands. 2017. *The Fate of NAFTA: Possible Scenarios and their Implications for Canada*. Vancouver: Fraser Institute.

Glyn, A. 2006. *Capitalism Unleashed: Finance Globalization and Welfare*. New York: Oxford University Press.

Godechot, O. 2012. "Is Finance Responsible for the Rise in Wage Inequality in France?" *Socio-Economic Review* 10 (3): 447–70. https://doi.org/10.1093/ser/mws003.

Godechot, O. 2016. "Financialization Is Marketization! A Study of the Respective Impacts of Various Dimensions of Financialization on the Increase in Global Inequality." *Sociological Science* 3 (30): 495–519. https://doi.org/10.15195/v3.a22.

Godley, W., and M. Lavoie. 2007. *Monetary Economics: An Integrated Approach to Credit, Money, Income, Production and Wealth*. Basingstoke, UK: Palgrave Macmillan.

Goeman, M. 2013. *Mark My Words: Native Women Mapping Our Nations*. Minneapolis: University of Minnesota Press.

Goeman, M. 2017. "Ongoing Storms and Struggles: Gendered Violence and Resource Exploitation." In *Critically Sovereign: Indigenous Gender, Sexuality, and Feminist Studies*, edited by J. Barker, 70–99. Durham, NC: Duke University Press.

Goldfinch, S. 1998. "Remaking New Zealand's Economic Policy: Institutional Elites as Radical Innovators." *Governance* 11 (2): 177–207.

Good, D. 2003. *The Politics of Public Management: The HRDC Audit of Grants and Contributions*. Toronto: University of Toronto Press.

Goodwin, C. 1961. *Canadian Economic Thought: The Political Economy of a Developing Nation, 1814–1914*. Durham, NC: Duke University Press.

Gordon, M. 1981. *Government in Business*. Montreal: C.D. Howe Institute.

Gordon, T., and J.R. Webber. 2008. "Imperialism and Resistance: Canadian Mining Companies in Latin America." *Third World Quarterly* 29 (1): 63–87. https://doi.org/10.1080/01436590701726509.

Goswami, M. 2004. *Producing India*. Chicago: University of Chicago Press.

Grady, J., and M. Simms. 2018. "Trade Unions and the Challenge of Fostering Solidarities in an Era of Financialisation." *Economic and Industrial Democracy* 40 (3): 490–510. https://doi.org/10.1177%2F0143831X18759792.

Graefe, P. 2007. "Political Economy and Canadian Public Policy." In *Critical Policy Studies*. , edited by M. Orsini and M. Smith, 19–64. Vancouver: UBC Press.

Graefe, P., and C.-A. Hudson. 2018. "Poverty Policy in Ontario: You Can't Eat Good Intentions." In *Divided Province: Ontario Politics in the Age of Neoliberalism*, edited by G. Albo, and B. Evans, 309–332. Montreal; Kingston, ON: McGill-Queen's University Press.

Graefe, P., and A. Orasch. 2013. "Family Policy in Ontario and Quebec: Different from Afar or Far from Different?" In *Quebec-Ontario Relations: A Shared Destiny?* edited by J.-F. Savard, A. Brassard, and L. Côté, 145–66. Quebec City: Presses de l'Université du Québec.

Granatstein, J.L. 2002. "A Friendly Agreement in Advance: Canada-US Defense Relations, Past, Present, and Future." C.D. Howe Institute Commentary 166. Toronto: C.D. Howe Institute.

Grant, G.1965. *Lament for a Nation: The Defeat of Canadian Nationalism*. Montreal; Kingston, ON: McGill-Queens University Press.

Gray, H. 1971 *Foreign Direct Investment in Canada*. Ottawa: Supply and Services Canada.

Green, D.A., and B.M. Sand. 2015a. "Has the Canadian Labour Market Polarized?" *Canadian Journal of Economics* 48 (2): 612–46. https://doi .org/10.1111/caje.12145

Green, D.A., and B.M. Sand. 2015b. "Has the Canadian Labour Market Polarized?" In *Income Inequality: The Canadian Story*, edited by D. Green, C. Riddell, and F. St-Hilaire, 217–28. Montreal: Institute for Research on Public Policy.

Green, J.A. 2003. "Decolonization and Recolonization in Canada." In *Changing Canada: Political Economy as Transformation*, edited by L. Vosko, and W. Clement, 51–78. Montreal; Kingston, ON: McGill-Queen's University Press.

Green, J.A. 2015. "Reconciliation Is a Verb." *Rabble.ca*, 8 October. Online at http://rabble.ca/blogs/bloggers/views-expressed/2015/10/reconciliation -verb, accessed 30 November 2018.

Green, J.A., ed. 2017. *Making Space for Indigenous Feminism*. Halifax, NS: Fernwood.

Green, J.A. 2019. "Enacting Reconciliation." In *Visions of the Heart: Issues Involving Indigenous People in Canada*. 5th ed., edited by G. Starblanket, and D. Long, 237–251. Toronto: Oxford University Press.

Gregory, R.J. 1991. "The Attitudes of Senior Public Servants in Australia and New Zealand: Administrative Reform and Technocratic Consequence." *Governance* 4 (3): 295–331.

Grinspun, R., and R. Kreklewich. 1994. "Consolidating Neoliberal Reforms: 'Free Trade' as a Conditioning Framework." *Studies in Political Economy* 43 (1): 33–61. https://doi.org/10.1080/19187033.1994.11675388.

Grundy, J., A.M. Noack, L.F. Vosko, R. Casey, and R. Hii. 2017. "Enforcement of Ontario's Employment Standards Act: The Impact of Reform." *Canadian Public Policy* 43 (3): 190–201. https://doi.org/10.3138/cpp.2016-064.

Guay, L., and P. Hamel. 2014. *Cities and Urban Sociology*. Toronto: Oxford University Press.

Guerriero, M. 2012. "The Labour Share of Income around the World: Evidence from a Panel Dataset." Paper prepared for the 4th Economic Development International Conference of GREThA/GRES "Inequalities and Development: New Challenges, New Measurements? Bordeaux, France, 13–15 June. Online at http://piketty.pse.ens.fr/files/Guerriero2012.pdf, accessed 28 June 2018.

Guest, D. 1980. *The Emergence of Social Security in Canada*. Vancouver: UBC Press.

Guest, D. 1997. *The Emergence of Social Security in Canada*. 3rd ed. Vancouver: UBC Press.

Guo, C., and W. Bielefeld. 2014. *Social Entrepreneurship: An Evidence-based Approach to Creating Social Value*. San Francisco: Jossey-Bass.

Guttmann, R. 2016. *Finance-Led Capitalism: Shadow Banking, Re-Regulation, and the Future of Global Markets*. New York: Palgrave Macmillan.

Hacker, J., and P. Pierson. 2010a. *Winner-Take-All Politics: How Washington Made the Rich Richer – And Turned Its Back on the Middle Class*. New York: Simon & Schuster.

Hacker, J., and P. Pierson. 2010b. "Winner-Take-All Politics: Public Policy, Political Organization, and the Precipitous Rise of Top Incomes in the United States." *Politics and Society* 38 (2): 152–204. https://doi.org/10.1177/0032329210365042.

Hacker, J., and P. Pierson. 2016. *American Amnesia: How the War on Government Led Us to Forget What Made America Prosper*. New York: Simon and Schuster.

Hackworth, J. 2007. *The Neoliberal City: Governance, Ideology, and Development in American Urbanism*. Ithaca, NY: Cornell University Press.

Hackworth, J. 2008. "The Durability of Roll-Out Neoliberalism under Centre-Left Governance: The Case of Ontario's Social Housing Sector." *Studies in Political Economy* 81 (1): 7–26. https://doi.org/10.1080/19187033.2008.11675071.

Haley, B. 2011. "From Staples Trap to Carbon Trap: Canada's Peculiar Form of Carbon Lock-In." *Studies in Political Economy* 88 (1): 97–132. https://doi.org/10.1080/19187033.2011.11675011.

Halligan, J. 1995. "Policy Advice and Public Service." In *Governance in a Changing Environment*, edited by D. Savoie, and G. Peters, 138–72. Montreal; Kingston, ON: McGill-Queen's University Press.

Haluza-DeLay, R., and A. Carter. 2016. "Social Movements Scaling Up: Strategies and Opportunities in Opposing the Oil Sands Status Quo." In *First World Petro-Politics: The Political Ecology and Governance of Alberta*, edited by L. Adkin, 456–98. Toronto: University of Toronto Press.

Hamouda, O.F. 1998. "On Rae's Methodology of Economics." In *The Economics of John Rae*, edited by O.F. Hamouda, C. Lee, and D. Mair, 39–64. London Routledge.

Hamouda, O.F., C. Lee, and D. Mair, eds. 1998. *The Economics of John Rae*. London Routledge.

Hansen, E.D. 2001. *European Economic History: From Mercantilism to Maastricht and beyond*. Copenhagen: Copenhagen Business School Press.

Hart, J. 1990. "The Executive Establishment and Executive Leadership: A Comparative Perspective." *Governance* 3 (3): 249–63. https://doi.org/10.1111/j.1468-0491.1990.tb00121.x.

Hart, M. 1994. *Decision at Midnight: Inside the Canada-US Free Trade Negotiations*. With B. Dymond and C. Robertson. Vancouver: UBC Press.

Harvey, D. 1973. *Social Justice and the City*. Baltimore: Johns Hopkins University Press.

Harvey, D. 1982. *Limits to Capital*. Oxford: Oxford University Press.

Harvey, D. 2005a. *A Brief History of Neoliberalism*. Oxford: Oxford University Press.

Harvey, D. 2005b. *The New Imperialism*. Oxford: Oxford University Press.

Head, B. 2008. "Three Lenses of Evidence Based Policy." *Australian Journal of Public Administration* 67 (1): 1–11. https://doi.org/10.1111/j.1467-8500.2007.00564.x.

Heaman, E.A. 2014. "Macdonald and Fiscal Realpolitik." In *MacDonald at 200: New Reflections and Legacies*, edited by P. Dutil and R. Hall, 149–74. Toronto: Dundurn.

Heaman, E.A. 2017. *Tax, Order and Good Government: A New Political History of Canada, 1867–1917*. Montreal; Kingston, ON: McGill-Queens University Press.

Hein, E. 2015. "Finance-Dominated Capitalism and Re-distribution of Income: A Kaleckian Perspective." *Cambridge Journal of Economics* 39 (3): 907–34. https://doi.org/10.1093/cje/bet038.

Heintzman, R. 1979. "Efficiency and Community." *Journal of Canadian Studies* 14 (3): 1–147. https://doi.org/10.3138/jcs.14.3.1.

Heisz, A. 2015. *Trends in Income Inequality in Canada and Elsewhere*. Montreal: Institute for Research on Public Policy.

Helleiner, E. 2006. *Towards North American Monetary Union?* Montreal; Kingston, ON: McGill-Queen's University Press.

Helleiner, Eric. 2019. "Conservative Economic Nationalism and the National Policy: Rae, Buchanan, and Early Protectionist Thought." *Canadian Journal of Political Science* 52 (3): 521–38.

Helleiner, E., and A. Rosales. 2017. "Peripheral Thoughts for Global IPE: Latin American Ideational Innovation and the Diffusion of the Nineteenth Century Free Trade Doctrine." *International Studies Quarterly* 61: 924–34. https://doi.org/10.1093/isq/sqx063.

Henley, K. 1989. "The International Roots of Economic Nationalist Ideology in Canada, 1846–1885." *Journal of Canadian Studies* 24 (4): 107–21. https://doi.org/10.3138/jcs.24.4.107.

Hennebry, J. 2012. *Permanently Temporary? Agricultural Migrant Workers and their Integration in Canada.* Montreal: Institute for Research on Public Policy.

Hennessey, P. 1997. "The Essence of Public Service." *John L. Manion Lecture Series.* Ottawa: Canadian Centre for Management Development.

Hennessy, T., R. Tranjan, and S. Block. 2018. "Ontario budget throws down the election gauntlet." *Behind the Numbers*, 28 March. Online at http://behindthenumbers.ca/2018/03/28/ontario-budget-placeholder/.

Heron, C., and R. Storey, eds. 1986. *On the Job: Confronting the Labour Process in Canada.* Montreal; Kingston, ON: McGill-Queen's University Press.

Heynen, N., J. McCarthy, S. Prudham, and P. Robbins, eds. 2007. *Neoliberal Environments: False Promises and Unnatural Consequences.* London: Routledge.

High, S. 2003. *Industrial Sunset: The Making of North America's Rust Belt, 1969–1984.* Toronto: University of Toronto Press.

Hill, N., A. Alook, and I. Hussey. 2017. "How Gender and Race Shape Experiences of Work in Alberta's Oil Industry." *Parkland Blog.* Edmonton: Parkland Institute.

Hiller, H. 2010a. "Canadian Urbanization in Historical and Global Perspective." In *Urban Canada.* 2nd ed., edited by H. Hiller, 2–17. Toronto: Oxford University Press.

Hiller, H. 2010b. "The Dynamics of Canadian Urbanization." In *Urban Canada.* 2nd ed., edited by H. Hiller, 18–39. Toronto: Oxford University Press.

Hobsbawm, E.J. 1969. *Industry and Empire.* Harmondsworth, UK: Penguin Books.

Holmes, J. 1983. "Industrial Reorganization, Capital Restructuring and Locational Change: An Analysis of the Canadian Automobile Industry in the 1960s." *Economic Geography* 59 (3): 251–71. https://doi.org/10.2307/143415.

Hood, C. 1991. "A Public Management for All Seasons?" *Public Administration* 69 (1): 3–19.

Hood, C., and M. Jackson. 1991. "The New Public Management: A Recipe for Disaster?" *Canberra Bulletin of Public Administration* 69 (1): 3–19. https://doi.org/10.1111/j.1467-9299.1991.tb00779.x.

Hood, D. 2014. "Why Are Some Canadian Companies Paying Almost No Tax?" *Canadian Business*, 27 February.

Hopkin, J., and J. Lynch. 2016. "Winner-Take-All Politics in Europe? European Inequality in Comparative Perspective." *Politics & Society* 44 (3): 335–43. https://doi.org/10.1177/0032329216656844.

Horak, M. 2013. "State Rescaling in Practice: Urban Governance Reform in Toronto." *Urban Research and Practice* 6 (3): 311–28.

Horn, L. 2012. *Regulating Corporate Governance in the EU*. Basingstoke, UK: Palgrave Macmillan.

Howlett, D. 2017. "Canada's tax system is still subsidizing the ultra rich." *Tyee*, 6 June.

Howlett, M. 2009. "Policy Analytical Capacity and Evidence-based Policy-making: Lessons from Canada." *Canadian Public Administration* 25 (2): 153–75. https://doi.org/10.1111/j.1754-7121.2009.00070_1.x.

Howlett, M., and A. Migone. 2013a. "The Permanence of Temporary Services: The Reliance of Canadian Federal Departments on Policy and Management Consultants." *Canadian Public Administration* 56 (3): 369–90. https://doi .org/10.1111/capa.12026.

Howlett, M., and A. Migone. 2013b. "Searching for Substance: Externalization, Politicization and the Work of Canadian Policy Consultants 2006–2013." *Central European Journal of Public Policy* 7 (1): 112–33.

Howlett, M., and A. Migone. 2014. "Assessing Contract Policy Work: Overseeing Canadian Policy Consultants." *Public Money & Management* 34 (3): 173–80. https://doi.org/10.1080/09540962.2014.908007.

Howlett, M., A. Netherton, and M. Ramesh. 1999. *The Political Economy of Canada: An Introduction*. Oxford: Oxford University Press.

Howlett, M., and M. Ramesh. 1992. *The Political Economy of Canada*. Toronto: McClelland and Stewart.

Hudson, C.-A., and P. Graefe. 2011. "The Toronto Origins of Ontario's 2008 Poverty Reduction Strategy: Mobilizing Multiple Channels for Progressive Social Policy Change." *Canadian Review of Social Policy* 65–66: 1–15.

Huertas-Noble, C., C. Adams, S. Edel, A. Jones, C. Michael, M. Peck, J. Whitlow, and M. Risser. 2016. "Worker-Owned and Unionized Worker-Owned Cooperatives: Two Tools to Address Income Inequality." *Clinical Law Review* 22: 325–58. Online at https://community-wealth.org/content /worker-owned-and-unionized-worker-owned-cooperatives-two-tools -address-income-inequality.

Hufbauer, G.C., C. Cimino, and T. Moran. 2014. "NAFTA at 20: Misleading Charges and Positive Achievements." In *NAFTA 20 Years Later*, 6–29. Washington, DC: Peterson Institute for International Economics.

Hughes, O.E. 2003. *Public Administration and Public Management*. 3rd ed. Basingstoke, UK: Palgrave Macmillan.

Hulchanski, D.J. 2010. *The Three Cities within Toronto: Income Polarization among Toronto's Neighbourhoods*. Toronto: University of Toronto Press.

Hulchanski, D.J. 2015. *Divided Cities: A Legacy of the Late 20th Century?* Toronto: University of Toronto Press.

Hunt, S. 2013. "In Her Name: Relationships as Law." Online at https:// intercontinentalcry.org/name-relationships-law-sarah-hunt-tedxvictoria -2013/, accessed 30 November, 2018.

Hunt, S. 2015. "Violence, Law, and the Everyday Politics of Recognition." Presentation to the Native American and Indigenous Studies Association Annual Meeting (NAISA).

Hunt, S., and C. Holmes. 2015. "Everyday Decolonization: Living a Decolonizing Queer Politics." *Journal of Lesbian Studies* 19 (2): 154–72. https://doi.org/10.1080/10894160.2015.970975.

Hurl, C., and B. Christensen. 2015. "Building the New Canadian Political Economy." *Studies in Political Economy* 96 (1): 167–93. https://doi.org/10.1080/19187033.2015.11674942.

Hussey, I. 2020. "The Future of Alberta's Oil Sands Industry: More Production, Less Capital, Fewer Jobs." Edmonton: Parkland Institute. https://www.parklandinstitute.ca/the_future_of_albertas_oil_sands_industry.

Hussey, I., N. Hill, and A. Alook. 2017. "Ten Things to Know about Indigenous People and Resource Extraction in Alberta." *Parkland Blog*. Edmonton: Parkland Institute.

Hymer, S. 1966. "Direct Foreign Investment and the National Economic Interest." In *Nationalism in Canada*, edited by P. Russell. Toronto: McGraw-Hill.

Ibbitson, J. 1997. *Promised Land: Inside the Mike Harris Revolution*. Scarborough, ON: Prentice Hall.

Iliopoulos, C., and V. Valentinov. 2017. "Member Preference Heterogeneity and System-Lifeworld Dichotomy in Cooperatives: An Exploratory Case Study." *Journal of Organizational Change Management* 30 (7): 1063–80. https://doi.org/10.1108/JOCM-12-2016-0262.

Imagine Canada. n.d. *Sector Source*. Ottawa: Imagine Canada. Online at http://sectorsource.ca/research-and-impact/sector-impact.

InfluenceMap. 2016. "How Much Big Oil Spends on Obstructive Climate Lobbying." Online at https://influencemap.org/site/data/000/173/Lobby_Spend_Report_March_2016.pdf, accessed 8 August 2018.

Ingham, G. 2008. *Capitalism*. Cambridge, UK: Polity.

Innis, H. [1929] 1956. "The Teaching of Economic History in Canada." In *Essays in Canadian Economic History*, edited by M.Q. Innis. Toronto: University of Toronto Press.

Innis, H. 1930. *The Fur Trade in Canada: An Introduction to Canadian Economic History*. New Haven, CT: Yale University Press.

Innis, H. [1937] 1956. "An Introduction to Canadian Economic Studies." In *Essays in Canadian Economic History*, edited by M.Q. Innis. Toronto: University of Toronto Press.

Innis, H. 1940. *The Cod Fisheries: The History of an International Economy*. New Haven, CT: Yale University Press.

Innis, H. [1948] 1956. "Great Britain, the United States and Canada." In *Essays in Canadian Economic History*, edited by M.Q. Innis. Toronto: University of Toronto Press.

Innis, H. [1950] 1972. *Empire and Communications*, revised by M.Q. Innis. Toronto: University of Toronto.

Innis, H. 1956. *The Fur Trade in Canada: An Introduction to Canadian Economic History*. Toronto: University of Toronto Press.

Innis, H. 1975. *The Fur Trade in Canada: An Introduction to Canadian Economic History*. Rev. ed. Toronto: University of Toronto Press.

International Co-operative Alliance. 2020. "Co-operative Identity, Values, & Principles." Online at https://www.ica.coop/en/cooperatives/cooperative-identity, accessed 10 May 2020.

International Labour Organization. 2011. *Global Wage Report 2010/11*. Geneva: International Labour Organization.

International Labour Organization. 2017. *World Employment Social Outlook: Trends 2017*. Geneva: International Labour Organization. Online at http://www.ilo.org/wcmsp5/groups/public/-dgreports/-dcomm/-publ/documents/publication/wcms_541211.pdf.

International Monetary Fund. 2012. *Global Financial Stability Report*. Washington, DC: International Monetary Fund.

International Monetary Fund. 2017. *World Economic Outlook, October 2017*. Washington, DC: International Monetary Fund.

Jackson, A., and M. Thomas. 2017. *Work and Labour in Canada: Critical Issues*. Toronto: Canadian Scholars' Press.

James, R.W. 1965. *John Rae: Political Economist*, vol. 1. Toronto: University of Toronto Press.

James, R.W. 1998. "Birthday Greetings to John Rae." In *The Economics of John Rae*, edited by O.F. Hamouda, C. Lee, and D. Mair, 21–36. London: Routledge.

Jenson, J. 1990. "Representations in Crisis: The Roots of Canada's Permeable Fordism." *Canadian Journal of Political Science* 23 (4): 653–84. https://doi.org/10.1017/s0008423900020795.

Jenson, J. 2002. "Against the Current: Child Care and Family Policy in Quebec." In *Child Care Policy at the Crossroads: Gender and Welfare State Restructuring*, edited by S. Michel and R. Mahon, 309–32. New York: Routledge.

Jenson, J. 2004. *Canada's New Social Risks: Directions for a New Social Architecture*. Ottawa: Canadian Policy Research Networks.

Jenson, J. 2012. "Redesigning Citizenship Regimes after Neoliberalism: Moving towards Social Investment." In *Towards A Social Investment Welfare State? Ideas, Policies and Challenges*, edited by N. Morel, B. Palier, and J. Palme, 61–88. Bristol: Policy Press.

Jenson, J. 2013. "Historical Transformations of Canada's Social Architecture: Institutions, Instruments and Ideas." In *Inequality and the Fading of Redistributive Politics*, edited by K. Banting and J. Myles, 43–64. Vancouver: UBC Press.

Jenson, J., R. Mahon, and S. Phillips. 2003. "No Minor Matter: The Political Economy of Childcare in Canada." In *Changing Canada: Political Economy as Transformation*, edited by C. Clement and L. Vosko, 135–60. Montreal; Kingston, ON: McGill-Queen's University Press.

Jessop, B. 2000. "The Crisis of the National Spatio-Temporal Fix and the Tendential Ecological Dominance of Globalizing Capitalism." *International Journal of Urban and Regional Research*. 24 (2): 323–60. https://doi.org /10.1111/1468-2427.00251.

Jessop, B. 2002a. *The Future of the Capitalist State*. Cambridge: Polity Press.

Jessop, B. 2002b. "Liberalism, Neoliberalism, and Urban Governance: A State Theoretical Approach." *Antipode* 34 (3): 452–72. https://doi .org/10.1111/1467-8330.00250.

Jessop, B. 2016. "The Heartlands of Neoliberalism and the Rise of the Austerity State." In *The Handbook of Neoliberalism*, edited by K. Birch, S. Springer, and J. MacLeavy, 410–21. New York: Routledge.

Jesuit, D., and A. Williams. 2018. *Public Policy, Governance and Polarization: Making Governance Work*. London: Routledge.

Jevons, S. 1876. "The Future of Political Economy." *Fortnightly Review* 20: 617–33.

Jiang, W. 2018. "Under USMCA, Canada is neither strong nor free." *Globe and Mail*, 3 October. Online at https://www.theglobeandmail.com/opinion /article-under-usmca-canada-is-neither-strong-nor-free/.

Jobin, S. 2015 "Cree Economic Relationships, Governance, and Critical Indigenous Political Economy in Resistance to Settler-Colonial Logics." PhD diss., University of Alberta. Online at https://era.library.ualberta.ca /items/2d7491be-d605-4b13-a206-1764184218c2.

Johnston, P. 1983. *Aboriginal Children and the Child Welfare System*. Toronto: Canadian Council on Social Development.

Johnston, R. 2013. "The Party System, Elections and Social Policy." In *Inequality and the Fading of Redistributive Politics*, edited by K. Banting and J. Myles, 187–209. Vancouver: UBC Press.

Joy, M., P. Marier, and A.-M. Séguin. 2018. "La démarche villes-amies des aînés: un remède universel pour vieillir chez soi?" In *Les vieillissement sous la loupe: entre mythes et réalités*, edited by V. Billette, P. Marier, and A.-M. Séguin, 75–84. Laval, QC: Presses de l'Université Laval.

Joy, M., and J. Shields. 2013. "Social Impact Bonds: The Next Phase of Third Sector Marketization?" *Canadian Journal of Nonprofit and Social Economy Research* 4 (2): 39–55. https://doi.org/10.22230/cjnser.2013v4n2a148.

Joy, M., and J. Shields. 2016. "The Immorality of Innovation – the Tale of Social Impact Bonds." *Policy & Politics: Journal Blog*, October. Online at https:// policyandpoliticsblog.com/2016/10/05/the-immorality-of-innovation-the-tale-of-social-impact-bonds/.

Joy, M., and J. Shields. 2017. "Austerity and the Non-profit Sector: The Case of Social Impact Bonds." In *The Austerity State*, edited by S. McBride, and B. Evans, 309–29. Toronto: University of Toronto Press.

Joy, M., and J. Shields. 2018. "Austerity in the Making: Reconfiguring Social Policy through Social Impact Bonds." *Policy & Politics*, March. Online at https://doi.org/10.1332/030557318X15200933925397.

Joy, M., J. Shields, and S.M. Cheng. 2019. "Social Innovation Labs: A Neoliberal Austerity Driven Process or Democratic Intervention?" *Alternate Routes: A Journal of Critical Social Research* 30 (2): 35–54.

Joy, M., and R. Vogel. 2015. "Toronto's Governance Crisis: A Global City Under Pressure." *Cities* 49 (December): 35–52. https://doi.org/10.1016/j.cities.2015.06.009.

Justice, D.H. 2010. "Notes toward a Theory of Anomaly." *GLQ: A Journal of Lesbian and Gay Studies* 16 (1–2): 207–42. https://doi.org/10.1215/10642684-2009-020.

Kalleberg, A.L. 2009. "Precarious Work, Insecure Workers: Employment Relations in Transition." *American Sociological Review* 74 (1): 1–22. https://doi.org/10.1177/000312240907400101.

Kalmi, P. 2007. "The Disappearance of Co-Operatives from Economic Textbooks." *Cambridge Journal of Economics* 31 (4): 625–47. https://doi.org/10.1093/cje/bem005.

Karpilow, Q., I. Solomon, A.V. Calderón, M. Pérez-Rocha, and S. Trew. 2014. *NAFTA: 20 Years of Costs to Communities and the Environment*. Sierra Club, Sierra Club Canada, Mexican Action Network on Free Trade, Institute for Policy Studies, Council of Canadians.

Katz-Rosene, R., and M. Paterson. 2018. *Thinking Ecologically about the Global Political Economy*. London: Routledge.

Kealey, G. 1980. *Toronto Workers Respond to Industrial Capitalism, 1867–1892*. Toronto: University of Toronto Press.

Kealey, G. 1995. "The Canadian State's Attempt to Manage Class Conflict, 1900–48." In *Workers and Canadian History*, edited by G. Kealey, 125–47. Montreal; Kingston, ON: McGill-Queen's University Press.

Keating, T., and Murray, R.W. 2014. "Mutual Constitution or Convenient National Interest? The Security Strategies of Canada and the United States since 1991." *Canadian Foreign Policy Journal* 20 (3): 247–58. https://doi.org/10.1080/11926422.2014.977312.

Keil, R. 2009. "The Urban Politics of Roll-with-It Neoliberalization." *City* 13 (2–3): 230–45. https://doi.org/10.1080/13604810902986848.

Keil, R., D.V.J. Bell, P. Penz, and L. Fawcett, eds. 1998. *Political Ecology: Global and Local*. London: Routledge.

Kellogg, P. 2005. "Kari Levitt and the Long Detour of Canadian Political Economy." *Studies in Political Economy* 76 (Autumn): 31–60. https://doi.org/10.1080/19187033.2005.11675122.

Kellogg, P. 2015. *Escape from the Staple Trap: Canadian Political Economy after Left Nationalism*. Toronto: University of Toronto Press.

Kelly, K., and T. Caputo. 2012. *Community: A Contemporary Analysis of Policies, Programs, and Practices*. Toronto: University of Toronto Press.

Kendall, J. 2008. "Voluntary Welfare." In *The Student's Companion to Social Policy*, edited by P. Alcock, M. May, and K. Lingson, 212–18. Oxford: Blackwell.

Kent, T. 1988. *A Public Purpose*. Montreal; Kingston, ON: McGill-Queen's University Press.

Kipfer, S. 2002. "Urbanization, Everyday Life and the Survival of Capitalism: Lefebvre, Gramsci and the Problematic of Hegemony." *Capitalism, Nature, Socialism* 13 (2): 117–49. https://doi.org/10.1080/10455750208565482.

Kipfer, S., and R. Keil. 2002. "Toronto Inc.? Planning the Competitive City in the New Toronto." *Antipode* 34 (2): 227–64. https://doi.org/10.1111/1467-8330.00237.

Kirkpatrick, L.O., and M.P. Smith. 2011. "The Infrastructural Limits to Growth: Rethinking the Urban Growth Machine in Times of Fiscal Crisis." *International Journal of Urban and Regional Research* 35 (3): 477–503. https://doi.org/10.1111/j.1468-2427.2011.01058.x.

Kitchener. 2017. "Love My Hood." Kitchener, ON: City of Kitchener. Online at https://www.lovemyhood.ca/en/index.aspx#.

Klassen, J. 2014. *Joining Empire: The Political Economy of the New Canadian Foreign Policy*. Toronto: University of Toronto Press.

Klein, N. 2014. *This Changes Everything: Capitalism vs. the Climate*. Toronto: Alfred A. Knopf Canada.

Knox, J.H. 2004. "Separated at Birth: The North American Agreements on Labor and the Environment." *Loyola of Los Angeles International and Comparative Law Review* 26 (3): 359–87.

Kocka, J. 1980. "The Rise of the Modern Industrial Enterprise in Germany." In *Managerial Hierarchies*, edited by A. Chandler, and H. Daems. Cambridge, MA: Harvard University Press.

Kollmeyer, C., and J. Peters. 2019. "Financialization and the Decline of Organized Labor: A Study of 18 Advanced Capitalist Countries, 1970–. 2012." *Social Forces* 98 (1): 1–30. https://doi.org/10.1093/sf/soy105.

Kovach, M. 2013. "Treaties, Truths and Transgressive Pedagogies: Re-imagining Indigenous Presence in the Classroom." *Socialist Studies* 9 (1): 109–27. https://doi.org/10.18740/s4ks36.

KPMG. 2016. "Focus on Tax: KPMG's Guide to International Tax Competitiveness." Online at https://assets.kpmg/content/dam/kpmg/mx/pdf/2016/08/Focus-on-Tax-2016.pdf, accessed 29 July 2018.

Kramer, R., and T. Mitchell. 2010. *When the State Trembled: How A.J. Andrews and the Citizens' Committee Broke the Winnipeg General Strike*. Toronto: University of Toronto Press.

Krikorian, J.D. 2012. *International Trade Law and Domestic Policy: Canada, the United States, and the WTO*. Vancouver: UBC Press.

Krugman, P.R. 2012. *End this Depression Now!* New York: W.W. Norton.

Krugman, P.R., M. Obstfeld, and M.J. Melitz. 2018. *International Trade: Theory and Policy*. 11th ed. Boston: Pearson Education.

Kuokkanen, R. 2011. "From Indigenous Economies to Market-Based Self-governance: A Feminist Political Economy Analysis." *Canadian Journal of Political Science* 44 (2): 275–97. https://doi.org/10.1017/s0008423911000126.

Kwok, S.-M., and M.A. Wallis. 2008. *Daily Struggles: The Deepening Racialization and Feminization of Poverty in Canada*. Toronto: Canadian Scholars' Press.

Laforest, R. 2011a. "L'étude du tiers secteur au Québec: comment saisir la spécificité québécoise." *Politique et Sociétés* 30 (1): 43–55. https://doi.org/10.7202/1006058ar.

Laforest, R. 2011b. *Voluntary Sector Organizations and the State: Building New Relations*. Vancouver: UBC Press.

Laidlaw, A. 1980. *Co-Operatives in the Year 2000*. Geneva: International Co-operative Alliance.

Laing, S. 1842. *Notes of a Traveler on the Social and Political State of France, Prussia, Switzerland, Italy, and Other Parts of Europe*. London: Longman, Brown, Green, and Longman's.

Laing, S. 1852. *Observations on the Social and Political State of Denmark, and the Duchies of Sleswick and Holstein in 1851: Being the Third Series of The Notes of a Traveller on the Social and Political State of the European People*. London: Longman, Brown, Green, and Longmans.

Langille, D, 1987. "The Business Council on National Issues and the Canadian State." *Studies in Political Economy* 24 (1): 41–85.

Lapavitsas, C. 2014. *Profiting Without Producing: How Finance Exploits Us All*. New York: Verso.

Larner, W. 2000. "Neo-liberalism: Policy, Ideology, Governmentality." *Studies in Political Economy* 63 (1): 5–25. https://doi.org/10.1080/19187033.2000.11675231.

LaRocque, E. 2017. "Métis and Feminist." In *Making Space for Indigenous Feminisms*. 2nd ed., edited by J. Green, 122–45. Halifax, NS: Fernwood.

Lavoie, M., and M. Seccareccia. 2006. "The Bank of Canada and the Modern View of Central Banking." *International Journal of Political Economy* 35 (1): 58–82. https://doi.org/10.2753/ijp0891-1916350103.

Lavoie, M., and M. Seccareccia. 2013. "Reciprocal Influences: A Tale of Two Central Banks on the North American Continent." *International Journal of Political Econom*. 42 (3): 63–84. https://doi.org/10.2753/ijp0891-1916420304.

Lavoie, M., and M. Seccareccia. 2016. "Money and Banking." In *An Introduction to Macroeconomics: A Heterodox Approach to Economic Analysis*, edited by L.-P. Rochon and S. Rossi, 97–116. Cheltenham, UK: Edward Elgar.

Lawrence, B., and K. Anderson. 2003. *Strong Women Stories: Native Vision and Community Survival*. Toronto: Sumach Press.

Lawrence, B., and K. Anderson. 2005. "Introduction to Indigenous Women: The State of Our Nations." *Atlantis: Critical Studies in Gender, Culture & Social Justice* 29 (2): 1–8.

Lawson, M. 2018. *Reward Work, Not Wealth*. Cowley, UK: Oxfam UK. Online at https://oi-files-d8-prod.s3.eu-west-2.amazonaws.com/s3fs-public/file_attachments/bp-reward-work-not-wealth-220118-en.pdf, accessed July 14, 2018.

Laxer, G. 1989. *Open for Business*. Toronto: Oxford University Press.

Laxer, G. 2015. *After the Sands: Energy and Ecological Security for Canadians*. Madeira Park, BC: Douglas & McIntyre.

Laxer, R, ed. 1973. Canada Ltd.: The Political Economy of Dependency. Toronto: McClelland and Stewart.

Lazonick, W. 2014. "Profits without Prosperity." *Harvard Business Review*. September, 46–55.

Leblond, P., and J. Fabian. 2017. "Modernizing NAFTA: A New Deal for the North American Economy in the Twenty-first Century." CIGI Papers 123. Waterloo, ON: Centre for International Governance Innovation.

Lee, M. 2010. *Canada's Regulatory Obstacle Course: The Cabinet Directive on Streamlining Regulation and the Public Interest*. Ottawa: Canadian Centre for Policy Alternatives.

Lee, M., and B. Campbell. 2006. *Putting Canadians at Risk*. Ottawa: Canadian Centre for Policy Alternatives.

Lefebvre, H. 1970. *La révolution urbaine*. Paris: Gallimard

Le Gales, P. 2016. "Neoliberalism and Urban Change: Stretching a Good Idea Too Far?" *Territory, Politics, Governance* 4 (2): 154–72. https://doi.org/10.108 0/21622671.2016.1165143.

Leitner, H. 1990. "Cities in Pursuit of Economic Growth: The Local State as Entrepreneur." *Political Geography Quarterly* 9 (2): 146–70. https://doi.org/10.1016/0260-9827(90)90016-4.

Leitner, H., E.S. Sheppard, K. Sziarto, and A. Marinjanti. 2007. "Contesting Urban Futures: Decentering Neoliberalism." In *Contesting Neoliberalism: Urban Frontiers*, edited by H. Leitner, J. Peck, and S. Sheppard, 1–25. New York: Guilford Press.

Lemieux, T., and C. Riddell, 2016. "Who Are Canada's Top 1 Percent?" In *Income Inequality: The Canadian Story*, edited by D. Green, C. Riddell, and F. St-Hilaire, 103–56. Montreal: Institute for Research on Public Policy.

Lennox, P. 2009. *At Home and Abroad: The Canada-US Relationship and Canada's Place in the World*. Vancouver: UBC Press

Leslie, P. 1987. *Federal State, National Economy*. Toronto: University of Toronto Press.

Lévesque, B. 2014. "L'institutionnalisation des services de garde à la petite enfance à partir de l'économie sociale." In *L'innovation sociale: les marches d'une construction théorique et pratique.*, edited by B. Lévesque, J.-L. Klein, and J.-M. Fontan, 267–301. Quebec City: Presses de l'Université du Québec.

Levitt, K. 1970. *Silent Surrender: The Multinational Corporation in Canada*. Toronto: Macmillan.

Lewchuk, W., M. Lafleche, S. Procyk, C. Cook, D. Dyson, L. Goldring, K. Lior, A. Meisner, J. Shields, A. Tambureno, and P. Viducis. 2016. "The Precarity Penalty: How Insecure Employment Disadvantages Workers and Their Families." *Alternative Routes: A Journal of Critical Social Research* 27: 87–108.

Lewchuk, W., S. Procyk, and J. Shields. 2017. "Origins of Precarity: Families and Communities in Crisis." In *Precarious Employment: Cases, Consequences, and Remedies*, edited by S. Procyk, W. Lewchuk, and J. Shields, 2–12. Halifax, NS: Fernwood.

Lin, K.-H. 2016. "The Rise of Finance and Firm Employment Dynamics." *Organization Science*. 27 (4,): 972–88. https://doi.org/10.1287/orsc.2016.1073.

Lin, K.-H., and D. Tomaskovic-Devey. 2013. "Financialization and U.S Income." *American Journal of Sociology* 118 (5): 1284–329. https://doi .org/10.1086/669499.

List, F. [1841] 1885. *The National System of Political Economy*. Translated by S.S. Lloyd. London: Longmans, Green.

Logan, J.R., and H.L. Molotch. 1987. *Urban Fortunes: The Political Economy of Place*. Berkeley: University of California Press.

Loomer, G. 2015. "The Disjunction between Corporate Residence and Corporate Taxation: Is Improvement Possible?" *Canadian Tax Journal* 61 (1): 91–132.

Lorimer, J. 1970. *The Real World of City Politics*. Toronto: James Lewis and Samuel.

Lower, A. 1946. *Colony to Nation: A History of Canada*. Toronto: Longmans Green.

Lowndes, V. 2016. "Narrative and Storytelling." In *Evidence-Based Policy Making in the Social Sciences: Methods that Matter*, edited by G. Stoker and M. Evans, 103–22. Bristol: Policy Press.

Luxton, M. 2006. "Feminist Political Economy in Canada and the Politics of Social Reproduction." In *Social Reproduction: Feminist Political Economy Challenges Neo-Liberalism*, edited by K. Bezanson and M. Luxton, 11–44. Montreal; Kingston, ON: McGill-Queen's University Press.

MacArthur, J. 2016. *Empowering Electricity: Co-Operatives, Sustainability, and Power Sector Reform in Canada*. Vancouver: UBC Press.

MacDermid, R. 2009. *Funding City Politics: Municipal Campaign Funding and Property Development in the Greater Toronto Area*. Toronto: Centre for Social Justice.

Macdonald, D. 2014. *Outrageous Fortune: Documenting Canada's Wealth Gap*. Ottawa: Canadian Centre for Policy Alternatives.

Macdonald, D. 2017. *Addicted to Debt: Tracking Canada's Rapid Accumulation of Private Sector Debt*. Ottawa: Canadian Centre for Policy Alternatives.

Macdonald, D. 2018. *Climbing Up and Kicking Down: Executive Pay in Canada*. Ottawa: Canadian Centre for Policy Alternatives.

MacDowell, L.S. 1978. "The Formation of the Canadian Industrial Relations System during World War Two." *Labour* 3: 175–96.

Macionis, J.J., and V.N. Parrillo. 2009. *Cities and Urban Life*. 5th ed. New York: Prentice Hall.

Mackenzie, H. 2012. *Canada's CEO Elite 100: The 0.01%*. Ottawa: Canadian Centre for Policy Alternatives.

Mackenzie, H. 2017. *Throwing Money at the Problem: 10 Years of Executive Compensation*. Ottawa: Canadian Centre for Policy Alternatives.

Mackintosh, W.A. 1934. *Prairie Settlement, the Geographical Setting*. Toronto: Macmillan.

Mackintosh, W.A. 1939. *The Economic Background of Dominion-Provincial Relations*. Study Prepared for the Royal Commission on Dominion-Provincial Relations. Ottawa: J.O. Patenaude.

MacNeil, R. 2014. "The Decline of Canadian Environmental Regulation: Neoliberalism and the Staples Bias." *Studies in Political Economy* 93 (1): 81–106. https://doi.org/10.1080/19187033.2014.11674965.

Macpherson, C.B. 1957. "The Social Sciences." In *The Culture of Contemporary Canada*, edited by J. Park. Ithaca, NY: Cornell University Press.

Macpherson, C.B. 1962. *The Political Theory of Possessive Individualism: From Hobbes to Locke*. Toronto: University of Toronto Press.

MacPherson, C.B. 1978. *Property: Mainstream and Critical Positions*. Toronto: University of Toronto Press.

MacPherson, I. 2009. *A Century of Co-operation*. Ottawa: Canadian Co-operative Association.

Maddison, A. 2001. *The World Economy: A Millennial Perspective*. Paris: Organisation for Economic Co-operation and Development.

Mahon, R. 1990. "The Waffle and Canadian Political Economy." *Studies in Political Economy* 32: (1): 187–94. https://doi.org/10.1080/19187033.1990.11675491.

Mahon, R. 2002. "Child Care: Toward What Kind of 'Social Europe?" *Social Politics* 9 (3): 343–79. https://doi.org/10.1093/sp/9.3.343.

Mahon, R. 2008. "Varieties of Liberalism: Canadian Social Policy from the 'Golden Age' to the Present." *Social Policy and Administration* 42 (4): 342–61. https://doi.org/10.1111/j.1467-9515.2008.00608.x.

Mann, G. 2017. *In the Long Run We Are All Dead*. London: Verso.

Marginson, P. 2016. "Governing Work and Employment Relations in an Internationalized Economy: The Institutional Challenge." *ILR Review* 69 (5): 1033–55. https://doi.org/10.1177/0019793916654891.

Marshall, H., F. Southard, and K. Taylor. 1976, *Canadian-American Industry*. Toronto: McClelland and Stewart.

Marutto, P. 2005. "Charity and Public Welfare in History: A Look at Ontario 1830–1950." *Phillanthropist* 19 (3): 159–67.

Marx, K. [1867] 1977. *Capital*, vol. 1. Moscow: Progress Publishers.

Marx, K., and F. Engels. 1848. *The Communist Manifesto*. Online at https://www.marxists.org/archive/marx/works/download/pdf/Manifesto.pdf.

Massey, D. 1984. *Spatial Divisions of Labour*. London: Macmillan.

Matthew, R.A., and V. Bransburg. 2017. "Democratizing Caring Labor: The Promise of Community-Based, Worker-Owned Childcare Cooperatives." *Affilia* 32 (1): 10–23. https://doi.org/10.1177/0886109916678027.

May, T., and B. Perry. 2005. "The Future of Urban Sociology." *Sociology* 39 (2): 343–70. https://doi.org/10.1177/0038038505050544.

Mayer, J. 2016. *Dark Money: The Hidden History of the Billionaires Behind the Rise of the Radical Right*. New York: Doubleday.

McAlevey, J.F. 2016. *Organizing for Power in the New Gilded Age*. Oxford: Oxford University Press.

McArthur, J.W., and K. Rasmussen. 2017. *Who and What Gets Left Behind? Assessing Canada's Domestic Status on Sustainable Development Goals*. Washington, DC: Brookings Institution.

McBride, S. 1992. *Not Working: State, Unemployment, and Neoconservatism in Canada*. Toronto: University of Toronto Press.

McBride, S. 1996. "The Political Economy Tradition and Canadian Policy Studies." In *Policy Studies in Canada: The State of the Art*, edited by L. Dobuzinskis, M. Howlett, and D. Laycock, 49–66. Toronto: University of Toronto Press.

McBride, S. 2003. "Quiet Constitutionalism in Canada: The International Political Economy of Domestic Institutional Change." *Canadian Journal of Political Science* 36 (2): 251–73. https://doi.org/10.1017/s0008423903778603.

McBride, S. 2005. *Paradigm Shift*. 2nd ed. Halifax, NS: Fernwood.

McBride, S. 2006. "Reconfiguring Sovereignty: NAFTA Chapter 11 Dispute Settlement Procedures and the Issue of Public-Private Authority." *Canadian Journal of Political Science* 39 (4): 755–75. https://doi.org/10.1017/s0008423906060331.

McBride, S. 2012. "The Scope and Limits of a Public-Private Hybrid: Dispute Settlement under NAFTA Chapter 19." *New Political Economy* 17 (2): 117–35. https://doi.org/10.1080/13563467.2010.540321.

McBride, S. 2017. *Working? Employment Policy in Canada*. Toronto: Rockmills.

McBride, S., and B. Evans. 2017. *The Austerity State*. Toronto: University of Toronto Press.

McBride, S., and J. Shields. 1997. *Dismantling a Nation: The Transition to Corporate Rule*. Halifax, NS: Fernwood.

McBride, S., and J. Shields, 2004. *Dismantling a Nation: The Transition to Corporate Rule*. 2nd ed. Halifax, NS: Fernwood.

McBride, S., and H. Whiteside. 2011. *Private Affluence, Public Austerity.* Halifax, NS: Fernwood.

McCabe, A., and J. Phillimore. 2018. *Community Groups in Context: Local Activities and Actions.* Bristol: Policy Press.

McCallum, M.E. 1995. "Labour and the Liberal State: Regulating the Employment Relationship, 1867–1920." *Manitoba Law Journal* 23: 574–93.

McCollum, E. 2010. "Notes in the Margins: The Social Economy in Economics and Business Textbooks." In *Researching the Social Economy,* edited by L. Mook, J. Quarter, and S. Ryan, 154–75. Toronto: University of Toronto Press.

McCormack, G., and T. Workman. 2015. *The Servant State.* Halifax, NS: Fernwood.

McDowell, L. 1983. "Towards an Understanding of the Gender Division of Urban Space." *Environment and Planning D: Society and Space* 1 (1): 59–72. https://doi.org/10.1068/d010059.

McGregor, J. 2018. "Why NAFTA's unloved investor-state dispute chapter may be in trouble." *CBC News,* 8 September. Online at https://www.cbc.ca/news/politics/nafta-isds-weekend-1.4814141.

McInnis, P.S. 2002. *Harnessing Labour Confrontation: Shaping the Postwar Settlement in Canada, 1943–1950.* Toronto: University of Toronto Press.

McInnis, P.S. 2012. "'Hothead Troubles': Sixties-Era Wildcat Strikes in Canada." In *Debating Dissent: Canada and the Sixties,* edited by L. Campbell, L. Clément, and G. Kealey, 155–70. Toronto: University of Toronto Press.

McKeen, W., and A. Porter. 2003. "Politics and Transformation: Welfare State Restructuring in Canada." In *Changing Canada: Political Economy as Transformation,* edited by W. Clement and L. Vosko, 109–34. Montreal; Kingston, ON: McGill-Queen's University Press.

McLeod, N., and N. Starblanket. 2014. "Finding the Stars in The Blanket of the Valley." In *The Land Is Everything: Treaty Land Entitlement,* edited by T. Hubbard and M. Poitras. Saskatoon, SK: Office of the Treaty Commissioner.

McMurtry, J.J. 2010a. "Introducing the Social Economy in Theory and Practice." In *Living Economics: Canadian Perspectives on the Social Economy, Co-operatives, and Community Development,* edited by J.J. McMurtry, 1–34. Toronto: Emond Montgomery.

McMurtry, J.J., ed. 2010b. *Living Economics: Canadian Perspectives on the Social Economy, Co-operatives, and Community Development.* Toronto: Emond Montgomery.

McNally, D. 1981. "Staple Theory as Commodity Fetishism: Marx, Innis and Canadian Political Economy." *Studies in Political Economy* 6 (1): 35–63. https://doi.org/10.1080/19187033.1981.11675700.

McQuaig, L. 1991. *The Quick and the Dead: Brian Mulroney, Big Business and the Seduction of Canada.* Toronto: Penguin Books.

Mercille, J., and E. Murphy. 2018. "Market, Non-Market and Anti-Market Processes in Neoliberalism." *Critical Sociology*. https://doi.org/10.1177 %2F0896920518788391.

Mertins-Kirkwood, H. 2018. *Making Decarbonization Work for Workers: Policies for a Just Transition to a Zero-Carbon Economy in Canada*. Ottawa: Canadian Centre for Policy Alternatives.

Metzler, M. 2006. "The Cosmopolitanism of National Economics: Friedrich List in a japanese Mirror." In *Global History*, edited by A.G. Hopkins, 98–130. Basingstoke, UK: Palgrave Macmillan.

Meyers, J.S.M., and S.P. Vallas. 2016. "Diversity Regimes in Worker Cooperatives: Workplace Inequality under Conditions of Worker Control." *Sociological Quarterly* 57 (1): 98–128. https://doi.org/10.1111/tsq.12114.

Milberg, W., and D. Winkler. 2013. *Outsourcing Economics: Global Value Chains in Capitalist Development*. New York: Cambridge University Press.

Milbourne, L. 2013. *The Voluntary Sector in Transition: Hard Times or New Opportunities?* Bristol: Policy Press.

Miliband, R. 1969. *The State in Capitalist Society*. London: Quartet Books.

Milicevic, A.S. 2001. "Radical Intellectuals: What Happened to the New Urban Sociology?" *International Journal of Urban and Regional Research* 25 (4): 759–83. https://doi.org/10.1111/1468-2427.00343

Mill, J.S. 1848. *Principles of Political Economy with Some of Their Applications to Social Philosophy*. London: Longmans, Green, Reader, and Dyer.

Miller, G.R. 2012. "'Gender Trouble': Investigating Gender and Economic Democracy in Worker Cooperatives in the United States." *Review of Radical Political Economics* 44 (1): 8–22. https://doi.org/10.1177/0486613411418049.

Milligan, C., and D. Conradson. 2011. "Contemporary Landscapes of Welfare: The 'Voluntary' Turn?" In *Landscapes of Voluntarism: New Spaces of Health, Welfare and Governance*, edited by C. Milligan and D. Conradson, 1–14. Bristol: Policy Press.

Million, D. 2013. *Therapeutic Nations: Healing in an Age of Indigenous Human Rights*. Tuscon: University of Arizona Press.

Mills, C.W. 1956. *The Power Elite*. New York: Oxford University Press.

Milward, A., and S.B. Saul. 1977. *The Development of the Economies of Continental Europe 1850–1914*. London: George Allen & Unwin.

Minami, R., K. Kwan, F. Makino, and J. Seo. 1995. "Japanese Experience in Technology: A Survey." In *Acquiring, Adapting and Developing Technologies*, edited by R. Minami, K. Kwan, F. Makino, and J. Seo, 1–28. London: Macmillan.

Minsky, H.P. 1982. *Can "It" Happen Again? Essays on Instability and Finance*. New York: M.E. Sharpe.

Molk, P. 2014. "The Puzzling Lack of Cooperatives." *Tulane Law Review* 88: 899–958.

Monad, D. 1996. *Store Wars: Shopkeepers and the Culture of Mass Marketing, 1890–1939*. Toronto: University of Toronto Press.

Montgomery, D. 1979. *Workers' Control in America*. Cambridge: Cambridge University Press.

Montreal. 2017. Commission sur le développement social et la diversité montréalaise. "Montréal de tous les possibles." Online at http://ville .montreal.qc.ca/pls/portal/docs/PAGE/COMMISSIONS_PERM_V2_FR /MEDIA/DOCUMENTS/MEM_CJEIM_20170119-1.PDF.

Moody, K. 2017. *On New Terrain: How Capital Is Reshaping the Battleground of Class War*. Chicago: Haymarket.

Morck, R.K. 2010. "Shareholder Democracy in Canada." NBER Working Paper 16558. Cambridge, MA: National Bureau of Economic Research. Online at http://www.nber.org/papers/w16558.pdf, accessed 18 August 2018.

Morck, R.K., M. Percy, G.Y. Tian, and B. Yeung. 2005. "The Rise and Fall of the Widely Held Firm: A History of Corporate Ownership in Canada." In *A History of Corporate Governance Around the World*, edited by R.K. Morck, 65–147. Chicago: University of Chicago Press.

Morck, R.K., D. Strangeland, and B. Yeung. 2000. "Inherited Wealth, Corporate Control and Economic Growth: The Canadian Disease." In *Concentrated Corporate Ownership*, edited by R.K. Morck, 319–72. Cambridge, MA: National Bureau of Economic Research.

Moreno, K.A.V., J. Shields, and J. Drolet. 2018. "Settling Immigrants in Neoliberal Times: NGOs and Immigrant Well-being in Comparative Context." *Alternate Routes: A Journal of Critical Social Research* 29: 65–89.

Morison, J. 2000. "The Government–Voluntary Sector Compacts: Governance, Governmentality, and Civil Society." *Journal of Law and Society* 27 (1): 98–132. https://doi.org/10.1111/1467-6478.00148.

Morton, D. 1998. *Working People: An Illustrated History of the Canadian Labour Movement*. Montreal; Kingston, ON: McGill-Queen's University Press.

Moulton, D. 1974. "Ford Windsor 1945." In *On Strike: Six Key Labour Struggles in Canada, 1919–1949*, edited by I. Abella, 129–62. Toronto: James Lewis and Samuel.

Mowery, D., and R. Nelson, eds. 1999. *Sources of Industrial Leadership: Studies of Seven Industries*. Cambridge: Cambridge University Press.

Mulgan, R. 2007. "Truth in Government and the Politicization of Public Service Advice." *Public Administration* 85 (3): 569–86. https://doi .org/10.1111/j.1467-9299.2007.00663.x.

Murphy, B., and M. Veall. 2015. "A Tale of Two Cities? The Surge Of Top Incomes At The City Level In Canada." In *Thinking Outside the Box: Innovation in Policy Ideas*, edited by K.G. Banting, R.P. Chaykowski, and S.F. Lehrer, 347–63. Montreal; Kingston, ON: McGill-Queen's University Press.

Murphy, B., M. Veall, and M. Wolfson. 2015. "Top-End Progressivity and Federal Tax Preferences in Canada: Estimates from Personal Income Tax Data." *Canadian Tax Journal* 63 (3): 661–88.

Narvaiza, L., C. Aragon-Amonarriz, C. Iturrioz-Landart, J. Bayle-Cordier, and S. Stervinou. 2017. "Cooperative Dynamics during the Financial Crisis: Evidence from Basque and Breton Case Studies." *Nonprofit and Voluntary Sector Quarterly* 46 (3): 505–24. https://doi.org/10.1177/0899764016661775.

Naylor, R.T. 1972. "The Rise and Fall of the Third Commercial Empire of the St. Lawrence." In *Capitalism and the National Question in Canada*, edited by G. Teeple, 1–43. Toronto: University of Toronto Press.

Naylor, R.T. 1997. *The History of Canadian Business, 1867–1914*. Montreal: Black Rose.

Neamtan, N. 2010. "The Social Economy in Quebec: Towards a New Political Economy." In *Researching the Social Economy*, edited by L. Mook, J. Quarter, and S. Ryan, 63–83. Toronto: University of Toronto Press.

Neill, R. 1972. *A New Theory of Value: The Canadian Economics of H.A. Innis*. Toronto: University of Toronto Press.

Neill, R. 1991. *A History of Canadian Economic Thought*. London: Routledge.

Neill, R. 1998. "Europe in America: Veblen and His Canadian Connections." In *The Economic Mind in America*, edited by M. Rutherford, 167–89. London: Routledge.

Neill, R., and G. Paquet. 1993. "L'économie hérétique: Canadian Economics before 1967." *Canadian Journal of Economics* 26 (1): 3–13. https://doi.org/10.2307/135840.

Neilson, D., and T. Stubbs. 2016. "Competition States in the Neo-Liberal Era." *Competition and Change* 20 (2): 122–44. https://doi.org/10.1177/1024529415623917.

Nelles, H.V. 1974. *The Politics of Development: Forests, Mines and Hydro-electric Power in Ontario, 1849–1941*. Toronto: Macmillan.

Nelson, D. 1995. *Managers and Workers: The Origins of the Twentieth-Century Factory System in the United States 1880–1920*. Madison: University of Wisconsin Press.

Nelson, R. 1993. *National Innovation Systems*. New York: Oxford University Press.

Neville, K.J., and E. Weinthal. 2016. "Scaling Up Site Disputes: Strategies to Redefine 'Local' in the Fight against Fracking." *Environmental Politics* 25 (4): 569–92. https://doi.org/10.1080/09644016.2016.1154124.

Newhouse, D. 2000. "Modern Aboriginal Economies: Capitalism with a Red Face." *Journal of Aboriginal Economic Development* 1 (2): 55–61.

Newman, J., A. Cherney, and B. Head. 2017. "Policy Capacity and Evidence-based Policy in the Public Service." *Public Management Review* 19 (2): 157–74. https://doi.org/10.1080/14719037.2016.1148191.

Niosi, J. 1985. *Canadian Multinationals*. Toronto: Garamond Press.

Noël, A. 2013. "Quebec's New Politics of Redistribution." In *Inequality and the Fading of Redistributive Politics*, edited by K. Banting and J. Myles, 256–83. Vancouver: UBC Press.

Noël, A., G. Boismenu, and L. Jalbert. 1993. "The Political Foundations of State Regulation in Canada." In *Production, Space, Identity: Canadian Political Economy Faces the Twenty-First Century*, edited by R. Mahon, J. Jenson, and M. Bienefeld, 171–94. Toronto: Canadian Scholars' Press.

Norrie, K., D. Owram, and J.C. Herbert Emery. 2002. *A History of the Canadian Economy*. Toronto: Nelson.

North, P. 2011. "Geographies and Utopias of Cameron's Big Society." *Social & Cultural Geography* 12 (8): 817–27. DOI: 10.1080/14649365.2011.618889.

Nowland-Foreman, G. 1996. "Governments, Community Organisations and Civil Society – A Beginner's Guide to Dissection of a Golden Goose." *Jobs Letter*, New Zealand. Online at www.jobsletter.org.nz/art/artn0001.htm.

Oakes, G. 1997. Treaty No. 4 Elders' Forum, May 22–24, 1997, Nekaneet ReCreation Centre, Saskatchewan, personal transcripts.

O'Connor, J. 1973. *The Fiscal Crisis of the State*. New York: St Martin's Press.

Odagiri, H., and A. Goto. 1993. "The Japanese System of Innovation: Past, Present, and Future." In *National Innovation Systems: A Comparative Analysis*, edited by R. Nelson, 76–114. New York: Oxford University Press.

OECD (Organisation for Economic Co-operation and Development). 2003. *The Non-Profit Sector in a Changing Economy*. Paris: OECD.

OECD. 2011. *Divided We Stand: Why Inequality Keeps Rising*. Paris: OECD.

OECD. 2015. *In It All Together: Why Less Inequality Benefits All*. Paris: OECD.

OECD. 2018a. *Main Science and Technology Indicators*. Paris: OECD.

OECD. 2018b. *Statutory Corporate Income Tax Rate*. Paris: OECD.

Oliver, C. 2005. "The Treadmill of Production under NAFTA." *Organization & Environment* 18 (1): 55–71. https://doi.org/10.1177/1086026604270461.

Oliver, J. 1956. *History of American Technology*. New York: Ronald Press.

Ommer, R., B. Neis, and D. Brake. 2017. *Asking the Big Questions: Reflections on a Sustainable Post Oil-Dependent Newfoundland and Labrador*. St John's, NL: Royal Society Atlantic and Memorial University.

Ontario Liberal Party. 2003. *Achieving Our Potential: The Ontario Liberal Plan for Economic Growth, Book #3*. Toronto: Ontario Liberal Party.

Oosterlynck, S. 2012. "Path Dependence: A Political Economy Perspective." *International Journal of Urban and Regional Research* 36 (1): 158–65. https://doi.org/10.1111/j.1468-2427.2011.01088.x.

Osberg, L. 2008. *A Quarter Century of Economic Inequality: 1981–2006*. Ottawa: Canadian Centre for Policy Alternatives.

Osborne, D., and T. Gaebler, 1992. *Reinventing Government: How the Entrepreneurial Spirit Is Transforming the Public Sector*. Reading, MA: Addison Wesley.

O'Shaughnessy, S., and G. Doğu. 2016. "The Gendered and Racialized Subjects of Alberta's Boomtown." In *First World Petro-Politics: The Political Ecology and Governance of Alberta*, edited by L. Adkin, 263–96. Toronto: University of Toronto Press.

Ostrom, E 1990. *Governing the Commons: The Evolution of Institutions for Collective Action*. Cambridge: Cambridge University Press.

Ott, J.S., ed. 2001. *The Nature of the Nonprofit Sector*. Boulder, CO: Westview Press.

Ottawa. 2010. *Poverty Affects Us All: A Community Approach to Poverty Reduction*. Ottawa: City of Ottawa. Online at https://app06.ottawa.ca/calendar/ottawa/citycouncil/cpsc/2010/01-21/04%20-%20Poverty%20Reduction%20Strategy-eng.pdf.

Oved, M.C., T.A.A. Heaps, and M. Yow. 2017. "The high cost of low corporate taxes." *Toronto Star*, 14 December.

Oxfam. 2004. *Like Machines in the Fields: Workers without Rights in American Agriculture*. Boston: Oxfam America.

Oxfam. 2017. "An Economy for the 99%." Online at https://d1tn3vj7xz9fdh.cloudfront.net/s3fs-public/file_attachments/bp-economy-for-99-percent-160117-en.pdf, accessed 14 July 2018.

Paddison, R., and E. McCann, eds. 2014. *Cities and Social Change: Encounters with Contemporary Urbanism*. London: SAGE.

Page, B., and R. Walker. 1991. "From Settlement to Fordism: The Agro-Industrial Revolution in the American Midwest." *Economic Geography* 67 (4): 281–315. https://doi.org/10.2307/143975.

Palan, R., R. Murphy, and C. Chavagneux. 2013. *Tax Havens: How Globalization Really Works*. Ithaca, NY: Cornell University Press.

Palmer, B.D. 1979. *A Culture in Conflict: Skilled Workers and Industrial Capitalism in Hamilton, Ontario, 1860–1914*. Montreal; Kingston, ON: McGill-Queen's University Press.

Palmer, B.D. 1987a. "Labour Protest and Organization in Nineteenth-Century Canada, 1820–1890." *Labour* 20 (Fall): 61–83. https://doi.org/10.2307/25142849.

Palmer, B.D. 1987b. *Solidarity: The Rise and Fall of an Opposition in British Columbia*. Vancouver: New Star.

Palmer, B.D. 1992. *Working Class Experience: Rethinking the History of Canadian Labour, 1800–1991*. Toronto: McClelland & Stewart.

Palmer, B.D. 2003. "What's Law Got to Do with It? Historical Considerations on Class Struggle, Boundaries of Constraint, and Capitalist Authority." *Osgood Hall Law Journal* 41: 465–90. https://doi.org/10.1163/9789004243866_016.

Palmer, B.D. 2009. *Canada's 1960: The Ironies of Identity in a Rebellious Era*. Toronto: University of Toronto Press.

Panitch, L., ed. 1977a. *The Canadian State: Political Economy and Political Power*. Toronto: University of Toronto Press.

Panitch, L. 1977b. "The Role and Nature of the Capitalist State." In *The Canadian State: Political Economy and Political Power*, edited by L. Panitch, 3–27. Toronto: University of Toronto Press.

Panitch, L. 1981. "Dependency and Class in Canadian Political Economy." *Studies in Political Economy* 6 (1): 7–33. https://doi.org/10.1080/19187033.1981.11675699.

Panitch, L. 1991. "Dependency and Class in Canadian Political Economy." In *Perspectives on Canadian Economic Development*, edited by G. Laxer, 267–94. Toronto: Oxford University Press.

Panitch, L., and S. Gindin. 2012. *The Making of Global Capitalism*. London: Verso.

Panitch, L., and D. Swartz. 2003. *From Consent to Coercion: The Assault on Trade Union Freedoms*. Toronto: Garamond.

Parfitt, B. 2019. *Captured: British Columbia's Oil and Gas Commission and the Case for Reform*. Vancouver: Canadian Centre for Policy Alternatives.

Park, L., and F. Park. 1962. *Anatomy of Big Business*. Toronto: Progress Books.

Parlee, B. 2016. "Mobilizing to Address the Impacts of Oil Sands Development: First Nations in Environmental Governance." In *First World Petro-Politics: The Political Ecology and Governance of Alberta*, edited by L. Adkin, 329–55. Toronto: University of Toronto Press.

Patterson, B. 2016. "Council of Canadians Call for Fair Trade, Rejects Racism in Anti-Free Trade Arguments." Council of Canadians, 2 July Online at https://canadians.org/blog/council-canadians-calls-fair-trade-rejects-racism-anti-free-trade-arguments, accessed 19 March 2018.

Pearce, J. 2003. *Social Enterprise in Anytown*. London: Calouste Gulbenkian Foundation.

Peck, J. 2010. *Constructions of Neoliberal Reason*. Oxford: Oxford University Press.

Peck, J. 2014. "Entrepreneurial Urbanism: Between Uncommon Sense and Dull Compulsion." *Geografiska Annaler B* 96: 396–401. https://doi.org/10.1111/geob.12061.

Peck, J., and N. Theodore. 2015. *Fast Policy: Experimental Statecraft at the Thresholds of Neoliberalism*. Minneapolis: University of Minnesota Press.

Peck, J., and A. Tickell. 2002. "Neoliberalizing Space." *Antipode* 34 (3): 380–404. https://doi.org/10.1111/1467-8330.00247.

Peck, J., and A. Tickell. 2007. "Conceptualizing Neoliberalism: Thinking Thatcherism." In *Contesting Neoliberalism: Urban Frontiers*, edited by H. Leitner, J. Peck, and S. Sheppard, 26–50. New York: Guilford Press.

Peck, J., and H. Whiteside, 2016. "Financializing Detroit." *Economic Geography* 92 (3): 235–68. https://doi.org/10.1080/00130095.2015.1116369.

Pedwell, T. 2018. "Liberals table back-to-work legislation to force end to Canada Post strike." *Toronto Star*, 22 November.

Perelman, M. 2000. *The Invention of Capitalism: Classical Political Economy and the Secret History of Primitive Accumulation*. Durham, NC: Duke University Press.

Perl, A., and D.J. White. 2002. "The Changing Role of Consultants in Canadian Policy Analysis." *Policy & Society* 21 (1): 49–73. https://doi.org/10.1016/s1449-4035(02)70003-9.

Perotti, E. 2014. "The Political Economy of Finance." *Capitalism and Society* 9 (1). https://doi.org/10.2139/ssrn.2222630.

Peters, B.G. 1991. "The European Bureaucrat: The Applicability of 'Bureaucracy and Representative Government' to Non-American Settings." In *The Budget-Maximizing Bureaucrat: Appraisals and Evidence*, edited by A. Blais, and S. Dion, 303–53. Pittsburgh: University of Pittsburgh Press.

Peters. B.G., and J. Pierre. 2004. "Politicization of the Civil Service: Concepts, Causes, Consequences." In Politicization of the Civil Service in Comparative Perspective: The Quest for Control, edited by B.G. Peters, and J. Pierre, 1–13. New York: Routledge.

Peters, B.G., and V. Wright. 1996. "Public Policy and Administration, Old and New." In *A New Handbook of Political Science*, edited by R. Goodin and H.D. Klingemann, 628–41. Oxford: Oxford University Press.

Peters, J. 2011. "The Rise of Finance and the Decline of Organised Labour in the Advanced Capitalist Countries." *New Political Economy* 16 (1): 73–99. https://doi.org/10.1080/13563461003789746.

Peters, J., ed. 2012. *Boom, Bust and Crisis: Labour, Corporate Power and Politics in Canada*. Halifax, NS: Fernwood.

Phillips, P. 1979. "The National Policy Revisited." *Journal of Canadian Studies* 14 (3): 3–13. https://doi.org/10.3138/jcs.14.3.3.

Phillips, P. 1991. "New Staples and Mega-Projects: Reaching the Limits to Sustainable Development." In *The New Era of Global Competition: State Policy and Market Power*, edited by D. Drache and M. Gertler, 229–46. Montreal; Kingston, ON: McGill-Queen's University Press.

Phillips, P. 1999. "Why Were We Bombing Yugoslavia?" *Studies in Political Economy* 60 (1): 85–98.

Phillips, P. 2003. *Inside Capitalism*. Halifax, NS: Fernwood.

Phillips, S. 2007. "Policy Analysis and the Voluntary Sector: Evolving Policy Styles." In *Policy Analysis in Canada: The State of the Art*, edited by L. Dobuzinskis, M. Howlett, and D. Laycock, 497–522. Toronto: University of Toronto Press.

Phillips, S.D. 2009. "The Harper Government and the Voluntary Sector: Whither a Policy Agenda?" In *The New Federal Policy Agenda and the Voluntary Sector: On the Cutting Edge*, edited by R. Laforest, 7–34. Montreal; Kingston, ON: McGill-Queen's University Press.

Pierce, J., and K.J. Bentham. 2003. *Canadian Industrial Relations*. Toronto: Pearson.

Piketty, T. 2014. *Capital in the Twenty-First Century*. Cambridge, MA: Harvard University Press

Pineault, É. 2018. "The Capitalist Pressure to Extract: The Ecological and Political Economy of Extreme Oil in Canada." *Studies in Political Economy* 99 (2): 1–21. https://doi.org/10.1080/07078552.2018.1492063

Piven, F.F., and R. Cloward. 1977. *Poor People's Movements: Why They Succeed, How They Fail*. New York: Random House.

Piven, F.F., and R. Cloward. 1982. *The New Class War: Reagan's Attack on the Welfare State and Its Consequences*. New York: Pantheon Books.

Poelzer, G., and K.S. Coates. 2015. *From Treaty Peoples to Treaty Nation: A Road Map for All Canadians*. Vancouver: UBC Press.

Polanyi, Karl. [1944] 2001. *The Great Transformation: The Political and Economic Origins of Our Time*. Boston: Beacon Press.

Pollitt, C. 1990. *Managerialism and the Public Service: The Anglo-American Experience*. Oxford: Blackwell.

Poloz, S. 2018. "Canada's Economy and Household Debt: How Big Is the Problem?" Remarks before the Yellowknife Chamber of Commerce, Yellowknife, NT, 1 May.

Pomfret, R. 1993. *The Economic Development of Canada*. Toronto: Nelson.

Popeski, R. 2015. "Harper's tough stance on Ukraine out of step with international reality." *CBC News*, 1 October. Online at http://www.cbc.ca/news/canada/manitoba/stephen-harper-ukraine-opinion-1.3251864.

Porter, A. 2015. "Austerity, Social Program Restructuring, and the Erosion of Democracy: Examining the 2012 Employment Insurance Reforms." *Canadian Review of Social Policy* 71: 21–52.

Porter, D. 2017. *The Day After NAFTA: Economic Impact Analysis*. Toronto: Bank of Montreal.

Porter, J. 1965. *The Vertical Mosaic: An Analysis of Social Class and Power in Canada*. Toronto: University of Toronto Press.

Porter, T. 2004. *Globalization and Finance*. Malden, MA: Polity Press.

Porter, T. 2014. "Canada, the FSB, and the International Institutional Respone to the Current Crisis." In *Crisis and Reform: Canada and the International Financial System*, edited by R. Medhora and D. Rowlands, 71–86. Montreal; Kingston, ON: McGill-Queen's University Press.

Poulantzas, N. 1973. *Political Power and Social Classes*. London: New Left Books.

PEPSO (Poverty and Employment Precarity in Southern Ontario). 2013. *It's More than Poverty: Employment Precarity and Household Well-being*. Online at https://socialsciences.mcmaster.ca/pepso/documents/2013_itsmorethanpoverty_report.pdf.

Powell, M. 2007. "The Mixed Economy of Welfare and the Social Division of Welfare." In *Understanding the Mixed Economy of Welfare*, edited by M. Powell, 1–21. Bristol: Policy Press.

Preibisch, K. 2010. "Pick-Your-Own Labor: Migrant Workers and Flexibility in Canadian Agriculture." *International Migration Review* 44 (2): 404–11. https://doi.org/10.1111/j.1747-7379.2010.00811.x.

Preibisch, K., and L. Binford. 2007. "Interrogating Racialized Global Labour Supply: An Exploration of the Ethnic Replacement of Foreign Agricultural Workers in Canada." *Canadian Review of Sociology and Anthropology* 44 (1): 5–36. https://doi.org/10.1111/j.1755-618x.2007.tb01146.x.

Preibisch, K., and G. Otero. 2014. "Workplace Health and Safety for Migrant and Immigrant Laborers." *Rural Sociology* 79 (2): 174–99. https://doi.org/10.1111/ruso.12043.

Pringle, D. 2018. "The 1998 Canadian Bank Merger Decision and the 2008 Financial Crisis: Factual and Counterfactual Investigations." PhD diss., Carleton University.

Procyk, S., W. Lewchuk, and J. Shields, eds. 2017. *Precarious Employment: Causes, Consequences and Remedies*. Halifax, NS: Fernwood.

Pryke, S. 2012. "Economic Nationalism: Theory, History and Prospects." *Global Policy* 3 (3): 281–91. https://doi.org/10.1111/j.1758-5899.2011.00146.x.

Public Policy Forum. 1995. *The Public Service of Ontario and the Challenge of Restructuring: Summary of Proceedings*. 8 November. Ottawa: Public Policy Forum.

Pugliese, D. 2017. "Chrystia Freeland's granddad was indeed a Nazi collaborator: So much for Russian disinformation." *Ottawa Citizen*, 8 May. Online at https://ottawacitizen.com/news/national/defence-watch/chrystia-freelands-granddad-was-indeed-a-nazi-collaborator-so-much-for-russian-disinformation.

Purcell, M. 2002. "Excavating Lefebvre: The Right to the City and Its Urban Politics of the Inhabitant." *GeoJournal* 58 (October): 99–108. https://doi.org/10.1023/b:gejo.0000010829.62237.8f.

Putnam, R.D. 2000. "Thinking about Social Change in America." In *Bowling Alone: The Collapse and Revival of American Community*, 15–30. New York: Simon & Schuster.

Quarter, J. 1992. *Canada's Social Economy: Co-Operatives, Non-Profits and Other Community Enterprises*. Toronto: Jamers Lorimer.

Quarter, J., and L. Mook. 2010. "An Interactive View of the Social Economy." *Canadian Journal of Social Economy and Non-profit Research* 1 (1): 8–22.

Quiggin, J. 2012. *Zombie Economics: How Dead Ideas Still Walk among Us*. Princeton, NJ: Princeton University Press.

Rae, J. [1834] 1964. *Statement of Some New Principles on the Subject of Political Economy*. New York: Augustus Kelley.

Raventós, D., and J. Wark. 2018. *Against Charity*. Chico, CA: AK Press.

Rea, K.J. 1985. *The Prosperous Years: The Economic History of Ontario 1939–1975*. Toronto: University of Toronto Press.

Recollet, K. 2015. "Glyphing Decolonial Love through Urban Flash Mobbing and Walking with Our Sisters." *Curriculum Inquiry* 45 (1): 129–45. https:// doi.org/10.1080/03626784.2014.995060.

Remes, J. 2014. "A Tale of Two Mexicos: Growth and Prosperity in a Two-Speed Economy." In *NAFTA 20 Years Later*. PIIE Briefing 14-3, 30–6. Washington, DC: Peterson Institute for International Economics.

Renders, A. 2018. "Canadian corporations are suing feveloping countries for billions of dollars." *National Observer*, 10 April.

Restakis, J. 2010. *Humanizing the Economy: Co-Operatives in the Age of Capital.* Gabriola Island, BC: New Society Publishers.

Rhodes, R.A.W. 1994. "The Hollowing Out of the State: The Changing Nature of the Public Service in Britain." *Political Quarterly* 65 (2): 138–51. https:// doi.org/10.1111/j.1467-923x.1994.tb00441.x.

Rice, J.J., and Prince, M.J. 2013. *Changing Politics of Canadian Social Policy.* 2nd ed. Toronto: University of Toronto Press.

Richards, B. 2012. "Status of Co-Operatives in Canada: Report of the Special Committee on Co-Operatives." Ottawa: Government of Canada. Online at http://www.parl.gc.ca/content/hoc/Committee/411/COOP/Reports /RP5706528/cooprp01/cooprp01-e.pdf.

Richardson, J. 1992. "Free Trade: Why Did It Happen?" *Canadian Review of Sociology and Anthropology* 29 (3): 307–28.

Robbins, P. 2012. *Political Ecology: A Critical Introduction.* 2nd ed. Malden, MA: J. Wiley & Sons.

Robert, J. 1998. *In the Shadow of Empire: Canada for Americans.* New York: Monthly Review Press.

Roberts, A., and R. Kwon. 2017. "Finance, Inequality and the Varieties of Capitalism in Post-industrial Democracies." *Socio-Economic Review* 15 (3): 511–38. https://doi.org/10.1093/ser/mwx021.

Roelants, B., D. Dovgan, H. Eum, and E. Terrasi. 2012. *The Resilience of the Cooperative Model.* European Confederation of Cooperatives and Worker-Owned Enterprises Active in Industry and Services. Online at https:// www.ess-europe.eu/sites/default/files/report_cecop_2012_en_web.pdf.

Roman, R., and Velasco Arregui, E. 2013. *Continental Crucible: Big Business, Workers and Unions in the Transformation of North America.* Halifax, NS: Fernwood.

Roman, R., and Velasco Arregui, E. 2015. *Continental Crucible: Big Business, Workers and Unions in the Transformation of North America.* 2nd ed. Black Point, NS: Fernwood.

Rosenberg, N. 1976. "Karl Marx on the Economic Role of Science." *Perspectives on Technology.* New York: Cambridge University Press.

Rosenbluth, G. 1957. *Corporate Concentration in Canadian Manufacturing Industries.* Princeton, NJ: Princeton University Press.

Ross, S. 2013. "Social Unionism and Union Power in Public Sector Unions." In *Public Sector Unions in the Age of Austerity*, edited by S. Ross and L. Savage, 57–68. Halifax, NS: Fernwood.

Ross, S., L. Savage, E. Black, and J. Silver. 2015. *Building a Better World: An Introduction to the Labour Movement in Canada*. Halifax, NS: Fernwood.

Rowat, D. 1955. *Your Local Government: A Sketch of the Municipal System in Canada*. Toronto: Macmillan.

Russell, B. 1990. *Back to Work? Labour, State and Industrial Relations in Canada*. Toronto: Nelson.

Russell, E., and Dufour, M. 2016. "Why the Rising Tide Doesn't Lift All Boats: Wages and Bargaining Power in Neoliberal Canada." *Studies in Political Economy* 97 (1): 37–55. https://doi.org/10.1080/07078552.2016.1174462.

Russell, P., ed. 1966. *Nationalism in Canada*. Toronto: McGraw-Hill.

Rutherford, T., and J. Holmes. 2014. "Manufacturing Resiliency: Economic Restructuring and Automotive Manufacturing in the Great Lakes Region." *Cambridge Journal of Regions, Economy and Society* 7 (3): 359–78. https://doi.org/10.1093/cjres/rsu014.

Ryerson, S.B. 1973. *Unequal Union: Roots of Crisis in the Canadas 1815–1873*. Toronto: Progress Books.

Saez, E., and M. Veall. 2005. "The Evolution of High Incomes in Northern America: Lessons from Canadian Evidence." *American Economic Review* 95 (3): 831–49. https://doi.org/10.1257/0002828054201404.

Saint-Martin, D. 1998. "The New Managerialism and the Policy Influence of Consultants in Government: An Historical–Institutionalist Analysis of Britain, Canada and France." *Governance* 11 (3): 319–56. https://doi.org/10.1111/0952-1895.00074.

Saint-Martin, D. 1999. "The Formation of the New Entrepreneurial State and the Growth of Modern Management Consultancy." In *Public Policy and Political Ideas*, edited by D. Braun and A. Busch. Northampton, MA: Edward Elgar.

Salamon, L.M. 1995. *Partners in Public Service: Government-Non-Profit Relations in the Modern Welfare State*. Baltimore: Johns Hopkins University Press.

Salverda, W., B. Nolan, D. Checchi, I. Marx, A. McKnight, G. Toth, and H. van de Werhorst, eds. 2014. *Changing Inequalities in Rich Countries: Analytical and Comparative Perspectives*. New York: Oxford University Press.

Sancton, A., and W. Magnusson, eds. 1983. *City Politics*. Toronto: University of Toronto Press.

Sangster, J. 2004. "'We No Longer Respect the Law': The Tilco Strike, Labour Injunctions, and the State." *Labour* 53 (Spring): 47–87. https://doi.org/10.2307/25149446.

Sangster, J. 2010. *Transforming Labour: Women and Work in Post-war Canada*. Toronto: University of Toronto Press.

Sapers, H. 2016. *Annual Report of the Office of the Correctional Investigator 2015–2016*. Ottawa: Office of the Correctional Investigator. Online at http://www.oci-bec.gc.ca/cnt/rpt/annrpt/annrpt20152016-eng.aspx#s7, accessed 30 November 2018.

Sapinski, J.P. 2016. "Constructing Climate Capitalism: Corporate Power and the Global Climate Policy-Planning Network." *Global Networks* 16 (1): 89–111. https://doi.org/10.1111/glob.12099.

Sassen, S. 1991. *The Global City: New York, London, Tokyo*. Princeton, NJ: Princeton University Press.

Sassen, S. 2005. "The Global City: Introducing a Concept." *Journal of World Affairs* 11 (2): 27–43.

Savage, L., and C.W. Smith. 2017. *Unions in Court: Organized Labour and the Charter of Rights and Freedoms*. Vancouver: UBC Press.

Savoie, D.J. 1993. *Globalization and Governance*. Ottawa: Canadian Centre for Management Development.

Savoie, D.J. 1995. "Globalization, Nation States, and the Civil Service." In *Governance in a Changing Environment*, edited by G.B. Peters and D.J. Savoie, 82–112. Montreal; Kingston, ON: McGill-Queen's University Press.

Schmidt, R. 1981. "Canadian Political Economy: A Critique." *Studies in Political Economy* 6 (1): 65–92. https://doi.org/10.1080/19187033.1981.11675701.

Schwartz, R. 2017. *Toward a Trade and Indigenous People's Chapter in a Modernized NAFTA*. CIGI Papers 144. Waterloo, ON: Centre for International Governance Innovation. Online at https://www.cigionline.org/publications/moving-toward-trade-and-indigenous-peoples-chapter-modernized-nafta.

Schwartz, Z. 2018. "Is Alberta dominated by oil? Do unions run Ontario? Find out the top donors in provincial politics." *National Post*, 29 March.

Scott, K. 2005. *The World We Have: Towards a New Social Architecture*. Ottawa: Canadian Council on Social Development.

Seccareccia, M. 2012. "Financialization and the Transformation of Commercial Banking: Understanding the Recent Canadian Experience before and during the International Financial Crisis." *Journal of Post Keynesian Economics* 35 (2): 277–300. https://doi.org/10.2753/pke0160-3477350206.

Seccareccia, M. 2014. "Banking Sector Viability and Fiscal Austerity: From Rhetoric to the Reality of Bank Behavior." *Journal of Economic Issues* 48 (2): 567–74. https://doi.org/10.2753/jei0021-3624480233.

Senghaas, D. 1985. *The European Experience: A Historical Critique of Development Theory*. Leamington Spa, UK: Berg Publishers.

Sengupta, U. 2015. "Indigenous Cooperatives in Canada: The Complex Relationship between Cooperatives, Community Economic Development, Colonization, and Culture." *Journal of Entrepreneurial and Organizational Diversity* 4 (1): 121–52. https://doi.org/10.5947/jeod.2015.007.

Sewell, J. 1972. *Up Against City Hall*. Toronto: James Lewis and Samuel.

Shaffer, Edward. 1980. "Class and Oil in Alberta." In *Oil and Class Struggle*, edited by P. Nore and T. Turner, 252–71. London: Zed Press.

Sharpe, A. 2001. "Review Article on *The World Economy: A Millennial Perspective* by Angus Maddison." *International Productivity Monitor* 3 (Fall): 69–78. https://doi.org/10.1080/15357449.2002.11069142.

Shaxson, N. 2012. *Treasure Islands: Tax Havens and the Men Who Stole the World*. New York: Random House.

Shields, J. 2014. "Constructing and 'Liberating' Temporariness in the Canadian Nonprofit Sector: Neoliberalism and Nonprofit Service Providers." In *Liberating Temporariness? Migration, Work and Citizenship in and Age of Insecurity*, edited by R. Latham, V. Preston, and L. Vosko, 255–81. Montreal; Kingston, ON: McGill-Queen's University Press.

Shields, J., and B.M. Evans. 1998. *Shrinking the State: Globalization and the "Reform" of Public Administration*. Halifax, NS: Fernwood.

Shields, J., D. Baines, and I. Cunningham. 2017. "Precarious Undertakings: Serving Vulnerable Communities through Non-profits Work." In *Precarious Employment: Causes, Consequences and Remedies*, edited by S. Procyk, W. Lewchuk, and J. Shields, 31–43. Halifax, NS: Fernwood.

Shragge, E., and J.-M. Fontan, eds. 2000. *Social Economy: International Debates and Perspectives*. Montreal: Black Rose.

Shrivastava, M., and L. Stefanick, eds. 2015. *Alberta Oil and the Decline of Democracy in Canada*. Edmonton: AU Press.

Shrybman, S. 1993. "Trading Away the Environment." In *The Political Economy of North American Free Trade*, edited by R. Grinspun and M. Cameron, 271–94. New York: St Martin's Press.

Simpson, A. 2008. "From White into Red: Captivity Narratives as Alchemies of Race and Citizenship." *American Quarterly* 60 (2): 251–57. https://doi.org/10.1353/aq.0.0003.

Simpson, A. 2016. "The State Is a Man: Theresa Spence, Loretta Saunders and the Gender of Settler Sovereignty." *Theory & Event* 19 (4).

Simpson, L.B. 2017. *As We Have Always Done: Indigenous Freedom through Radical Resistance*. Minneapolis: University of Minnesota Press.

Sinclair, S. 2018a. *Canada's Track Record under NAFTA Chapter 11*. Ottawa: Canadian Centre for Policy Alternatives.

Sinclair, S. 2018b. *Saving NAFTA Chapter 19: Was It Worth It?* Ottawa: Canadian Centre for Policy Alternatives.

Sinclair, S., S. Trew, and H. Mertins-Kirkwood. 2017. "Renegotiating NAFTA: CCPA Submission to Global Affairs Canada on the Renegotiation and Modernization of the North American Free Trade Agreement (NAFTA)." Ottawa: Canadian Centre for Policy Alternatives. Online at https://www.policyalternatives.ca/publications/reports/renegotiating-nafta.

Skerrett, K., C. Roberts, J. Weststar, and S. Archer, eds. 2018. *The Contradictions of Pension Fund Capitalism*. Ithaca, NY: Cornell University Press.

Slinn, S. 2004. "An Empirical Analysis of the Effects of the Change from Card-Check to Mandatory Vote Certification." *Canadian Labour and Employment Law Journal* 11: 259–301.

Slowey, G., and L. Stefanick. 2015. "Development at What Cost? First Nations, Ecological Integrity, and Democracy." In *Alberta Oil and the Decline of Democracy in Canada*, edited by M. Shrivastava and L. Stefanick, 195–224. Edmonton: AU Press.

Smardon, B. 2014. *Asleep at the Switch*. Montreal; Kingston, ON: McGill-Queen's University Press.

Smiley, D. 1975. "Canada and the Quest for a National Policy." *Canadian Journal of Political Science* 8 (1): 40–62. https://doi.org/10.1017/s0008423900045224.

Smith, C.W. 2014. "'We Didn't Want to Totally Break the Law': Industrial Legality, the Pepsi Strike, and Workers' Collective Rights in Canada." *Labour* 74: 89–121.

Smith, C.W. 2019. "The Ghosts of Wagnerism: Organized Labour, Union Strategies, and the Charter of Rights and Freedoms." *Canadian Journal of Law and Society* 34 (1): 99–120. https://doi.org/10.1017/cls.2019.9.

Smith, C.W., and L. Savage. 2018. "Back-to-work legislation may come back to haunt Justin Trudeau." *Conversation*, 6 December. Online at http://theconversation.com/back-to-work-legislation-may-come-back-to-haunt-justin-trudeau-107779.

Smith, C.W., and A. Stevens. 2018. "The Architecture of Modern Anti-unionism in Canada: Class Struggle and the Erosion of Workers' Collective Freedoms." *Capital and Class* 42 (4): 1–28. https://doi.org/10.1177/0309816818815262.

Smith, D.E. 1989. "Feminist Reflections on Political Economy." *Studies in Political Economy* 30 (Autumn): 37–59. https://doi.org/10.1080/19187033.1989.11675506.

Smith, J. 2014. "An 'Entirely Different' Kind of Union: The Service, Office, and Retail Workers' Union of Canada (SORWUC), 1972–1986." *Labour* 73: 23–65.

Smith, S.C., and J. Rothbaum. 2013. "Cooperatives in a Global Economy: Key Economic Issues, Recent Trends, and Potential for Development." IZA Policy Paper 68. Online at https://www.econstor.eu/bitstream/10419/91777/1/pp68.pdf.

Sobering, K. 2016. "Producing and Reducitng Gender Inequality in a Worker-Recovered Co-Operative." *Sociological Quarterly* 57 (1): 129–51. https://doi.org/10.1111/tsq.12112.

Speers, K. 2007. "The Invisible Public Service: Consultants and Public Policy in Canada." In *Policy Analysis in Canada: The State of the Art*, edited by L.

Dobuzinskis, M. Howlett, and D. Laycock, 220–31. Toronto: University of Toronto Press.

Stam, L. 2018. "Everything You Ever Wanted to Know about Bill 148 but Were Too Afraid to Ask." *Employment & Human Rights Law in Canada*, 30 May. Online at https://www.canadaemploymenthumanrightslaw.com/2018/05/everything-ever-wanted-know-bill-148-afraid-ask/.

Standing, G. 2011. *The Precariat: The New Dangerous Class*. New York: Bloomsbury Academic.

Standing, G. 2016. *The Corruption of Capitalism: Why Rentiers Thrive and Work Does Not Pay*. London: Biteback.

Stanford, J. 1993 "Investment." In *Canada under Free Trade*, edited by D. Cameron and M. Watkins, 151–72. Toronto: James Lorimer.

Stanford, J. 1999. *Paper Boom: Why Real Prosperity Requires a New Approach to Canada's Economy*. Ottawa: Canadian Centre for Policy Alternatives.

Stanford, J. 2008. "Staples, Deindustrialization, and Foreign Investment: Canada's Economic Journey Back to the Future." Studies in Political Economy 82 (1): 7–34. https://doi.org/10.1080/19187033.2008.11675062.

Stanford, J. 2010. "The Geography of Auto Globalization and the Politics of Auto Bailouts." *Cambridge Journal of Regions, Economy and Society* 3 (3): 383–405. https://doi.org/10.1093/cjres/rsq025.

Stanford, J. 2011. "Having Their Cake and Eating It Too: Business Profits, Taxes, and Investment in Canada – 1961 through 2010." Ottawa: Canadian Centre for Policy Alternatives.

Stanwick, H. 2000. "A Megamayor for All People? Voting Behaviour and Electoral Success in the 1997 Toronto Municipal Election." *Canadian Journal of Political Science* 33 (3): 549–68. https://doi.org/10.1017/s0008423900000196.

Stapleton, J. 2019. *The Working Poor in the Toronto Region*. Toronto: Metcalf Foundation.

Starblanket, G. 2017. "Being Indigenous Feminists: Resurgences against Contemporary Patriarchy." In *Making Space for Indigenous Feminism*. 2nd ed., edited by J. Green. Halifax, NS: Fernwood.

Starblanket, G. 2019. "The Numbered Treaties and the Politics of Incoherency." *Canadian Journal of Political Science* 52 (3): 443–59. https://doi.org/10.1017/S0008423919000027.

Starblanket, G., and H. Stark. 2018. "Towards a Relational Paradigm – Four Points for Consideration: Knowledge, Gender, Land, and Modernity." In *Resurgence and Reconciliation: Indigenous-Settler Relations and Earth Teachings*, edited by J. Tully, J. Borrows, and M. Asch, 175–208. Toronto: University of Toronto Press.

Stark, H.K. 2012. "Marked by Fire: Anishinaabe Articulations of Nationhood in Treaty Making with the United States and Canada." *American Indian Quarterly*, 36 (2): 119–49. https://doi.org/10.5250/amerindiquar.36.2.0119.

Stark, H.K. 2017. "Changing the Treaty Question: Remedying the Right(s) Relationship." In *The Right Relationship: Reimagining the Implementation of Historical Treaties*, edited by J. Borrows and M. Coyle, 248–76. Toronto: University of Toronto Press.

Stasiulis, D. 1997. "The Political Economy of Race, Ethnicity and Migration." In *Understanding Canada: Building on the New Canadian Political Economy*, edited by W. Clement, 141–71. Montreal; Kingston, ON: McGill-Queen's University Press.

Statistics Canada. 1973. *Quarterly Estimates of the Canadian Balance of International Payments*. Third Quarter. Ottawa.

Statistics Canada. 1991. *Science Statistics* 15 (3). Ottawa.

Statistics Canada. 2018. "The Fall and Rise of Canada's Top Income Earners." *Canadian MegaTrends*. Ottawa. Online at https://www.statcan.gc.ca /pub/11-630-x/11-630-x2016009-eng.htm, accessed 21 April 2018.

Statistics Canada. 2019. "Non-profit Institutions and Volunteering: Economic Contribution, 2007–2017." *Daily*, 5 March.

Steedman, M. 1986. "Skill and Gender in the Canadian Clothing Industry, 1890–1940." In *On the Job: Confronting the Labour Process in Canada*, edited by C. Heron and R. Storey, 152–76. Montreal; Kingston, ON: McGill-Queen's University Press.

Stephens, H. 2018. "USMCA's fine print giving US the right to veto." *Globe and Mail*, 2 October.

Stevenson, G. 1977. "Federalism and the Political Economy of the Canadian State." In *The Canadian State: Political Economy and Political Power*, edited by L. Panitch, 71–100. Toronto: University of Toronto Press.

Stewart, W. 1977. *Strike!* Toronto: McClelland and Stewart.

Stewart-Harawira, M. 2005. *The New Imperial Order: Indigenous Responses to Globalization*. London: Zed Books.

Stewart-Harawira, M. 2013. "Challenging Knowledge Capitalism: Indigenous research in the 21st Century." *Socialist Studies* 9 (1): 39–51. https://doi .org/10.18740/s43s3v.

Stiglitz, J.E. 2013. *The Price of Inequality: How Today's Divided Society Endangers Our Future*. New York: W.W. Norton.

Stoker, G., and M. Evans. 2016. "Evidence-based Policy Making and Social Science." In *Evidence-based Policy Making in the Social Sciences: Methods that Matter*, edited by G. Stoker, and M. Evans, 15–28. Bristol: Policy Press.

Storper, M. 2016. "The Neo-liberal City as Idea and Reality." *Territory, Politics, Governance* 4 (2): 241–63. https://doi.org/10.1080/21622671.2016.1158662.

Streeck, W. 2014. *Buying Time: The Delayed Crisis of Democratic Capitalism*. New York: Verso.

Sullivan, H. 2009. "Social Capital." In *Theories of Urban Politics*. 2nd ed., edited by J. Davies and D.L. Imbroscio, 221–38. Los Angeles: SAGE.

Suzack, C., S.M. Huhndorf, J. Perreault, and J. Barman, eds. 2011. *Indigenous Women and Feminism: Politics, Activism, Culture.* Vancouver: UBC Press.

Swartz, D., and R. Warskett. 2012. "Canadian Labour and the Crisis of Solidarity." In *Rethinking the Politics of Labour,* edited by S. Ross, and L. Savage, 18–32. Halifax, NS: Fernwood.

Swift, R., ed. 2013. *The Great Revenue Robbery.* Toronto: Between the Lines.

Szreter, S., and A. Ishkanian. 2012. "Introduction: What Is Big Society? Contemporary Social Policy in a Historical and Comparative Perspective." In *The Big Society Debate: A New Agenda for Social Welfare?* edited by S. Szreter, and A. Ishkanian, 1–24.Cheltenham, UK: Edward Elgar.

Tabb, W.K. 1982. *The Long Default: New York City and the Urban Fiscal Crisis.* New York: Monthly Review Press.

Taft, K. 2017. *Oil's Deep State.* Toronto: James Lorimer.

Task Force on the Structure of Canadian Industry. 1968. *Foreign Ownership and the Structure of Canadian Industry.* Ottawa: Supply and Services Canada.

Taylor, D.W. 1991. *Business and Government Relations.* Toronto: Gage.

Taylor, M. 2002. "Government, the Third Sector and the Contract Culture: The UK Experience So Far." In *Dilemmas of the Welfare Mix: The New Structure of Welfare in an Era of Privatization,* edited by U. Ascoli, and C. Ranci, 77–108. New York: Kluwer Academic /Plenum.

Teeple, G., ed. 1972. *Capitalism and the National Question in Canada.* Toronto: University of Toronto Press.

Tester, F. 1991. "Canada and the Global Crisis in Resource Development." In *The New Era of Global Competition: State Policy and Market Power,* edited by D. Drache and M. Gertler, 399–414. Montreal; Kingston, ON: McGill-Queen's University Press.

Tester, F., and Kulchyski, P. 2011. *Tammarniit (mistakes): Inuit Relocation in the Eastern Arctic, 1939–63.* Vancouver: UBC Press.

Thomas, K. 2015. *Dollars, Democracy and Disclosure: Should Investors Demand Better Disclosure from Canadian Corporations on Political Spending?* Vancouver: Shareholder Association for Research & Education.

Thomas, M. 2009. *Regulating Flexibility: The Political Economy of Employment Standards.* Montreal; Kingston, ON: McGill-Queen's University Press.

Thomas, M., L. Vosko, O. Lyubchenko, and C. Fanelli, eds. 2019. *New Canadian Political Economy.* Montreal; Kingston, ON: McGill-Queen's University Press.

Thompson, J.A. 2014. *Making North America: Trade, Security, and Integration.* Toronto: University of Toronto Press.

Thompson, S., M. Rony, J. Temmer, and D. Wood. 2014. "Pulling in the Indigenous Fishery Cooperative Net: Fishing for Sustainable Livelihoods and Food Security in Garden Hill First Nation, Manitoba, Canada." *Journal of Agriculture, Food Systems, and Community Development* 4 (43): 177–92. https://doi.org/10.5304/jafscd.2014.043.016.

Thorns, D.C. 2002. *The Transformation of Cities: Urban Theory and Urban Life.* London: Palgrave Macmillan.

Toennies, F. 1956. *Community and Society.* East Lansing: Michigan State University Press

Tomas, A. 2006. "Recent Trends in Corporate Finance Some Evidence from the Canadian System of National Accounts." Ottawa: Statistics Canada.

Tomlins, C. 1985. "The New Deal, Collective Bargaining, and the Triumph of Industrial Pluralism." *Industrial and Labor Relations Review* 39 (1): 19–34. https://doi.org/10.2307/2523535.

Toronto. 2015. *TO Prosperity: Toronto Poverty Reduction Strategy.* Toronto: City of Toronto. Online at https://www.toronto.ca/city-government /accountability-operations-customer-service/long-term-vision-plans -and-strategies/poverty-reduction-strategy/.

Toronto. 2017. *Report for Action: TO Prosperity: Toronto Poverty Reduction Strategy.* Toronto: City of Toronto. Online at https://www.toronto.ca /legdocs/mmis/2016/ex/bgrd/backgroundfile-98561.pdf.

Toronto Foundation. 2017. *Vital Signs.* Online at https://torontofoundation. ca/wp-content/uploads/2018/01/TF-VS-web-FINAL-4MB.pdf.

Traves, T. 1979. *The State and Enterprise: Canadian Manufacturers and the Federal Government 1917–1931.* Toronto: University of Toronto Press.

Trotsky, L. [1906/1930] 1962. *The Permanent Revolution and Results and Prospects.* London: Labor.

Truth and Reconciliation Commission. 2015. *Canada's Residential Schools: Reconciliation. The Final Report of the Truth and Reconciliation Committee of Canada.* Montreal; Kingston, ON: McGill-Queen's University Press.

Tucker, E. 1991. "That Indefinite Area of Toleration": Criminal Conspiracy and Trade Unions in Ontario, 1837–77." *Labour* 27: 15–54. https://doi .org/10.2307/25130244.

Tucker, E. 2014. "Shall Wagnerism Have No Domain?" *Just Labour: Canadian Journal of Work and Society* 21 (Spring): 1–27. https://doi .org/10.25071/1705-1436.11.

UFCW Canada. 2011. *UFCW Canada Report on the Status of Migrant Farm Workers in Canada, 2010–2011: UFCW Canada and the Agricultural Workers Alliance.* Online at http://www.ufcw.ca/templates/ufcwcanada/images /awa/publications/UFCW-Status_of_MF_Workers_2010-2011_EN.pdf, accessed 22 September 2014.

Unifor. 2014. "Imagining a Fair Trade Future." Unifor Discussion Paper. Vancouver: Unifor, Canadian Council, Research Department. Online at https://www.unifor.org/en/take-action/campaigns/peoples -trade?v=take_action, accessed 6 April 2018.

United Kingdom. 1990. *Seeking Help from Management Consultants*. London: Her Majesty's Treasury.

United States. 2016. Department of State. *Treaties in Force : A List of Treaties and Other International Agreements of the United States in Force on January 1, 2016*. Washington, DC.

United States. 2017a. Congressional Budget Office "International Comparisons of Corporate Income Tax Rates." Washington, DC. Online at https://www.cbo.gov/system/files/115th-congress-2017-2018/reports/52419 -internationaltaxratecomp.pdf, accessed 2 August 2018.

United States. 2017b. Office of Management and Budget. *2017 Draft Report to Congress on the Benefits and Costs of Federal Regulations and Agency Compliance with the Unfunded Mandates Reform Act*. Online at https://www.whitehouse.gov/wp-content/uploads/2017/12/draft_2017_cost _benefit_report.pdf.

United Way of Greater Toronto. 2002. *A Decade of Decline: Poverty and Income Inequality in the City of Toronto in the 1990s*. Toronto: UWGTA.

Urquhart, I. 2018. *Costly Fix: Power, Politics, and Nature in the Tar Sands*. Toronto: University of Toronto Press.

Useem, M. 1984. *The Inner Circle: Large Corporations and the Rise of Business Political Activity in the U.S. and the U.K.* New York: Oxford University Press.

Vaillancourt, Y., F. Aubry, C. Jetté, and L. Tremblay. 2002. "Regulation Based on Solidarity: A Fragile Emergence in Quebec". In *Social Economy: Health and Welfare in Four Canadian Provinces*, edited by Y. Vaillancourt, and L. Tremblay, 29–69. Halifax, NS: Fernwood.

Vancouver. 2015. "A Healthy City for All: Healthy City Strategy – Four Year Action Plan, 2015–2018, Phase 2." Online at https://vancouver.ca/files /cov/Healthy-City-Strategy-Phase-2-Action-Plan-2015-2018.pdf.

van der Zwan, N. 2014. "Making Sense of Financialization." *Socio-Economic Review* 12 (1): 99–129. https://doi.org/10.1093/ser/mwt020.

Veall, M.R. 2012. "Top Income Shares in Canada: Recent Trends and Policy Implications." *Canadian Journal of Economics* 45 (4): 1247–72. https://doi .org/10.1111/j.1540-5982.2012.01744.x.

Vieta, M., and F. Duguid. 2020. "Canada's co-operatives: Helping communities after the coronavirus," *Conversation*, 19 April. Online at https://theconversation.com/canadas-co-operatives-helping-communities -during-and-after-the-coronavirus-135477, accessed 10 May 2020.

Vieta, M., J. Quarter, and A. Moskovskaya. 2016. "Participation in Worker Cooperatives." In *The Palgrave Handbook of Volunteering, Civic Participation, and Nonprofit Associations*, 436–53. https://doi.org/https://doi.org /10.1007/978-1-137-26317-9_21.

Villarreal, M.A., and Fergusson, I.F. 2014.*NAFTA at 20: Overview and Trade Effects*. Washington, DC: Congressional Research Service.

Online at http://digitalcommons.ilr.cornell.edu/cgi/viewcontent
.cgi?article=2272&context=key_workplace.

Vitali, S., J.B. Glattfelder, and S. Battiston. 2011. "The Network of Global
Corporate Control." *PLOS ONE* 6 (10): e25995. https://doi.org/10.1371
/journal.pone.0025995.

Vogt, R. 1999. *Whose Property?* Toronto: University of Toronto Press.

Volscho, T.W., and N.J. Kelly. 2012. "The Rise of the Super-Rich: Power
Resources, Taxes, Financial Markets, and the Dynamics of the Top
1 Percent, 1949 to 2008." *American Sociological Review* 77 (5): 679–99.
https://doi.org/10.1177/0003122412458508.

Vosko, L. 2000. Temporary Work: The Gendered Rise of a Precarious
Employment Relationship. Toronto: University of Toronto Press.

Vosko, L. 2002. "The Pasts (and Futures) of Feminist Political Economy in
Canada: Reviving the Debate." *Studies in Political Economy* 68 (1): 55–83.
https://doi.org/10.1080/19187033.2002.11675191.

Vosko, L. 2006a. "Precarious Employment: Towards an Improved
Understanding of Labour Market Insecurity." In *Precarious Employment:
Understanding Labour Market Insecurity in Canada*, edited by L. Vosko, 3–39.
Montreal; Kingston, ON: McGill-Queen's University Press.

Vosko, L., ed. 2006b. *Precarious Employment: Understanding Labour Market
Insecurity in Canada*. Montreal; Kingston, ON: McGill Queen's University
Press.

Vosko, L. 2013. "'Rights without Remedies': Enforcing Employment
Standards in Ontario by Maximizing Voice among Workers in Precarious
Jobs." *Osgoode Hall Law Journal* 50 (4): 845–74.

Vosko, L., J. Grundy, and M.P. Thomas, 2016. "Challenging New Governance:
Evaluating New Approaches to Employment Standards Enforcement in
Common Law Jurisdictions." *Economic and Industrial Democracy* 37 (2):
373–98. https://doi.org/10.1177/0143831x14546237.

Vosko, L, J. Grundy, E. Tucker, M.P. Thomas, A.M. Noack, R. Casey, M.
Gellatly, and J. Mussell. 2017. "The Compliance Model of Employment
Standards Enforcement: An Evidence-based Assessment of Its Efficacy in
Instances of Wage Theft." *Industrial Relations Journal* 48 (3): 256–73. https://
doi.org/10.1111/irj.12178.

Vosko, L., and M. Thomas. 2014. "Confronting the Employment Standards
Enforcement Gap: Exploring the Potential for Union Engagement with
Employment Law in Ontario, Canada." *Journal of Industrial Relations* 56 (5):
631–52. https://doi.org/10.1177/0022185613511562.

Waldinger, R., and M. Bozorgmehr, eds. 1996. *Ethnic Los Angeles*. New York:
Russell Sage Foundation.

Walkom, T. 2018. "Why did Canada expel four Russian diplomats? Because
they told the truth." *Toronto Star*, 5 April. Online at https://www.thestar

.com/opinion/star-columnists/2018/04/05/why-did-canada-expel-four
-russian-diplomats-because-they-told-the-truth.html.

Wallace, I., and R. Shields. 1997. "Contested Terrains: Social Space and the Canadian Environment." In *Understanding Canada: Building on the New Canadian Political Economy*, edited by W. Clement, 386–408. Montreal; Kingston, ON: McGill-Queen's University Press.

Wallis, M.A., and S.M. Kwok, eds. 2008. *Daily Struggles: The Deepening Racialization and Feminization of Poverty in Canada*. Toronto: Canadian Scholars' Press.

Wallis, M.A., L. Sunseri, and G.-E. Galabuzi. 2010. *Colonialism and Racism in Canada: Historical Traces and Contemporary Issues*. Toronto: Nelson.

Walmsley, T., and P. Minor. 2017. *Reversing NAFTA: A Supply Chain Perspective*. Boulder, CO: ImpactECON.

Walton, J. 1993. "Urban Sociology: The Contribution and Limits of Political Economy." *Annual Review of Sociology* 19: 301–20. https://doi.org/10.1146 /annurev.so.19.080193.001505.

Waring, M. 1990. *If Women Counted: A New Feminist Economics*. San Francisco: Harper.

Warnock, J. 2004. *Saskatchewan: The Roots of Discontent and Protest*. Montreal: Black Rose.

Watkins, M. 1963. "A Staple Theory of Economic Growth." *Canadian Journal of Economics and Political Science* 29 (2): 141–58. https://doi .org/10.2307/139461.

Watkins, M. 1978. "The Economics of Nationalism and the Nationality of Economics." *Canadian Journal of Economics* 11: S87–120. https://doi .org/10.2307/134515.

Watkins, M. 1981. "The Staples Theory Revisited." In *Culture, Communication, and Dependency: The Tradition of H.A. Innis*, edited by W. Melody, L. Salter, and P. Heyer. Norwood, NJ: Ablex.

Watkins, M. 1982. "The Innis Tradition in Canadian Political Economy." *Canadian Journal of Political and Social Theory* 6 (1–2): 12–34.

Watkins, M. 1989. "The Political Economy of Growth." In New Canadian Political Economy, edited by W. Clement and G. Williams, 16–35. Montreal; Kingston, ON: McGill-Queen's University Press.

Watkins, M. 1997. "Introduction to the 1997 Edition." *History of Canadian Business, 1867–1914*. Montreal: Black Rose.

Watkins, M. 2006. "Forward to the Carleton Library Edition," vol. 1, *The History of Canadian Business, 1867–1914*. Montreal; Kingston, ON: McGill-Queen's University Press.

Watson, A. 2006. *Marginal Man: The Dark Vision of Harold Innis*. Toronto: University of Toronto Press.

Weber, M. [1905] 2009. *The Protestant Ethic and the Spirit of Capitalism*. New York: W.W. Norton.

Weil, D. 2014. *The Fissured Workplace: Why Work Became So Bad for So Many and What Can Be Done to Improve It*. Cambridge, MA: Harvard University Press.

Weisbrot, M., L. Merling, V. Mello, S. Lefebvre, and J. Sammut. 2017. *Did NAFTA Help Mexico? An Update After 23 Years*. Washington, DC: Center for Economic and Policy Research.

Wekerle, G.R. 2010. "Gender and the Neoliberal City: Urban Restructuring, Social Exclusion and Democratic Participation." In *Urban Canada*. 2nd ed., edited by H. Hiller, 211–33. Toronto: Oxford University Press.

Whitaker, R. 1977. "Images of the State in Canada." In *The Canadian State*, edited by L. Panitch, 28–71. Toronto: University of Toronto Press.

White, G. 1997. "Transition: The Tories Take Power." In *Revolution at Queen's Park: Essays on Governing Ontario*, edited by S. Noel. Toronto: James Lorimer.

White, G. 2001. "Adapting the Westminster Model: Provincial and Territorial Cabinets in Canada." *Public Money and Management* 21 (2): 17–24. https://doi.org/10.1111/1467-9302.00255.

White, L.A. 2017. *Constructing Policy Change: Early Childhood Education and Care in Liberal Welfare States*. Toronto: University of Toronto Press.

White, K. 2018. "A Brief Survey of Indigenous Co-ops in Canada." Co-operatives First. https://cooperativesfirst.com/blog/2018/07/20/context-and-opportunity-a-brief-survey-of-indigenous-co-ops-in-canada/.

Whiteside, H. 2009. "Canada's Health Care 'Crisis': Accumulation through Dispossession and the Neoliberal Fix." *Studies in Political Economy* 84 (1): 79–100. https://doi.org/10.1080/19187033.2009.11675047.

Whiteside, H. 2012. "Crises of Capital and the Logic of Dispossession and Repossession." *Studies in Political Economy*. 89 (1): 59–78. https://doi.org/10.1080/19187033.2012.11675001.

Whiteside, H. 2015. *Purchase for Profit: Public-Private Partnerships and Canada's Public Health Care System*. Toronto: University of Toronto Press.

Whiteside, H. 2016. *About Canada: Public-Private Partnerships*. Halifax, NS: Fernwood.

Whiteside, H. 2017a. "The Canada Infrastructure Bank: Private Finance as Poor 'Alternative.'" *Studies in Political Economy* 98 (2): 223–37. https://doi.org/10.1080/07078552.2017.1343008.

Whiteside, H. 2017b. "The State's Estate: Devaluing and Revaluing 'Surplus' Public Land in Canada." *Environment & Planning A*, 2 August. Online at http://journals.sagepub.com/doi/10.1177/0308518X17723631.

Whiteside, H. 2018a. "Austerity as Epiphenomenon? Public Assets Before and Beyond 2008." *Cambridge Journal of Regions, Economy and Society* 11 (3): 409–25. https://doi.org/10.1093/cjres/rsy022.

Whiteside, H. 2018b. "Public Works: Better, Cheaper, Faster Infrastructure." *Studies in Political Economy* 99 (1): 2–19. https://doi.org/10.1080/07078552.2 018.1440988.

Whittington, L. 2012. "Jim Flaherty and Mark Carney take on corporate Canada." *Toronto Star*, 28 August.

Wiebe, S.M. 2016. *Everyday Exposure: Indigenous Mobilization and Environmental Justice in Canada's Chemical Valley*. Vancouver: UBC Press.

Wilkins, M. 1970. *The Emergence of Multinational Enterprise*. Cambridge, MA: Harvard University Press.

Wilkins, M. 1988. "European and North American Multinationals, 1870–1914: Comparisons and Contrasts." In *The End of Insularity: Essays in Comparative Business History*, edited by R.P.T. Davenport-Hines and G. Jones. London: Frank Cass.

Williams, G. 1992. "Greening the New Canadian Political Economy." *Studies in Political Economy* 37 (1): 5–30. https://doi.org/10.1080/19187033.1992.1167 5432.

Williams, G. 1994. *Not for Export*. Toronto: McClelland and Stewart.

Wilson, A. 2008. "N'tacinowin inna nah': Our Coming in Stories." *Canadian Woman Studies* 26 (3): 193–9.

Wilson, E., and A. Doing. 1996. "The Shape of Ideology: Structure, Culture and Policy Delivery in the New Public Sector." *Public Money and Management* 16 (2): 53–61. https://doi.org/10.1080/09540969609387921.

Wilson, S. 2018. "Feminist Energy Futures." Online at http://feministenergyfutures.ca/.

Wolfe, D. 2018. *Creating Digital Opportunity for Canada*. Toronto: Brookfield Institute for Innovation + Entrepreneurship and Innovation Policy Lab, Munk School of Global Affairs.

Wolfe, P. 2006. "Settler Colonialism and the Elimination of the Native." *Journal of Genocide Research* 8 (4): 387–409. https://doi.org/10.1080/14623520601056240.

Wolfson, M., M. Veall, N. Brooks, and B. Murphy. 2016. "Piercing the Veil: Private Corporations and the Income of the Affluent." *Canadian Tax Journal* 64 (1): 1–30.

Wood, E.M. 2002. *The Origin of Capitalism: A Longer View*. London: Verso.

Woods, H.D. 1955. "Canadian Collective Bargaining and Dispute Settlement Policy: An Appraisal." *Canadian Journal of Economics and Political Science* 21 (4): 447–65. https://doi.org/10.2307/138124.

World Bank. 2016. "Foreign Direct Investment, Net Inflows." Online at https://data.worldbank.org/indicator/BX.KLT.DINV.CD.WD.

Wray, L.R. 2012. "Imbalances? What Imbalances? A Dissenting View." Working Paper Series. Annandale-on-Hudson, NY: Levy Economics Institute of Bard College.

Wright, E.O. 2010. *Envisioning Real Utopias*. London: Verso.

Wuttunee, W. 2010. "Aboriginal Perspectives on the Social Economy." In *Living Economics: Canadian Perspectives on the Social Economy*, edited by J.J. McMurtry. Toronto: Emond Montgomery.

Yalnizyan, A. 2010. *The Rise of Canada's Richest 1%*. Ottawa: Canadian Centre for Policy Alternatives.

Young, R., and C. Leuprecht. 2006. *Canada: The State of the Federation 2004: Municipal-Federal-Provincial Relations in Canada*. Montreal; Kingston, ON: McGill-Queen's University Press.

Zhang, B. 2018. "Bombardier scores shocking victory over Boeing in trade dispute involving Delta jets." *Bloomberg*, 26 January. Online at http://www.businessinsider.com/itc-vote-us-government-bombardier-delta-over-boeing-2018-1.

Zini, S. 2016. *Exporter le New Deal: les normes du travail dans la politique commerciale des États-Unis*. Quebec City: Presses de l'Université du Québec.

Zucman, G. 2015. *The Hidden Wealth of Nations: The Scourge of Tax Havens*. Chicago: University of Chicago Press.

Zukin, S. 1995. *The Cultures of Cities*. Cambridge, MA: Blackwell.

Zukin, S. 2009. *Naked City: The Death and Life of Authentic Urban Places*. London: Oxford University Press.

Contributors

Jamie Brownlee obtained his PhD in sociology and political economy from Carleton University, where he currently teaches and conducts research in the areas of Canadian and international political economy, higher education, corporate crime, environmental politics and climate change, and access to information law. He is the author of *Ruling Canada: Corporate Cohesion and Democracy* (2005) and *Academia, Inc.: How Corporatization Is Transforming Canadian Universities* (2015). He is also co-editor of *Corporatizing Canada: Making Business Out of Public Service* (2018) and *Access to Information and Social Justice: Critical Research Strategies for Journalists, Scholars, and Activists* (2015).

Angela V. Carter is an Associate Professor in the Department of Political Science at the University of Waterloo. She has researched environmental policy regimes surrounding oil extraction in Canada's primary oil-producing provinces (Alberta, Newfoundland and Labrador, and Saskatchewan). Her recent publications focus on government policy approaches and social movement opposition to fracking and on variations in provincial oil sector emissions policies. She is now extending this work in an international comparative project on supply-side climate policy, focused on the conditions necessary to wind down fossil fuel extraction in developed-world states.

Elaine Coburn is in the Department of International Studies at the bilingual Glendon campus of York University and cross-appointed to the graduate program in Gender, Feminist and Women's Studies. She is the editor of *More Will Sing Their Way to Freedom: Indigenous Resistance and Resurgence*. Her work is concerned with unjust inequalities and efforts to challenge these, especially through critical engagement with Indigenous, antiracist, and feminist historical materialist perspectives. Recently, she returned to work on international financial institutions, seeking to understand gender mainstreaming at the International Monetary Fund.

Bryan Evans is Professor, Department of Politics and Public Administration, Ryerson University. His most recent publications include *The Public Sector in an Age of Austerity* (with Carlo Fanelli, co-editor, 2018); *Austerity: The Lived Experience* (2017); *The Austerity State* (with Stephen McBride, co-editor, 2017); and *The End of Expansion? The Political Economy of Canadian Provinces and Territories in a Neo-liberal Era* (with Charles Smith, co-editor). Prior to his appointment at Ryerson University in 2003, he worked as a policy advisor and senior manager at the Ontario Legislative Assembly and later with the Ontario Public Service.

Carlo Fanelli is Assistant Professor and Coordinator of Work and Labour Studies in the Department of Social Science at York University. He is the author of *Megacity Malaise: Neoliberalism, Public Services and Labour in Toronto*, and co-editor (with Bryan Evans) of *The Public Sector in an Age of Austerity: Perspectives from Canada's Provinces and Territories*.

Gavin Fridell is a Canada Research Chair in International Development Studies at Saint Mary's University and a member of the Advisory Council of the Canadian Fair Trade Network. He has published three books and numerous articles on fair trade and free trade, drawing on research on coffee in Mexico and fruit in St Vincent and the Grenadines. He holds a PhD in political science from York University, and in 2015 was inducted as a member of the College of New Scholars of the Royal Society of Canada.

Peter Graefe teaches in the Department of Political Science at McMaster University. His research interests include economic and social development policies in Quebec, social assistance policy in Ontario, and intergovernmental relations in Canadian social policy.

Eric Helleiner is a Professor in the Department of Political Science and Balsillie School of International Affairs at the University of Waterloo. His latest books include *Forgotten Foundations of Bretton Woods* (Cornell University Press, 2014) and *The Status Quo Crisis* (Oxford University Press, 2014), as well as the co-edited volume *Governing the World's Biggest Market* (with Stefano Pagliari and Irene Spagna, Oxford University Press, 2018). He is currently researching a global history of ideologies about the world economy.

Carol-Anne Hudson is a PhD Candidate in Political Science at McMaster University. Her research and publications focus on social policies related to poverty reduction, income inequality, and community breakdown.

Meghan Joy is an Assistant Professor in the Department of Political Science at Concordia University. Her research explores the politics of population aging, theories and practice of progressive politics and policy in cities, and the political economy of the non-profit sector.

Julie L. MacArthur is a Senior Lecturer in Politics and International Relations and the Master of Public Policy program at the University of Auckland, where she teaches public policy and environmental politics. She is the author of *Empowering Electricity: Co-operatives, Sustainability and Power Sector Reform in Canada* (UBC Press, 2016), as well as numerous articles and book chapters on sustainable community development, participatory governance, and comparative energy policy. She is also a research associate with the University of Auckland's Energy Centre, Public Policy Institute, and was the coordinator of the New Zealand Politics Association's Environmental Politics and Policy Network from 2014 to 2018.

Stephen McBride is Professor of Political Science and Canada Research Chair in Public Policy and Globalization at McMaster University. His current research focuses on the politics of austerity and on the decline of democracy. He is the author or editor of several books dealing with issues of international and Canadian political economy. Recent titles include *Working? Employment Policy in Canada* (Rock's Mills Press, 2017) and two volumes on austerity, both co-edited with Bryan Evans, *The Austerity State* (University of Toronto Press, 2017) and *Austerity: The Lived Experience* (University of Toronto Press, 2017).

John Peters is an Associate Professor of Labour Studies at Laurentian University. His research focuses on economic globalization, inequality, and labour market deregulation. He has recently completed a manuscript entitled *Jobs with Inequality: Financialization, Post-Democracy, and Labour Market Deregulation in Canada* (under review, University of Toronto Press) and is currently examining the impacts of austerity as well as the policies required to improve jobs and employment.

David Pringle is an Ottawa-based economist, having worked for more than ten years in the federal Department of Finance and Statistics Canada. From 2014 to 2018, he served as the chair of the Progressive Economics Forum. In 2018, he defended his doctorate on Canada's banking system at Carleton University 's School of Public Policy and

Administration. His principal areas of research are the political economy of Canadian finance and regulatory and governance issues in Canadian public administration.

Mario Seccareccia is currently Professor Emeritus of Economics at the University of Ottawa, where he taught for forty years, from 1978 to 2018. Between 1988 and 2006, he also taught at the Labour College of Canada. He has authored or edited over a dozen books and monographs, published over one hundred academic articles in scientific-refereed journals or chapters of books, and edited or co-edited over forty special issues of scientific journals in economics. He has also been editor of the *International Journal of Political Economy* since 2002. His principal areas of research are monetary economics and macroeconomics, the history of economic thought and methodology, labour economics, and Canadian economic history.

John Shields is a Professor in the Department of Politics and Public Administration at Ryerson University. His recent research has examined precarious employment, the public policy of immigration and settlement, the politics of social impact bonds, and critical non-profit sector studies. His most recent volumes are *Precarious: Causes, Consequences and Remedies* (with Stephanie Procyk and Wayne Lewchuk, 2017); *Precarious Work and the Struggle for Living Wages, Alternate Routes: A Journal of Critical Social Research*, Volume 27 (with Carlo Fanelli, 2016); and *Immigrant Experiences in North America: Understanding Settlement and Integration* (with Harald Bauder, 2015).

Bruce Smardon is Associate Professor in the Department of Politics, York University. He is the author of articles in *Studies in Political Economy* (2010 and 2011) and *Asleep at the Switch* (2014), which won the 2015 Smiley Prize, awarded by the Canadian Political Science Association for the best book on Canadian politics and government in 2014.

Charles W. Smith is an Associate Professor of Political Science at St Thomas More College, University of Saskatchewan. His research interests focus on the intersection of law, class, and politics. He has written several articles on the political economy of labour and on labour law. His most recent book is *Unions in Court: Organized Labour and the Charter of Rights and Freedoms* (with Larry Savage, 2017). He is also co-editor of *Labour/Le Travail*, Canada's foremost labour history and labour studies journal.

Gina Starblanket is an Assistant Professor in the Department of Political Science at the University of Calgary. Gina is Cree/Saulteaux and a member of the Star Blanket Cree Nation in Treaty 4 territory in Saskatchewan. She holds a PhD and MA from the University of Victoria and a BA (Honours) from the University of Regina. Her work is centered in Indigenous political theory and takes up questions of treaty implementation, gender, feminism, identity, decolonization, Indigenous resurgence, and relationality.

Heather Whiteside is Associate Professor of Political Science at the University of Waterloo and Fellow at the Balsillie School of International Affairs. Her research and writing centre on theories and practices of privatization, financialization, and fiscal austerity. Her books are *Capitalist Political Economy* (2020); *About Canada: Public-Private Partnerships* (2016); *Purchase for Profit* (2015); and *Private Affluence, Public Austerity* (2011). She has also published in journals such as *Review of International Political Economy, Cambridge Journal of Regions, Economy and Society, Urban Studies, Economic Geography,* and *Studies in Political Economy.* She is co-coordinator of the Waterloo Political Economy Group (WatPEG) and an Associate Editor of the journal *Studies in Political Economy* (SPE).

Index